Collins

NICHOLSON

W0009905

WATERWAYS

North West & the Pennines

CONTENTS

Map data

Published by Nicholson
An imprint of HarperCollins Publishers
Westerhill Road, Bishopbriggs, Glasgow G64 2QT
www.harpercollins.co.uk

Waterways guides published by Nicholson since 1969
This edition first published by Nicholson and Ordnance Survey 1997
New edition published by Nicholson 2000, 2003, 2006, 2009, 2012, 2015, 2019

Wildlife text from *Collins Complete Guide to British Wildlife* and *Collins Wild Guide*.

This product uses map data licensed from Ordnance Survey © Crown copyright and database rights (2018) Ordnance Survey (100018598)

The representation in this publication of a road, track or path is no evidence of the existence of a right of way.

Researched and written by Jonathan Mosse.

The publishers gratefully acknowledge the assistance given by Canal & River Trust and their staff in the preparation of this guide. Grateful thanks are also due to the Environment Agency, members of the Inland Waterways Association, and CAMRA representatives and branch members.

Photographs reproduced by kind permission of:
Jonathan Mosse p47, 69–91, 93–148, 90, 98, 136, 142, 148, 149–163, 159, 164–174, 165, 171, 179, 175–186, 186, 187–205, 192, 201, 206–214, 208; Alamy 14, MSP Travel Images, 15–25 David Williams, 22 Brian Holding, 27–45 Roy Conchie, 46–55 Alan Wrigley, 49 PrimrosePix, 56–63 John Morrison, 65–68 Steven Gillis HD9 Imaging, 125 Jason Smalley Photography, 204 Rory Prior, 216 John Keates; Paul Huggins (www.paulhugginsphotography.com) 42, 43, 72, 76 (Heron); Shutterstock 68 Andre Nekrassov, 76 Borislav Borisov (Woodpecker), 200 Areipa.it, 215–227 brinkstock, 217 Karel Gallas

A catalogue record for this book is available from the British Library

Printed in China

ISBN 978-0-00-830939-8

10 9 8 7 6 5 4 3 2 1

MIX
Paper from
responsible sources
FSC
www.fsc.org **FSC™ C007454**

This book is produced from independently certified FSC™ paper to ensure responsible forest management.

For more information visit: www.harpercollins.co.uk/green

▌INTRODUCTION

Wending their quiet way through town and country, the inland navigations of Britain offer boaters, walkers and cyclists a unique insight into a fascinating, but once almost lost, world. When built this was the province of the boatmen and their families, who lived a mainly itinerant lifestyle: often colourful, to our eyes picturesque but, for them, remarkably harsh. Transporting the nation's goods during the late 1700s and early 1800s, negotiating locks, traversing aqueducts and passing through long narrow tunnels, canals were the arteries of trade during the initial part of the industrial revolution.

Then the railways came: the waterways were eclipsed in a remarkably short time by a faster and more flexible transport system, and a steady decline began. In a desperate fight for survival canal tolls were cut, crews toiled for longer hours and worked the boats with their whole family living aboard. Canal companies merged, totally uneconomic waterways were abandoned, some were modernised but it was all to no avail. Large scale commercial carrying on inland waterways had reached the finale of its short life.

At the end of World War II a few enthusiasts roamed this hidden world and harboured a vision of what it could become: a living transport museum which stretched the length and breadth of the country; a place where people could spend their leisure time and, on just a few of the wider waterways, a still modestly viable transport system.

The restoration struggle began and, from modest beginnings, Britain's inland waterways are now seen as an irreplaceable part of the fabric of the nation. Long-abandoned waterways, once seen as an eyesore and a danger, are recognised for the valuable contribution they make to our quality of life, and restoration schemes are integrating them back into the network. Let us hope that the country's network of inland waterways continues to be cherished and well-used, maintained and developed as we move through the 21st century.

If you would like to comment on any aspect of the guides, please write to Nicholson Waterways Guides, Collins, Westerhill Road, Bishopbriggs, Glasgow G64 2QT or email nicholson@harpercollins.co.uk.

Also available:

Collins NICHOLSON

Waterways guides and map

1 **Grand Union, Oxford & the South East**

2 **Severn, Avon & Birmingham**

3 **Birmingham & the Heart of England**

4 **Four Counties & the Welsh Canals**

6 **Nottingham, York & the North East**

7 **River Thames & the Southern Waterways**

Norfolk Broads

Inland Waterways Map of Great Britain

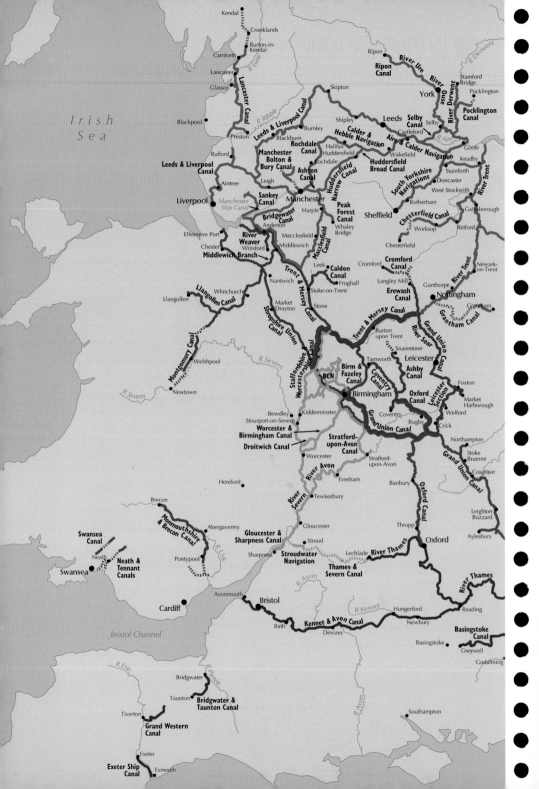

The Waterways of Britain

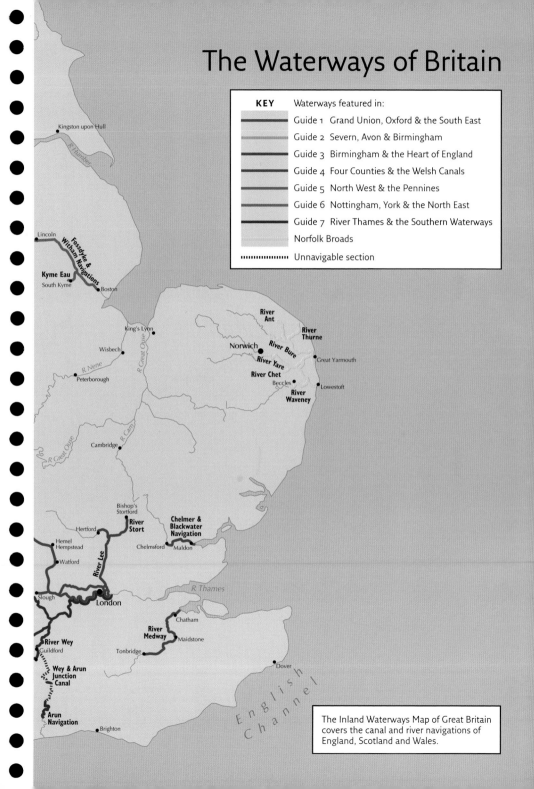

KEY — Waterways featured in:

Guide 1 Grand Union, Oxford & the South East
Guide 2 Severn, Avon & Birmingham
Guide 3 Birmingham & the Heart of England
Guide 4 Four Counties & the Welsh Canals
Guide 5 North West & the Pennines
Guide 6 Nottingham, York & the North East
Guide 7 River Thames & the Southern Waterways
Norfolk Broads
.... Unnavigable section

The Inland Waterways Map of Great Britain
covers the canal and river navigations of
England, Scotland and Wales.

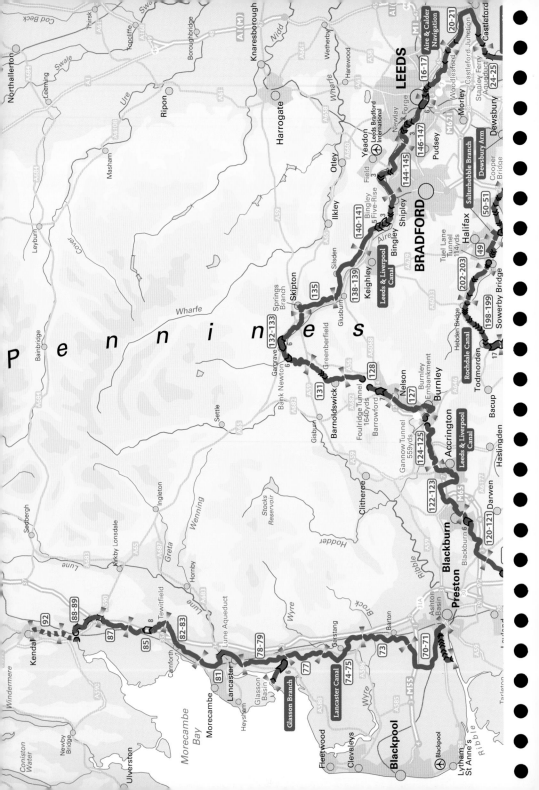

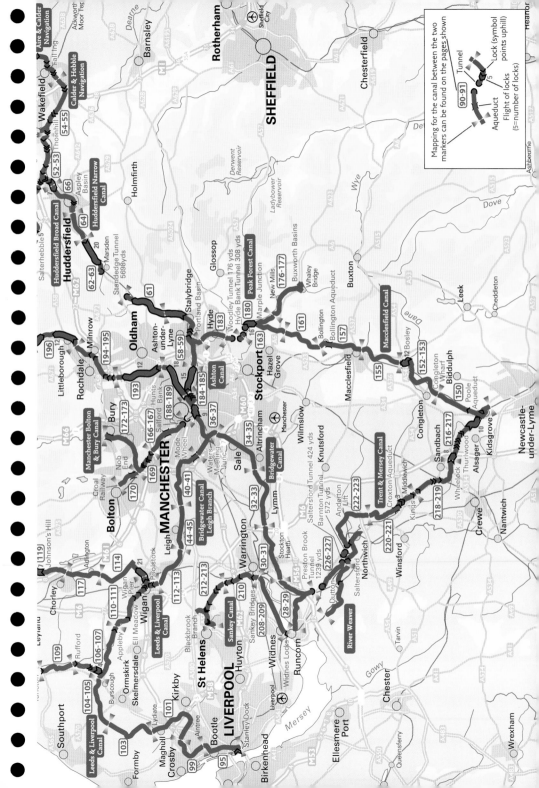

Mapping for the canal between the two markers can be found on the pages shown

90-91 Tunnel
Lock (symbol points uphill)
5
Aqueduct Flight of locks (5=number of locks)

SHEFFIELD

Sheffield City

Chesterfield

Rotherham

Barnsley

Wakefield

Aire & Calder Navigation
Fall Ing
Ackworth Moor Top
Dearne

Calder & Hebble Navigation 54-55
Thornhill
52-53

Derwent Reservoir

Ladybower Reservoir

Dove

Wye

Leek

Cheddleton

Ashbourne

Huddersfield Broad Canal 66
Aspley Basin
64
Huddersfield Narrow Canal
62-63
HUDDERSFIELD
Salterhebble 5
20 Marsden
Standedge Tunnel 5698yds

Holmfirth

Glossop

Buxton

Woodley Tunnel 176 yds
Hyde Bank Tunnel 308 yds
Peak Forest Canal
176-177
Buxworth Basins
Whaley Bridge
New Mills
Marple Junction
180
161
Bollington Aqueduct
Bollington
157
Macclesfield Canal
Macclesfield
155
12 Bosley
152-153
Congleton Wharf
150
Poole Aqueduct
Biddulph

61
Stalybridge
Portland Basin
Hyde 183
Ashton-under-Lyne
58-59
194-195
Oldham
12
Ashton Canal
163
Stockport
Hazel Grove
Marple

Milnrow
196
Littleborough 12
Rochdale
193
Bury
172-173
166-167
188-189
184-185
36-37
34-35
Altrincham
Sale
32-33
Lymm
Knutsford
Saltersford Tunnel 424 yds
Barnton Tunnel 572 yds
Anderton Lift
222-223
Croxton Aqueduct
Middlewich
Trent & Mersey Canal
220-221
Winsford
Northwich
218-219
Wheelock
Thurlwood 8
Alsager 10
Sandbach
216-217
Kidsgrove
Newcastle-under-Lyme
Congleton
Crewe
Nantwich

Manchester Bolton & Bury Canal
Nob End
169
170
Bolton
Croal Railway
Bury
Hunts Bank
Salford Bank
Mode Wheel
MANCHESTER
Waters Meeting Junc.
Leigh
Bridgewater Canal Leigh Branch
44-45
40-41
Bridgewater Canal
Manchester
Wilmslow
Hazel Grove
9
15
18
16

196

7 (119)
Johnson's Hill
Adlington
117
114
Chorley
Poolstock
Wigan Pier
21
110-111
Leeds & Liverpool Canal
112-113
Wigan
Appleby
Ell Meadow
Leeds & Liverpool Canal
109
Rufford
106-107
104-105
Burscough
Ormskirk
Skelmersdale
Southport
Leyland

Stockton Heath
30-31
28-29
Warrington
212-213
210
Sankey Canal
208-209
Sankey Bridges
St Helens
Huyton
Widnes
Widnes Locks
Runcorn
River Weaver
226-227
Dutton
Saltersford
Preston Brook Tunnel 1239 yds
Kings
M6
M62
M57

103
Maghull
Lydiate
Aintree
101
Kirkby
Crosby
Bootle
99
95
Stanley Dock
Liverpool
LIVERPOOL
Birkenhead
Formby
Blackbrook Branch

Ellesmere Port
Queensferry
Chester
Tarvin
Gowy
Mersey

Wrexham

GENERAL INFORMATION FOR WATERWAYS USERS

INTRODUCTION

Boaters, walkers, fishermen, cyclists and gongoozlers (on-lookers) all share in the enjoyment of our quite amazing waterway heritage. Canal & River Trust (CRT) and the Environment Agency, along with other navigation authorities, are empowered to develop, maintain and control this resource. It is to this end that a series of guides, codes, and regulations have come into existence over the years, evolving to match a burgeoning – and occasionally conflicting – demand. Set out in this section are key points as they relate to everyone wishing to enjoy the waterways.

The *Boater's Handbook* is available from all navigation authorities. It contains a complete range of safety information, boat-handling know-how, warning symbols and illustrations, and can be downloaded from www.canalrivertrust.org. uk/boating/navigating-the-waterways/boaters-handbook. It is complemented by this excellent video relating specifically to safe lock operation: www.youtube.com/watch?v=3UIW7VotJpM.

CONSIDERATE BOATING

Considerate Boating gives advice and guidance to all waterway users on how to enjoy the inland waterways safely and can be downloaded from www.canalrivertrust.org.uk/boating/navigating-the-waterways/considerate-boating. It is also well worth visiting www.considerateboater.com. These publications are also available from the Customer Services Team which is staffed *Mon–Fri, 08.00–18.00*. The helpful staff will answer general enquiries and provide information about boat licensing, mooring, boating holidays and general activities on the waterways. They can be contacted on 0303 040 4040; customer. services@canalrivertrust.org.uk; Canal & River Trust, Head Office, First Floor North, Station House, 500 Elder Gate, Milton Keynes MK9 1BB. Visit www.canalrivertrust.org.uk for up to date information on almost every aspect of the inland waterways from news and events to moorings.

Emergency Helpline Available from Canal & River Trust outside normal office hours on weekdays and throughout weekends. If lives or property are at risk or there is danger of serious environmental contamination then contact 0800 47 999 47 immediately for emergency help.

ENVIRONMENT AGENCY

The Environment Agency (EA) manages around 600 miles of the country's rivers, including the Thames and the River Medway. For general enquiries or to obtain a copy of the *Boater's Handbook*, contact EA Customer Services on 03708 506 506; enquiries@environment-agency. gov.uk. To find out about their work nationally (or to download a copy of the *Handbook*) and for lots of other useful information, visit www.gov. uk/government/organisations/environment-agency. The website www.visitthames.co.uk provides lots on information on boating, walking, fishing and events on the river.

Incident Hotline The EA maintain an Incident Hotline. To report damage or danger to the natural environment, damage to structures or water escaping, telephone 0800 80 70 60.

LICENSING – BOATS

The majority of the navigations covered in this book are controlled by CRT and the EA and are managed on a day-to-day basis by local Waterway Offices (you will find details of these in the introductions to each waterway). All craft using the inland waterways must be licensed and charges are based on the dimensions of the craft. In a few cases, these include reciprocal agreements with other waterway authorities (as indicated in the text). CRT and the EA offer an optional Gold Licence which covers unlimited navigation on the waterways of both authorities. Permits for permanent mooring on CRT waterways are issued by CRT.

Contact Canal & River Trust Boat Licensing Team on 0303 040 4040; www.canalrivertrust. org.uk/boating/licensing; Canal & River Trust Licensing Team, PO Box 162, Leeds LS9 1AX.

For the Thames and River Medway contact the EA. River Thames: 0118 953 5650; www.gov.uk/government/organisations/ environment-agency; Environment Agency, PO Box 214, Reading RG1 8HQ. River Medway: 01732 223222 or visit the website.

BOAT SAFETY SCHEME

CRT and the EA operate the Boat Safety Scheme aimed at maintaining boat safety standards and featuring four-yearly testing, primarily intended to identify third party risks. A Boat Safety Scheme Certificate (for new boats, a Declaration of

Conformity) is necessary to obtain a craft licence from all navigation authorities. CRT also requires proof of insurance for Third Party Liability for a minimum of £2,000,000 for powered boats. The scheme is gradually being adopted by other waterway authorities. Contact details are: 0333 202 1000; www.boatsafetyscheme.org; Boat Safety Scheme, First Floor North, Station House, 500 Elder Gate, Milton Keynes MK9 1BB. The website offers useful advice on preventing fires and avoiding carbon monoxide poisoning.

TRAINING
The Royal Yachting Association (RYA) runs one and two day courses leading to the Inland Waters Helmsman's Certificate, specifically designed for novices and experienced boaters wishing to cruise the inland waterways. For details of RYA schools, telephone 023 8060 4100 or visit www.rya.org.uk. The practical course notes are available to buy. Contact your local boat clubs, too. The National Community Boats Association (NCBA) run courses on boat-handling and safety on the water. Telephone 0845 0510649 or visit www. national-cba.co.uk.

LICENSING – CYCLISTS
You no longer require a permit to cycle on those waterways under the control of Canal & River Trust. However, you are asked to abide by the ten point Greenway Code for Towpaths available at www.canalrivertrust.org.uk/see-and-do/cycling which also provides a wide range of advice on cycling beside the waterways. Cycling along the Thames towpath is generally accepted, although landowners have the right to request that you do not cycle. Some sections of the riverside path, however, are designated and clearly marked as official cycle ways. No permits are required but cyclists must follow London's Towpath Code on Conduct at all times.

TOWPATHS
Few, if any, artificial cuts or canals in this country are without an intact towpath accessible to the walker at least and the Thames is the only river in the country with a designated National Trail along its path from source to sea (for more information visit www.nationaltrail.co.uk). However, on some other river navigations, towpaths have on occasion fallen into disuse or, sometimes, been lost to erosion. The indication of a towpath in this guide does not necessarily imply a public right of way or mean that a right to cycle along it exists.

Horse riding and motorcycling are forbidden on all towpaths.

INDIVIDUAL WATERWAY GUIDES
No national guide can cover the minutiae of detail concerning every waterway, and some CRT Waterway Managers produce guides to specific navigations under their charge. Copies of individual guides (where available) can be obtained from the relevant CRT Waterway Office or downloaded from www.waterscape.com/things-to-do/boating/guides. Please note that times – such as operating times of bridges and locks – do change year by year and from winter to summer. For free copies of a range of helpful leaflets for all users of the River Thames – visit www.visitthames.co.uk/about-the-river/publications.

STOPPAGES
CRT and the EA both publish winter stoppage programmes which are sent out to all licence holders, boatyards and hire companies. Inevitably, emergencies occur necessitating the unexpected closure of a waterway, perhaps during the peak season. You can check for stoppages on individual waterways between specific dates on www.canalrivertrust.org.uk/notices/winter, lockside noticeboards or by telephoning 0303 040 4040; for stoppages and river conditions on the Thames, visit www.gov.uk/river-thames-conditions-closures-restrictions-and-lock-closures or telephone 0845 988 1188.

NAVIGATION AUTHORITIES AND WATERWAYS SOCIETIES
Most inland navigations are managed by CRT or the EA, but there are several other navigation authorities. For details of these, contact the Association of Inland Navigation Authorities on 0844 335 1650 or visit www.aina.org.uk. The boater, conditioned perhaps by the uniformity of our national road network, should be sensitive to the need to observe different codes and operating practices.

The Canal & River Trust is a charity set up to care for England and Wales' legacy of 200-year-old waterways, holding them in trust for the nation forever, and is linked with an ombudsman. CRT has a comprehensive complaints procedure and a free explanatory leaflet is available from Customer Services. Problems and complaints should be addressed to the local Waterway Manager in the first instance. For more information, visit their website.

The EA is the national body, sponsored by the Department for Environment, Food and Rural Affairs, to manage the quality of air, land and water in England and Wales. For more information, visit its website.

The Inland Waterways Association (IWA) campaigns for the use, maintenance and restoration of Britain's inland waterways, through branches all over the country. For more information, contact them on 01494 783453; iwa@waterways.org.uk; www.waterways.org.uk; The Inland Waterways Association, Island House, Moor Road, Chesham HP5 1WA. Their website has a huge amount of information of interest to boaters, including comprehensive details of the many and varied waterways societies.

STARTING OUT
Extensive information and advice on booking a boating holiday is available from the Inland Waterways Association, www.visitthames.co.uk and www.canalrivertrust.org.uk/boating/boat-trips-and-holidays. Please book a waterway holiday from a licensed operator – this way you can be sure that you have proper insurance cover, service and support during your holiday. It is illegal for private boat owners to hire out their craft. If you are hiring a holiday craft for the first time, the boatyard will brief you thoroughly. Take notes, follow their instructions and do ask if there is anything you do not understand. CRT have produced a 40 min DVD which is essential viewing for newcomers to canal or river boating. Available to view free at www.canalrivertrust.org.uk/boatersdvd or obtainable (charge) from the CRT Customer Service Centre 0303 040 4040; www.canalrivertrust.org.uk/shop.

PLACES TO VISIT ALONG THE WAY
This guide contains a wealth of information, not just about the canals and rivers and navigating on them, but also on the visitor attractions and places to eat and drink close to the waterways. Opening and closing times, and other details often change; establishments close and new ones open. If you are making special plans to eat in a particular pub, or visit a certain museum it is always advisable to check in advance.

MORE INFORMATION
An internet search will reveal many websites on the inland waterways. Those listed below are just a small sample:

National Community Boats Association is a national charity and training provider, supporting community boat projects and encouraging more people to access the inland waterways. Telephone 0845 0510649; www.national-cba.co.uk.
National Association of Boat Owners is dedicated to promoting the interests of private boaters on Britain's canals and rivers. Visit www.nabo.org.uk.
www.canalplan.org.uk is an online journey-planner and gazetteer for the inland waterways.
www.canals.com is a valuable source of information for cruising the canals, with loads of links to canal and waterways related websites.
www.ukcanals.net lists services and useful information for all waterways users.

GENERAL CRUISING NOTES
Most canals and rivers are saucer shaped, being deepest at the middle. Few canals have more than 3-4ft of water and many have much less. Keep to the centre of the channel except on bends, where the deepest water is on the outside of the bend. When you meet another boat, keep to the right, slow down and aim to miss the approaching craft by a couple of yards. If you meet a loaded commercial boat keep right out of the way and be prepared to follow his instructions. Do not assume that you should pass on the right. If you meet a boat being towed from the bank, pass it on the outside. When overtaking, keep the other boat on your right side.

Some CRT and EA facilities are operated by pre-paid cards, obtainable from CRT and EA regional and local waterways offices, lock keepers and boatyards. Weekend visitors should purchase cards in advance. A handcuff/anti-vandal key is commonly used on locks where vandalism is a problem. A watermate/sanitary key opens sanitary stations, waterpoints and some bridges and locks. Both keys and pre-paid cards can be obtained via CRT Customer Service Centre.

Safety
Boating is a safe pastime. However, it makes sense to take simple safety precautions, particularly if you have children aboard.
• Never drink and drive a boat – it may travel slowly, but it weighs many tons.
• Be careful with naked flames and never leave the boat with the hob or oven lit. Familiarise yourself and your crew with the location and operation of the fire extinguishers.

- Never block ventilation grills. Boats are enclosed spaces and levels of carbon monoxide can build up from faulty appliances or just from using the cooker.
- Be careful along the bank and around locks. Slipping from the bank might only give you a cold-water soaking, but falling from the side of, or into a lock is more dangerous. Beware of slippery or rough ground.
- Remember that fingers and toes are precious! If a major collision is imminent, never try to fend off with your hands or feet; and always keep hands and arms inside the boat.
- Weil's disease is a particularly dangerous infection present in water which can attack the central nervous system and major organs. It is caused by bacteria entering the bloodstream through cuts and broken skin, and the eyes, nose and mouth. The flu-like symptoms occur two-four weeks after exposure. Always wash your hands thoroughly after contact with the water. Visit www.leptospirosis.org for details.

Speed

There is a general speed limit of 4 mph on most CRT canals and 5 mph on the Thames. There is no need to go any faster – the faster you go, the bigger a wave the boat creates: if your wash is breaking against the bank, causing large waves or throwing moored boats around, slow down. Slow down also when passing engineering works and anglers; when there is a lot of floating rubbish on the water (try to drift over obvious obstructions in neutral); when approaching blind corners, narrow bridges and junctions.

Mooring

Generally you may moor where you wish on CRT property, as long as you are *not causing an obstruction*. Do not moor in a winding hole or junction, the approaches to a lock or tunnel, or at a water point or sanitary station. On the Thames, generally you have a right to anchor for 24 hours in one place provided no obstruction is caused, however you will need explicit permission from the land owner to moor. There are official mooring sites along the length of the river; those provided by the EA are free, the others you will need to pay for. Your boat should carry metal mooring stakes, and these should be driven firmly into the ground with a mallet if there are no mooring rings. Do not stretch mooring lines across the towpath and take account of anyone who may walk past. Always consider the security of your boat when there is no one aboard. On tideways and commercial waterways it is advisable to moor only at recognised sites, and allow for any rise or fall of the tide.

Bridges

On narrow canals slow down well in advance and aim to miss one side (usually the towpath side) by about 9 inches. *Keep everyone inboard when passing under bridges and ensure there is nothing on the roof of the boat that will hit the bridge.* If a boat is coming the other way, the craft nearest to the bridge has priority. Take special care with moveable structures – the crew member operating the bridge should be strong and heavy enough to hold it steady as the boat passes through.

Going aground

You can sometimes go aground if the water level on a canal has dropped or you are on a particularly shallow stretch. If it does happen, try reversing *gently*, or pushing off with the boat hook. Another method is to get your crew to rock the boat from side to side using the boat hook, or move all crew to the end opposite to that which is aground. Or, have all crew leave the boat, except the helmsman, and it will often float off quite easily.

Tunnels

Again, ensure that everyone is inboard. Make sure the tunnel is clear before you enter, and use your headlight. Follow any instructions given on notice boards by the entrance.

Fuel

Diesel can be purchased from most boatyards and some CRT depots. To comply with HMRC regulations you must declare an appropriate split between propulsion and heating so that the correct level of VAT can be applied. However, few boatyards stock petrol. Where a garage is listed under a town or village's facilities petrol (and DERV) are available.

Water

It is advisable to top up daily.

Pump out

Self-operated pump out facilities are available at a number of locations on the waterways network. These facilities are provided by CRT and can be operated via a 25-unit prepayment card. Details of how to buy a pump out card either

11

online, by phone or in person are available from www.canalrivertrust.org.uk. The cards provide for one pump out or 25 units of electricity. Cards can be obtained from CRT Waterway Offices, some Marinas and boatyards, shops and cafés.

Boatyards

Hire fleets are usually turned around at a weekend, making this a bad time to call in for services.

VHF Radio

The IWA recommends that all pleasure craft navigating the larger waterways used by freight carrying vessels, or any tidal navigation, should carry marine-band VHF radio and have a qualified radio operator on board. In some cases the navigation authority requires craft to carry radio and maintain a listening watch. Two examples of this are for boats on the tidal River Ouse wishing to enter Goole Docks and the Aire & Calder Navigation, and for boats on the tidal Thames, over 45ft, navigating between Teddington Lock and Limehouse Basin.
VHF radio users must have a current operator's certificate. The training is not expensive and will present no problem to the average inland waterways boater. Contact the RYA (see Training) for details.

PLANNING A CRUISE

Don't try to go too far too fast. Go slowly, don't be too ambitious, and enjoy the experience. Mileages indicated on the maps are for guidance only. A *rough* calculation of time taken to cover the ground is the lock-miles system:

Add the number of *miles* to the number of *locks* on your proposed journey, and divide the resulting figure by three. This will give you an approximate guide to the number of *hours* your travel will take.

TIDAL WATERWAYS

The typical steel narrow boat found on the inland waterways is totally unsuitable for cruising on tidal estuaries. However, the adventurous will inevitably wish to add additional 'ring cruises' to the more predictable circuits of inland Britain. Passage is possible in most estuaries if careful consideration is given to the key factors of weather conditions, tides, crew experience, the condition of the boat and its equipment and, perhaps of overriding importance, the need to take expert advice.

In many cases it will be prudent to employ the skilled services of a local pilot. Within the text, where inland navigations connect with a tidal waterway, details are given of sources of advice and pilotage. It is also essential to inform your insurance company of your intention to navigate on tidal waterways as they may very well have special requirements or wish to levy an additional premium. This guide is to the inland waterways of Britain and therefore recognizes that tideways – and especially estuaries – require a different approach and many additional skills. We do not hesitate to draw the boater's attention to the appropriate source material.

LOCKS AND THEIR USE

A lock is a simple and ingenious device for transporting your craft from one water level to another. When both sets of gates are closed it may be filled or emptied using gates, or ground paddles, at the top or bottom of the lock. These are operated with a windlass. On the Thames, the locks are manned all year round, with longer hours from April to October. You may operate the locks yourself at any time.

If a lock is empty, or 'set' for you, the crew open the gates and you drive the boat in. If the lock is full of water, the crew should check first to see if any boat is waiting or coming in the other direction. If a boat is in sight, you must let them through first: do not empty or 'turn' the lock against them. This is not only discourteous, and against the rules, but wastes precious water.

In the diagrams the *plan* shows how the gates point uphill, the water pressure forcing them together. Water is flooding into the lock through the underground culverts that are operated by the ground paddles: when the lock is 'full', the top gates (on the left of the drawing) can be opened. One may imagine a boat entering, the crew closing the gates and paddles after it.

In the *elevation*, the bottom paddles have been raised (opened) so that the lock empties. A boat will, of course, float down with the water. When the lock is 'empty' the bottom gates can be opened and the descending boat can leave.

Remember that when going *up* a lock, a boat should be tied up to prevent it being thrown about by the rush of incoming water; but when going *down* a lock, a boat should never be tied up or it will be left high and dry.

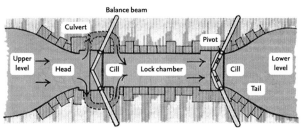

Ground paddles open. Water fills the chamber through the culverts.

Gate paddles closed, retaining water in the lock chamber.

A plan of a lock filling.

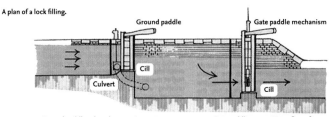

Ground paddles closed preventing water from the upper level filling the chamber.

Gate paddles open. Water flows from the chamber to the lower level.

An elevation of a lock emptying.

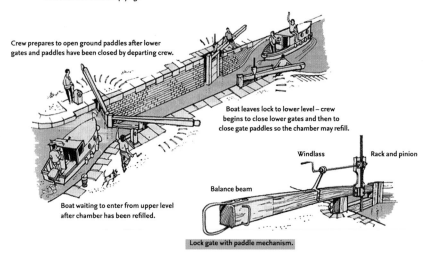

Crew prepares to open ground paddles after lower gates and paddles have been closed by departing crew.

Boat leaves lock to lower level – crew begins to close lower gates and then to close gate paddles so the chamber may refill.

Boat waiting to enter from upper level after chamber has been refilled.

Lock gate with paddle mechanism.

- Make safety your prime concern. *Keep a close eye on young children.*
- Always take your time, and do not leap about.
- Never open the paddles at one end without ensuring those at the other end are closed.
- Keep to the landward side of the balance beam when opening and closing gates. Whilst it may be necessary to put your back behind the balance beam to gain a better purchase when starting to close a gate, always move to the correct position as soon as possible.

- Never leave your windlass slotted onto the paddle spindle – it will be dangerous should anything slip.
- Keep your boat away from the top and bottom gates to prevent it getting caught on the gate or the lock cill.
- Never drop the paddles – always wind them down.
- Be wary of fierce *top gate* paddles, especially in wide locks. Operate them slowly, and close them if there is *any* adverse effect.
- Always follow the navigation authority's instructions, where given on notices or by their staff.

13

Sunset from Ferrybridge Lock on the Aire & Calder Navigation

AIRE & CALDER NAVIGATION

MAXIMUM DIMENSIONS

River Lock to tail of Leeds Lock
Length: 141' 0"
Beam: 17' 9"
Headroom: 11' 9"
Draught: 7' 7"

Leeds Lock to Castleford
Length: 200' 0"
Beam: 20' 0"
Headroom: 11' 9"
Draught: 8' 2"

Castleford to Wakefield
Length: 141' 0"
Beam: 17' 9"
Headroom: 11' 10"
Draught: 7' 7"

MANAGER

0303 040 4040;
www.canalrivertrust.org.uk/contact-us/
ways-to-contact-us

MILEAGE

LEEDS to
Castleford: 10 miles, 5 locks
Wakefield: 17½ miles, 10 locks including Fall Ing

SAFETY NOTES

CRT produce an excellent set of *Cruising Notes* for pleasure boaters using this navigation, obtainable by contacting the Waterway Unit Manager's office above, or downloadable from www. waterscape.com/boatersguides. This is both a commercial waterway and one developed from a river navigation: both pose their own disciplines highlighted in the notes.
Each lock on the waterway has a set of traffic lights both upstream and downstream of the lock chamber. The purpose of these lights is to convey instructions and advice to approaching craft.

Red light
Stop and moor up on the lock approach. The lock is currently in use.

Amber light *(between the red and green lights)*
The lock keeper is not on duty. You will need to self-operate.

Green light
Proceed into lock.

Red & green lights together
The lock is available for use. The lock keeper will prepare and operate the lock for you.

Flashing red light
Flood conditions – unsafe for navigation.

Most lock approach moorings are immediately upstream and downstream of the lock chamber. However, **please note:**

1   Knostrop Lock downstream approach mooring is located alongside the lock bullnose.

2   Locks at Leeds, Lemonroyd, Castleford, Woodnook and Broadreach allow access to river sections of the navigation. For interpretation of river level gauge boards *see* Safety Notes in the introduction to the Calder & Hebble Navigation on page 46.

3   There is a safe haven mooring immediately upstream of Lemonroyd Lock.

All locks between Leeds and Wakefield (except Fall Ing Lock) are equipped with VHF Marine Band Radio. They monitor and operate on channel 74. In an emergency non-VHF users contact the manager's office or out of office hours telephone 0800 47 999 47.

The River Aire was first made navigable to Leeds in 1700, and rapidly became a great commercial success, taking coal out of the Yorkshire coalfield and bringing back raw wool, corn and agricultural produce. Improvements were then made to the difficult lower reaches, with first Selby and later Goole becoming Yorkshire's principal inland port. The opening of the New Junction Canal in 1905 further secured its suitability for commercial traffic, which until recently amounted to some 2 million tonnes a year, mainly coal, sand and petroleum. With the completion of coal extraction at the St Aidens opencast site, together with the unacceptably high sulphur content of the material from Kellingley colliery, coal carrying came to an abrupt halt. With the amalgamation of the two aggregate giants – Lafarge and Tarmac – a similar fate met the long established sand and gravel freight from Besthorpe to Whitwood, when Tarmac (now responsible for all quarrying operations within the group) elected to move aggregate required in the Leeds area by road from their pit near Ripon.

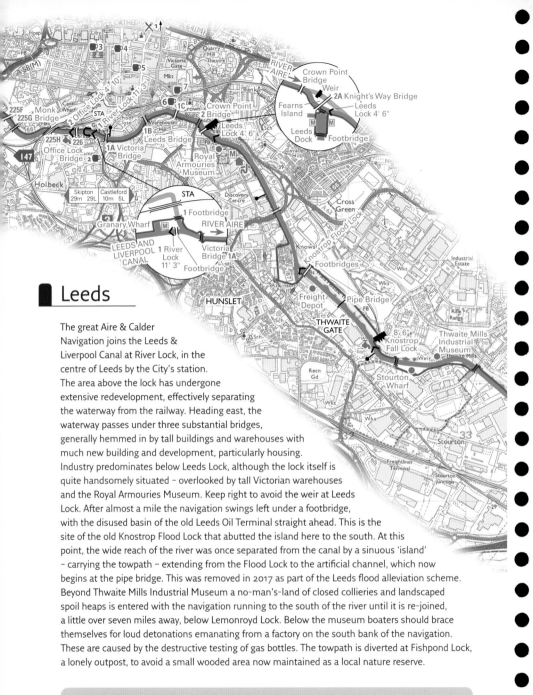

Leeds

The great Aire & Calder Navigation joins the Leeds & Liverpool Canal at River Lock, in the centre of Leeds by the City's station. The area above the lock has undergone extensive redevelopment, effectively separating the waterway from the railway. Heading east, the waterway passes under three substantial bridges, generally hemmed in by tall buildings and warehouses with much new building and development, particularly housing. Industry predominates below Leeds Lock, although the lock itself is quite handsomely situated – overlooked by tall Victorian warehouses and the Royal Armouries Museum. Keep right to avoid the weir at Leeds Lock. After almost a mile the navigation swings left under a footbridge, with the disused basin of the old Leeds Oil Terminal straight ahead. This is the site of the old Knostrop Flood Lock that abutted the island here to the south. At this point, the wide reach of the river was once separated from the canal by a sinuous 'island' – carrying the towpath – extending from the Flood Lock to the artificial channel, which now begins at the pipe bridge. This was removed in 2017 as part of the Leeds flood alleviation scheme. Beyond Thwaite Mills Industrial Museum a no-man's-land of closed collieries and landscaped spoil heaps is entered with the navigation running to the south of the river until it is re-joined, a little over seven miles away, below Lemonroyd Lock. Below the museum boaters should brace themselves for loud detonations emanating from a factory on the south bank of the navigation. These are caused by the destructive testing of gas bottles. The towpath is diverted at Fishpond Lock, a lonely outpost, to avoid a small wooded area now maintained as a local nature reserve.

WALKING AND CYCLING

The towpath from Leeds to Mickletown is now part of the Trans Pennine Trail (National Cycle Route 67) and is well used by walkers and cyclists alike. There are two excellent interpretation boards between Victoria and Crown Point Bridges – entitled 'Eye on the Aire' – depicting local activity in times gone by.

NAVIGATIONAL NOTES

1 All the locks on the Aire & Calder operate mechanically. Lock keepers move from lock to lock, primarily to operate them for commercial traffic. They will assist boaters through locks whenever possible but all locks can now be self-operated. Obey the traffic light signals.

2 Remember that this is a river navigation. Many of the locks are accompanied by large weirs, so keep a sharp lookout for the signs which direct you safely into the locks.

3 When the river level rises after prolonged heavy rain, the flood gates will be closed. Pleasure craft should stay put until they are advised by a lock keeper that it is safe to proceed.

4 This is still a commercial waterway capable of carrying 600-tonne barges. Keep a lookout for them, and give them a clear passage. Moor carefully, using bollards or fixed rings rather than mooring stakes, since the wash from these craft can be substantial.

5 It is anticipated that soon after this guide is published aggregate traffic will be operating on the canal between Goole and Wharfs at Fleet (see page 20) and Stourton, opposite Thwaite Mills Industrial Museum.

5 Leeds Rowing Club run regular training sessions between Knostrop and Fishponds Locks *Apr-Oct, Mon-Fri 06.00-08.00 & 16.00-21.00; additional Wed session 12.00-16.00. Also Sat-Sun 08.00-16.00*. Be prepared to slow down and give way.

7 Mooring is available at Granary Wharf, Fearns Wharf, Brewery Wharf, Leeds Lock and Knostrop Lock.

BOAT TRIPS
Kirkstall Flyboat 26 Canal Wharf, Holbeck, Leeds LS11 5PS (0113 245 6195; www.tripboat.co.uk) is a restaurant boat seating up to 44 persons. Licensed bar and food available. Café open *Mon-Fri 08.00-14.00*. Yorkshire Hire Cruisers also operate a free water taxi service aboard *Twee* and *Drie daily* between the new southern station exit and Leeds Dock.

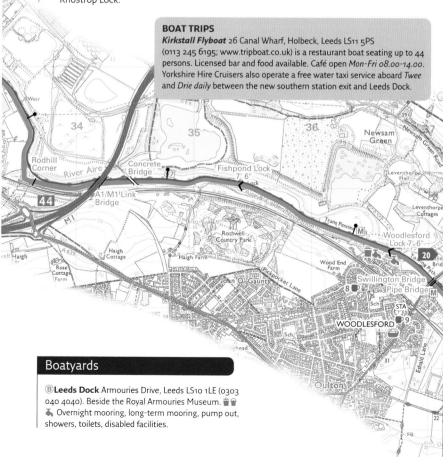

Boatyards

Ⓑ**Leeds Dock** Armouries Drive, Leeds LS10 1LE (0303 040 4040). Beside the Royal Armouries Museum. 🚽🚿 Overnight mooring, long-term mooring, pump out, showers, toilets, disabled facilities.

Leeds

W. Yorks. All services. A vast industrial city that was a wool centre in the Middle Ages and has continued to grow to prosperity under the textile and clothing trades; indeed Marks & Spencer started business here with a stall in the market. Montague Burton also became established in the city, building what was to become, by 1921, the largest clothing factory in the world. However the last few years have brought substantial changes, with old industries being replaced by new, and the atmosphere is one of growth and prosperity. The great town hall in Victoria Square (walk north from Victoria Bridge and turn left at Great George Street) stands as a magnificent monument to Victorian civic pride. It was designed by Cuthbert Brodrick and opened in 1858. Looking at the Corinthian columns on all sides and the clock tower some 255ft high, it is hard to believe that Brodrick was only 29 years old when he submitted his plans. As a measure of this man's self-confidence, note that he also designed the organ, installed in 1859, which itself weighs almost 70 tonnes, has 6,500 pipes and stands 50ft high. The light and airy Corn Exchange (north of Leeds Bridge along Call Lane and now a shopping arcade) built in 1861 is also Brodrick's work. Always the cultural centre of Yorkshire, the city hosts an international concert season and an international piano competition. It has several splendid theatres, including The Grand in Briggate, modelled on La Scala, Milan; the City Varieties, the oldest surviving music hall in the country; and the Leeds Playhouse Repertory Theatre. Also impressive is the way, perhaps unique in the development of northern industrial towns, that contemporary and Victorian buildings stand harmoniously side by side. There are several splendid parks and rich museums, and excellent shopping facilities, including the ornate Victorian Queens and County arcades. Headingley, the home of Yorkshire cricket and a test match venue, attracts an enthusiastic following in the area, and of course the city's association with football and rugby teams is known worldwide. Boaters should try to spend a day here if they possibly can – there are good moorings on the Leeds & Liverpool Canal by Office Lock, or above Leeds Lock. *See also* page 135 (Leeds & Liverpool Canal) for information on Leeds Industrial Museum and Abbey House Museum.

Metro. The area is well served by an excellent, cheap bus and train service which offers a variety of Day Rover tickets. Telephone 0113 245 7676 or visit www.wymetro.com for details.

Tourist Information Centre Headrow, Leeds LS1 3AA (0113 378 6977; www.visitleeds.co.uk/maps-and-more/Tourist-Information-Centre.aspx‡). *Open Mon-Sat 10.00-17.00 & Sun 11.00-15.00.*

Henry Moore Institute 74 The Headrow, Leeds LS1 3AH (0113 246 7467; www.henry-moore.org). Walk north from Victoria Bridge. Award-winning institute housing four galleries showing temporary sculpture exhibitions of all periods and nationalities. Shop. *Open Tue-Sun 11.00-17.30 (Wed 20.00).* Free.

City Art Gallery The Headrow, Leeds LS1 3AA (0113 378 5350; www.leeds.gov.uk/museumsandgalleries/Home). Fine collections of paintings, watercolours, sculpture. *Open Tue-Sat 10.00-17.00 & Sun 11.00-15.00.* Free.

Leeds-Settle-Carlisle Line From Leeds City Station LS1 4DT (www.settle-carlisle.co.uk). The 70 miles from Settle to Carlisle is said to be one of the most memorable rail journeys in the world, so this would make an excellent day trip away from the boat. There is a *daily* passenger service between Leeds and Carlisle with no need to book. *Every Sat and Sun, May-Oct* there are free guided walks from trains on the line (www.foscl.org.uk/guided-walks/current-leaflet). Coach tours around the Yorkshire Dales also connect. Details from leaflets at the station or Tourist Information Centre.

Middleton Railway The Station, Moor Road, Hunslet, Leeds LS10 2JQ (0113 271 0320; 0845 680 1758; www.middletonrailway.org.uk). Built in 1758 to link Leeds with the Middleton Colliery, this is considered to be the world's oldest railway. It operates at *weekends (including B Hol Mon) and Wed during school holidays* from the industrial suburb of Hunslet, where steam engines were once built. Charge.

Royal Armouries Armouries Drive, Leeds LS10 1LT (0113 220 1999; www.royalarmouries.org/leeds). Beside Leeds Lock with moorings in Clarence Dock, adjacent to the complex. The emphasis is on participation in this massive, interactive museum reputed to be Britain's largest post-war leisure development. Five themed galleries unfold stories of weapons, battles, tournaments, falconry and the Wild West. See, touch, smell and handle before retiring to watch the skills of an armourer or experience the tranquillity of a Japanese tea garden. *Open daily 10.00-17.00. Closed 24-26th Dec.* Two cafés and a bistro. Free.

Thackray Medical Museum 141 Beckett Street, Leeds LS9 7LN (0113 244 4343; www.thackraymedicalmuseum.co.uk). A hands-on experience covering the history of medicine from Victorian times to the present day. This award-winning museum introduces you to Sherlock Bones and his tour of the Giant Gut, allows you to experience surgery without anaesthetics in 'Pain, Pus and Blood' and lets you assist Mrs Hirst with her 12th child. A truly participative establishment. Shop and café. *Open daily 10.00-17.00 – allow 3 hours for your visit.* Bus Nos 4, 4C, 22, 42, 50, 50A, 88. Information hotline 0113 245 7084. Charge (tickets valid for 12 months).

Leeds Town Hall The Headrow, Leeds LS1 3AD (0113 376 0318; www.leedstownhall.co.uk). Built in 1858, Queen Victoria performed the official opening. Today it is a venue for concerts of all types of music and light entertainment.

Leeds Corn Exchange 42 Call Lane, Leeds LS1 7BR (0113 234 7900; www.cornx.net; www.leedscornexchange.co.uk). A Grade 1 listed Victorian building, restored to its original splendour. There are plans to turn the building into a focus for food, with a restaurant and food and drink retailers, as well as cookware and kitchen appliances.

The Grand Theatre 46 New Briggate, Leeds LS1 6NZ (0844 848 2700; www.leedsgrandtheatre.com) Theatre and opera house, showing ballet as well as all types of shows. Also workshops and special events.

The City Varieties Music Hall Swan Street, Leeds LS1 6LG (0113 243 0808; www.cityvarieties. co.uk/Online/default.asp). Pantomine and all kinds of variety shows in a grade II listed building where variety shows have been held since 1865.

Headingley Carnegie Stadium St Michael's Lane, Headingley, Leeds LS6 3BR (0344 248 6651; www.therhinos.co.uk). Home to theYorkshire County Cricket Club since 1891.

Thwaite Mills Watermill Thwaite Lane, Stourton, Leeds LS10 1RP (0113 378 2983; www.leeds.gov.uk/thwaitemills). A canalside flint and china stone-grinding mill built in 1872 and powered by two waterwheels until 1975, when they were washed away, bringing closure a year later. *Open Sat-Sun 12.00-16.00; Tue-Fri 10.00- 17.00 during school holidays & Mon B Hols.* Charge.

Tropical World Princes Avenue, Roundhay, Leeds LS8 2ER (0113 237 0754; www.tropicalworld. leeds.gov.uk). A wide selection of buses from the city centre serves this tropical paradise featuring butterflies, exotic blooms and colourful fish. This is also one of Europe's largest parks, with woodland walks, scented gardens (including National Collections), canal gardens, waterfalls and a ruined castle. *Open 10.00-18.00 (16.00 in winter) daily except Christmas.* Charge.

● **Woodlesford**
W. Yorks. PO, tel, stores, butcher, baker, fish & chips, takeaways, off-licence, garage, library, station. Good moorings above the lock and nearby pubs make this a popular stopping place for boaters. There is a very popular bird hide adjacent to the canal. *Gas* is available at Woodlesford Motor Spares in the centre of the village. Stores *open daily 07.00-23.00.*

Pubs and Restaurants (pages 16-17)

A fine city such as Leeds has many pubs and restaurants. The following is a selection of those fairly close to the navigation.

✕♀ 1 **Hansa's Gujarati Vegetarian Restaurant** 72-74 North Street, Leeds LS2 7PN (0113 244 4408; www.hansasrestaurant.com). Worth seeking out for excellent, home-cooked dishes with an Indian flavour. A unique establishment serving Indian vegetarian cuisine from the State of Gujarat in a split-level restaurant with an elegant, homely atmosphere. Families warmly welcomed. *Open Mon-Sat 17.00-22.00 (Sat 23.00) & Sun 12.00-14.00.*

● 2 **The Grove** Back Row, Holbeck, Leeds LS11 5PL (0113 243 2085; www.thegroveinnleeds.co.uk). Small traditional ale house dispensing a choice of eight real ales and real cider. Breakfast available *Mon-Fri 08.30-11.00 and L 12.00-15.00.* An eclectic range of music is on offer *six nights a week,* including a *Fri* folk club. Dogs welcome, outside seating. Traditional pub games, real fires and Wi-Fi. *Open daily 11.00-00.00.*

● 3 **Foley's Tap House** 159 The Headrow, Leeds LS1 5RG (0113 242 9674; www.mrfoleysleeds.co.uk). Situated in a splendid Grade II listed building, this hostelry serves up to 12 real ales and 20 ciders and perries. Pies and home-made cakes available at the bar. Dog-friendly. Wi-Fi. *Open Sun-Thu 12.00-23.00 (Sun 22.00) & Fri-Sat 11.00-01.00.*

● 4 **The Adelphi Hotel** 3-5 Hunslet Road, Leeds LS10 1JQ (0113 245 6377; www.theadelphileeds. co.uk). South of Leeds Bridge. A superbly restored and very grand Victorian pub, with lots of etched glass and mahogany. Listed inside and out. Real ale and appetising food *daily 12.00-22.00 (Sun 21.00).* Children welcome, dogs in taproom only. Outside seating. *Regular* entertainment. Wi-Fi. *Open daily 12.00-23.00 (Fri-Sat 00.30).*

● ✕ 5 **Whitelock's Ale House** 4 Turks Yard, Briggate, Leeds LS1 6HB (0113 245 3950; www. whitelocksleeds.com). North of Leeds Bridge.

An unspoilt Edwardian pub, one of the first buildings to have electricity. Reputedly the oldest pub in the city (its first licence was granted in 1715) and described by John Betjeman as 'the very heart of Leeds', this hostelry serves up to eight real ales, real cider and food *daily 12.00-21.00 (Sun 20.00).* Dog-friendly and outside seating. Real fires and Wi-Fi. *Open Mon-Sat 11.00-00.00 (Fri-Sat 01.00) & Sun 11.00-23.00.*

● 6 **Duck & Drake** 43 Kirkgate, Leeds LS2 7DR (0113 245 5432; www.duckndrake.co.uk). Real ales, real cider and music are the focus of this traditional, two-roomed Victorian hostelry with live bands *most nights.* Dog-friendly, outside seating. Real fires and Wi-Fi. *Open Mon-Sat 10.00-23.00 (Fri-Sat 00.00) & Sun 11.00-23.00.*

● 7 **The Palace** Kirkgate, Leeds LS2 7DJ (0113 244 5882; www.thepalaceleeds.co.uk). Straightforward, no-frills pub dispensing 10 real ales, real cider and food *daily 10.00-22.00* including breakfast *until 12.00.* Courtyard seating, sports TV and Wi-Fi. *Open Mon-Sat 10.00-23.30 (Fri-Sat 00.00) & Sun 10.00-22.30.*

● 8 **The Two Pointers** 69 Church Street, Woodlesford, Leeds LS26 8RE (0113 282 1884). A smart, friendly village pub - with a coffee shop *open 08.00-16.00* - serving real ale. Garden. Traditional pub games, sports TV, *occasional* live music and Wi-Fi. *Open daily 11.00-23.30 (Sat-Sun 12.00).*

● ✕ 9 **The Midland Hotel** 97 Aberford Road, Woodlesford, Leeds LS26 8LQ (0113 282 1398; www. midlandhotelleeds.co.uk). Friendly establishment serving real ale and food *Mon-Sat L and E & Sun 12.00-17.00* - including breakfast *until 11.45.* Family-friendly and garden. Traditional pub games, sports TV and Wi-Fi. B&B. *Open Mon 10.00-23.00; Tue-Sun 09.00-23.00 (Fri-Sat 00.00).*

Adjacent ✕ **Coffee Shop**. Shop *open daily 12.00- 20.00 (Sun 17.00).*

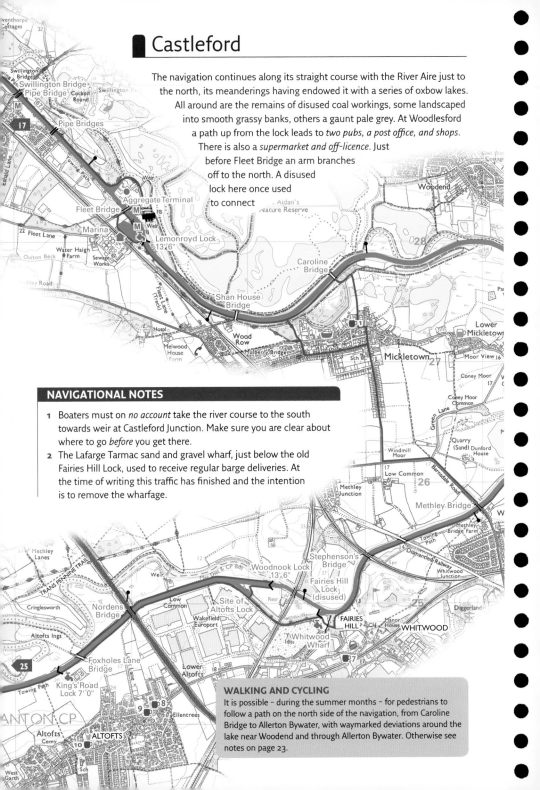

Castleford

The navigation continues along its straight course with the River Aire just to the north, its meanderings having endowed it with a series of oxbow lakes. All around are the remains of disused coal workings, some landscaped into smooth grassy banks, others a gaunt pale grey. At Woodlesford a path up from the lock leads to *two pubs, a post office, and shops*. There is also a *supermarket and off-licence*. Just before Fleet Bridge an arm branches off to the north. A disused lock here once used to connect

NAVIGATIONAL NOTES

1. Boaters must on *no account* take the river course to the south towards weir at Castleford Junction. Make sure you are clear about where to go *before* you get there.
2. The Lafarge Tarmac sand and gravel wharf, just below the old Fairies Hill Lock, used to receive regular barge deliveries. At the time of writing this traffic has finished and the intention is to remove the wharfage.

WALKING AND CYCLING

It is possible – during the summer months – for pedestrians to follow a path on the north side of the navigation, from Caroline Bridge to Allerton Bywater, with waymarked deviations around the lake near Woodend and through Allerton Bywater. Otherwise see notes on page 23.

with the river. Enclosed within the arm is an aggregate wharf and concrete plant replacing, what for many years had been an oil depot serviced by barges which today – with their tanks cut open to form holds – deliver sea-dredged sand and gravel loaded at Hull. The river by Fleet Lock was the site of a disastrous breach which occurred in March 1988, when the ground separating it from the adjacent St Aidens open-cast mine collapsed and the water poured in. Apparently the river below the breach flowed backwards for half a day, such was the volume of water consumed, and the workforce only just managed to rescue the two large draglines. There are *visitor and long-term moorings* available in the marina above the new Lemonroyd Lock (combining the old Lemonroyd Lock with the now-vanished Kippax Lock). Rejoining the river at Lemonroyd Lock, the mining village of Allerton Bywater appears at the end of the newly constructed section of waterway. There is a welcome waterside pub here but mooring outside has become difficult. Should you stop, make sure you moor securely, since passing commercial craft can emerge and cause a considerable wash. There is a waterways 'crossroads' at Castleford.

Navigators heading towards Sowerby Bridge should turn right here and must on no account go straight across – since that way leads to

continued in Book 6

the huge Castleford Weir. To the left, through the Flood Lock, are a *sanitary station*, *showers* and good *moorings*, beyond which lies the route to Sheffield (*see* Book 6), Goole, Hull, York, the River Trent and ultimately the North Sea. Large commercial craft may still emerge from here, so boats travelling downstream on either the rivers Aire or Calder, though not entering the flood lock, must still observe the traffic signals to avoid collision with vessels leaving the lock. Entering the River Calder, navigators will notice that its course here has been straightened, as the oxbow lakes either side will testify. After ducking under a large road bridge and two railway bridges, a path which gives access to the New Wheatsheaf pub can be seen heading east from the aggregate wharf. Your nose will also tell you there is a large sewage works here. Pressing on, the large, deep mechanised Woodnook Lock is reached. This replaced the earlier Fairies and Altofts locks (now disused) to the south. By comparing the sizes of the locks, an impression of the improvements carried out on the navigation during the last 100 years can be gained. Beyond the large motorway bridge is King's Road Lock (also mechanised) and paths from here lead to Altofts, although there is little reason to walk the ½ mile or so, except for supplies.

Temple Newsam House and Garden

Temple Newsam Road, off Selby Road, Leeds LS15 0AE (0113 336 7460; www.leeds.gov.uk/museumsandgalleries/templenewsamhouse/Home). Walk north from Swillington Bridge, fork left after the river – 2 miles. A superb Tudor/Jacobean house in 900 acres of parkland. Magnificent Georgian and Regency interiors. Walks in park and woods, magnificent displays of roses and rhododendrons in gardens. Regular events and activities. House *open Tue-Sun (& Mon in school holidays) 10.00-17.00*. Park and garden *open all year*. Charge for house.

Temple Newsam Farm A working rare breeds farm – home to 400 animals. Sheep, pigs, goats, chickens, ducks and largest Vaynol herd in the world. Three-hundred-year-old Great Barn and other traditional farm buildings housing a collection of old agricultural tools and machinery. *Open Tue-Sun 10.00-17.00 (16.00 winter)*. Shop and café. Charge.

Mickletown

W. Yorks. PO, tel, stores, off-licence, hardware, takeaway. Claimed by the locals to be the second largest village in England – it is suggested that Wroxham in Norfolk is the largest – Mickletown has clearly had its problems since the neighbouring colliery closed. The stores are *open 08.00-21.00 daily.*

Allerton Bywater

W. Yorks. PO, tel, stores, butcher, chemist, fish & chips, takeaway, off-licence. A mining village, but the pit is now closed. Coal was once loaded from wagons onto barges from a small staithe here.

Castleford

W. Yorks. All services. Once the Roman settlement of *Lagentium*, now a busy industrial town which has grown up at this important waterways junction, it is also the birth place of the sculptor Henry Moore.

Castleford Museum Carlton Street, Castleford WF10 1BB (01977 722085; www.wakefield.gov.uk/events-and-culture/museums/castleford-museum). In the library. Recently refurbished and extended, the museum presents the history of Castleford from the Bronze Age to the present day. There are objects from when the settlement was an important Roman town, not forgetting marbles, rugby, mining, pottery and glass. The early life of Henry Moore is also depicted. *Open Mon-Tue & Thu-Sat 09.30-17.00 (Sat 16.00).*

Diggerland Willowbridge Lane, Whitwood, Castleford WF10 5NW (0871 227 7007; www.diggerland.com). Approximately 1 mile south east of Whitwood Wharf, on A655, opposite Castleford Rugby Union Football ground. The ultimate adventure for children old and young – everything from mini-tractors and digger driving through to dumper truck racing – with some fairground rides thrown in for good measure! *Open daily 10.00-1700 (16.00 in winter)*. Charge.

Altofts

W. Yorks. PO, tel, stores, off-licence, fish & chips, delicatessen, station (1 mile distant at Normanton). Originally a mining village and now a suburb of Wakefield. There was once a pub by the river, but it is now a private house. There are still three pubs in the village. The stores are open *05.30-23.00.*

Stanley Ferry Aqueduct

Pubs and Restaurants (pages 20–21)

🍺 1 **The Commercial** 12 Main Street, Mickletown LS26 9JE. Busy, two-roomed local serving real ale. Dog- and child-friendly, garden. Quiz *Thu* and live music *Fri*. Traditional pub games, newspapers, sports TV and Wi-Fi. *Open Mon-Wed 14.00-00.00 (Mon 15.00) & Thu-Sun 12.00-00.00.*

🍺✗ 2 **The Boat** Boat Lane, Allerton Bywater, Castleford WF102BX (01977 514808). An attractive riverside pub where once a ferry operated carrying miners and boat horses across the river. Real ales. Food is available *daily 12.00-19.30 (Sun 18.00)*. Dog- and child-friendly, riverside seating. Traditional pub games, *occasional* live music, real fires, sports TV and Wi-Fi. *Open 12.00-23.00 (Sun 22.30).*

🍺 3 **The Anchor** Victoria Street, Allerton Bywater, Castleford WF10 2DF (01977 603119). Friendly two-roomed local serving real ale. Dog- and family-friendly, garden. Sports TV and Wi-Fi. *Open Mon-Thu 16.00-23.00 & Thu-Sun 12.00-23.00.*

🍺✗ 4 **The Victoria Hotel** 63 Main Street , Allerton Bywater, Castleford WF10 2BZ (01977 516438). Friendly, modernised local dispensing real ale and food *Wed-Fri E; Sat L and E & Sun 12.00-18.00*. Dog- and family-friendly, garden. *Occasional* live music, real fires, sports TV and Wi-Fi. *Open Mon-Tue 15.00-23.00; Wed-Thu 14.00-00.00 & Fri-Sun 12.00-00.00.*

🍺 5 **The Griffin** Lock Lane, Castleford WF10 2LB (01977 731706). Friendly local serving real ale and food *Mon-Tue & Thu-Sat 08.00-14.00; Fri-Sat 17.00-19.00 & Sun 11.00-16.00*. Dog- and child-friendly, outdoor seating. Traditional pub games and sports TV. *Open daily 11.00-01.00.*

🍺 6 **The Junction** 109 Carlton Street, Castleford WF10 1EE (01977 277750; www. thejunctionpubcastleford.com). A warm, friendly welcome awaits the visitor to this community pub that takes its real ale seriously, serving beer from the wood. Entertainment comes in the form of bar billiards, conversation and general banter. Dogs and children *(during the day)* welcome. Live music *Fri*. Real fires and Wi-Fi. *Open Mon-Thu 14.00-21.00 (Thu 23.00); Fri-Sat 12.00-23.30 & Sun 12.00-21.00.*

🍺✗ 7 **The New Wheatsheaf** Altofts Lane, Whitwood, Castleford WF10 5QB (01977 553052; www.wheatsheaf.com). Large, brightly decorated traditional pub, where someone clearly takes a great pride in their flower arrangements. A wide range of food is available *Mon-Sat L and E & Sun 12.00-20.00*. Family-friendly. *Open daily 10.00-00.00 (Sun 22.30).*

🍺 8 **The Miners Arms** 169 Church Road, Altofts WF6 2QR. ½ mile south of Nordens Bridge, along Lock Lane. Friendly community pub with an enclosed garden. Children welcome. Sports TV. *Open Mon-Sat 16.00-00.00 (Fri-Sat 01.00) & Sun 12.00-01.00.*

🍺 9 **The Poplar Inn** 151 Church Road, Altofts WF6 2QN (01924 893416). Almost opposite the Miners Arms. Lively village local serving real ale and with barbecues *in summer*. Large garden and children's play area. Quiz *Thu*, bands *Sat* & karaoke *Sun*. *Open Mon-Fri 15.00-23.00 (Fri 14.00) & Sat-Sun 12.00-23.00.*

🍺 10 **The Horse & Jockey** 47 Church Road, Altofts WF6 2NU (01924 892994). Village local – the oldest pub in the Altofts – with outside seating and *occasional* live music. *Open Mon-Fri 16.00-23.00 & Sat-Sun 12.00-23.30 (Sun 22.30).*

WALKING AND CYCLING

Currently there is no continuous towpath from Caroline Bridge to Castleford so walkers and cyclists wishing to follow the navigation are presented with two choices:

1 Leave the towpath ½ mile east of Shan Bridge and follow the Trans Pennine Trail signs onto Mickletown Road and thence to the junction of Savile Road and Church Road. Turn left along Savile Road and right along Pinfold Lane at the T junction. At the main road (Barnsdale Road) turn left and follow this road – along the pavement – round a sharp right-hand bend (ignore the left-hand turning here into Micklefield) and then south to Methley Bridge over the Wakefield Branch of the Aire & Calder Canal. Join the towpath here and follow it east into Castlefield. For those following this diversion in reverse (i.e. from Castleford) leave the navigation at Barnsdale Road Bridge and head south, over the river and turn right along Savile Road. Immediately past the roundabout look for a Public Footpath sign leading you back onto the river bank.

2 Follow the directions above to Methley Bridge where, by turning west along the towpath, it is possible to reach Wakefield and, with the assistance of the excellent Metro bus/rail system (0113 245 7676; www. wymetro.com) complete a circular walk/ride that might have commenced in Leeds.
N.B. A section of the towpath Methley Bridge to Wakefield is only cyclable with care and at the cyclist's own risk!

3 A third option is to make use of the Trans Pennine Trail throughout its route in the Leeds area. Starting at Crown Point Bridge (*see* page 16 near the city centre), it follows the canal to Mickletown (*see* 1 above) where, by following the excellent waymarking west along a minor road and a disused railway line, it heads into Wakefield making use of a further section of canal (the Aire & Calder Wakefield Branch) at Stanley Ferry. This is part of Euro-route E8 (ultimately running from the west coast of Ireland to Istanbul). For further information (free) and detailed guides (charge) contact the Trans Pennine Trail Officer on 01226 772574 or visit www.transpenninetrail.org.uk.

Wakefield

Birkwood Lock was for a long time the last mechanised lock when travelling upstream. At Stanley Ferry the canal is diverted over the new aqueduct, which stands alongside the original and was opened in 1981. The original aqueduct was thought to be at risk from the large craft which can now navigate here. There is a Canal & River Trust repair yard and lock gate building workshop immediately before the aqueduct, and *a marina with a pub* beyond. This has been built in a defunct loading basin beside the splendid, stone wharf office. It was here that empty 'Tom Puddings' were hauled onto railway wagons and, after loading at the nearby colliery, re-launched en route for Goole. After Ramsden's Swing Bridge (*sanitary station, pump out and showers*) the navigation continues in a dead straight line, passing Broadreach Flood Lock and Heath Old Hall before turning west to join the Calder & Hebble at Fall Ing Lock. There are craft moored here by an old loading chute, a *picnic area* and convenient *pub*. Below Wakefield Flood Lock the river is navigable for a short distance towards the weir, although much cluttered by large craft undergoing refurbishment at the boatyard here. Leaving Wakefield you pass under a splendid curving brick railway viaduct known locally as 'the 99 arches'. A careful count will reveal only 95.

Stanley Ferry Aqueduct

It is a good idea to moor at Stanley Ferry Marina and walk to the road bridge for a full view of this fine structure – a trough suspended from a two-pin cast iron arch – built on the same principle as the Sydney Harbour Bridge, which it predates by 100 years. Nearly 7000 tons of Bramley Fall stone and 1000 tons of cast iron were used in its construction. The first boat to pass across it was the *James*, a schooner of 160 tons drawn by three grey horses, on 8 August 1839. The 700 men who worked on it were fed at the nearby public houses, one of which, The Ship, still stands. Designed by George Leather, the strength of the structure was severely tested when, soon after opening, the largest flood for 20 years caused the river below actually to flow into the trough. The towpath is carried on a separate steel girder structure designed to protect the aqueducts during such floods. The concrete aqueduct was built in 1981, and the original, by its side, is still in water.

NAVIGATIONAL NOTES

1 Take heed of the notices and flood indicator boards at the locks. Pleasure craft should only proceed if the water level is in the *green* or *amber* sectors. Amber indicates that the river is above normal levels and that boaters should proceed with caution to and THROUGH the next lock.

2 Most locks on the Calder & Hebble have a unique type of paddle gear, consisting of a small perforated wheel which is turned using a 'handspike'. These are obtainable from boatyards on the navigation. Or a piece of 3" x 2" hardwood, 3ft long (and planed down to size), will do just as well.

3 When coming downstream (from Sowerby Bridge direction) keep a sharp lookout for the entrance to Wakefield Flood Lock. There is a large weir on the river, a short distance beyond the boatyard, by the bridge.

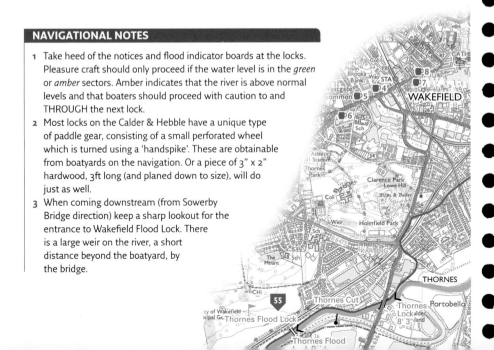

WALKING AND CYCLING

1 At Stanley Ferry the Trans Pennine Trail (*see* page 17) joins the towpath and it continues south east of Broadreach Lock over the river footbridge and under the railway arches. Once under the railway bridge, those wishing to follow the navigation into Wakefield – and beyond – should bear round to the right and back onto the river bank. In the wooded area, around Heath Old Hall, it may be necessary in the summer to make a slight detour along tracks to avoid the dense vegetation. A slightly longer detour at this point could bring you to the excellent Kings Arms, in the delightful village of Heath itself (*see* page 26).

2 At Wakefield Flood Lock cross over the navigation and head north along Bridge Street to cross the river. Bear left on to Thornes Lane and follow this road along the river bank. Stay on Thornes Lane when it meets Thornes Lane Wharfe and turns away from the river. Go under two railway bridges and turn left at the roundabout, past The Queen's Arms and under a third railway bridge. Turn left down Holmfield Lane (there is a *takeaway* on the corner) and then right past the industrial units along Green End Lane. Rejoin the navigation at Thornes Lock.

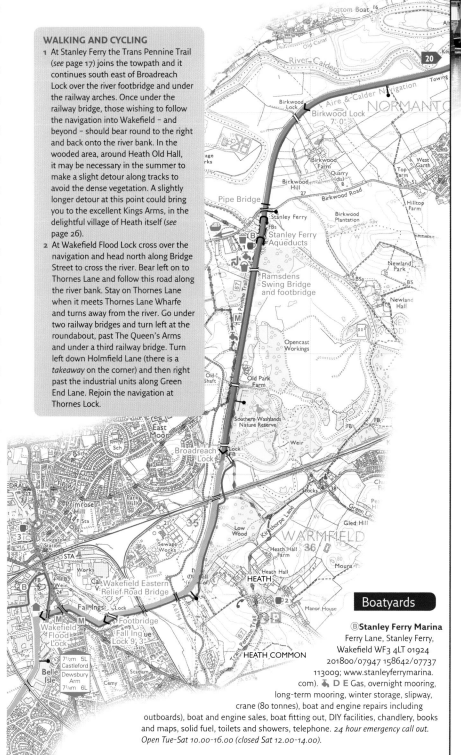

Boatyards

Ⓑ **Stanley Ferry Marina**
Ferry Lane, Stanley Ferry, Wakefield WF3 4LT 01924 201800/07947 158642/07737 113009; www.stanleyferrymarina. com). 🛠 D E Gas, overnight mooring, long-term mooring, winter storage, slipway, crane (80 tonnes), boat and engine repairs including outboards), boat and engine sales, boat fitting out, DIY facilities, chandlery, books and maps, solid fuel, toilets and showers, telephone. *24 hour emergency call out. Open Tue-Sat 10.00-16.00 (closed Sat 12.00-14.00).*

25

Wakefield

W. Yorks. All services. The city centre is north of the navigation. The regional capital of West Yorkshire, it gained city status in 1888 when the cathedral was granted its charter. Mainly 15th-C Perpendicular in style, the cathedral's 247ft spire is a landmark for miles around. On a much smaller scale, but perhaps of equal interest, is the Chantry Chapel of St Mary, a rare 14th-C example of a bridge chapel, just a short walk north of Fall Ing, by the weir. Industrial pollution has meant that the entire front of the building has had to be replaced twice in the last two centuries: the original now graces the entrance to a boathouse at Kettlethorpe. The city itself is set on a hill, and still contains some quiet streets and dignified Georgian houses, notably those in St John's Square, with its delightful church and handsome council buildings. Wakefield's prosperity was founded on the textile and engineering industries, both of which have taken a battering in recent years. However, the city has been successful in attracting new industry, such as Coca Cola/Schweppes; and the vast and spectacular Ridings shopping complex has created many new jobs.

The Hepworth Wakefield Gallery Walk, Wakefield WF1 5AW (01924 247360; www.hepworthwakefield. org). Contemporary art gallery and museum, including work from Wakefield's art collection and works by Barbara Hepworth. Café, shop, regular events and nearby children's play area. *Open daily 10.00-17.00.* Free.

The Theatre Royal & Opera House 12 Drury Lane, Wakefield WF1 2TE (01924 211311; www. theatreroyalwakefield.co.uk). Provides a lively and varied programme of entertainment.

Yorkshire Sculpture Park at Bretton Hall, West Bretton WF4 4LG (01924 832631; www.ysp.co.uk). displays some important works by Barbara Hepworth and Henry Moore, both local artists. *Open daily 10.00-17.00.* Free.

Wakefield Museum Burton Street, Wakefield WF1 2DD (01924 302104; www.wakefield.gov.uk/ events-and-culture/museums/wakefield-museum). Local history and archaeology, excavations from Sandal Castle, and the Waterton collection of exotic birds and animals. The building, designed in 1820, was originally a music Saloon. *Open Mon-Fri 09.00-17.00 (Wed-Thu 19.00) & Sat 09.00-16.00.* Free.

Heath Village 2 miles east of Wakefield. A beautifully preserved village with some 18th-C merchants' houses amongst other substantial buildings. Heath Hall is a fine Georgian house by John Carr (1753) with carved woodwork and moulded plaster ceilings. The gas-lit King's Arms pub is a gem (*see below*).

Pubs and Restaurants (pages 24-25)

X 1 The Stanley Ferry Ferry Lane, Stanley Ferry, Wakefield WF3 4LT (01924 290596; www. hungryhorse.co.uk/pubs/west-yorkshire/stanley-ferry). One of the old converted wharf-side buildings. Restaurant with bar serving food *daily 11.00-22.00 (Sat-Sun 10.00).* Indoor and outdoor play areas. Garden. Traditional pub games and Wi-Fi. *Open 11.00-23.00 (Sat-Sun 10.00).*

X 2 The King's Arms Heath Village, near Wakefield WF1 5SL (01924 377527; www. thekingsarmsheath.co.uk). Overlooking the common, originally built as houses in the 18th C and converted into a pub in 1841. A wide choice of real ale is served in an exceptional setting with a gas-lit, wood-panelled bar, a range of different rooms, stone-flagged floors, and full of antiques. Open fire, excellent bar and restaurant food *Mon-Thu L and E & Fri-Sun 12.00-21.00 (Sun 19.00).* Real cider. Dog- and child-friendly, walled gardens. *Occasional* live music, real fires and Wi-Fi. *Open 12.00-23.00 (Fri-Sat 00.00).*

3 Fernandes Brewery Tap 5 Avison Yard, Kirkgate, Wakefield WF1 1UA (01924 386348; www. ossett-brewery.co.uk/pubs/fernandes-brewery-tap--bier-keller-wakefield). Once a malt store and conditioning room for Beverley Brewery – and a malt kiln before that – this pub resurrects the original brewer's name and now dispenses both the present incumbent's own beers and that of guests. A dearth of electronic machines; brewery memorabilia and an open fire *in winter* makes this popular hostelry a real ale drinker's dream. Pets welcome and *Wed* quiz. Real cider. Wi-Fi. *Open Mon-Thu 16.00-23.00 (Thu 11.30) & Fri-Sun 12.00-00.30 (Sun 23.00).*

4 Henry Boon's 130 Westgate, Wakefield WF2 9SR (01924 378126). West of the cathedral, next to the prison. Fine traditional brewery tap for Clark's Brewery, also serving other real ales in an enthusiasts' pub, together with food *Mon-Thu and Sat-Sun 11.00-14.00 & Fri 18.00-19.00.* Dog-friendly. Traditional pub games, sports TV and Wi-Fi. *Open 11.00-23.00 (Fri-Sat 01.00).*

5 The Redoubt 28 Horbury Road, Wakefield WF2 8TS (01924 377085). Little changed in 150 years, this heritage pub dispenses real ales. Family-friendly, garden and you can bring your own food. *Open Mon-Thu 14.00-23.00 & Fri-Sun 12.00-23.00 (Sun 22.30).*

6 The Waterloo 101 Westgate End, Westgate Common, Wakefield WF2 9RL (01924 376717). This pub sports appealing interior woodwork, a striking mural on its gable end and serves real ale. Outside seating and large-screen TV. *Open Mon-Thu and Sun 10.00-00.00 & Fri-Sat 10.00-02.00.*

7 Harry's Bar 107B Westgate, Wakefield WF1 1EL (01924 373773). Tucked away down a narrow passage, this one-roomed hostelry serves an interested variety of real ales together with real cider. Real fires and pub games. Outdoor drinking area and live music *Mon & Wed. Open Mon-Thu 17.00-00.00; Fri-Sat 16.00-01.00 & Sun 12.00-00.00.*

8 The Ruddy Duck Bridge Street, Wakefield WF1 5JR (01924 379079; www.ruddyduckpubwakefield. co.uk). Majoring on food, this family pub serves real ale and food *all day, every day.* Garden and Wi-Fi. *Open Mon-Fri 10.00-00.30 (Fri-Sat 01.30) & Sun 11.00-00.30.*

BRIDGEWATER CANAL

MAXIMUM DIMENSIONS

Length: 70'
Beam: 14' 9"
Headroom: 8'
Draught: 2' 6"

LICENCES

The Bridgewater Canal Company Limited,
Peel Dome, Intu Trafford Centre,
Manchester M17 8PL
Enquiries: 0161 629 8266/8432;
www.bridgewatercanal.co.uk.

All craft using the canal must be licensed. They must also be insured against third party risks which should include the cost of salvage and removal of wreck. Any boat holding a Canal & River Trust canal and river licence may cruise on the Bridgewater Canal for up to seven consecutive days free of charge. However, return within 28 days requires a permit (charge) available through the website, by telephone or from the Enforcement Officer on the bank.

MILEAGE

PRESTON BROOK to:
Lymm: 10½ miles
Waters Meeting, junction with
Leigh Branch: 22 miles

CASTLEFIELD JUNCTION, start of
Rochdale Canal: 23½ miles, no locks

DUCIE STREET JUNCTION, start of
Ashton Canal: 25 miles (Rochdale Canal, 9 locks)
Preston Brook to Runcorn: 4¾ miles, no locks
Leigh Branch: 10¾ miles, no locks

The Bridgewater Canal received Royal Assent on 23 March 1759, four years after the Sankey Brook, or St Helens, Canal and 18 years after the Newry Canal (once known as Black Pig's Dyke), which linked Lough Neagh to the sea below Newry, in Northern Ireland, and was probably the first 'modern' canal in the British Isles. The Bridgewater was built by Francis Egerton, third Duke of Bridgewater, to enable coal from his mines at Worsley to be transported to Manchester and sold cheaply. His agent was John Gilbert and his engineer was James Brindley, who designed a lockless contour canal which crossed the River Irwell on a stone aqueduct – a revolutionary concept and one that was ridiculed by many sceptics. However, the line was open to Castlefield by the end of 1765.

While the canal was under construction, there began the excavation of a remarkable system of underground canals to serve the Duke's mines, reached through two entrances at Worsley Delph. Eventually 46 miles of underground canal were built, some on different levels and linked by an ingenious inclined plane built along a fault in the sandstone. The craft used in the mines were known as 'starvationers', double-ended tub boats which could carry up to 12 tons of coal. This whole system remained in use until the late 19th C.

In 1762 the Duke received sanction to extend his canal to the Liverpool tideway at Runcorn – this was later amended in order to connect with the new Trent & Mersey Canal at Preston Brook. The route between Liverpool and Manchester was opened in 1776, although Brindley did not live to see its completion. In 1795 the Duke, then 60 years old, received the Royal Assent for the final part of the network, which linked Worsley to the Leeds & Liverpool Canal at Leigh.

The coming of the railways did not initially affect the prosperity of the canal. In 1872 the newly formed Bridgewater Navigation Company purchased the canal for £1,120,000, and they in turn sold it to the Manchester Ship Canal Company in 1885. When the building of the new Ship Canal meant that Brindley's original stone aqueduct over the River Irwell was replaced, its successor, the Barton Swing Aqueduct, was no less outstanding than the original, being a steel trough closed by gates at each end, pivoting on an island in the Ship Canal.

The Bridgewater Canal is a tribute to its builders in that it continued to carry commercial traffic until 1974 – indeed its wide gauge, lock-free course and frequent use of aqueducts makes many later canals seem retrograde. It is now an oasis of tranquillity amidst the burgeoning new industry of Manchester.

Preston Brook

Although the main line of the Bridgewater once locked down to the Mersey in Runcorn, this is now a dead end, with the locks being closed in 1966. It does, however, still make an interesting diversion – there is a *supermarket, PO* and *chemist* south of Bridge 73. What is now the main canal route to Manchester bears to the right immediately after the big M56 motorway bridge, and its direct course to the south of the Mersey affords good views of the Manchester Ship Canal. The canal frontage at Moore is attractive, with moored boats, a *PO, shop and off-licence,* and a *telephone box* right by the canal.

Boatyards

Ⓑ**Claymoore Canal Holidays** The Wharf, Preston Brook WA4 4BA (01928 717273; www.claymoore.co.uk). 🚽🛒 D Pump out, gas, narrowboat and day-hire craft (2–10 berth boats), overnight mooring, boat repairs, engine repairs, toilets, books, maps, gifts. *Open daily 09.30-17.00.*

Ⓑ**Preston Brook Marina** Preston Brook WA7 3AF (01928 719081). 🚽🛒🛠 Pump out, secure long-term mooring, slipways, toilets, showers.

Ⓑ**Boat and Butty Company** Ockleston's Wharf, Ringway Road, Runcorn WA7 5QN (07976 303696). 🚽🛒🛠Pump out, secure long-term mooring, winter storage, DIY facilities.

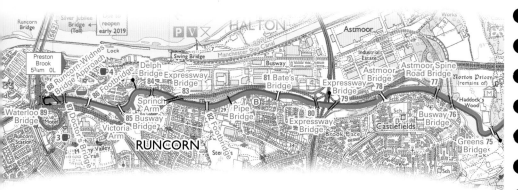

- **Preston Brook Tunnel**
  1239yds long and forbidden to unpowered craft. *A notice indicates when you may enter – see page 202.*
- **Preston Brook**
  Cheshire. *PO, tel, stores.* A village which grew to serve the canal, where goods were transshipped from wide beam craft of the north west to narrowboats of the Midlands. Unfortunately, little remains as evidence of this activity, and the M56 dominates.
  Norton Priory Museum and Gardens Windmill Hill, Runcorn WA7 1SX (01928 569895; www.nortonpriory. org). Access from mooring north east of bridge 75. Only the undercroft survives from the 12th C. A recorded commentary describes points of interest. Walled garden, pleasant woodland and sculpture gardens. Regular events and hands-on activities for children. Seasonal fruit and vegetables for sale. Café and tea rooms (in walled garden). Buildings, Ruins and Museum *open daily Apr-Oct 10.00-17.00 & Nov-Mar 11.00-16.00* and Walled Garden *open Apr-Oct 12.00-16.00. Charge.*
- **Runcorn**
  Cheshire. *All services.* The old town is to be found down by the docks, where the elegant curved 1092ft single span of the steel road bridge (built 1961), with the railway beside,

leaps over the Ship Canal and the Mersey. The massive flight of 10 double locks which connected the Bridgewater Canal to the Mersey was abandoned in 1966 and filled in, much to the dismay of industrial archaeologists and canal enthusiasts. Since 1964 Runcorn has been a 'new town', its rapid growth being carefully planned.
- **Daresbury**
  Cheshire. *PO box, tel.* Half-a-mile up the road from Keckwick Bridge, this was the birthplace of Charles Lutwidge Dodgson, better known as Lewis Carroll. The church of All Saints Daresbury Lane WA4 4AE (01925 740348/07778 859935; www.daresburycofe.org.uk) has a pretty Lewis Carroll memorial window in the Daniell Chapel, where he is shown with characters from *Alice in Wonderland:* the Dormouse, the Mad Hatter and the Cheshire Cat. This window was designed by Geoffrey Webb, and was dedicated in 1934. The original church on this site dates from the 12thC, and was a daughter house of nearby Norton Priory (*see above*). The present tower dates from around 1550, with the rest of the church being rebuilt in the 1870s. The fine oak pulpit, dating from 1625, and the rood screen incorporated into the panelling behind the altar, are both worth a look. *The church is open daily 10.00-22.00 (Sun 14.00).*

Pubs and Restaurants

◗✕ 1 **The Ring O' Bells** 7 Chester Road, Daresbury, Warrington WA4 4AJ (01925 740256; www. chefandbrewer.com/pubs/cheshire/ring-o-bells). There has been an ale house here since 1641, although this building dates from 1841. The adjoining stables are older than the pub: to the other side the old Petty Sessions room has been incorporated. Pleasantly busy, with a relaxed atmosphere and open fires. Real ale and food available *daily 12.00-22.00 (Sun 21.30)*. Dog- and family-friendly, garden. Real fires and Wi-Fi. *Open 12.00-23.00 (Sun 22.30).*

◗✕ 2 **The Red Lion** 119 Runcorn Road, Moore, Warrington WA4 6UD (01925 740101). Well-beamed, smart hostelry serving real ale and food *12.00-21.00 (Sun-Mon 20.00)*. *Regular* quiz nights and *occasional* live music. Dog- and child-friendly, garden. Wi-Fi. *Open daily 12.00-23.00 (Sun 22.30).*

There are plenty of pubs in Runcorn, including:

◗ 3 **The Lion Hotel** 100 Greenway Road, Runcorn WA7 5AG (01928 574129). Close to the station, and enjoying a new lease of life, this pub serves an ever-changing choice of real ale and real cider. Sports TV. *Open Mon-Thu 16.00-23.00 (Thu 00.00) Fri-Sat 14.00-00.00 & Sun 12.00-23.00.*

◗ 4 **The Ferry Boat** 10 Church Street, Runcorn WA7 1LR (01928 583380; www.jdwetherspoon.co.uk/home/pubs/the-ferry-boat). Celebrating the ferry service, that used to cross the Mersey between Runcorn and Widnes, this one-time cinema lies in the centre of the old town and serves real ale and cider, together with food *daily 08.00-22.00*. Children welcome. Outside seating and Wi-Fi. *Open 08.00-00.00 (Fri-Sat 01.00).*

WALKING AND CYCLING

The towpath is in good condition throughout, but is only open to walkers. The towpath on the main line forms part of the Cheshire Ring Canal Walk, which makes a circuit with the Ashton, Peak Forest, Macclesfield and Trent & Mersey canals. Leaflets giving details of cycle routes in Runcorn can be downloaded from www3.halton.gov.uk/Pages/traffic/pdfs/RuncornCyclemap.pdf. A cyclists map and Guide to Runcorn can be obtained from www.cycling.org.uk. The Trans Pennine Trail is a 350-mile national route which crosses Runcorn on its way from Liverpool to Warrington. Maps and an Official Accommodation and Visitor Guide are available from www.transpenninetrail.org.uk, www.sustrans.org.uk or Trans Pennine Trail Barnsley Council, PO Box 634, Barnsley S70 9GG (01226 772574; www.barnsley.gov.uk).

Stockton Heath

A short rural stretch is interrupted by the estate village of Higher Walton, which can be seen among trees, and this is followed by a secluded tree-lined length in a shallow cutting before the outskirts of Stockton Heath are approached. The building occupied by Thorn Marine was once a fodder store, stables and staff house for the packet boats (more recently it was

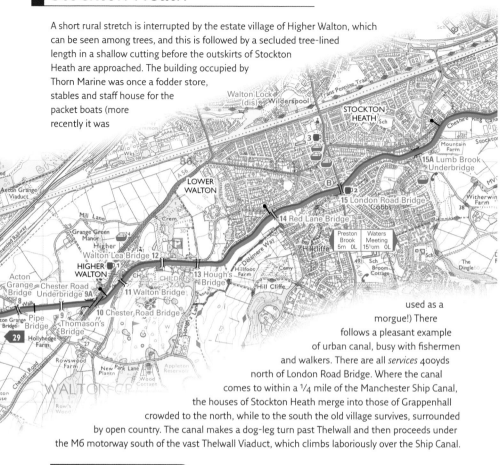

used as a morgue!) There follows a pleasant example of urban canal, busy with fishermen and walkers. There are all *services* 400yds north of London Road Bridge. Where the canal comes to within a ¼ mile of the Manchester Ship Canal, the houses of Stockton Heath merge into those of Grappenhall crowded to the north, while to the south the old village survives, surrounded by open country. The canal makes a dog-leg turn past Thelwall and then proceeds under the M6 motorway south of the vast Thelwall Viaduct, which climbs laboriously over the Ship Canal.

Boatyards

Ⓑ**Thorn Marine** London Road, Stockton Heath, Warrington WA4 6LE (01925 265129; www.thornmarine.co.uk). 🛟🔧D Pump out, gas, day-boat hire, boat safety examiner, Gas Safe registered, boat and engine repairs, chandlery, toilets, books, maps and gifts, solid fuels. Public telephone and shopping centre *nearby. Open daily 09.00-17.00*

● **Higher Walton**
Cheshire. PO box, tel. A pretty, late-Victorian estate village among trees.
Walton Hall and Gardens Walton Lea Road, Higher Walton, Warrington WA4 6SN (01925 262908; www.warrington.gov.uk/waltongardens). Thirty two acres of parkland and gardens *open from dawn to dusk.* Facilities include children's zoo, outdoor games, heritage centre, play area, café and Ranger Service organising activities for the public and groups. Café *open daily 10.00-15.00 (16.00 in school holidays).* Zoo *open daily 10.30-17.00 (winter 16.00)* and Park *open daily 08.00-dusk.* Free entry – charge for parking only.

● **Stockton Heath**
Cheshire. PO, tel, stores, banks, chemists, fish & chips, off-licence, takeaways, library. A useful selection of shops and services north of London Road Bridge 15. An outer suburb of Warrington, England's centre for vodka distilling and a useful place for supplies.
Stockton Quay London Bridge 15. The terminus of the canal from 1771 to 1776, before the Duke of Bridgewater completed his route from Manchester to Runcorn, and consequently a major transshipment point with stables, yards, wharves, warehouses and a canal company office. Passenger packet boat services also ran from here from 1771 to the mid 1880s, one of the craft being the renowned *Duchess-Countess.*

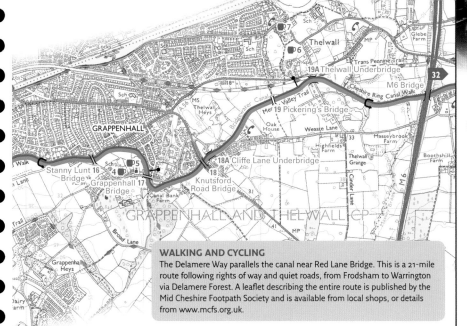

WALKING AND CYCLING

The Delamere Way parallels the canal near Red Lane Bridge. This is a 21-mile route following rights of way and quiet roads, from Frodsham to Warrington via Delamere Forest. A leaflet describing the entire route is published by the Mid Cheshire Footpath Society and is available from local shops, or details from www.mcfs.org.uk.

● Grappenhall

Cheshire. PO box, tel, library. A fine group of buildings on cobbled streets survive around the church of St Wilfred, where the village stocks remain. There are two excellent pubs, which makes a stop here very worthwhile.

● Thelwall

Cheshire. PO box, tel. A pretty village with its name now indelibly linked with a motorway viaduct.

Pubs and Restaurants

● ✕ 1 The Walton Arms 148 Old Chester Road, Higher Walton, Warrington WA4 6TG (01925 262659; www.vintageinn.co.uk/restaurants/north-west/thewaltonarms). This 19th-C, brick-built, mock-Tudor pub serves real ale, real cider and food *daily 12.00-22.00 (Sun 21.30)*. Dog- and child-friendly, garden. Sports TV and Wi-Fi. *Open 12.00-23.00.*

● ✕ 2 The London Bridge 163 London Road, Appleton, Warrington WA4 5BG (01925 267904; www.londonbridgeinn.co.uk). A homely and welcoming pub with a canalside terrace, offering real ale and food *daily 12.00-21.00 (Sun 20.00)*. Dog- and family-friendly. Quiz *Tue & Sun.* Occasional live music, real fires and Wi-Fi. *Open Sun-Thu 11.00-23.00 (Thu 23.30) & Fri-Sat 00.00.*

● 3 The Red Lion 60 London Road, Stockton Heath WA4 6HN (01925 861041; www.thwaitespubs.co.uk/red-lion-inn-stockton-heath). Two-hundred-year-old, Georgian coaching inn, still dispensing real ales and food *daily 12.00-19.00*. Dog- and child-friendly *(until 19.00)* garden. Live music *Fri.* Traditional pub games (including crown bowling) newspapers and sports TV. *Open Mon-Thu 11.00-23.00 & Fri-Sun 12.00-01.00 (Sun 23.00).*

● ✕ 4 The Rams Head Church Lane, Grappenhall, Warrington WA4 3EP (01925 262814; www.ramshead-inn.co.uk). A comfortable old-fashioned pub on a cobbled street in a conservation village dispensing real ale and food *Mon-Tue L and E; Wed-Sat 12.00-21.00*

(Fri-Sat 22.00) & *Sun 12.00-20.00*. Dog- and child-friendly, garden. Traditional pub games, *occasional* live music, real fires and Wi-Fi. *Open daily 12.00-23.00 (Fri-Sat 00.00).*

● ✕ 5 The Parr Arms Grappenhall Lane, Grappenhall, Warrington WA4 3EP (01925 212120; www.theparrarms.co.uk). A comfortable and homely pub on the cobbled street, right beside the church, serving real ale and food available *12.00-21.00 (Sun 20.30)*. Dog- and child-friendly, garden. Newspapers, real fires and Wi-Fi. *Open 12.00-23.00 (Sun 22.30).*

● ✕ 6 Little Manor Bell Lane, Thelwall, WA4 2SX (01925 212070; www.brunningandprice.co.uk/littlemanor). Set in large, pleasant grounds – and originally built for the Percival family in 1660 – this fine building now dispenses real ales and excellent food *daily 12.00-21.30 (Sun 21.00)*. Well-behaved dogs and children welcome. Traditional pub games, newspapers, real fires and Wi-Fi. *Open 10.30-23.00 (Sun 22.30).*

● 7 The Pickering Arms 1 Bell Lane, Thelwall WA4 2SU (01925 861262; www.pickeringarmsthelwall.co.uk). This Grade II listed building exudes an understated elegance, dispensing real ales and appetising, good value food *Mon-Fri L and E & Sat-Sun 12.00-21.00 (Sun 20.00)*. Dog- and child-friendly, garden. Quiz *Thu.* Traditional pub games, *occasional* live music, newspapers, real fires and Wi-Fi. *Open daily 12.00-23.00 (Fri-Sat 23.30).*

31

Lymm

There are fine views of the distant Pennines to the north before the canal makes a very pleasing passage through the heart of Lymm, where the streets come right down to the water's edge. There are convenient *24 hour moorings* here. The canal then passes the village of Oughtrington *(boater facilities include pump out, laundry, coal, gas, toilets and showers – open Mon-Sat*

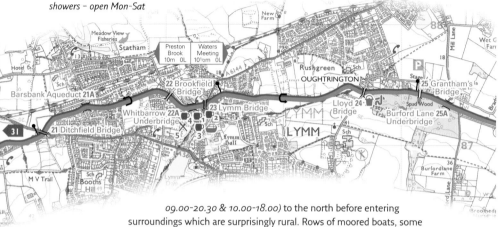

09.00-20.30 & 10.00-18.00) to the north before entering surroundings which are surprisingly rural. Rows of moored boats, some in an advanced state of decay, announce the presence of three useful boatyards and a fine pub, with a free ferry for towpath walkers. The fields then gently fall away into the valley of the River Bollin, which the Bridgewater crosses on a large embankment, with expansive views of the Manchester Ship Canal and Dunham Park. Dunham Underbridge is a new concrete and steel construction, built to replace the original stone trough which breached disastrously in August 1971 and resulted in a two-year closure and repairs amounting to £250,000 at the time. There are good moorings by Dunham Town Bridge. There are also two excellent farm shops – Little Heath WA14 4SE (0161 928 0520; www.littleheathfarmshop.co.uk) *open Mon-Sat 10.00-18.00 & Sun 10.00-17.00* (close to the Axe and Cleaver Hotel) and Ash Farm WA14 5SG (0161 928 1230; www.facebook.com/pages/category/Ice-Cream-Shop/Dunham-Massey-Farm-Ice-Cream-172736049751319) *open daily 12.00-18.00* (just north of the Vine Inn) – the latter majoring on home-made ice cream.

● **Lymm**
Cheshire. PO, tel, stores, banks, chemists, butcher, baker, fish & chips, takeaways, delicatessen, library. The 17th-C Lymm Cross stands just a few yards from the canal in the centre of this hilly and attractive little town. The dam at the back of the town was built to carry the turnpike road over a sharp ravine, thus creating a pleasant lake in the process.
● **Bollington**
Cheshire. A compact and attractive village, with a fine old pub and a converted mill.
Dunham Massey Hall Woodhouse Lane, Altrincham WA14 4SJ (0161 941 1025; www.nationaltrust.org.uk/dunham-massey). Once the seat of the Earl of Stamford, this beautiful 18th-C house by John Norris stands in a wooded and well-stocked deer park, landscaped by George Booth, the Second Earl of Warrington, and now considered to be one of the north west's great plantsman's gardens. A sumptuous interior contains collections of Huguenot

silver, paintings and walnut furniture. There is also an 18th-C orangery, an Elizabethan mount and a well-house. Concerts are staged in the gallery; exhibitions, fairs and services are held in the house and chapel; and there is a short programme of interesting conducted walks. Access is via Bollington, over the footbridge near the Swan with Two Nicks pub. House and garden *open all year*, telephone or check website for times. Admission charge. Restaurant and shop.
● **Dunham Town**
Cheshire. PO box, tel, stores, farm shops. A small, scattered, farming village with a pub. The shop is *open daily 08.00-12.00 (Sat-Sun 09.00).*

> **WALKING AND CYCLING**
> From Lymm Dam it is possible to access an excellent footpath network, details from 01925 443322; www.warrington.gov.uk.

Boatyards

Ⓑ**Hesford Marine** Warrington Lane, Lymm WA13 0SW (01925 754639; www.hesfordmarine.com). **D** Gas, long-term mooring, winter storage, slipway, crane (20 tons), covered hard standing, shot blasting, boat sales and repairs, engine repairs, chandlery, toilets, small selection of books, maps and gifts, DIY facilities.

Ⓑ**Lymm Marina Boat Sales** Warrington Lane, Lymm WA13 0SW (01925 752945/07798 752945; www.lmbs.co.uk). New boat sales – sailaway and fully fitted, long-term mooring, winter storage, 20-ton boat lift. *Open Thu-Fri & some Sats 10.00-16.30.*

Pubs and Restaurants

⬛ 1 **The Golden Fleece** 41 The Cross, Lymm WA13 0HR (01925 755538; www.greeneking-pubs.co.uk/pubs/cheshire/golden-fleece). A picturesque canalside pub, serving real ale and food *12.00-21.00 (Sun 20.00)*. Dog- and family-friendly, garden. *Quiz Tue* & live music *Fri*. Traditional pub games, sports TV and Wi-Fi. *Open Sun-Thu 12.00-23.00 (Sun 22.30) & Fri-Sat 12.00-00.00.*

⬛ 2 **The Bull's Head** 32 The Cross, Lymm WA13 0HU (01925 753614). A cosy traditional village local serving real ale. Dogs and children welcome. Garden. Traditional pub games, real fires, sports TV and Wi-Fi. *Open daily 12.00-00.00 (Fri-Sat 01.00).*

⬛✕ 3 **The Spread Eagle** 47 Eagle Brow, Lymm WA13 0AG (01925 757467; www.spreadeaglelymm.co.uk). Traditional local serving real ale and home-cooked food *daily 12.00-21.00 (Sun 19.00)*. Child- and dog-friendly. Garden. Open fires, large screen TV, traditional pub games, newspapers and Wi-Fi. *Occasional* live music. *Open Mon-Sat 11.00-23.30 & Sun 12.00-22.30.*

⬛ 4 **The Brewery Tap** 18 Bridgewater Street, Lymm WA13 0AB (01925 755451; www.lymmbrewing.co.uk). Established in the old post office, this friendly hostelry serves a range of real ales from its own microbrewery in the cellar. Renown local pies available. Dog- and child-friendly (*until 19.00*) outside seating. Traditional pub games, newspapers, real fires and Wi-Fi. *Open Sun-Wed 12.00-23.00 & Thu-Sat 12.00-23.30 (Thu 00.00).*

✕♀ 5 **Bowden's Wine Bar and Tapas** 16 Bridgewater Street, Lymm WA13 0AB (01925 754852; www.bowdenstapas.com/home/4575009693). Centrally-placed wine and tapas bar serving real ale and wine (you can also bring your own wine) together with food *Wed-Fri 17.00-21.30 (Sat 22.00) & Sun 13.00-17.00*. Bar open

Wed-Sat 17.00-23.00 (Sat 16.00) & Sun 13.00-20.00.

⬛✕ 6 **The Barn Owl Inn** Agden Wharf, Warrington Lane, Lymm WA13 0SW (01925 752020; www.thebarnowlinn.co.uk). A friendly pub with an excellent reputation for its food, serving real ales and meals *Mon-Fri L* and *E & Sat-Sun 12.00-20.30 (Sun 20.00)*. Dog- and child-friendly, patio. *Occasional Sat* live music and Wi-Fi. *Open daily 12.00-23.00.*

⬛ 7 **Ye Olde No. 3** Lymm Road, Little Bollington, WA14 4TA (01925 756754; www.yeoldeno3.com/index). An attractive former coaching inn with no less than three ghosts, which now serves a good selection of real ales. Food is available *daily 12.00-20.00 (Sun 19.00)* and there is a canalside garden with play area. Dogs welcome. Quiz *Sun* & Karaoke *Fri*. Real fires. *Open 12.00-23.00 (Fri-Sat 00.00).*

⬛✕ 8 **The Swan With Two Nicks** Park Lane, Little Bollington, WA14 4TJ (0161 928 2914; www.swanwithtwonicks.co.uk). A fine, comfortable and cosy pub with a friendly atmosphere, serving real ale. Extensive menu for upmarket bar food and à la carte *daily 12.00-21.00 (Sun 20.00)*. Gluten-free options available. Dog- and family-friendly. Open fires and garden. Wi-Fi. *May close early on quiet winter evenings* so it is advisable to telephone to check.

⬛ 9 **The Axe and Cleaver** School Lane, Dunham Massey, WA14 4SE (0161 928 3391; www.chefandbrewer.com). Chain pub serving real ales and food *daily 12.00-22.00 (Sun 21.30)*. Family-friendly with a garden. Open fires, newspapers and Wi-Fi. *Open 12.00-23.00 (Sun 22.30).*

⬛ 10 **The Vine Inn** Barns Lane, Dunham Massey WA14 5RU (0161 928 3275). Very inexpensive real ale dispensed in a relaxed, friendly atmosphere together with food *Tue & Thu-Sun 12.00-17.30 (Sun 17.00) and Wed 12.00-14.30)*. Dog- and family-friendly, large garden. Traditional pub games and Wi-Fi. *Open daily 11.00-23.00 (Sun 12.00).*

⬛✕ 11 **The Rope & Anchor** Paddock Lane, Dunham Massey, WA14 5RP (0161 927 7901; www.theropeandanchor.co.uk). Large pub with extensive gardens and play area, serving real ale and food *daily 12.00-21.30 (Sun 21.00)*. Real fires, newspapers and Wi-Fi. *Open 11.00-23.00.*

33

Sale

Beyond Seamon's Moss Bridge 29, where a *PO, chemist, stores and a takeaway* will be found to the south, buildings close in upon the canal, and the countryside rapidly disappears from view. Among the many industrial buildings, both old and new, stands the superb Victorian Linotype Factory, dated 1897, where metal printing type was manufactured. The Metrolink tramway closes in from the south east and escorts the canal all the way through Sale and on into Stretford. At Sale Bridge the area around the imposing Town Hall has been rebuilt, and a couple of *pubs and a restaurant*, along with the Robert Bolt Theatre and The Waterside Arts Centre, take full advantage of their canal frontage. There is another canalside *pub* before the waterway is crossed by the M60 motorway, which then crosses the River Mersey. A large expanse of graves opposite the Watch House Cruising Club heralds the entrance to Stretford.

Pubs and Restaurants

1 **The Railway** 153 Manchester Road, Broadheath WA14 5NT (0161 941 3383). Once set in a row of cottages, this Grade II listed, traditional, multi-room pub dispenses real ale, together with real conversation. Family-friendly, outside seating. Traditional pub games and real fires. *Open daily 12.00-23.30.*

2 **The Old Packet House** 1 Navigation Road, Broadheath WA14 1LW (0161 929 1331; www. theoldpackethouse.co.uk). An excellent choice of real ales, together with good value food *(L daily and E Tue-Thu.* Dog- and family-friendly, canalside seating. Quiz *Mon* & Karaoke *Fri*. Traditional pub games, real fires, sports TV and Wi-fi. *Open Sun-Thu 12.00-23.00 (Sun 22.30) & Fri-Sat 12.00-00.00 (Sat 11.00).*

3 **The Block & Gasket** 11-13 School Road, Sale M33 7XY (0161 976 4174). Large open-plan bar serving real ale and food *daily 09.00-21.00 (Sat-Sun 10.00).* Family-friendly. *Open Mon-Thu 09.00-23.00 (Thu 00.00) Fri-Sat 09.00-02.00 (Sat 10.00) & Sun 10.00-23.00.*

4 **The JP Joule** 2A Northenden Road, Sale M33 3BR (0161 962 9889; www. jdwetherspoon.com/pubs/all-pubs/england/manchester/the-j-p-joule-sale). Popular , town-centre pub on two levels dispensing real ales, real cider and food *daily 08.00-23.00.* Children welcome *until 21.00,* outside seating. Wi-Fi. *Open 08.00-00.00 (Fri-Sat 01.00).*

5 **The King's Ransom** Brittania Road, Sale M33 2AA; www.greeneking-pubs.co.uk/pubs/greater-manchester/kings-ransom). Much of this pub is in fine converted canalside brick buildings, which were at one time part of a coal yard. They extend under the railway, so the pub is larger than you might think. Real ale is served, and food is available *11.00-22.00 (Fri-Sun 21.00).* Family-friendly, outdoor seating. Sports TV and Wi-fi. *Open daily 11.00-00.00 (Fri-Sat 02.00).*

6 **The Bridge Inn** Dane Road, Sale M33 7QH (0161 962 3030; www.thebridgesale.co.uk). Comfortable, canalside pub offering real ale and food *Mon-Fri 12.00-21.00 (Fri-22.00) & Sat-Sun 09.30-22.00 (Sun 20.00)* – breakfast *until 11.00.* Dog- and family-friendly, canalside seating. Quiz *Mon* & Poker *Thu. Occasional* live music and sports TV. *Open Mon-Fri 12.00-23.00 (Fri 00.00) & Sat-Sun 10.00-00.00 (Sun 22.30).*

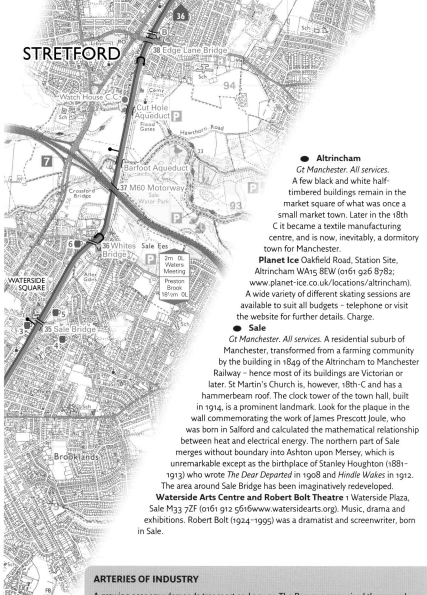

STRETFORD

● **Altrincham**
Gt Manchester. All services.
A few black and white half-timbered buildings remain in the market square of what was once a small market town. Later in the 18th C it became a textile manufacturing centre, and is now, inevitably, a dormitory town for Manchester.
Planet Ice Oakfield Road, Station Site, Altrincham WA15 8EW (0161 926 8782; www.planet-ice.co.uk/locations/altrincham). A wide variety of different skating sessions are available to suit all budgets – telephone or visit the website for further details. Charge.

● **Sale**
Gt Manchester. All services. A residential suburb of Manchester, transformed from a farming community by the building in 1849 of the Altrincham to Manchester Railway – hence most of its buildings are Victorian or later. St Martin's Church is, however, 18th-C and has a hammerbeam roof. The clock tower of the town hall, built in 1914, is a prominent landmark. Look for the plaque in the wall commemorating the work of James Prescott Joule, who was born in Salford and calculated the mathematical relationship between heat and electrical energy. The northern part of Sale merges without boundary into Ashton upon Mersey, which is unremarkable except as the birthplace of Stanley Houghton (1881–1913) who wrote *The Dear Departed* in 1908 and *Hindle Wakes* in 1912. The area around Sale Bridge has been imaginatively redeveloped.
Waterside Arts Centre and Robert Bolt Theatre 1 Waterside Plaza, Sale M33 7ZF (0161 912 5616www.watersidearts.org). Music, drama and exhibitions. Robert Bolt (1924–1995) was a dramatist and screenwriter, born in Sale.

ARTERIES OF INDUSTRY

A growing economy demands transport and power. The Romans recognised these needs and built the Caer-dyke, a part of which still survives as the Fossdyke Navigation, to the west of Lincoln. They realised a horse can pull only 2 tons on a good road, but up to 100 tons on a waterway.

Edward the Confessor ordered improvements on the Thames, Severn, Trent and Yorkshire Ouse, and it was about this time that an artificial cut, a revolutionary idea at the time, was made to improve navigation on the Itchen. The development of the 'flash' lock, where a weir was used to build up a head of water which was then released to propel craft over an obstruction, was eventually superseded by the 'pound' lock, still in use today.

But it was the Newry Canal, the Sankey Brook and the Bridgewater Canal, which was built to serve the Duke's mines at Worsley and was still in commercial use until the 1970s, which heralded the start of the Canal Age.

At Waters Meeting, marked with a fine vortex sculpture hidden amongst the bushes, the original main line of the canal is joined – to the north west is Barton, Leigh and the connection with the Leeds & Liverpool Canal; to the east is the centre of Manchester and the Rochdale Canal which crosses the hills to Rochdale and into Yorkshire beyond. The Bridgewater's route passes close to Manchester United football ground, where the new stand of this famous club towers above the canal, and the magnificent Salford Quays. Old Trafford cricket ground, the home of Lancashire Cricket Club and a Test Match venue, is a little further south. Near bridge 95 there is a fine mural, painted in 1993 by Walter Kershaw, depicting transport and industry. More empty docks are passed following the well-painted Throstle Nest Footbridge. The Manchester Ship Canal is now very close – indeed just across the towpath – with good views of the City Park buildings and the distant city centre. The new Metrolink towers above, before crossing high above Pomona Lock – the connection with the Ship Canal. Have a look on the towpath side for the circular overflow weir by bridge 97, and notice the disused basins beyond the towpath. These are followed by a railway bridge, more overgrown basins and the remains of the Hulme Lock Branch – the original junction with the Ship Canal. The excitingly restored Castlefield Junction is then reached. It is well worth stopping here to explore the basins under the railway bridge, and to visit the *pubs and restaurants* and you can moor on the stretch below Grocers Warehouse. The first of the the nine wide locks of the Rochdale Canal is right beside the restored Merchants' Warehouse. The gear is anti-vandal locked, so you will need to use a Watermate key. The canal now passes between the backs of tall buildings and beneath elaborate railway arches, all of which have a certain faded grandeur. Tantalising glimpses of Victorian buildings invite exploration, but be wary of mooring away from Castlefield. You then pass the gay village, adjacent to Chorlton Street Lock, before finally the canal crawls under an 18-storey office block where you will find the top lock amidst concrete pillars.

Ahead lies the Rochdale Canal (*see page 179*). Sharp right and left turns bring you to the start of the Ashton Canal, and the climb to Fairfield Junction (*see page 167*).

NAVIGATIONAL NOTES

1 *See* Navigational Notes on page 185 if you intend to proceed up the Rochdale 9 – Locks 92–84.
2 To use Pomona lock see www.bridgewatercanal.co.uk/media/BoatingPDFs/Terms_and_Conditions_Use_of_Upper_Reach.pdf.

Boatyards

See page 193, for details of
Ⓑ**New Islington Marina** at Ducie Street Junction.

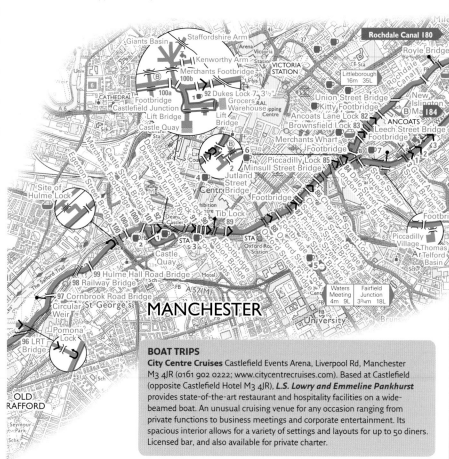

BOAT TRIPS

City Centre Cruises Castlefield Events Arena, Liverpool Rd, Manchester M3 4JR (0161 902 0222; www.citycentrecruises.com). Based at Castlefield (opposite Castlefield Hotel M3 4JR), *L.S. Lowry and Emmeline Pankhurst* provides state-of-the-art restaurant and hospitality facilities on a wide-beamed boat. An unusual cruising venue for any occasion ranging from private functions to business meetings and corporate entertainment. Its spacious interior allows for a variety of settings and layouts for up to 50 diners. Licensed bar, and also available for private charter.

● **Manchester**
All services. One of Britain's finest Victorian cities, a monument to 19th-C commerce and the textile boom, its size increasing remorselessly with the building of the canals, and later railways. Unfortunately virtually no early buildings survived the city's rapid growth, although there is an incredible wealth of Victorian architecture surviving, in spite of redevelopment. The town hall and surrounding streets are a particularly rich area (north of Oxford Street Bridge). St Peter's Square, by the town hall, was the site of the 'Peterloo Massacre' in 1819, when a meeting demanding political reform was brutally dispersed by troops carrying drawn sabres. Eleven people were killed and many more were injured. The Free Trade Hall, once the home of the Hallé Orchestra, is a little further along the road. Built in 1856, it was badly

damaged in World War II, but was subsequently re-built to its original Palladian design. There is theatre, ballet and cinema, art galleries, and a wealth of interesting buildings, Victorian shopping arcades, many pubs with a choice of good beer and a variety of restaurants just a short walk from the canal. Sporting facilities are excellent, partly as a consequence of Manchester being the venue for the 2002 Commonwealth Games. The new developments at Salford Quays, on the Manchester Ship Canal, are quite breathtaking, and the building work continues elsewhere.

Imperial War Museum North Quay West, Trafford Wharf Road, Manchester M17 1TZ (0161 836 4000; www.iwm.org.uk/visits/iwm-north). Right beside the Ship Canal, in a stunning building by Daniel Libeskind, clad in shimmering aluminium and representing a world shattered by war. Visitors enter through the 55-metres-high air shaft, giving fine views over the city. Exhibitions depict weapons, aircraft, the experience of war, science and war, interactive collections and a spectacular audio-visual display. Shop and café. *Open daily 10.00-16.30.* Free.

Metrolink The new electric 'supertram'. G-Mex is a station close to the canal (G-Mex, Deansgate Railway Station, Manchester, M3 4LG), near to the second lock, if you fancy a ride. Information on (0161 205 2000; www.tfgm.com/public-transport/tram).

Manchester Visitor Information Centre 1 Piccadilly Gardens, Manchester M1 1RG (0871 222 8223; www.visitmanchester.com). *Open Mon-Sat 09.30-17.00 & Sun 10.30-16.30.*

● **Manchester Ship Canal**
The Harbour Master, Manchester Ship Canal Company, Eastham Locks, Queen Elizabeth II Dock, Eastham (0151 327 1461; www.shipcanal.co.uk). The canal was opened in 1894 at a cost of £15½ million and carries ships up to 15,000 tons displacement. It is 36 miles long and connects the tidal Mersey at Eastham to Manchester. The Weaver Navigation, the Bridgewater Canal and the Shropshire Union Canal connect with it. All craft using the canal must be licensed. They must also be insured against third party risks which should include the cost of salvage and removal of wreck. There is a charge for the use of Pomona Lock, and advance notice is required – telephone 0161 629 8266. Any boat holding a Canal & River Trust canal and river licence may cruise on the Bridgewater Canal for seven consecutive days free of charge (but *see* introduction on page 27).

See pages 190 and 191 for further details of Manchester attractions.

Pubs and Restaurants (pages 36-37)

There are many fine pubs in Manchester. Those close to the canal include:

🍺 1 **Dukes 92** 18-25 Castle, Castlefield, Manchester M3 4LZ (0161 839 8642; www.dukes92.com). Serving real ale, this very popular modern bar was once a stable for the nearby Merchant's Warehouse. Bar and restuarant meals, together with speciality cheese and paté available *Mon-Fri 12.00-22.00 (Fri 22.30) & Sat-Sun 10.30-23.00 (Sun 21.30)*. Family- and dog-friendly (outside) canalside patio. Newspapers and *occasional Sun* live music. *Open Mon-Thu 11.00-23.00 (Thu 00.00) Fri-Sat 11.00-01.00 & Sun 10.30-21.30.*

🍺✕ 2 **The Wharf** 6 Slate Wharf, Manchester M15 4ST (0161 220 2960; www.brunningandprice.co.uk/thewharf). Housed in a purpose-built building beside Castlefield Basin, this busy pub serves a wide range of real ales, together with real cider, wines and malt whiskies. Food is available *12.00-22.00 (Sun 21.30)* and there is extensive outside seating. Well-behave children and dogs welcome. Real fires, traditional pub games, *Fri* acoustic music, newspapers and Wi-Fi. *Open Mon-Sat 10.30-23.00 (Fri-Sat 00.00) & Sun 10.30-22.30.*

🍺 3 **The Knott Bar** 374 Deansgate, Manchester M3 4LY (0161 839 9229; www.knottbar.co.uk). Close to Deansgate railway station. A deservedly popular pub serving a wide and ever-changing range of real ales. Also real cider, lagers and bottled beers. Excellent food is available (with a children's menu and vegan options) *daily 12.00-22.00*. Dog- and child-friendly (*until 20.00*) outdoor balcony. Traditional pub games and Wi-Fi. *Open Sun-Thu 12.00-23.30 (Thu 00.00) & Fri-Sat 12.00-00.30.*

🍺 4 **The Rising Sun** 22 Queen Street, Manchester M2 5HX (0161 834 1193). ½ mile north of Deansgate Tunnel, just off Deansgate itself. Traditional city pub, offering visitors a warm welcome, serving a wide range of real ales and a real cider. Food available *Tue-Fri 12.00-14.30*. Dog-friendly. *Open Mon-Sat 12.00-23.00 (Fri-Sat 00.00)*.

🍺 5 **Joshua Brooks** 106 Princess Street, Manchester M1 6NG (0161 273 7336; www.joshuabrooks.co.uk). 300yds south of Princess Street Bridge. Popular city-centre venue, which is a pub by day and a club by night, serving a good selection of real ales and cider, together with food *11.00-19.00 (Sat-Sun 17.00)*. Outdoor seating and sports TV. *Open Mon-Fri 11.00-15.00 (Thu-Fri 16.00) & Sat-Sun 12.00-16.00 (Sun 15.00)*.

🍺 6 **The Waterhouse** 67-71 Princess Street, Manchester M2 4EG (0161 200 5380; www.jdwetherspoon.co.uk/home/pubs/the-waterhouse). ¼ mile north of Princess Street Bridge. This former row of Georgian cottages now dispenses a range of beers, including those from local microbreweries. Also real cider. Food is available *daily 08.00-23.00*. Family-friendly, garden, real fires and Wi-Fi. *Open 08.00-00.00*.

🍺 7 **The Jolly Angler** 47 Ducie Street, Ancoats, Manchester M1 2JW (0161 236 5307; www.hydesbrewery.com/pub-details/?id=26). Near the junction. A small, plain and friendly pub offering real ale and run by the same family for many years. Impromptu music and a *regular* folk club. Real fires. *Opening hours vary* according to trade but *17.30-00.00* would be typical of a weekday.

See also **Pubs and Restaurants** on page 189.

NAVIGATIONAL NOTES

MANCHESTER SHIP CANAL

Harbour Master, Queen Elizabeth II Dock, Eastham, Wirral (0151 327 1461; www.shipcanal.co.uk). The ship canal currently carries an increasing annual tonnage of approximately 2,500 vessel movements per year. A great deal of it is hazardous, petro-chemical traffic and therefore a no smoking régime is enforced. The canal company is happy to allow pleasure boats use on the understanding that certain conditions are adhered to. It is not a navigation for the novice boater and should be viewed as a daytime transit corridor for the experienced boat owner (not hire boater) to access the River Weaver, the River Mersey and the Shropshire Union Canal. In essence the company's requirements are as follows:

1   The boat must carrying at least £3 million third party insurance cover.
2   The boat is subject to an annual Certificate of Seaworthiness carried out by an MSC approved surveyor (listed in the Pleasure Craft Transit Notes). This is not required for the passage from Pomona Lock east to The Manchester, Bolton & Bury Canal.
3   The appropriate fee is paid by cheque, currently set at £29 Weston Marsh Lock to Ellesmere Port and £143 Manchester to Ellesmere Port. Transit through Pomona Lock is £25 each way.
4   The boater must contact the harbourmaster at least 48hrs in advance of passage to obtain copies of:
    a)   Pleasure Craft Transit Notes (or visit www.waterways.org.uk and search on 'Manchester Ship Canal').
    b)   Port of Manchester Navigation By-laws.
    At this juncture boaters can discuss appropriate times of arrival and departure to coincide with scheduled shipping movements.
5   At all times the boater is required to act in a responsible manner and be aware that this is a *daytime* transit route only, with no lay-by facilities. Boaters should familiarise themselves with the geography of the canal before setting out. A schematic map of the canal is appended to the Pleasure Craft Transit Notes.
6   VHF radio equipment is desirable (the Manchester Ship Canal Company call on channel 14 in the canal; channel 7 in the River Mersey and operate on channels 14 and 20) and if not available a mobile phone should be considered essential. (Eastham VTS – 0151 327 1242; Latchford Locks – 01925 635249).

The above synopsis is a brief note of the essential requirements and should be read in conjunction with **The Transit Notes** and **Navigation Bylaws** referred to in 4 above. Also available from the MSC at Peel Dome are notes for the transit of Pomona Lock and 'The Upper Reach', for which a Certificate of Seaworthiness is NOT required.

Weston Marsh Lock Weston Marsh Lock, for access to the Manchester Ship Canal, must be booked *48hrs ahead* and is available *weekdays 08.00-16.30 (all year round), & weekends 08.00-16.30 (from Apr-Oct only) when it must be booked before 16.30 on the proceeding Thursday. The Saturday and Sunday access is operated on a first come first served basis once in any weekend period.* Telephone 0303 040 4040 to make a booking.

All relevant paperwork for passage on the Manchester Ship Canal must be in place prior to making a booking for Weston Marsh Lock. VHF Channel for the River Weaver is 74.

Ellesmere Port Bottom Lock Entry into the Manchester Ship Canal from the Shropshire Union is restricted by a swing bridge over the first lock (adjacent to the Holiday Inn) which is not under the control of CRT. Boaters wishing to enter the canal must first contact Ellesmere Port & Neston Borough Council (0151 356 6543) to make arrangements for the bridge to be swung. They require *eight hours* notice and will make a charge for weekend operation. Any difficulties in obtaining assistance should be referred to CRT at Northwich (0303 040 4040; enquiries.northwalesborders@canalrivertrust.org.uk).

Bridgewater and Rochdale Canals   Waters Meeting

39

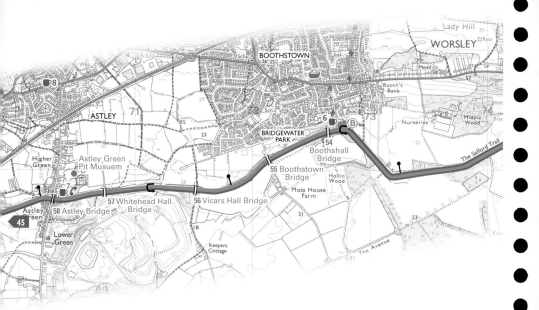

Worsley

This is a surprisingly interesting section of waterway, well worth visiting for its own sake and a useful link with the Leeds & Liverpool Canal. What was the original line of the Bridgewater Canal leaves Waters Meeting through the vast Trafford Park Industrial Estate to cross the Manchester Ship Canal on the impressive Barton Swing Aqueduct, after passing an incongruous landscaped pagoda, and an even more incongruous 'lighthouse' at Parrin Lane Bridge. Curving through the suburbs of Salford and the leafy expanse of Broadoak Park, the navigation reaches the village of Worsley and what was the entrance to the underground mines which provided its raison d'être. It is well worth stopping to take a look around the Delph, to see at first hand what brought about the canals' construction, and a sturdy brick fountain built in 1905 to commemorate the Third Duke of Bridgewater in the park to the east of bridge 51. You will also notice that dissolved iron ore colours the canal bright ochre around here. After Worsley the M60 motorway and its attendant slip roads cross the canal as the Bridgewater then heads west through open country now only hinting at its industrial past. There is, however, more solid evidence of the area's mining connections at Astley, where it's worth stopping for a short while to visit the Colliery Museum. You will see the pit-head gear as you approach. North of Bridge 54, west along A572, there is a useful selection of *shops* including a *PO, stores, chemist, off-licence, takeaway, fish & chips and library*. There are also *fish & chips and a Chinese takeaway* 100yds north of Bridge 58.

Boatyards

®**Worsley Dry Docks** The Boatyard, Worsley Road, Worsley M28 2WN (0161 793 6767). **D** Gas, hull surveys, Boat Safety Certification, dry docks, overnight & short-term mooring, winter mooring, hull blacking, chandlery, emergency docking, anodes supplied and fitted, breakdown advice. ®**Bridgewater Marina** 14 Quayside Close, Boothstown, Worsley M28 1YB (0161 702

8622//07713 098032; www.bridgewatermarina. co.uk). By bridge 54. 🛈🛈🛠**D** Pump out, gas, day-boat hire and holiday hire with disabled access, overnight and long-term mooring, winter storage, boat sales and repairs, boat building, engine repairs, chandlery, toilets, showers, solid fuel, DIY facilities. *Emergency call out.*

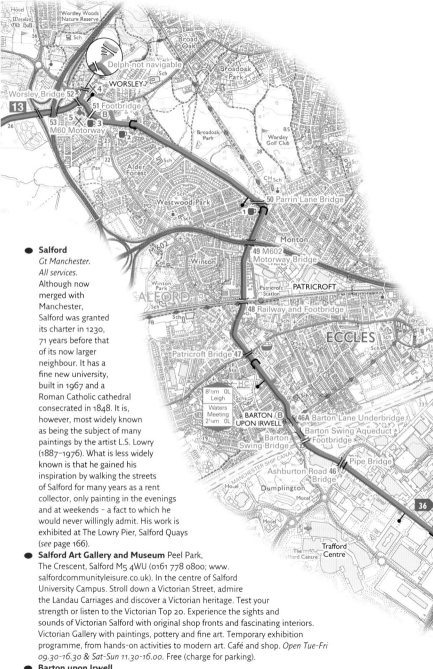

● **Salford**
Gt Manchester.
All services.
Although now
merged with
Manchester,
Salford was granted
its charter in 1230,
71 years before that
of its now larger
neighbour. It has a
fine new university,
built in 1967 and a
Roman Catholic cathedral
consecrated in 1848. It is,
however, most widely known
as being the subject of many
paintings by the artist L.S. Lowry
(1887–1976). What is less widely
known is that he gained his
inspiration by walking the streets
of Salford for many years as a rent
collector, only painting in the evenings
and at weekends – a fact to which he
would never willingly admit. His work is
exhibited at The Lowry Pier, Salford Quays
(*see* page 166).

● **Salford Art Gallery and Museum** Peel Park,
The Crescent, Salford M5 4WU (0161 778 0800; www.
salfordcommunityleisure.co.uk). In the centre of Salford
University Campus. Stroll down a Victorian Street, admire
the Landau Carriages and discover a Victorian heritage. Test your
strength or listen to the Victorian Top 20. Experience the sights and
sounds of Victorian Salford with original shop fronts and fascinating interiors.
Victorian Gallery with paintings, pottery and fine art. Temporary exhibition
programme, from hands-on activities to modern art. Café and shop. *Open Tue-Fri*
09.30-16.30 & Sat-Sun 11.30-16.00. Free (charge for parking).

● **Barton upon Irwell**
Gt Manchester. Tel, stores, garage. In an interesting position overlooking the two canals. The richly
decorated Catholic Church of the City of Mary Immaculate is by Pugin, 1867, and is considered to be one of
his best works. Indeed the architect can be found featured in a painting on the south wall of the chancel.

Barton Aqueduct

One of the wonders of the waterways, it carries the Bridgewater Canal over the Manchester Ship Canal. Designed by Sir Edward Leader Williams, it was built in the early 1890s in a bold style comparable to contemporary railway engineering. Gates seal off the 235ft-long 1450-ton section that swings at right angles to the Ship Canal over a central island. It replaced Brindley's earlier aqueduct, built in 1761 and which carried the canal in a trough over 66oft long and 39ft above the Irwell, truly a wonder in its day. The aqueduct operates *Apr-Sep 09.15-21.00 & Oct-Mar 09.15-16.30*. The aqueduct is usually *closed for maintenance during the last two weeks of March* – telephone 0161 629 8200 for details.

Patricroft

Gt Manchester. All services. Here are the Bridgewater Mills, established in 1836 by Nasmyth, who invented the steam hammer.

Eccles

Gt Manchester. All services. The town peaked as a cotton and silk weaving centre between 1870–90, and little has happened since, although its name will always be remembered in connection with the famous cakes – round pastry filled with currants. The Church of St Mary has its origins in the 10th C, although the present sandstone building dates from the late 15th C.

Worsley

Gt Manchester. PO box, tel, stores, garage (distant). There are more facilities approximately 1 mile to the north east. An attractive estate village dating from the 18th–19th C, and widely recognised as the place which triggered the 'canal age', in spite of the fact that the Bridgewater was not the first modern canal in the British Isles. Coal had been mined in Worsley since the 14th C, originally from the surface, and later by sinking shafts. It is thought that a drainage sough, common in underground workings, may have provided the germ of the idea for an underground canal network which could be used to bring the coal out. John Gilbert, the Duke of Bridgewater's agent, probably designed the system, which included an inclined plane on a 1 in 4 gradient 453ft long and 6oft wide. Work started at the same time on the building of the canal to Manchester, and eventually 46 miles of tunnels were hewn out. A particular kind of simple double-ended tub boat was used underground, called a 'starvationer'. These carried up to 12 tons of coal. The old canal basin at Worsley Delph, with its entrance tunnels to the mines, is still intact, and information boards help to explain its workings. On the canal, look out for the Boathouse, built by Lord Ellesmere to house the royal barge, prepared for Queen Victoria's visit in 1851, and Duke's Wharf, an old oil store. Close by is Worsley Old Hall, the half-timbered Court House and The Old Reading Room, which was originally a nailers shop, shown on a plan of 1785 and painted on a Wedgwood dinner service presented to Queen Catherine II of Russia. The church, by George Gilbert Scott, 1846, has a spire decorated with crockets and gargoyles – inside there is a rich collection of monuments to the Dukes of Bridgewater.

Astley Green

Gt Manchester. Tel. Canalside mining village dominated by a gaunt red-brick Victorian church.

Astley Green Colliery Museum Higher Green Lane, Astley Green, Tyldesley M29 7JB (01942 895841; www.lancashireminingmuseum.org). To the north of the canal, perched on the edge of Chat Moss. The colliery was originally owned by the Pilkington Colliery Company, a branch of the Clifton and Kearsley Coal Company, which commenced the sinking of the first of two shafts in 1908. There are various pit relics to explore, plus a superb engine house containing a 3,300 HP twin tandem compound engine by Yates & Thom of Blackburn. This once wound the 8 ton lift which transported the miners to their work 873yds underground, at a maximum speed of 82ft per second (55mph!). Astley Green Colliery is situated in an area that was once full of collieries, but over the years they have all been closed, and demolished. There is now only one headgear and engine house left in Lancashire – this one, which ceased commercial activity in 1970. Being restored by the Red Rose Steam Society, it remains as a valuable reminder of life and work in this area in the recent past. *Open Tue-Thu & Sat-Sun 13.30-17.00.* Donations.

WALKING AND CYCLING

Broadoak Park, to the north of Parrin Lane Bridge 50, contains some pleasant paths, suitable for a short walk. Bridgewater Park, Boothstown, has a few paths which can be enjoyed, while to the south of the canal is an area known as Chat Moss, a surprisingly remote area about 7,000 years old, and which was not reclaimed until the late 18th C. Close to the canal it consists mainly of reclaimed open-cast mine workings. A path from bridge 56 gives restricted access.

BIRD LIFE

Mallard ducks are widespread and familiar. The colourful male has a yellow bill and a green, shiny head and neck, separated from the chestnut breast by a white collar. Its plumage is otherwise grey-brown except for a black stern and white tail. The female has an orange bill and mottled brown plumage. In flight both sexes have blue and white speculum (patch on trailing edge of inner wing).

WILDLIFE

As water quality has improved, many different species of wildlife are being spotted in the Manchester Ship Canal (*see page 38*), including the *Grey Seal*. This large mammal is streamlined in water, but extremely cumbersome on land. It is frequently seen 'bottling', with its head and neck clear of the water. The coat colour is extremely variable, but usually some shade of blue-grey; the background colour of the male is generally darker than that of the female. Both sexes show an irregular and individually unique pattern of blotches and spots on their coats.

Pubs and Restaurants (pages 40–41)

X 1 Crompton's at the Waterside 1 Parrin Lane, Monton M30 8AN (0161 788 8788; www.watersidebarrestaurant.com). Restaurant/bar offering a varied menu available *12.00-21.00 (Sun 20.00)*. Children welcome. Large garden. *Open Tue–Sun from 12.00 (closed Mon except B Hols)*.

2 The Barton Arms 2 Stableford, Barton Road, Worsley M28 2ED (0161 728 6157; www.emberinns.co.uk/the-barton-arms-worsley). An excellent selection of real ale is served in this modern pub, which majors on food available *daily 10.00-22.00*. Dog- and child-friendly, garden. Real fires and Wi-Fi. *Open 10.00-23.00*.

3 The Bridgewater Hotel 23 Barton Road, Worsley M28 2PD (0161794 6206; www.greeneking-pubs.co.uk/pubs/lancashire/bridgewater). Large, comfortable pub serving real ale and food *daily 11.00-22.00*. Family-friendly, garden. Real fires, sports TV and Wi-Fi. *Open 10.00-23.00 (Fri-Sat 00.00)*.

X 4 Tung Fong 2 Worsley Road, Worsley M28 2NL (0161 794 5331; www.tung-fong.co.uk). Smart Chinese restaurant, with interesting décor. *Open daily 17.30-23.30*.

X 5 George's Dining Room & Bar 17-21 Barton Road, Worsley M28 2PD (0161 794 5444; www.georgesworsley.co.uk). Named after the famous Victorian architect, Sir George Gilbert Scott (who designed St Marks – the village church) this contemporary restaurant serves a modern British menu together with an array of cocktails and fine wines. Food is available *10.00-22.00 (Sun 21.00)*. Bar *open 10.00-23.00 (Fri-Sat 00.00)*.

6 The Moorings 2 Quayside Close, Boothstown, Manchester M28 1YB (0161 703 8895; www.fayre-square.com/pub/moorings-boothstown-worsley/p1595). By Bridge 54. In a lovely spot overlooking open country and the canal, on the corner of the Bridgewater Park Nature Reserve. Serving real ale and food available *daily 12.00-22.00 (Sun 21.30)*. Family-friendly with canalside seating. Mooring and Wi-Fi. *Open daily 11.00-23.00 (Sun 22.30)*.

7 The Old Boathouse Inn 164 Higher Green Lane, Astley, Tyldesley M29 7JB (01942 883300; www.oldboathouseastley.co.uk). A comfortable canalside pub with a garden, serving real ale and food *Mon-Thu L and E & Fri-Sun 12.00-21.00 (Sun 20.00)*. Dog- and child-friendly, garden. Quiz *Tue* & live music *Fri*. Traditional pub games, newspapers, real fires and Wi-Fi. *Open daily 12.00-00.00*.

8 The Bull's Head 504 Manchester Road, Astley, Tyldesley M29 7BP (01942 887109; www.emberinns.co.uk/nationalsearch/northwest/the-bulls-head-astley). A large, comfortable establishment beside the village green serving real real ales and food *daily 12.00-22.00*. Dog-friendly, garden. Children *over 14* when dining. Quiz *Wed*. Newspapers and Wi-Fi. *Open 11.30-23.00 (Thu-Sat 00.00)*.

CHAT MOSS DESCRIBED

From hence [Warrington], on the road to Manchester, we passed the great bog or waste called Chatmos, the first of that kind that we see in England, from any of the south parts hither. It extends on the left-hand of the road for five or six miles east and west, and they told us it was, in some places, seven or eight miles from north to south. The nature of these mosses, for we found there are many of them in this country, is this, and you will take this for a description of all the rest. The surface, at a distance, looks black and dirty, and is indeed frightful to think of, for it will bear neither horse or man, unless in an exceedingly dry season, and then not so as to be passable, or that any one should travel over them. What nature meant by such a useless production, 'tis hard to imagine; but the land is entirely waste, except for the poor cottager's fuel, and the quantity used for that is very small.

Daniel Defoe, around 1720.

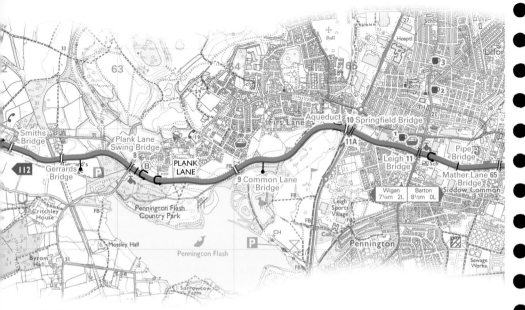

Leigh

After the excitement and interest of Barton, Worsley and Astley Green, the canal now passes through pleasant open country and reclaimed land towards the mill town of Leigh, where it transforms into the Leeds & Liverpool Canal, continuing the route to Wigan. Raised canal banks reveal past problems of subsidence in this area, caused by old mine workings. At Leigh the canal passes a sturdy warehouse by bridge 66 before it becomes the Leeds & Liverpool – the familiar stop plank cranes of the Bridgewater finish here, and signs announce you are back in Canal & River Trust territory. Wigan is 7¼ miles away (*see* page 110).

Leigh
Gt Manchester. All services. Once the archetypal mill town, most of the tall buildings and chimneys have now been demolished to be replaced with ubiquitous new developments. However, in the market place you can see the fine Edwardian baroque town hall, built 1904-7, facing the battlemented church of St Mary.

Boatyards

Ⓑ**Pennington Wharf Marina** Plank Lane, Leigh WN7 4QD (01257 481054; www.bwml.co.uk/pennington-wharf-marina). Moorings and some other boater facilities. Visit website or telephone for further details.

Pubs and Restaurants

🍺 1 **The Waterside Inn** Twist Lane, Leigh WN7 4DB (01942 605005; www.greeneking-pubs.co.uk/pubs/lancashire/waterside-inn). This pub is situated within very handsome grade II listed canalside buildings, one a two-storey stone warehouse dated 1821, the other a brick warehouse dated 1894. A distinctive wooden tower adjoins. Real ale is served, and food is available *daily 11.00-21.00*. Open fires, a garden, moorings and family-friendly. *Weekend discos 'til late.* Wi-Fi. *Open 11.00-23.00 (Fri-Sat 03.00).*

🍺 2 **The White Lion** 6A Leigh Road, Leigh WN7 1QL (07713 863835). Situated opposite Leigh's historic parish church, this friendly pub dispenses six real ales from local and regional microbreweries. Outside seating, traditional pub games, newspapers, real fires, sports TV and Wi-Fi. *Open Mon-Fri 14.00-23.00 & Sat-Sun 12.00-23.00 (Sun 13.00).*

🍺 3 **The Thomas Burke** 20A Leigh Road, Leigh WN7 1QR (01942 685640; www.jdwetherspoon.com/pubs/all-pubs/england/lancashire/the-thomas-burke-leigh). Named in honour of a famous local tenor – the 'Lancashire Caruso' – this striking pub serves a large range of real ales and food daily *08.00-22.00*. Family-friendly, outside seating. Wi-Fi. *Open 08.00-00.00 (Fri-Sat 01.00).*

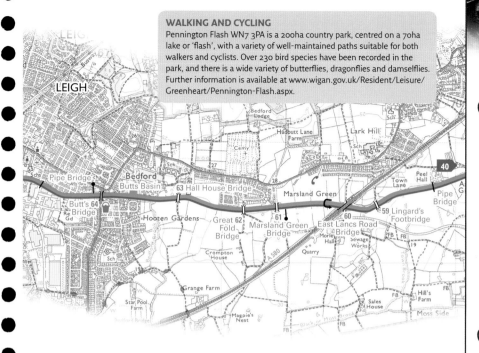

WALKING AND CYCLING

Pennington Flash WN7 3PA is a 200ha country park, centred on a 70ha lake or 'flash', with a variety of well-maintained paths suitable for both walkers and cyclists. Over 230 bird species have been recorded in the park, and there is a wide variety of butterflies, dragonflies and damselflies. Further information is available at www.wigan.gov.uk/Resident/Leisure/Greenheart/Pennington-Flash.aspx.

NAVIGATIONAL NOTE

Plank Lane Swing Bridge (which is in reality a lift bridge) is boater-operated and requires a Watermate Key. It is available for use at all times outside the periods *Mon-Fri 08.00-09.30 & 16.00-18.00*. Any difficulties contact CRT (0303 040 4040; www.canalrivertrust.org.uk/contact-us/ways-to-contact-us).

A VISIT TO THE MINES AT WORSLEY

'Arrived at Worsley, passing athwart the river Irwell, over which the canal runs, being raised on arches not less than fifty feet in height above that stream. Sent compliments to Mr Gilbert, the steward, asking the favour of seeing the duke's underground works, which was granted, and we stepped into the boat, passing into an archway partly of brick and partly cut through the stone, of about three and a half feet high; we received at entering six lighted candles. This archway, called a funnel, runs into the body of the mountain almost in a direct line three thousand feet, its medium depth beneath the surface about eighty feet; we were half an hour passing that distance. Here begins the first underground road to the pits, ascending to the wagon road, so called, about four feet above the water, being a highway for wagons, containing about a ton weight of the form of a mill-hopper, running on wheels, to convey the coals to the boats.

Arrived at the coal mine, which appearing about five feet through the roof, was supported by many posts, the area being about twenty feet square and the height scarce four. A hundred men are daily employed, and each turns out a ton a day; the miners' wages two shillings, and the laborers' about one shilling.'

Samuel Curwen, *Journal and Letters*, 7 June 1777.

CALDER & HEBBLE NAVIGATION

CALDER & HEBBLE NAVIGATION

Wakefield to Broad Cut
Length: 120'
Beam: 17' 6"
Headroom: 11' 10"
Draught: 6' 6"

Broad Cut to Sowerby Bridge
Length: 57' 6" (or 60' narrowboat)
Beam: 14' 2"
Headroom: 9' 4"
Draught: 3' 6"

HUDDERSFIELD BROAD CANAL

Length: 57' 6" (or 60' narrowboat)
Beam: 14' 2"
Headroom: 9' 6"
Draught: 2' 6"

MANAGER

0303 040 4040;
www.canalrivertrust.org.uk/contact-us/ways-to-contact-us

MILEAGE

WAKEFIELD to
Cooper Bridge: 13 miles, 13 locks
Sowerby Bridge: 23½ miles, 27 locks including Fall Ing
Huddersfield Broad Canal: 3¾ miles, 9 locks

SAFETY NOTES

1 Where locks give access onto river sections of the navigation, river level gauge boards are located at each lock chamber indicating the following:

   Green band – Normal river levels safe for navigation.

   Amber band – River levels are above normal. If you wish to navigate the river section you are advised to proceed on to and through the next lock.

   Red band – Flood conditions unsafe for navigation. Lock closed.

   In an emergency telephone the manager's office or out of office hours telephone 0800 47 999 47.

2 In times of flood, where the Rivers Calder and Hebble run in parallel with sections of the canal, beware of flood water overtopping the canal banks.

The construction of the Aire & Calder resulted in pressure to improve the Calder above Wakefield. After much opposition, the Calder & Hebble was built, with boats finally reaching Sowerby Bridge in the 1770s. The first survey had been made in 1740 and the Bill to implement it defeated by partisan landowners and millers. Sixteen years later John Smeaton produced a survey that was more acceptable and a Bill was finally passed in 1758. Construction was slow and conflict amongst the overseeing commissioners was rife. In 1765 Brindley was called upon to advise and Smeaton was dismissed. Three years later the position was reversed after serious flooding had damaged the recently completed navigation at Salterhebble. Further monies were raised to fund repairs and the waterway finally re-opened throughout in 1770.

From then on it was a case of continuous improvement and development with the addition of branch canals to profit from local pockets of trade. As always there were conflicts over water with mill owners, which curtailed some of the company's more ambitious plans to canalize large sections of the navigation but wherever possible the mills themselves were bought up. During the first half of 19th C, in line with developments on the Aire & Calder, further improvements were made (which included the cut at Horbury) but burgeoning railway competition severely blunted their impact. As a result the navigation was first leased to the Manchester & Leeds Railway and subsequently to the Aire & Calder. This second association led to a programme of lock enlargement under W.H. Bartholomew, which was of particular benefit to the section between Fall Ing Lock and Broad Cut Top Lock, above which the prevailing gauge remained consistent with the dimensions of the 57'x14' Yorkshire Keel. In 1885, on the expiry of the Aire & Calder's lease, the Calder and Hebble turned their attention to rebuilding their overbridges and establishing a carrying company: the Calder Carrying Co.

Beyond this there was little further investment, although the company continued to pay a dividend right through to Nationalization in 1948; often financed by the sale of assets. Never as successful as the Aire & Calder, it did, however, benefit from trade coming in from the Huddersfield Broad Canal and later, in 1811, from the Huddersfield Narrow. Commercial traffic ended in 1981, when the last coal barges unloaded at Thornhill Power Station. Becoming increasingly popular and yet still uncrowded, this waterway has much to offer, with great industrial interest and, in many places, considerable charm.

WALKING AND CYCLING

The Calder & Hebble, as its name suggests, is largely a river navigation and it incorporates a series of lock cuts where weirs have been constructed to maintain a navigable depth. This approach, whilst excellent for boaters, can pose problems for those following the waterway along the towpath. These problems are twofold: erosion of the river bank during times of flood and the need to cross the river at either the head or tail of a lock cut in order to remain with the navigation. When boats relied upon horse power, before the invention of the internal combustion engine, both towpaths and horse bridges were maintained in a usable condition. Subsequently both have suffered from the ravages of time and the vagaries of flood – hence the need to come up with some 'creative alternatives' as detailed below.

1 At Thornes Flood Lock (*see* page 49) follow the river south west and under the motorway bridge. Strike off west across the mown sward through the clumps of trees at almost any point before reaching Broad Cut Low Lock and head west to meet the railway line where it intersects the north bank of the river. The bridge here incorporates an enclosed walkway accessible to walkers and cyclists and, in conjunction with a lane running south, returns you to Broad Cut beside the Navigation pub.

2 At Ledgard Bridge 17 (*see* page 50) cross over the navigation, go under the railway and over the river and turn right. At Chadwick Lane fork right and go through the industrial estate with Ledgard Boats on your right. Pass Navigation Garage on the left and as the road swings left, take the stone path on the right back towards the river, to the left of the PFS Factory Unit.

3 Due to severe bank erosion, only a small section of the towpath between Cooper Bridge and Brighouse (*see* page 52) remains, therefore walkers and cyclists should leave the navigation at Cooper Bridge, briefly heading south west along the A6107, before turning right at the garage along Lower Quarry Road. Cross the railway bridge and fork right down a track under the line signposted to Bradley Hall Farm. Just before the farm turn right and rejoin the waterway at bridge 11, below Kirklees Top Lock.

Canal Basin, Sowerby Bridge

Sowerby Bridge

Leaving Sowerby Bridge, with its transshipment basins and imposing stone warehouses, the waterway is initially flanked by trees and tall buildings. To the west is the start of the Rochdale Canal, now fully restored, providing a third Pennine crossing and offering the opportunity for two dramatic northern cruising rings. A conspicuous building to the north is Wainhouse Tower, built in 1875 as a 253ft dyeworks chimney (but never used as such) and now converted into a viewing tower. A superb example of stonemasonry, it is *open on Bank Holidays* and there are 400 steps to be negotiated to the top! The navigation, now relatively narrow and accompanied by the river, clings to the side of a wooded hill, its clean water alive with fish, while the towpath throughout this section is excellent.

Boatyards

Ⓑ**Shire Cruisers** The Wharf, Sowerby Bridge, Halifax HX6 2AG (01422 832712; www. shirecruisers.co.uk). Facilities either here or in the basin. 🛁🚿♿D Gas, pump out, narrowboat hire, overnight mooring, long-term mooring, winter storage, slipway, crane, boat sales & repairs, chandlery, books, maps and gifts, boat fitting out, engine sales and repairs, toilets, DIY facilities, Gas Safe registered.

Halifax
W. Yorks. All services. Well known as the home of the Halifax Building Society, founded in 1853, which now has ultra-modern offices in Portland Place; it is worth the journey north from the canal to visit this industrial town. The parish church of St John the Baptist is Perpendicular in style, battlemented and with a mass of pinnacles, parapets and gargoyles.
Bankfield Museum Akroyd Park, Boothtown Road, Halifax HX3 6HG (01422 352334; www.museums. calderdale.gov.uk/visit/bankfield-museum). Magnificent 19th-C mill owner's residence housing a fascinating range of costumes from around the world, displayed in exotic surroundings. *Open Tue-Sat 10.00-16.00. Free.*
Eureka Museum for Children Discovery Road, Halifax HX1 2NE (01422 330069; www.eureka.org.uk). Hands-on museum designed for children to touch, listen and smell. Three main exhibition areas: Me and my body, Living and working together, and Invent, create, communicate. *Open during term time Tue-Fri 10.00-16.00 & Sat-Sun 10.00-17.00. During school holidays & B Hols daily 10.00-17.00. Charge.*
Piece Hall Blackledge, Halifax HX1 1RE (01422 525217; www.thepiecehall.co.uk). Built as a cloth hall in 1779, it is the last remaining manufacturers' hall in the country. Here weavers traded their products, the continuation of an industry that dates back to 1275 in Halifax. Now restored, the hall houses arts and craft shops, a museum, art gallery, cafés and restaurants. Gates *open at 07.00; shops 10.00-18.00 Apr-Oct (reduced hours in winter).*
Shibden Hall Folk Museum Lister's Road, Halifax HX3 6XG (01422 352246; www.museums.calderdale. gov.uk/visit/shibden-hall). A 15th-C building with 17th-C furniture and extensive folk Exhibits. Also a miniature railway, boating lake, play area, restored gardens, woodland and café. *Open Sat-Thu 10.00-17.00. Charge.*
Tourist Information Centre Central Library, Square Road, Halifax HX1 1UN (01422 368725; www. visitcalderdale.com/towns-villages/halifax). *Open Mon-Fri 09.30-18.30 (Wed 12.30) & Sat 09.30-16.00.*
Wainhouse Tower Wakefield Gate, Halifax HX2 7EN (01422 832174; www.calderdale.gov.uk/v2/ residents/leisure-and-culture/local-history-and-heritage/wainhouse-tower). *Open B Hols and Father's Day 11.00-16.00 (last ascent 15.30). Charge.* Private parties catered for. The *Aug B Hol opening* is in conjunction with Calderdale Heritage Walks who offer a selection of around 90 conducted walks in the area (www.calderdaleheritagewalks.org.uk). Charge.
Tourist Information Centre Halifax Visitor Centre, Halifax Library, Northgate, Halifax HX1 1UN (01422368725; www.visitcalderdale.com). *Open Mon, Tue, Thu & Fri 09.30-19.00 and Sat 09.30-17.00.*

Sowerby Bridge
W. Yorks. All services. Although this is an industrial town, the scale and grandeur of the surrounding landscape dominate the mill chimneys and factory roofs that are dotted about. This rare subservience to nature makes the town human and attractive. The 19th-C classical church is in a good position, overlooking the restored deep lock and tunnel.

Sowerby Bridge Basin
This great canal centre is a classic example of the functional tradition in industrial architecture, and has thankfully survived to be given a new life in restoration, while many other such examples have disappeared. The Rochdale Canal was built to accommodate vessels up to 72ft in length, so goods had to be transshipped here into the shorter Calder & Hebble before they could continue their journey; hence this important centre grew in stature.

Rochdale Canal
One of three canal routes across the Pennines, its 92 wide locks over a distance of 33 miles virtually guaranteed its ultimate commercial failure, closing in 1952. Re-opened on 1st July 2002, and connected to the Calder & Hebble Canal via a new tunnel and deep lock, it is once again possible to cruise across the Pennines to Manchester: hard work but the effort is amply rewarded.

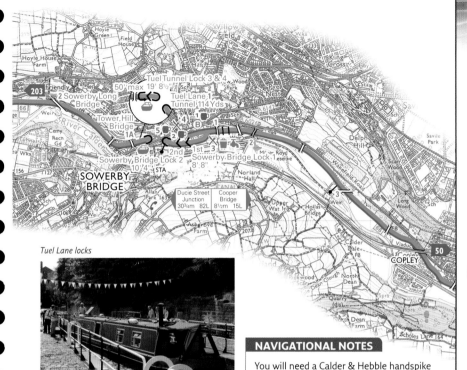

Tuel Lane locks

NAVIGATIONAL NOTES

You will need a Calder & Hebble handspike to operate the locks at Sowerby Bridge and subsequent locks to Wakefield. These can be obtained from local boatyards or a piece of 3"x 2" timber can be fashioned to suit.

Pubs and Restaurants

🍺 1 **The Navigation Inn** 47 Chapel Lane, Sowerby Bridge, Halifax HX6 3LF (01422 316073; www. thenavigationpub.co.uk). By bridge 1. Friendly canalside pub dating back to 15th C complete with inglenook fireplace and Victorian cast iron range. Real ale and food available *Mon-Sat 11.30-21.00 (Mon 20.30) & Sun 12.00-21.00*. Garden and real fires. *Open daily 11.00-22.00 (Sun 12.00)*.

🍺✕ 2 **The Moorings** No 1 Warehouse, Canal Basin, Sowerby Bridge, Halifax HX6 2AG (01422 833940; www.themooringspub.co.uk). A good choice of bar food is served together with real ale in this attractive coversion. Food is available *Mon-Sat 12.00-21.00 (Mon 20.30) & Sun 12.00-20.00*. Dog- and child-friendly. *Occasional* live music and Wi-Fi. *Open daily 12.00-23.00 (Sun 22.30)*.

✕♀ 3 **Tenujin** No 1 Warehouse, Canal Basin, Sowerby Bridge, Halifax HX6 2AG (01422 835500; www.temujinrestaurant.co.uk). Specialists in

Mongolian barbecues. Children welcome. *Open Mon-Thu 18.00-22.00; Fri L and E; Sat 12.00-23.00 & Sun 13.00-20.00.*

✕ 4 **Village Restaurant** 75 Wharf Street, Sowerby Bridge, Halifax HX6 2AF (01422 831654; www. javavillagerestaurant.co.uk). By the basin. A restaurant specialising in Indonesian and Indian food. Children welcome. *Open Mon- Fri L and E (not Mon L); Sat 17.00-01.00 & Sun 16.00-23.00.*

🍺 5 **The Commercial Inn** The Wharf, 31 Wharf Street, Sowerby Bridge HX6 2LA (01422 317350; www.jdwetherspoon.com/pubs/all-pubs/england/west-yorkshire/the-commercial-inn-sowerby-bridge). Modern pub, sitting atop Tuel Lane Tunnel, serving a wide range of real ales, real cider and inexpensive food *daily 08.00-23.00*. Family-friendly, outside seating. Real fire and Wi-Fi. *Open 08.00-00.00 (Fri-Sat 01.00).*

See also Pubs and Restaurants on page 205

Brighouse

Above the three picturesque Salterhebble Locks, the Salterhebble Branch leaves the main line and via Salterhebble Basin (now providing long-term *moorings and boater facilities*) once climbed to Halifax. Below the top two locks, the waterway swings left over a small aqueduct before negotiating the bottom lock which has its own electrically-powered guillotine gate, operated with a Watermate key. This was installed when the road was widened in the 1930s.

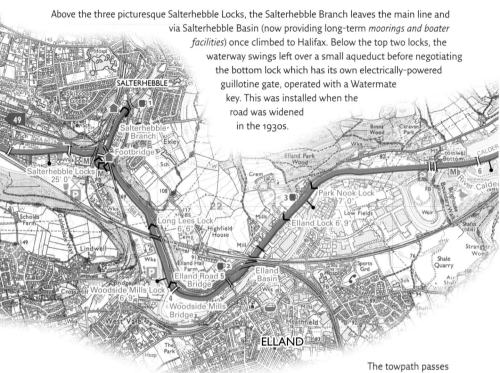

The towpath passes separately through its own narrow tunnel. Elland Basin, with its tastefully restored buildings and gardens, is worth more than a fleeting glance, however, and makes a good stopping place en route. During the winter floods of 2015, Elland Road Bridge was very nearly destroyed, cutting off connections with the village from the north. It has been completely rebuilt as a pastiche of the original. Have a look at the fine converted warehouse, with its covered dock, before pressing on to Elland and Park Nook Locks. A milestone right by Park Nook Lock reveals that you are now just 18 miles from Fall Ing, while flooded gravel pits nearby are used for water-skiing. At Brookfoot Lock there is evidence of a connection with the river giving some idea of how the navigation has evolved as canalised sections were progressively constructed. There are good *moorings* between the two Brighouse Locks and the passage through the town is pleasant, with gardens, seats and willow trees. Leaving the canal, the navigation enters the river, completely enclosed by factories.

● **Brighouse**
W. Yorks. All services. A woollen textile producing village transformed into an important canal port with the building of the Calder & Hebble Navigation. In the 19th C silk and cotton were also spun here. Now there seems to be plenty of thriving new industry. The canal bisects the town, passing very close to the market place. A large Victorian church at the top of the hill is surrounded by trees and flowers.
Smith Art Gallery Halifax Road, Brighouse HD6 2AF (01484 352334; www.calderdale.gov.uk; www.museums. calderdale.gov.uk/visit/smith-art-gallery). Permanent display of 19th-C art works and touring exhibitions. *Open Mon & Fri 10.00-17.00; Tue & Thu 10.00-16.00 & Sat 10.00-15.30.* Free.

- **Elland**

W. Yorks. PO, tel, stores, chemist, butcher, baker, hardware, fish & chips, takeaways, delicatessen, off-licence, cinema, library, garage. Elland has an enviable position on the steep south side of the Calder Valley, its narrow streets discourage through traffic, and its handsome church and terraces of stone houses give an air of tranquillity. The well-restored canal basin makes an excellent stopping point.

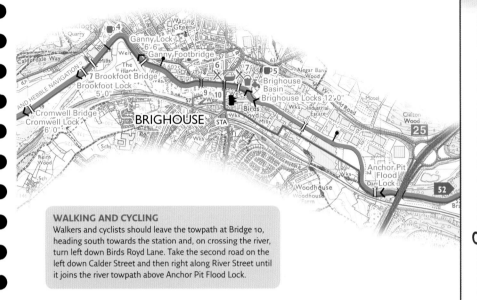

WALKING AND CYCLING
Walkers and cyclists should leave the towpath at Bridge 10, heading south towards the station and, on crossing the river, turn left down Birds Royd Lane. Take the second road on the left down Calder Street and then right along River Street until it joins the river towpath above Anchor Pit Flood Lock.

Pubs and Restaurants

1 The Watermill Huddersfield Road, Salterhebble, Halifax HX3 0QT (01422 347700; www.premierinn.com). Pub and hotel at the terminus of the Salterhebble Branch. Real ales served in this relaxed, family-orientated establishment. Food is available *daily 12.00-22.00 (Sun 21.30) – breakfast 06.00-10.30 (Sat-Sun 07.00-11.00)*. Outside seating and Wi-Fi. Mooring. B&B. *Open 12.00-23.00 Sun 22.30).*

2 The Barge & Barrel 10-12 Park Road, Elland HX5 9HP (01422 254604). An interesting choice of real ales is available largely featuring local micro-breweries together with food available *Tue-Fri L and E & Sat-Sun 12.00-17.00*. Dog- and family-friendly, canalside decking. Traditional pub games, real fires and Wi-Fi. *Open 12.00-23.00*.

3 The Colliers Arms 66 Park Road, Elland HX5 9HZ (01422 377058). Traditional canalside pub offering real ale. Children and dogs welcome. Canalside garden and open fires. Food available *Wed-Sun 12.00-20.00. Open Mon-Tue 16.00-23.00 & Wed-Sun 12.00-23.00 (Sun 12.00).*

4 The Red Rooster, 123 Elland Road, Brookfoot, Brighouse HD6 2QR (01484 713737/07825 128682). Purpose-built around 1900 to serve the local colliery wharf, this welcoming hostelry now dispenses an excellent selection of real ales, together with locally sourced pie and peas available *at all times*. Dog- and child-friendly, decked area. Traditional pub games, *occasional* live music and Wi-Fi. *Open Mon-Thu 16.00-23.00 & Fri-Sun 12.00-00.00 (Sun 22.30).*

5 The Richard Oastler Bethel Street, Brighouse HD6 1JN (01484 401756; www.jdwetherspoon.com/pubs/all-pubs/england/west-yorkshire/the-richard-oastler-brighouse). Housed in a former Grade II listed Methodist chapel, this establishment now serves real ciders and an excellent range of real ales, including a selection from local microbreweries. Children welcome, outside seating, large-screen TV and Wi-Fi. *Open 08.00-00.00 (Fri-Sat 01.00)* with food available all day.

6 Prego Huddersfield Road, Brighouse HD6 1JZ (01484 715566; www.waterfronthotel andvenue.co.uk/Prego-Restaurant). Italian and continental cuisine served in a sophisticated contemporary setting. *Open Mon-Fri L and E & Sat-Sun 12.00-20.00 (Sat 19.00)*. Breakfast 07.00-09.00 (Sat-Sun 08.00-10.00). B&B. Children welcome.

7 Jeremy's at the Boathouse The Boathouse, Wharf Street, Brighouse HD6 1PP (01484 719819; www.jeremysattheboathouse.co.uk). Informal bar and kitchen situated in the old Sagar boatbuilding works, serving a range of food – from afternoon tea to tapas – *daily 12.00-20.00 (Sun 18.00)* together with real ale, wine and cocktails. Live music *Fri-Sun. Open 11.00-00.00 (Sun 22.30).*

51

Cooper Bridge

The navigation passes under the M62 motorway bridge with Kirklees Park ranged across the hillside to the north. Cooper Bridge marks the junction of the Calder & Hebble with the Huddersfield Broad Canal (*see* page 64) which branches off to the south below the flood gates, overlooked by the tall chimney of Bottomley & Sons. Immediately to the south west of Cooper Bridge, along the A6107, there is a *24hr shop* in the *garage*. At Battyeford there is a short canal section which leaves the river opposite a large sewerage works. A fine display of roses suggests that they are not short of fertiliser!

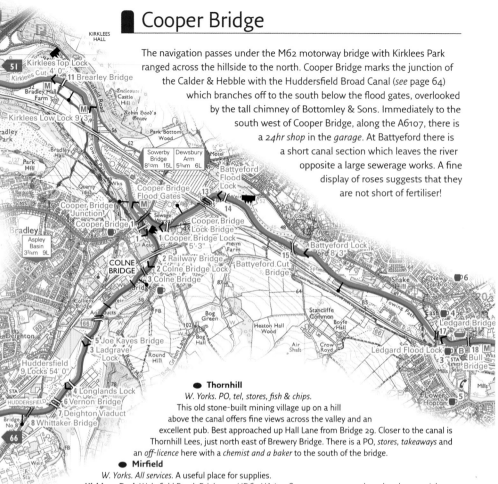

● **Thornhill**
W. Yorks. PO, tel, stores, fish & chips.
This old stone-built mining village up on a hill above the canal offers fine views across the valley and an excellent pub. Best approached up Hall Lane from Bridge 29. Closer to the canal is Thornhill Lees, just north east of Brewery Bridge. There is a PO, *stores, takeaways* and an *off-licence* here with a *chemist and a baker* to the south of the bridge.

● **Mirfield**
W. Yorks. All services. A useful place for supplies.
Kirklees Park Wakefield Road, Brighouse HD6 4HA (01484 414700; www.parksandgardens.org/places-and-people/site/7450). In the grounds are the modest ruins of a priory founded in the 12th C for Cistercian nuns. Most of the stones were incorporated in the construction of Kirklees Hall during the late 16th C. It is believed that Robin Hood died whilst at the priory but before so doing he shot two arrows from the window to mark his burial place. One landed in the River Calder and floated away, the other landed in the grounds of the park. A tablet marks the spot thought to be his grave.

NAVIGATIONAL NOTES

1 When coming downstream, look out for the entrance to Ledgard Bridge Flood Lock. A large weir awaits those who miss it. This warning applies equally to boaters leaving Shepley Bridge Lock and approaching Greenwood Flood Gates.
2 There are landing stages below the locks which you can use, as well as ladders in virtually all the locks.

BOAT TRIPS

Safe Anchor Shepley Bridge Marina, Huddersfield Road, Mirfield WF14 9HR (www.safeanchor.org.uk). An award-winning charity providing trips on the waterways for special needs groups, the socially disadvantaged and for those with health and mobility problems. The Trust runs five passenger craft, two of which are fully wheelchair accessible. The boats operate *Mar-Oct*.

At Shepley Bridge Lock the river is briefly re-joined on a sweeping bend, before the navigation enters another artificial cut. Between Greenwood Lock and Thornhill Flood Lock a short, wide, river section intervenes before the navigation enters another artificial channel near the site of the old Thornhill power station where barges used to unload coal. Soon the open industrial wasteland (for which there are large-scale redevelopment plans) gives way to a long deep, secluded cutting, spanned by tall bridges, and the previous wide horizons are strictly curtailed.

WALKING AND CYCLING
The towpath is generally good on the canal sections, less so (or indeed non-existent) on the river sections. See notes on page 47.

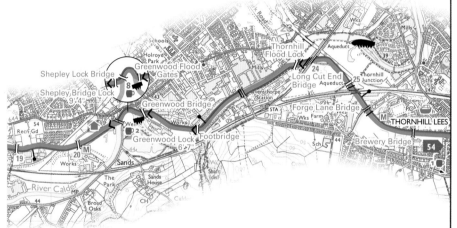

Pubs and Restaurants

🍺 1 **Savile Arms** 12 Church Lane, Thornhill, Dewsbury WF12 0JZ (01924 463738; www.savile-arms.co.uk). A genuine old village local that rather surprisingly shares consecrated ground with the nearby church, hence its other name – Church House. It dispenses an excellent range of real ales and totally eschews noisy machines. Traditional pub games and large garden – children welcome in the garden. Real fires and Wi-Fi. *Open Mon-Fri 17.00-23.00 (Fri 12.00) & Sat-Sun 12.00-23.00.* Homemade food available for groups with *advanced notice.*

🍺 2 **The Ship Inn** Steanard Lane, Shepley Bridge, Mirfield WF14 8HB (01924 493364; www. hungryhorse.co.uk/pubs/west-yorkshire/ship-inn). Large, smart and comfortable pub dispensing real ale. A carvery restaurant serves food *daily 09.30-22.00.* Children welcome. Garden, indoor and outdoor play area. Traditional pub games, pool and Wi-Fi. Dogs welcome. *Bar open 12.00-23.00 daily.*

🍺 3 **The Navigation Tavern** 6 Station Road, Mirfield WF14 8NL(01924 492476; www.realaletrail. net/mirfield). An excellent selection of real ales and real cider is dispensed in this canalside pub. There

is a garden and limited moorings. Large screen TV, traditional pub games and Wi-Fi. Children welcome *until 21.00.* Real fires and *occasional* live music. B&B. *Open daily 11.30-23.00 (Sun 12.00).*

🍺✕ 4 **The Railway** 212 Huddersfield Road, Mirfield WF14 9PX (01924 493299). Until recently known as the White Stag, this cosy pub serves real ale and food *12.00-20.00 (Fri-Sun 18.00).* Dog- and child-friendly, outside seating. Traditional pub games, newspapers, real fires and Wi-Fi. *Open daily 12.00-23.00.*

🍺 5 **The Flowerpot** 65 Calder Road, Mirfield WF14 8NN (01924 496939; www.ossett-brewery. co.uk/pubs/flowerpot-mirfield). Tastefully refurbished, this pub dispenses real ale, real cider and a pie & peas menu *Mon-Fri L.* Dog- and family-friendly, river terrace. Traditional pub games, real fires and Wi-Fi. *Open 12.00-00.30 (Fri-Sat 01.30).*

🍺✕ 6 **The Old Colonial** Dunbottle Lane, Mirfield WF14 9JJ (01924 496920; www.theoldcolonial. webplus.net). Once a club and now an excellent venue to enjoy a selection of real ales. Food available *Thu-Sun L and E (not Sun E).* Sun roasts are particular popular. Children welcome, garden. Traditional pub games, *occasional* live music, real fires and Wi-Fi. *Open Mon-Wed E; Thu-Sat L and E & Sun L.*

Horbury Bridge

Thornhill Double Locks mark the junction with the Dewsbury Arm, which branches off to Savile Town Basin where there is a *boatyard, moorings and a pub*. The towpath from Dewsbury to Broad Cut is in good condition. At the bridge, approaching Mill Bank Lock, look out for a milestone marked 'from Fall Ing 7 miles' on the towpath side. Next are the Figure of Three Locks followed by a tree-lined cutting. There are three locks on the navigation, with another now disused, which used to connect with the river. Is it this, or the fact that the river here makes the shape of a '3', which gives these locks their unusual name? Experts seem unable to agree. There are good moorings at Horbury Bridge and a *shop, post office and a takeaway* are close by. A short arm here used to connect with the river and this has now become an attractive long-term mooring with *showers* and the usual *boater facilities*. Remains of mooring staithes can be seen opposite the Navigation Inn and there was regular trade on this stretch until 1981, when West Country barges carried coal from the British Oak Colliery to Thornhill Power Station. The beautifully kept Broad Cut Low Lock marks the end of a 5-mile-long canal section with eight locks. Passing under the M1 motorway, the waterway makes a beeline for Thornes Flood Lock where the navigation enters a short cut and re-joins the river at Thornes Lock: only the northern-most chamber is now in use.

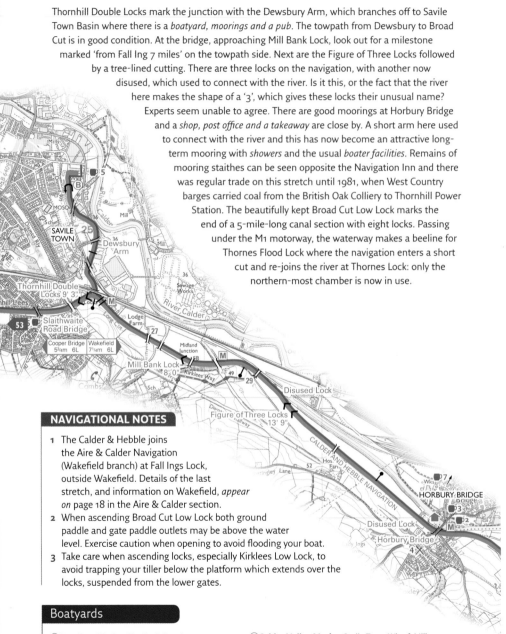

NAVIGATIONAL NOTES

1 The Calder & Hebble joins the Aire & Calder Navigation (Wakefield branch) at Fall Ings Lock, outside Wakefield. Details of the last stretch, and information on Wakefield, *appear on page 18 in the Aire & Calder section.*

2 When ascending Broad Cut Low Lock both ground paddle and gate paddle outlets may be above the water level. Exercise caution when opening to avoid flooding your boat.

3 Take care when ascending locks, especially Kirklees Low Lock, to avoid trapping your tiller below the platform which extends over the locks, suspended from the lower gates.

Boatyards

Ⓑ**Broadcut Marine** The Yard, Broadcut Road, Calder Grove, Wakefield WF4 3DS (01924 270070/07855 930051; www.broadcutmarine. co.uk). Marine engineering, boat repairs and restoration.

Ⓑ**Calder Valley Marine** Savile Town Wharf, Mill Street East, Dewsbury WF12 9BD (01924 467976; www. cvmarine.co.uk). 🏠🏠🛒 Gas, pump out, overnight mooring, long-term mooring, slipway, winter storage, boat and engine repairs, boat sales, books and maps, showers, laundry, toilets, solid fuel.

Pubs and Restaurants

🍺 1 **The Navigation Inn** Broad Cut Road, Calder Grove, Wakefield WF4 3DS (01924 2743610). A well-placed canalside pub serving real ales and inexpensive bar snacks and meals *L* and *E*. Family- and dog-friendly, large garden. Real fires. *Open Mon-Sat 10.00-00.30 (Fri-Sat 01.30) & Sun 12.00-00.00. PO, newsagent, fish & chips and a takeaway* just a short walk to the south.

🍺 2 **The Bingley Arms** 221 Bridge Road, Horbury, Wakefield WF4 5NL (01924 272838). A warm friendly establishment in another fine-looking building serving real ale, real cider and food *Fri-Sun L*. Family-friendly, garden. Traditional pub games, real fires and sports TV. *Open 12.00-23.00 Mon-Sat (Mon-Tue 16.00) & Sun 12.00-22.30.*

🍺 3 **The Horse & Jockey Inn** Bridge Road, Horbury Bridge WF4 5PP (01924 650321). Friendly pub serving real ale and food *Sun L* from a carvery. Children welcome. Traditional pub games and live music *Fri*. *Open Mon-Fri 16.00-23.00 (Fri 12.00) & Sat-Sun 12.00-00.00 (Sun 23.30).*

✗🍴 4 **Capri Bistro** 223 Bridge Road, Horbury WF4 5QA (01924 263090; www.caprirestaurant.co.uk). Italian restaurant and wine bar serving a range of pasta dishes, pizzas and appetising deserts. Children welcome. *Open Mon-Sat 18.00-22.30 (Sat 17.30) & Sun*

12.00-21.00. There is also a takeaway service (01924 277666) operating *from 16.30,* together with a café (01924 270065) offering breakfast, lunch and snacks *open Mon-Sat 08.30-15.30 & Sun 09.00-13.00.*

🍺 5 **The Leggers' Inn** Savile Town Wharf, 66 Mill Street East, Dewsbury WF12 9BD (01924 488153; www.leggersinn.co.uk). Real ale and real cider are available in this converted stables together with food *daily 12.00-20.00 (Sun 18.00).* Dog- and child-friendly, outside seating. Traditional pub games, *occasional* live music, real fires and Wi-Fi. *Open 11.00-23.00 (Fri-Sat 00.00).*

🍺 6 **The Nelson Inn** 145 Slaithwaite Road, Thornhill Lees, Dewsbury WF12 9DW (01924 461685). Real ales served in a 17th-C pub atop the canal. Food is available *Mon-Fri 16.00-20.00 & Sat-Sun 12.00-20.00.* Dog- and family-friendly, garden. Traditional pub games, newspapers, sports TV and Wi-Fi. *Open Mon-Fri 16.00-00.00 & Sat-Sun 12.00-00.00.* There is a *chemist, fish & chips and a takeaway* close by.

Also try: 🍺 7 **The Cricketers Arms** Cluntergate, Horbury WF4 5AG (01924 267032; www.beerhouses. co.uk/pub/the-cricketers-arms). Approximately 1 mile up the hill in Horbury itself.

● Horbury Bridge
W. Yorks. PO, tel, stores, off-licence, takeaway, garage. A useful selection of shops, pubs and a restaurant close to the canal. A mile or so up the hill, to the north east, is the small town of Horbury itself. The Hymn 'Onward Christian Soldiers' was written and first sung here by the Reverend S. Baring-Gould as a marching song for children.

National Coal Mining Museum for England Caphouse Colliery, New Road, Overton, Wakefield WF4 4RH (01924 848806; www.ncm.org.uk). On the A642, 2 miles south west of Horbury Bridge (bus service) and accessible by bus 263 from Huddersfield and Wakefield. Go 450ft underground to visit old- and new-style coalfaces. Audio-visual show, café, shop, picnic area. Wear warm clothes; not suitable for children under 5. *Open daily 10.00-17.00.* Free – but donations very welcome.

● Dewsbury
W. Yorks. All services, station. The compact and attractive town centre is 1 mile away from Savile Town Basin.
Dewsbury Arm WF12 9BB Extending for 3/4 mile to Savile Town Basin.

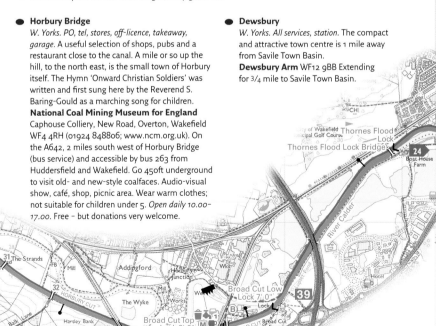

HUDDERSFIELD NARROW CANAL

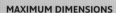

MAXIMUM DIMENSIONS

Length: 70'
Beam: 6' 10"
Headroom: 6' 2"
Draught: 3' 3"

MANAGER

0303 040 4040;
www.canalrivertrust.org.uk/contact-us/
ways-to-contact-us

MILEAGE

ASHTON-UNDER-LYNE
Junction with Peak Forest Canal to
Stalybridge: 2 miles
Mossley: 6 miles
Diggle: 8½ miles
Marsden: 12 miles
Linthaite: 16 miles
HUDDERSFIELD
Junction with Huddersfield Broad Canal: 19½ miles

Passage through Standedge Tunnel is on a chaperoned basis, allowing the helmsman to steer his vessel through the tunnel, accompanied by a member of the Canal & River Trust Tunnel Team. Transit is available *from late Mar to early Nov on Mon, Wed & Fri.* Bookings must be made *in advance* by telephoning 0303 040 4040 and the Standedge Customer Guidelines can be downloaded in pdf form from www.canalrivertrust.org.uk/media/original/30632-standedge-online-guidelines.pdf?v=c74c97. This provides full details of the transit, including a diagram setting out the limiting dimensions for craft wishing to undertake the passage.

Boats may travel no further than Lock 32E or 24W without having first made a booking.

One of three transPennine canals, and by far the shortest route, this waterway was conceived in 1793, at the height of 'Canal Mania' (the bulk of canal construction was concentrated into the 1790s), and encouraged by the success of the Ashton and Huddersfield Broad canals. Benjamin Outram was retained as engineer and he reported in favour of a narrow canal (in the interest of cost saving) following the route of the present navigation. There was the inevitable conflict with local mill owners over water supply and a total reservoir capacity of 20,000 locks full of water was provided by way of appeasement.

As always optimism was in far greater supply than the capital raised from the initial share issue following the enabling Act passed on 4 April 1794. The estimated cost was some £183,000, of which nearly one-third was allocated to the construction of a 3-mile tunnel under the Pennines. As work progressed the canal was opened in sections to generate income; the first section opened in March 1797 between Huddersfield and Slaithwaite and two more, linking Slaithwaite to Marsden and Ashton to Greenfield, were completed late in the following year. It was not until 12 years later that the first boat passed through the completed Standedge Tunnel.

From the outset the waterway was dogged by shoddy workmanship and flood damage. In its 436ft rise to the eastern tunnel portal at Marsden, the canal follows the Colne Valley, whilst from the west end of the summit pound – 645ft above sea level – it follows the Tame Valley, dropping 334ft in 8½ miles to Ashton-under-Lyne. Damage extended along 16 miles of canal after flooding during the winter of 1799 and Robert Whitworth, called in to report during Outram's absence through illness, observed that the masonry and earthworks along the navigation 'were the worst executed of any he had seen'. Benjamin Outram resigned in 1801 and he was not replaced, although subsequently, five years later, Thomas Telford was asked to survey the work to date and advise on its completion. Two further Acts were passed to raise more capital before the navigation was officially opened on 4 April 1811 at a final cost of over £300,000. However, this was only after another disastrous flood occasioned after Swellands Reservoir (recommended by Telford as an addition to Outram's design) burst its banks and inundated large areas of the Colne Valley. Six people were drowned and many factories and mills severely damaged.

High tolls, in conjunction with an additional charge levied on boats using the tunnel, suppressed use of the waterway and although individual communities along the route expanded and thrived, within the climate of industrial prosperity brought by the canal, profits were disappointing. With the reduction of dues in the 1830s, trade was greatly stimulated, only to fall in the face of the inevitable railway competition which came with the completion of the Leeds and Manchester Railway in 1841. Three years later the Huddersfield and Manchester Railway Company was formed with the aim of building a line closely following the route of the navigation, which it acquired in 1845. The existing canal tunnel at Standedge was linked at intervals by cross adits to the infant railway tunnel during construction, thereby greatly reducing time and expense. Subsequent railway tunnels, built as traffic increased, also benefited immensely from the existence of the canal tunnel.

Much trade was surrendered to the railways over the years and by the time of its official abandonment in 1944, regular cargoes were limited to coal and iron ore. The last end-to-end voyage was made by Robert Aickman and fellow IWA members, in *Ailsa Craig*, during 1948.

WALKING AND CYCLING

There is an interesting interpretation board beside the Roaches Lock pub (*see* page 61) detailing the industrial history of the area and setting out a short walk that takes in significant local features. The Oldham Way is a 40-mile trail, linking the newly opened Huddersfield Narrow and Rochdale canals, split up into seven more easily manageable sections. Visit the TIC for further details. The Medlock Valley Way leads walkers from the remote uplands of Saddleworth Moor above Oldham into the heart of Manchester linking meadows, rivers, moors, woodlands and canals along a trail of great diversity. Further information from local TICs. The Public Art Sculpture Trail links a number of pieces installed along the section of the canal running through Oldham. These images reflect life on the canal; they have been inspired by the geography of the area, by a local school and, in many cases, make use of recycled and reclaimed materials. Further details from local TICs and Brownhill Visitor Centre – *see* page 60. The Tameside Trail is a 40-mile circular walk that intersects with the canal at Division Bridge and broadly follows the Tameside boundary linking river valleys, country parks and other places of interest. Further details from Tameside Countryside Service (0161 330 9613; www.tameside.gov.uk/countryside). A section of the 268-mile-long Pennine Way runs through wild country along the eastern edge of Saddleworth Moor. *See* Leeds & Liverpool Canal, page 124 for further details.

To negotiate Standedge Tunnel, walkers and cyclists can make use of one of the several waymarked routes over the Pennines, commencing beside the Diggle Hotel. Walkers can also take a bus from Uppermill or a boat trip through the tunnel. Charge. See above for booking details.

The Colne Valley Circular Walk is 12 miles long and majors on the contrasts of impressive industrial buildings set against a backdrop of a striking river valley. Details from Huddersfield TIC (*see* page 66). The Kirklees Way beats the bounds of this eponymous district, totalling a demanding 72 miles. Again contrast abounds: landscape versus history, scenery versus industry. Details from Huddersfield TIC. The Marsden and Tunnel End Trail is a 'hands on' version of much that is depicted in The Old Goods Yard (*see* page 63 under Marsden Moor Estate) and as such is a fascinating insight into the area. There is a regular series of walks and events based on Marsden Moor Estate's 5,685 acres of unenclosed moorland. For a programme and copies of the trail detailed above, visit The Old Goods Yard or www.nationaltrust.org.uk/marsdenmoor, or telephone 01484 847016.

Apart from the range of walks detailed above, the presence of the transPennine railway line close to the waterway throughout makes planning expeditions along the canal straightforward. Trains run at frequent intervals, some stopping at all stations and some only at major stations. All trains carry bicycles free of charge although space is limited on First Transpennine Express services and it is advisable to book in advance during busy periods. Telephone 08457 48 49 50 for details.

To avoid the somewhat daunting trek over the top of Standedge Tunnel *see* note on page 63.

Stalybridge

The canal follows the River Tame east out of Portland Basin, crossing it just over 1 mile later to arrive at the first newly constructed lock in Stalybridge. In 1947 the section from here through the town was culverted and the enthusiasm for the recently exhumed navigation, ascending a series of locks amidst busy streets, is universal. Replacing a forgotten drain, there is now a vibrant waterway, a bustle of activity made colourful with boats: a scene reminiscent of a Dutch town, the canal its central focus, roads subservient. Good *moorings* are plentiful, well distributed between locks 4W and 8W. The Pennines beckon over the rooftops of Stalybridge, as the waterway continues on its steady climb towards Scout Tunnel, ducking directly between the legs of an unfortunately sited electricity pylon, more recently placed in its path. There are *showers and toilets* beside Grove Road Bridge 96. The climb is unremitting, though largely through leafy glades with just the occasional glimpses of open hill views, punctuated with the dereliction of past industry – largely coal mining. Throughout its ascent, the waterway remains discrete, almost shunning the outside world, winding through woods and passing several attractively sited, waterside picnic areas. Whilst road crossings do briefly intrude, it is the transPennine railway that keeps constant company with the waterway: a not altogether unwelcome diversion bringing a source of well-ordered activity and flashes of colour on a dull day.

● **Stalybridge**
Cheshire. PO, tel, stores, banks, chemists, fish monger, hardware, butcher, baker, greengrocer, delicatessen, fish & chips, takeaways, library, station. With the first mill completed in 1776, this was one of the original centres of textile production during the Industrial Revolution. 19th-C prosperity went on to transform a series of small, scattered rural communities into a prosperous industrial town, which the effects of the past 50 years of decline appear well on the way to reversing. See also page 182.

Pubs and Restaurants

1 The Station Buffet Bar Platform 4, Rassbottom Street, Stalybridge SK15 1RF (0161 303 0007; www.beerhouses.co.uk/pub/stalybridge-buffet-bar). The original station buffet, decorated with old railway photographs and memorabilia, and now dispensing an excellent range of real ales, cider and food *daily 12.00-19.00. Occasional* live music and a real fire. No electronic machines – just the rattle of passing trains. *Open Sun-Thu 12.00-23.00 (Tue-Thu 11.00) & Fri-Sat 11.00-00.00.*

2 Q Inn 3 Market Street, Stalybridge SK15 2AL (0161 303 9152; www.hydesbrewery.com/pub-details/?id=38). In the *Guinness Book of Records* as the pub with the shortest name in the UK. Real ales and food available *Wed-Sun 12.00-20.00 (Sun 14.00).* Family-friendly, garden. *Regular* live music. Sports TV and Wi-Fi. *Open Sun-Thu 12.00-23.00 (Wed-Thu 00.00) & Fri-Sat 12.00-01.30.*

3 The White House
1 Water Street, Stalybridge SK15 2AG (0161 303 2154; www.our-pub.co.uk/Pubs/WhiteHouse.php). Exposed brickwork, tiled floors and old cast iron radiators create the atmosphere in a pub serving real ales, real ciders and food *Sun 12.00-18.00.* Dog-friendly, beer garden. *Regular* live music. Traditional pub games, newspapers and sports TV. *Open Mon-Sat 12.00-23.30 (Fri-Sat 01.00) & Sun 12.00-23.00.*

4 The Society Rooms 49-51 Grosvenor Street, Stalybridge SK15 2JN (0161 338 9740; www.jdwetherspoon.co.uk/home/pubs/the-society-rooms-stalybridge). Occupying the old Co-op store, this friendly pub now purveys real ale, real cider and food available *daily 08.00-23.00.* Family-friendly, outside seating. Wi-Fi. *Open 08.00-00.00 (Fri-Sat 01.00).*

5 Bridge Beers 55 Melbourne Street, Stalybridge SK15 2JJ (07948 617145; www.bridgebeers.co.uk). A combined micro-pub and bottle shop run by an enthusiastic CAMRA member, serving real ales (by gravity) real cider and a selection of crisps, pork scratchings and nuts. Well-behaved children and small dogs welcome. Traditional pub games and newspapers. *Open Tue-Thu 12.00-19.00 (Thu 21.00) Fri-Sat 12.00-22.00 & second Sun of the month 12.00-17.00.*

See also **Pubs and Restaurants** on page 183.

59

Saddleworth

The Pennines rear up ahead, although their full impact is softened by the fringe of woodland accompanying the navigation up the valley. To the west the imposingly situated building of Quickwood church, with its needle-like spire, oversees the bustle of road, rail and waterway activity below. Impressive mills, now sadly decaying, line the canal as it winds its tortuous path towards Uppermill, where it is greeted by what appears to be a castle keep, complete with portcullis. Closer inspection reveals a somewhat elaborate stone facing, topped with iron railings and employed to disguise a concrete box culvert, with further embellishment to hide a vertical gas main! By now the scale of the textile industry is subdued by the imposing bulk of Saddleworth Moor, while the sprawling conurbation of Manchester gives way to a straggle of attractive villages, constructed in the local gritstone and strewn randomly over the surrounding hillsides. Looking back towards the smoking chimneys below, there are wide open views now appearing over the high ground that had seemed to pose such a formidable obstacle when viewed from Stalybridge. Beyond the striking Wool Road Transshipment Warehouse (all facilities including toilets) the waterway, still climbing relentlessly, breaks out alongside the railway and together they both pick their way across heathered moorland towards their interlaced passage, deep beneath the Pennines.

Mossley

Gt Manchester. PO, tel, stores, off-licence, chemist, butcher, fish & chips, DIY, takeaways, station. A small agricultural hamlet of 1,200 souls in 1821, Mossley had grown into a prosperous cotton town by 1885 with a population of 15,000. The shops, PO etc are all close to the station as are several additional pubs.

Mossley Industrial Heritage Centre Longlands Mill, Queen Street, Mossley OL5 9AH (01457 832813; www.emmausmossley.org.uk/heritage-centre). Memories abound and are brought to life in an old cotton spinning mill now owned by Emmaus, a charitable organisation which provides work and a home for people who would otherwise be homeless. The Centre now seeks to answer questions about past times in a boom era of cotton and woollen manufacture. Shop and café. Heritage Centre *open Wed–Sat 14.00–16.00*; Emmaus shop *open Mon–Sat 09.00–17.00 (Mon 10.00).* Café *open Mon–Sat 10.00–16.00.*

Greenfield

Gt Manchester. PO, tel, stores, chemist, fish monger, greengrocer, butcher, off-licence, library, station. Another cotton community attempting to adjust to the demise of a past prosperity. The nearest station to Uppermill is here and there is a useful coal merchant – The Saddleworth Coal Hut (01457 839902/ 01457 871267/07775 713792/07775 801413; www.seatonfuels.co.uk).

Uppermill

Gt Manchester. PO, tel, stores, bank, chemists, butchers, baker, fish & chips, hardware, takeaways, library, garage. A traditional Pennine village and once the centre of the local cotton and cottage weaving industry, it has become a focus for the tourist trade that has long supplanted all such activity. Now the largest settlement in Saddleworth, it only gained its supremacy in the late 18th C with the coming of the canal and turnpike road, ousting nearby Dobcross.

Saddleworth Museum and Gallery High Street, Uppermill, Oldham OL3 6HS (01457 874093; www.saddleworthmuseum.co.uk). By Wade Lock. A family-friendly museum full of intriguing objects from the past telling the story of the people who have created Saddleworth's landscape and character. Gallery with changing exhibitions, many of local interest. Shop. *Open Mon–Sat 13.00–16.00.* Charge. There is also a **Visitor Information Centre** and **Boat Trips** aboard Pennine *Moonraker Sat & Sun and daily during school holidays.*

Visitor Information Centre Saddleworth Museum & Art Gallery, High Street, Uppermill, Oldham OL3 6HS (01457 870336/870336; www.visitmanchester.com/visitor-information/saddleworth-tourist-information-centre-p24061). *Open daily 13.00–16.00.*

Dobcross

Gt Manchester. PO, tel, stores, off-licence. A delightful village, quintessentially Pennine, every building and winding narrow street a gem, the whole presided over by the charming Saddleworth Bank – now fulfilling a more homely role.

Brownhill Countryside Centre Wool Road, Dobcross, Oldham OL3 5PB (0161 770 5888; www.visitoldham.com/attractions/brownhill-countryside-centre-p84811). Wildlife and historical interpretation centre for the area with changing exhibitions and displays, a woodland 'crawly tunnel' for children, shop, café, toilets and a picnic area. *Open daily 09.00–19.00.*

Diggle

Gt Manchester. PO, tel, off-licence, takeaway, fish & chips. Together with its neighbours Dobcross and Delph, Diggle lay at the heart of local hand-weaving until, in the late 18th C, the Industrial Revolution spawned mills as the centres of production, sited further down the valley for easier access.

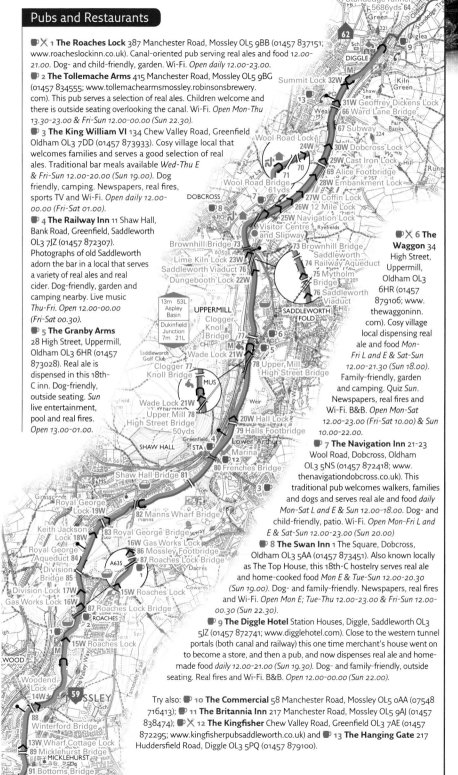

Pubs and Restaurants

🍴✕ 1 **The Roaches Lock** 387 Manchester Road, Mossley OL5 9BB (01457 837151; www.roacheslockinn.co.uk). Canal-oriented pub serving real ales and food 12.00-21.00. Dog- and child-friendly, garden. Wi-Fi. *Open daily 12.00-23.00.*

🍴 2 **The Tollemache Arms** 415 Manchester Road, Mossley OL5 9BG (01457 834555; www.tollemachearmsmossley.robinsonsbrewery. com). This pub serves a selection of real ales. Children welcome and there is outside seating overlooking the canal. Wi-Fi. *Open Mon-Thu 13.30-23.00 & Fri-Sun 12.00-00.00 (Sun 22.30).*

🍴 3 **The King William VI** 134 Chew Valley Road, Greenfield, Oldham OL3 7DD (01457 873933). Cosy village local that welcomes families and serves a good selection of real ales. Traditional bar meals available *Wed-Thu E & Fri-Sun 12.00-20.00 (Sun 19.00).* Dog friendly, camping. Newspapers, real fires, sports TV and Wi-Fi. *Open daily 12.00-00.00 (Fri-Sat 01.00).*

🍴 4 **The Railway Inn** 11 Shaw Hall, Bank Road, Greenfield, Saddleworth OL3 7JZ (01457 872307). Photographs of old Saddleworth adorn the bar in a local that serves a variety of real ales and real cider. Dog-friendly, garden and camping nearby. Live music *Thu-Fri. Open 12.00-00.00 (Fri-Sat 00.30).*

🍴 5 **The Granby Arms** 28 High Street, Uppermill, Oldham OL3 6HR (01457 873028). Real ale is dispensed in this 18th-C inn. Dog-friendly, outside seating. *Sun live entertainment, pool and real fires. Open 13.00-01.00.*

🍴✕ 6 **The Waggon** 34 High Street, Uppermill, Oldham OL3 6HR (01457 879106; www. thewaggoninn. com). Cosy village local dispensing real ale and food *Mon-Fri L and E & Sat-Sun 12.00-21.30 (Sun 18.00).* Family-friendly, garden and camping. Quiz *Sun.* Newspapers, real fires and Wi-Fi. B&B. *Open Mon-Sat 12.00-23.00 (Fri-Sat 10.00) & Sun 10.00-22.00.*

🍴 7 **The Navigation Inn** 21-23 Wool Road, Dobcross, Oldham OL3 5NS (01457 872418; www. thenavigationdobcross.co.uk). This traditional pub welcomes walkers, families and dogs and serves real ale and food *daily Mon-Sat L and E & Sun 12.00-18.00.* Dog- and child-friendly, patio. Wi-Fi. *Open Mon-Fri L and E & Sat-Sun 12.00-23.00 (Sun 20.00)*

🍴 8 **The Swan Inn** 1 The Square, Dobcross, Oldham OL3 5AA (01457 873451). Also known locally as The Top House, this 18th-C hostelry serves real ale and home-cooked food *Mon E & Tue-Sun 12.00-20.30 (Sun 19.00).* Dog- and family-friendly. Newspapers, real fires and Wi-Fi. *Open Mon E; Tue-Thu 12.00-23.00 & Fri-Sun 12.00-00.30 (Sun 22.30).*

🍴 9 **The Diggle Hotel** Station Houses, Diggle, Saddleworth OL3 5JZ (01457 872741; www.digglehotel.com). Close to the western tunnel portals (both canal and railway) this one time merchant's house went on to become a store, and then a pub, and now dispenses real ale and home-made food *daily 12.00-21.00 (Sun 19.30).* Dog- and family-friendly, outside seating. Real fires and Wi-Fi. B&B. *Open 12.00-00.00 (Sun 22.00).*

Try also: 🍴 10 **The Commercial** 58 Manchester Road, Mossley OL5 0AA (07548 716413); 🍴 11 **The Britannia Inn** 217 Manchester Road, Mossley OL5 9AJ (01457 838474); 🍴✕ 12 **The Kingfisher** Chew Valley Road, Greenfield OL3 7AE (01457 872295; www.kingfisherpubsaddleworth.co.uk) and 🍴 13 **The Hanging Gate** 217 Huddersfield Road, Diggle OL3 5PQ (01457 879100).

Marsden

It comes as almost something of a relief to leave the activity centred around the tunnel mouth and start the long steady descent into Huddersfield. Lock operation is no less arduous going downhill and there is a feeling akin to anti-climax as the waterway drops rapidly through a profusion of trees and almost into Sparth Reservoir. In places the hills lining the Colne Valley step back a little, leaving level grazing and fields for hay and silage making. The infant river is never far away and in places is separated only by a narrow band of trees. From time to time the landscape is punctuated by the gaunt remains of a splendid old mill as views open out briefly before the often tree-lined hills close in once again. *Gas* is available beside Shuttle Lock 24E. The railway shadows the canal into Slaithwaite where once again the harmony wrought by its focal position amidst shops and streets is most satisfactory.

Pubs and Restaurants

🍺 **1 The Railway** 34 Station Road, Marsden HD7 6DH (01484 841541). Beside Dirker Lock. Real ale is served in this traditional English pub. Home-made food is available *daily 12.00-21.00*. Dog- and child-friendly. Garden, Wi-Fi, traditional pub games and large-screen TV. *Open 11.00-23.00 (Fri-Sat 00.00).*

🍺 **2 The Shakespeare** 33 Peel Street, Marsden HD7 6BW (01484 844818). Village centre local serving real ale and showing sport on large-screen TVs. Dog- and family-friendly. Garden and traditional pub games. Wi-Fi. *Open Mon-Sat 11.00-23.00 (Fri-Sat 01.00) & Sun 12.00-22.30.*

🍺 **3 The Riverhead Brewery Tap** 2 Peel Street Marsden HD7 6BR (01484 844324). This lively brew-pub now dispenses real ciders and an excellent range of its own real ales from the brewery visible from the bar. Food available *Tue-Fri L and E & Sat-Sun 12.00-21.00 (Sun 20.00).* Dog- and family-friendly, outside drinking area. Newspapers and Wi-Fi. *Open 12.00-00.00.*

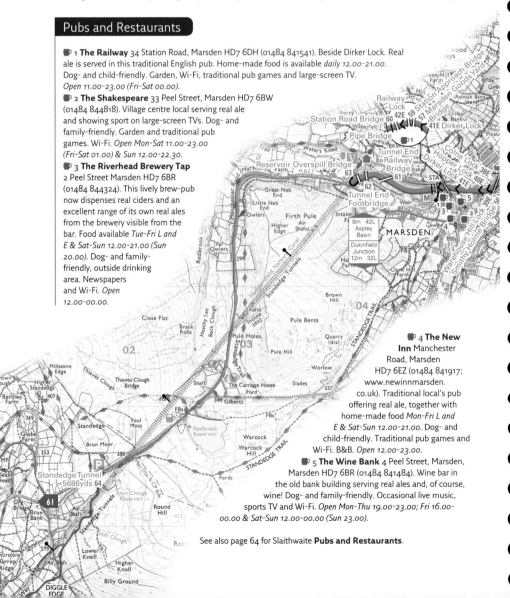

🍺 **4 The New Inn** Manchester Road, Marsden HD7 6EZ (01484 841917; www.newinnmarsden. co.uk). Traditional local's pub offering real ale, together with home-made food *Mon-Fri L and E & Sat-Sun 12.00-21.00.* Dog- and child-friendly. Traditional pub games and Wi-Fi. B&B. *Open 12.00-23.00.*

🍺 **5 The Wine Bank** 4 Peel Street, Marsden HD7 6BR (01484 841484). Wine bar in the old bank building serving real ales and, of course, wine! Dog- and family-friendly. Occasional live music, sports TV and Wi-Fi. *Open Mon-Thu 19.00-23.00; Fri 16.00-00.00 & Sat-Sun 12.00-00.00 (Sun 23.00).*

See also page 64 for Slaithwaite **Pubs and Restaurants**.

Marsden

W. Yorks. PO, tel, stores, chemist, greengrocer, off-licence, takeaways, fish & chips, library, station. Situated at an important transPennine crossing point, Marsden has always been a focus for the

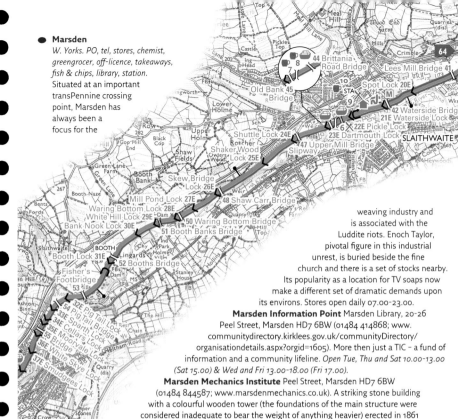

weaving industry and is associated with the Luddite riots. Enoch Taylor, pivotal figure in this industrial unrest, is buried beside the fine church and there is a set of stocks nearby. Its popularity as a location for TV soaps now make a different set of dramatic demands upon its environs. Stores open daily 07.00-23.00.

Marsden Information Point Marsden Library, 20-26 Peel Street, Marsden HD7 6BW (01484 414868; www. communitydirectory.kirklees.gov.uk/communityDirectory/ organisationdetails.aspx?orgid=1605). More then just a TIC – a fund of information and a community lifeline. *Open Tue, Thu and Sat 10.00-13.00 (Sat 15.00) & Wed and Fri 13.00-18.00 (Fri 17.00).*

Marsden Mechanics Institute Peel Street, Marsden HD7 6BW (01484 844587; www.marsdenmechanics.co.uk). A striking stone building with a colourful wooden tower (the foundations of the main structure were considered inadequate to bear the weight of anything heavier) erected in 1861 to provide education for the betterment of the working man. Now the library and community hall. Also home to the evergreen Mikron Theatre Company (when not touring the waterways on their boat *Tysley*) who can be contacted on 01484 843701; www.mikron.org.uk.

Marsden Moor Estate The Old Goods Yard, Station Road, Marsden HD7 6DH (01484 847016; www.nationaltrust.org.uk/marsden-moor-estate). Over 5,000 acres of moorland in the hands of the NT and accessible through a series of walks and trails. The exhibition in the Old Goods Yard, beside the towpath at Marsden Railway Station, uses a series of excellent displays to provide a wealth of information about every aspect of the area, from natural phenomena through to the relatively recent industrial impact of weaving, water, canal and railway. Free.

Standedge Tunnels At first sight there appears to be an indecently large number of tunnels connecting Diggle with Marsden. The canal tunnel came first, completed in 1811, followed by the single bore of the Huddersfield and Manchester Railway dating from 1845. Two years later this railway company was taken over by the LNWR who built a second single – and parallel – track to cope with increasing demand. In 1894 the present double track tunnel was constructed to cope with the burgeoning traffic. In all instances the canal tunnel, now owned by the railway company and connected to its tunnels by cross-adits, proved invaluable for spoil removal during construction.

Standedge Tunnel and Visitor Centre Waters Road, Marsden HD7 6NQ (01484 844298; www. canalrivertrust.org.uk/places-to-visit/standedge-tunnel-and-visitor-centre). All the superlatives marshalled within the confines of one extremely long tunnel: highest, longest and deepest in Britain and largely hewn out of solid rock. The centre offers the opportunity to get to grips with all the facts, figures and dates. *Opening times vary* so telephone for further details. Café, a walking trail and boat trips into (and sometimes through) the tunnel. Park at Marsden Railway Station and walk west along the towpath. A water taxi service operates at weekends (01457 871800; www2.huddersfieldcanal.com/tag/boat-trips).

BOAT TRIPS

Thirty-minute trips into Standedge Tunnel operate when the Visitor Centre (see above) is open starting at *12.00 Mon-Fri & 11.00 Sat-Sun*. Also rides on the *Marsden Shuttle* water taxi service as above – see website for timetable.

Slaithwaite

The railway, as enthusiastic a companion to the navigation as ever, shadows the canal into Slaithwaite where once again the harmony wrought by its focal position amidst shops and streets is most satisfactory. It is a matter of intense speculation as to why it took so long to replace a secret subterranean trickle with this overtly delightful scene. East of the settlement the waterway settles into a broader valley bottom and the hills become a little more submissive. Attractive tree-lined glades alternate with views of a still bold landscape and everywhere there are the gaunt remains of mills: reminders of this area's supremacy as a textile producer and the canal's real purpose. The descent into Huddersfield is steady and not without contrast – pretty stone bridges vie with an imposing railway viaduct and many of the locks (although still in need of more use) appear in attractive settings.

Slaithwaite

W. Yorks. PO, tel, stores, bank, chemist, greengrocer, butcher, off-licence, takeaways, fish & chips, hardware, station. Another settlement founded on the woollen and cotton industries with a fine Georgian church and the 16th-C Slaithwaite Hall. The juxtaposition of canal with the village streets is very pleasing. Stores *open daily 07.00-22.00.*

Linthwaite

W. Yorks. Tel. Although strung out and somewhat detached from the waterway, this village is not without charm and is home to several very striking (and very derelict) mills which tell of its former glory as a textile producer. Happily several of these structures are now undergoing renovation to fit them for their new rôle as appartments.

NAVIGATIONAL NOTES

See page 67.

Pubs and Restaurants (page 63)

XΨ **6 The Little Bridge** Britannia Road, Slaithwaite HD7 5HF (01484 846738; www.littlebridgewinebar. co.uk). Sandwiched between the canal and river, in the centre of the village, this relaxed establishment serves a good range of drinks and appetising food, freshly prepared from locally-sourced ingredients, available *Tue-Thu L and E & Fri-Sun L*. Real ale. *Open Tue-Sun 10.00-00.00 (Sun 22.30).*

🍺 **7 The Shoulder of Mutton** 9 Church Street, Slaithwaite HD7 5AS (01484 841436). Traditional pub serving real ale and food *Sun 12.00-18.00*. Dog- and family-friendly. Traditional pub games, *occasional* live music and Wi-Fi. *Open 12.00-00.00.*

🍺 **8 The Commercial Hotel** 1 Carr Lane, Slaithwaite HD7 5AN (01484 846258; www.commercial-slaithwaite. co.uk). Traditional pub, with a strong community focus, dispensing real cider and a wide range of real ales. Dog-friendly with an outdoor drinking area and traditional pub games. Wi-Fi. *Open 12.00-00.00 (Fri-Sat 01.00).*

X **9 The Captain's Table** 15 Carr Lane, Slaithwaite HD7 5AN (01484 841068). Fresh fish and chips with a difference. Eat in or take away. *Open Mon-Fri L and E & Sat 11.30-20.00.*

🍺 **10 The Silent Woman** Nabbs Lane, Slaithwaite HD7 5AY (01484 844286). A lively, welcoming pub serving real ale. Dog- and child-friendly. Traditional pub games, occasional live music, sports TV and Wi-Fi. *Open Mon-Fri 10.00-23.00 (Fri 01.00) & Sat-Sun 12.00-01.00.*

HUDDERSFIELD BROAD CANAL

MAXIMUM DIMENSIONS

Length: 57' 6"
Beam: 14' 2"
Headroom: 9' 6"
Draught: 2' 6''

MANAGER

0303 040 4040;
www.canalrivertrust.org.uk/contact-us/
ways-to-contact-us

MILEAGE

ASPLEY BASIN, HUDDERSFIELD to:
Cooper Bridge: 3¾ miles
Locks: 9

Travel through Standedge Tunnel is on a chaperoned basis, allowing the helmsman to steer his vessel through the tunnel, accompanied by a member of the Canal & River Trust Tunnel Team. Transit is available *from late Mar to early Nov on Mon, Wed & Fri*. Bookings must be made *in advance* by telephoning 0303 040 4040 and the Standedge Customer Guidelines can be downloaded in pdf form from www.canalrivertrust.org.uk/canals-and-rivers/huddersfield-narrow-canal#Standedge. This provides full details of the transit, including a diagram setting out the limiting dimensions for craft wishing to undertake the passage.

Boats may travel no further than Lock 32E or 24W without having first made a booking.

The Huddersfield Broad Canal was built to serve the rapidly expanding woollen industry of the 18th C. Known also as Sir John Ramsden's Canal, it was authorised in 1774 and completed in 1780. Costing £12,000, the waterway gave local textile manufacturers access to markets throughout Yorkshire as well as coal to feed the steam-driven mills. Despite the inevitable amalgamation with the competing railway company (the London and North Western Railway in 1847) the waterway remained a profitable concern until the late 1940s. It was conceived as a broad gauge canal to accommodate square-rigged, sailing keels or 'Yorkshire craft' – 58' 0" in length and 14' 0" beam. Due to the navigation's low bridges these had to be de-rigged at Cooper Bridge and bow hauled the remaining 3¾ miles. The Huddersfield Narrow Canal, completed some 30 years later, was built as a narrow gauge waterway unable to accept traffic from the Broad Canal; consequently warehousing and transshipment facilities were developed at Aspley Basin. The problem was partially overcome with the introduction of the West Riding narrowboat: a specially shortened craft able to negotiate locks on both systems. Immediately south west of Aspley Basin is a warehouse built prior to 1778 which is probably the oldest surviving example of such a building, demonstrating an early stage in the development of the large multi-storey warehouses of the 19th C. The crane beside it dates from the early 19th C.

Huddersfield

The two factory tunnels (now reduced to one) were an ingenious solution to recent building on the old canal line and, in conjunction with the re-siting of the locks, represent the very best in Northern pragmatism! However, it is with some relief that you leave the stygian gloom of the remaining tunnel – the towpath employs an above-ground and altogether less elegant solution to the blockage – and, winding between university buildings, arrive at Apsley Basin. Beyond is the remarkable Turnbridge Loco Liftbridge dating from 1865; you will need a Watermate key to unlock it. The outskirts of Huddersfield present a mix of industry, a new waste incineration plant and by way

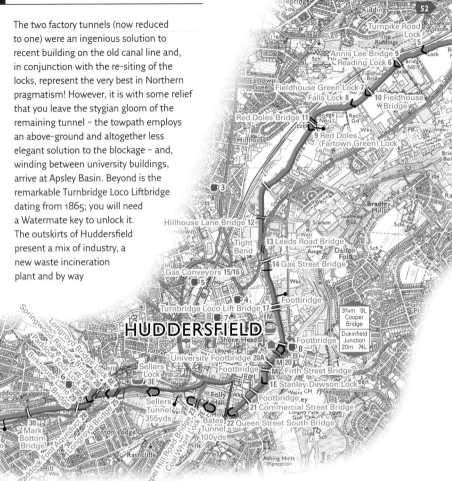

of relief, a vast expanse of green sports fields. The nine locks appear with a steady regularity and, passing through Cooper Bridge Lock, the canal finally enters a river section of the Calder & Hebble Navigation (*see page 50*). Before leaving this lock, boaters should be quite clear of the layout of the junction and of their intended passage.

Boatyards

Ⓑ**Aspley Wharf Marina** Apsley Basin, St Andrew's Road, Huddersfield HD1 6SD (01484 514123; www.aspleywharfmarina.co.uk). 🏠🛒🚿D Pump out, gas, overnight mooring, long-term mooring, slipway, chandlery, books, maps and gifts, solid fuel, boat repairs, marine engineering services, telephone, toilets, showers, laundry. *Open Apr-Nov, Mon-Sat 10.00-17.00 (Sat 14.00) & Dec-Mar, Mon, Wed and Fri 10.00-17.00.*

NAVIGATIONAL NOTES

1   When leaving or joining the Huddersfield Broad Canal at Cooper Bridge, take care to avoid the weir on the river just beyond the entrance to lock 1.

2   Lock 24E has a guillotine-type tailgate. Read the operating instructions before use.

WALKING AND CYCLING

Throughout both the Huddersfield Broad Canal and the adjoining Narrow Canal the towpath is in excellent condition making an attractive off-road trans-Pennine route for both walker and cyclist alike. To negotiate the section of canal in Huddersfield that tunnels under the floor of a factory, follow the copious blue and white signs along a succession of streets between Bridges 22 and 25.

Huddersfield

W. Yorks. All services. Huddersfield is in the best tradition of Victorian industrial towns: all built to a grand scale of dark local stone, in a happy mixture of 19th-C styles. The most striking part of the town is around the railway station, built in 1847 with its powerful classical façade of Corinthian columns, considered one of the finest examples of railway architecture. The renowned Huddersfield Choral Society operates from the 19th-C town hall. **Art Gallery** Princess Alexandra Walk, Huddersfield HD1 2SU (01484 221964; www.kirklees.gov.uk/beta/museums-galleries-history/huddersfield-art-gallery.aspx). Above the library. Presents an international programme embracing all media together with changing displays from the permanent collection. Shop. *Open Tue-Sat 11.00-16.00. Free.*
Castle Hill and Victoria Tower off Lumb Lane, Almondbury, Huddersfield HD4 6TA (07870 570914; communitydirectory.kirklees.gov.uk/communityDirectory/organisationdetails.aspx?orgid=2485). A striking local landmark occupied since the Stone Age and now topped by a Victorian tower. Splendid views and an exhibition tracing the hill's 4000 years of history. Bus number 341 from Huddersfield stops at the bottom of the hill. Open on occasional days throughout *the summer from Apr-Oct, 12.00-16.00.* Visit the website for further details. Charge.
Colne Valley Museum Cliffe Ash, Golcar, Huddersfield HD7 4PY (01484 659762; www.colnevalleymuseum.org.uk). The hand weaver's working life c.1850 depicted in a working exhibit in period settings. Also clog making by gas light and a range of changing craft exhibitions. Books, gifts and light refreshments available. *Open weekends and B Hols, Apr-Oct 14.00-17.00 & Nov-Mar 13.00-16.00.* Small charge.

Holmfirth Nr Huddersfield. An essential visit for all *Last of the Summer Wine* devotees, easily accessible by bus from Huddersfield. Exhibition gallery contains photographs and memorabilia dating from the series beginning in 1972. *Sat* craft market and galleries.
Holmfirth Tourist Information Centre 49-51 Huddersfield Road, Holmfirth HD9 3JP (01484 414868/221000; communitydirectory.kirklees.gov.uk/communityDirectory/venueDetails.aspx?venueID=1694). *Open Mon 09.30-19.00; Tue 09.30-13.30; Wed 13.00-17.30; Thu-Fri 09.30-17.30; Sat 10.00-16.00 & Sun 11.00-15.00 (seasonal).*
Kirklees Light Railway Park Mill Way, Clayton West, near Huddersfield HD8 9XJ (01484 865727; www.kirkleeslightrailway.com). Scenic ride on a narrow-gauge railway along a disused branch line. Children's playground and miniature fairground rides. Café. *Open weekends and most days throughout the summer.* Telephone for full details of event times. Charge. Bus nos. 80 or 81 from Huddersfield.
Tolson Museum Ravensknowle Park, Wakefield Road, Huddersfield HD5 8DJ (01484 223240; www.kirklees.gov.uk/beta/museums-galleries-history/tolson-museum.aspx). Fine Italianate mansion housing natural history, archaeology and local history exhibits. Workshops, events and children's activities. *Open Apr-Aug, Tue-Thu and B Hols 11.00-17.00 & Sat-Sun 12.00-17.00 and Sep-Mar, Tue-Thu 11.00-16.00 (during School Hols only) & Sat-Sun 12.00-16.00.* Free.
Tourist Information Centre Huddersfield Library, Princess Alexandra Walk, Huddersfield HD1 2SU (01484 223200; www.yorkshire.com/view/attractions/huddersfield/huddersfield-tourist-information-centre-1193630). *Open Mon 09.30-19.00; Tue-Fri 09.00-17.00 (Thu 19.00) and Sat 09.30-16.00.*

🍺 1 **The White Cross** 2 Bradley Road, Bradley, Huddersfield HD2 1XD (01484 425728). Dating from 1806, and once a Bentley Breweries house, this award-winning pub serves real ales and food *L Sun–Fri*. Outside seating, traditional pub games and Wi-Fi. *Mon-Sat 11.45-23.00 (Fri-Sat 00.00) & Sun 12.00-22.30.*

🍺✕ 2 **The Royal and Ancient Country Inn** 19 Dalton Bank Road, Colne Bridge, Huddersfield HD5 0RE (01484 425461; www.royal-ancient. co.uk). East of bridge 2. A fine pub, tastefully furnished, achieving a balance between genuine olde worlde and traditional comfort. An intimate, cosy atmosphere in the separate restaurant area, together with interesting wall decorations and an intriguing array of curios to captivate the eye. An elaborate, varied and exciting range of food is available in both the bar and restaurant *daily 12.00-21.00* and a good selection of real ales is dispensed from a bar dominated by a dark burr-oak post, uncarved, but appearing to depict the head of a Hereford bull. Children welcome as are well-behaved dogs (outside water provided). Patio seating. Open fires *in winter*. Wi-Fi. *Open Mon-Sat 11.30-23.00 (Fri-Sat 00.00) & Sun 12.00-22.30.*

🍺 3 **The Slubbers Arms** 1 Halifax Old Road, Hillhouse, Huddersfield HD1 6HW (01484 429032). ¼-mile west of Hillhouse Lane Bridge 12. With 150 years of history under its belt, this hostelry still dispenses real cider, perry and real Ales. Dog- and child-friendly *(until 20.00)* patio. Real fires. *Open Mon-Sat 16.00-23.00 (Fri-Sat 15.00) & Sun 14.00-23.00.*

🍺 4 **The Vulcan** 32 St Peters Street, Huddersfield HD1 1RA (01484 303040). Popular, town-centre pub serving a good selection of real ales and food *Mon-Sat 09.00-14.30 & Sun 11.00-17.00*. Child-friendly *(mornings and afternoons)* and outside seating. Traditional pub games, *Sun* live music and sports TV. *Open Sun-Fri 09.00-01.00 (Fri 02.00) & Sat 09.00-02.30.*

🍺 5 **The Sportsman** 1 St John's Road, Huddersfield HD1 5AY (01484 421929; www.beerhouses.co.uk/pub/the-sportsman). A CAMRA Conservation Heritage pub serving a wide range of real ales, real cider and food *Mon-Thu L & Fri-Sun 19.00 (Fri 21.00)*. Dog- and family-friendly *(until 18.00)* beer garden. *Occasional* live music, real fires and Wi-Fi. *Open 12.00-23.00 (Fri-Sat 00.00).*

There are plenty of **Pubs and Restaurants** in Huddersfield. These are just a selection close to Aspley Basin:

🍺 6 **The Rising Sun** 27 Crosland Hill Road, Crosland Hill Huddersfield HD4 5NZ (01484 653636). Community-driven local of the old school, serving real ales and with a hidden gem of a beer garden to the rear. Dog-friendly. Traditional pub games, sports TV and Wi-Fi. *Open 15.00-23.30 (Sat-Sun 12.00).*

🍺 7 **The Corner** 5 Market Walk, Huddersfield, HD1 2QA (www.thecornerhudds.co.uk). A light modern bar serving an excellent range of real ales and real ciders, together with imaginative food *Mon-Fri L and E (not Mon-Tue E) & Sat-Sun 12.00-17.00*. Dog- and family-friendly. Traditional pub games, *occasional* live music and Wi-Fi. *Open Mon-Sat 11.00-23.00 (Fri-Sat 00.00) & Sun 12.00-22.00.*

🍺 8 **The Aspley Table Table** Aspley Basin, St Andrews Way, Huddersfield HD1 6SB (01484 453310; www.tabletable.co.uk). Real ales and food available in both bar and restaurant *all day, every day*. Children welcome. Canalside seating and moorings. *Open Mon-Fri 06.30-23.00 & Sat-Sun 07.00-23.00 (Sun 22.30).*

WILDLIFE

The *Freshwater Crayfish* was formerly common and widespread, but has become somewhat scarce and endangered today. Its numbers are threatened by pollution and the disturbance of favoured river and stream habitats, and by competition from the introduced North American species. It needs fast-flowing, well-oxygenated water and, during the daytime, hides under stones, in holes in the bank and in gaps in dry-stone walls. During the restoration of the canal in Huddersfield, Canal & River Trust were able to create special habitat sites for the crayfish during construction of new tunnels built under factories that had been built over the canal. The crayfish has also successfully adopted the Rochdale Canal (*see page 172*).

▌LANCASTER CANAL

MAXIMUM DIMENSIONS	MANAGER
Preston to Tewitfield Length: 72' Beam: 14' Headroom: 8'	0303 040 4040; www.canalrivertrust.org.uk/contact-us/ways-to-contact-us
Glasson Branch Length: 70' Beam: 14' Headroom: 8'	**MILEAGE** PRESTON to Garstang: 16¹/₄ miles Junction with Glasson Branch: 24 miles
Ribble Link Length: 62' Beam: 10' 6' Headroom: 8' Draft: 2'	Lancaster: 29¹/₄ miles Carnforth: 37¹/₄ miles CANAL TERMINUS: 41¹/₄ No locks
	Glasson Branch: 2³/₄ miles, 6 locks Millennium Ribble Link: 4 miles, 9 locks

Construction on the Lancaster Canal began in 1792. The chosen route included several aqueducts, but only eight locks, at Tewitfield. By 1799 the canal between Tewitfield and Preston, including the aqueduct over the Lune, and the separate section between Clayton and Chorley, was opened. The route north was extended to Kendal in 1819, and the short, and very attractive, arm to Glasson Dock, falling through six locks, was opened in 1826, finally providing a direct link with the sea. In 1968 the canal north of Tewitfield was abandoned with the building of the M6 motorway (although eventual restoration now seems fairly certain), and the route in Preston was shortened by about a mile. What remains is remarkably rural, surprisingly quiet and worthy of exploration. The Ribble Link, opened in 2002, now provides a connection with the national network.

▌NAVIGATIONAL NOTES

1 You will need a Watermate key to use the locks on the Glasson Branch.
2 Those who wish to navigate the Ribble Link should visit www.canalrivertrust.org.uk/enjoy-the-waterways/canal-and-river-network/ribble-link/ribble-link-useful-information to download a variety of information including a Skippers Guide, general guidance notes and make an online booking. These are also obtainable by telephoning 0303 040 4040. *Passage can be booked up some time ahead, for this popular waterway, so advanced planning is necessary. Passage is free to CRT long term licence holders. Operating times are dictated by tides in the Ribble estuary, but a journey can be made during daylight hours as directed by CRT.* The staircase and sea lock are manned, and the link operates one way each day. There is no mooring on the Link. As the River Ribble is tidal, boats should carry, *as a minimum*: anchor, chain and warp, VHF radio or mobile phone, lifejackets for all on board, fire-fighting equipment, coastal flares. Your engine must be sufficiently powerful to cope with tidal conditions. Be sure to check that your boat insurance covers tidal waters.
3 If you need help or advice while on the River Ribble, contact Preston Riversway Control on VHF channel 16 (working on channel 14), or telephone 01772 726871.
4 If you wish to visit Preston Docks, contact Preston Riversway Control on 01772 726871.
5 Navigators entering the Rufford Branch of the Leeds & Liverpool from the sea should remember that they will need a Watermate key and a windlass to open the locks.
6 *At least 24hrs* notice of a booking cancellation must be given to CRT or a fee will be charged.

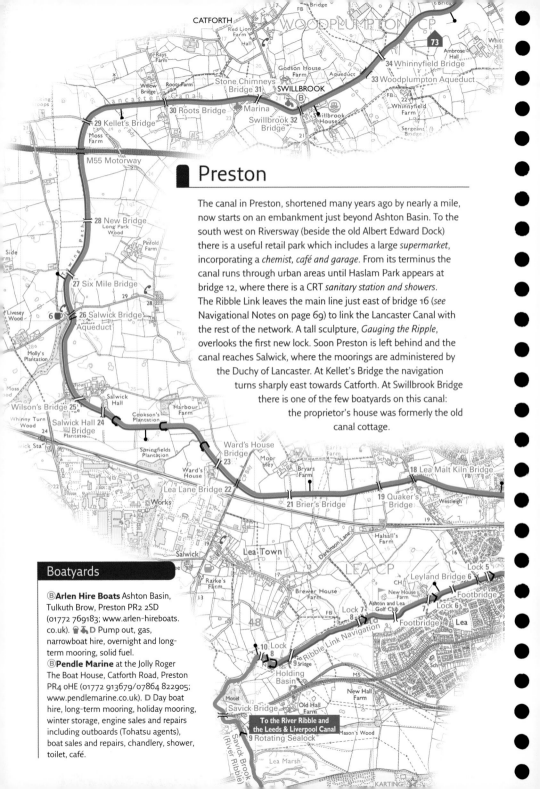

Preston

The canal in Preston, shortened many years ago by nearly a mile, now starts on an embankment just beyond Ashton Basin. To the south west on Riversway (beside the old Albert Edward Dock) there is a useful retail park which includes a large *supermarket*, incorporating a *chemist, café and garage*. From its terminus the canal runs through urban areas until Haslam Park appears at bridge 12, where there is a CRT *sanitary station and showers*. The Ribble Link leaves the main line just east of bridge 16 (*see* Navigational Notes on page 69) to link the Lancaster Canal with the rest of the network. A tall sculpture, *Gauging the Ripple*, overlooks the first new lock. Soon Preston is left behind and the canal reaches Salwick, where the moorings are administered by the Duchy of Lancaster. At Kellet's Bridge the navigation turns sharply east towards Catforth. At Swillbrook Bridge there is one of the few boatyards on this canal: the proprietor's house was formerly the old canal cottage.

Boatyards

Ⓑ**Arlen Hire Boats** Ashton Basin, Tulkuth Brow, Preston PR2 2SD (01772 769183; www.arlen-hireboats. co.uk). 🛁♨D Pump out, gas, narrowboat hire, overnight and long-term mooring, solid fuel.

Ⓑ**Pendle Marine** at the Jolly Roger The Boat House, Catforth Road, Preston PR4 0HE (01772 913679/07864 822905; www.pendlemarine.co.uk). D Day boat hire, long-term mooring, holiday mooring, winter storage, engine sales and repairs including outboards (Tohatsu agents), boat sales and repairs, chandlery, shower, toilet, café.

Preston

Lancs. All services. A large industrial town granted a Royal Charter by Henry II in 1179, with the right to hold a Guild Merchant. An outdoor market was also established and still thrives today. The teetotal movement was founded in Preston in 1834, and Joseph Livesey's Temperance Hotel (the world's first) used to stand at the corner of Church Street and North Road. There are many churches, such as St Walburge's (south east of the terminus), whose tall spires are a distinctive feature of the town. There is a good shopping precinct and a large modern bus station. Preston was awarded city status by the Queen in April 2002, in celebration of her Golden Jubilee.

Pubs and Restaurants

1 The Olde Dog & Partridge 44 Friargate, Preston PR1 2AT (01772 379339; www.dogandpartridgepreston.co.uk/index). Unpretentious, city-centre pub with a video jukebox dispensing real ales and good-value food *daily 09.00-20.00*. Dog- and family-friendly (in the daytime) patio seating. Live music *Fri-Sat*. Wi-Fi. *Open Mon-Sat 09.00-01.00 (Fri-Sat 02.00) & Sun 12.00-01.00.*

X 1 The Black Horse 166 Friargate, Preston PR1 2EJ (01772 204855; www.robinsonsbrewery.com/pubs-inns-and-hotels/find-a-pub/a-e/blackhorse). Historic, Arts and Crafts, Grade II listed hostelry (complete with a hall of mirrors seating area) serving a wide range of real ales and real ciders. Dog- and child-friendly. Traditional pub games, real fires and Wi-Fi. *Open Mon-Sat 10.30-23.30 (Fri-Sat 00.00) & Sun 12.00-22.00.*

Harris Museum & Art Gallery Market Square, Preston PR1 2PP (01772 258248; www.harrismuseum.org.uk). The largest gallery space in Lancashire, containing a specialised collection of the Devis family of painters and exhibits illustrating 18th-C and 19th-C art, including ceramics and costume. Shop, café and Wi-Fi. *Open 10.00-17.00 Sun-Mon 11.00). Free. Café open Mon-Sat 10.00-16.30 & Sun 11.00-15.30.*

Tourist Information Centre Town Hall, Lancaster Road, Preston PR1 2RL (01772 906900; www.preston.gov.uk/yourservices/events/visitor-information-centre). *Open Mon-Fri 09.00-17.00 (Thu 10.00).*

3 The Grey Friar 144 Friargate, Preston PR1 2EJ (01772 558542; www.jdwetherspoon.co.uk/home/pubs/the-grey-friar). Bustling, city-centre pub, in an ex-carpet store, serving real cider, a wide range of real ales and food *daily 08.00-23.00*. Family-friendly, outside seating and Wi-Fi. *Open 08.00-00.00 (Fri-Sat 01.00).*

4 The Old Vic 79 Fishergate, Preston, Lancashire PR1 2UH (01772 828519). Popular pub, close to the railway station, serving a wide range of real ales and food *daily 10.00-15.00*. Family-friendly *(mealtimes only)* and outside seating. Traditional pub games, newspapers, real fires, sports TV and Wi-Fi. *Open 10.00-23.00 Mon-Fri (Fri 00.00); Sat 11.00-00.00 & Sun 12.00-23.30.*

X 5 The Final Whistle Café Uclan Sports Arena Tom Benson Way, Preston PR2 1SG (01772 736901; www.facebook.com/FinalWhistleCafe). Convenient café beside Bridge 17, serving breakfasts, lunches, snacks, tea and coffee. Dog- and child-friendly. *Open Mon-Thu 10.30-20.00 (Mon 14.00) Fri 10.30-19.00 & Sat-Sun 09.30-15.30.*

X 6 The Hand & Dagger Treales Road, Salwick, Preston PR4 0SA (01772 690306; www.handanddagger.com). Once the Clifton Arms. A welcoming country pub serving real ale and freshly prepared food *Tue-Sun 12.00-21.00 (Sun 19.00)*. Dog- and child-friendly, garden. Traditional pub games, newspapers, real fires and Wi-Fi.

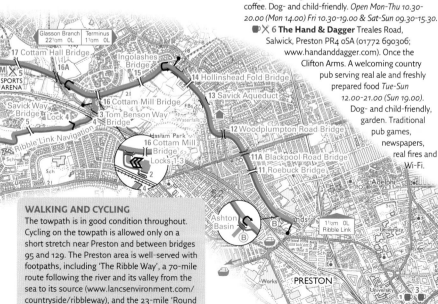

WALKING AND CYCLING

The towpath is in good condition throughout. Cycling on the towpath is allowed only on a short stretch near Preston and between bridges 95 and 129. The Preston area is well-served with footpaths, including 'The Ribble Way', a 70-mile route following the river and its valley from the sea to its source (www.lancsenvironment.com/countryside/ribbleway), and the 23-mile 'Round Preston Walk' – a booklet is available at the Tourist Information Centre.

Bilsborrow

Passing the marina at Moons Bridge, the canal gently meanders along its remote route to eventually enter the village of Bilsborrow on a minor embankment: the A6 joins the canal here, as does the West Coast Mainline to Scotland, and the M6. Generally these rival transport routes keep their distance and the canal is for the most part delightfully quiet, still passing through peaceful green farmland, while the foothills of the Pennines begin to converge from the east. 'Owd Nell's' and 'Guys Thatched Hamlet' provide a single colourful intrusion. The River Brock is crossed on an aqueduct, with a good view to the west. There is a handy *garage and shop (solid fuel)* at Bridge 49, with limited temporary *moorings* giving direct access.

Boatyards

Ⓑ**Moons Bridge Marina** Hollowforth Lane, Woodplumpton, Preston PR4 0BD (01772 690627; www.moonsbridgemarina.co.uk). **D** Gas, long-term mooring, winter storage, slipway, boat lift, boat and engine sales and repairs, chandlery, gifts, DIY facilities. *Summer opening Tue-Sun 10.00-16.00.*

ⒷB**Barton Grange Marina** Garstang Road, Bilsborrow PR3 0BT (01995 642926; www.bartongrange.co.uk/marina-lancaster-canal). 🚿🚽♿ . Pump out, short- and long-term moorings, toilets, showers, laundrette, barbeque facilities, Wi-Fi. Café and restaurant adjacent. *Open Mon-Sat 09.00-17.30 & Sun 10.30-16.30.* For Satnav use PR3 0RB.

Pubs and Restaurants

✖🍷 1 **Barton Bangla Brasserie** 913 Garstang Road, Barton, Preston PR3 5AB (01995 640236; www.bartonbanglabrasseriepreston.co.uk). Family orientated Indian restaurant offering à la carte, set menu and *Sun* buffet. *Open Mon-Fri 17.30-23.00 & Sat-Sun 15.00-23.00 (Sun 13.00).*

🍺✖ 2 **Owd Nell's** Canalside, St Michael's Road, Bilsborrow, Preston PR3 0RS (01995 640010; www.guysthatchedhamlet.co.uk). At bridge 44. A farmhouse-style thatched pub and restaurant complex, with all sorts of attractions. There are craft shops, a thatched terrace, a timber castle and games areas with cricket pavilion. Generous bar meals, with a children's menu *all day, every day*. When in season, local game features on the menu *daily 11.00-21.00*. Dog- and family-friendly, garden. Traditional pub games, sports TV and Wi-Fi. *Open 10.00-01.30 (Sun 01.00).*

🍺✖ 3 **The Roebuck** Garstang Road, Bilsborrow, Preston PR3 0RE (01995 640234; www.chefandbrewer.com/pubs/lancashire/roebuck). A pub/restaurant/lodge serving real ale and meals *daily 12.00-22.00 (Sun 21.00)*. Dog- and family-friendly, large garden. Newspapers, real fires and Wi-Fi. *Open 12.00-23.00 (Sun 22.00).*

🍺 4 **The White Bull** Garstang Road, Bilsborrow, Preston PR3 0RE (01995 643333). Friendly village local with an open fire, dispensing real ale and food *Mon-Sat 12.00-20.00 (Fri-Sat 21.00) & Sun 12.00-18.00*. Dog- and family-friendly, garden. Traditional pub games, *occasional* live music and Wi-Fi. Camping. *Open 12.00-23.00 (Fri-Sat 00.00).*

✖ 5 **Turners Fish & Chips** Garstang Road, Bilsborrow PR3 0RE (01995 640897; www.turnersfishandchips.co.uk). Friendly waitress-service providing an eat-in option. Children welcome. *Open Mon-Sat L and E (not Mon E).*

✖🍷 6 **The Riverside Café and Willow Restaurant** Garstang Road, Bilsborrow PR3 0BT (01995 642967; www.bartongrange.co.uk/restaurants). Light and spacious eatery beside the infant River Brock, serving breakfast, lunch and afternoon tea. Children's menu. Café *open Mon-Sat 09.00-17.00 & Sun 10.00-16.00* and Restaurant *open Mon-Sat 09.00-16.00 & Sun 10.00-16.00*. For Satnav use PR3 0RB.

BOAT TRIPS

1 The wide-beam boat *Jungle Queen* operates public trips from Guy's Thatched Hamlet *Jan-Mar, Sat-Sun 12.00–14.00*. The boat can also be chartered for private cruises. Contact Lancaster Canal Cruises, Olde Duncombe House, Bilsborrow Wharf, Garstang Road, Bilsborrow, PR3 0RE (01995 602943/07748 324221; www.party-boats.co.uk) for further details. Day boat hire, narrowboat hire and B&B also available.

2 Kingfisher Cruises 316 Blackpool Road, Fulwood, Preston PR2 3AE (01524 389410; https://www.kingfishercruise.co.uk). Operate the wide-beam boat *Kingfisher*, currently based at Barton Grange Garden Centre, Bilsborrow PR3 0RB, offering a range of different cruises. Telephone or visit their website for full details. Office *open May-Oct, Mon-Fri 10.00–16.00* & *Nov-Apr, Mon-Tue and Fri 10.00–16.00*.

3 There are several delightful, small hire boat operations strung out along the Lancaster Canal, providing an opportunity to get on the water for a day, a week, or even longer. These include:

i Snails Pace Narrowboats (07906 968668; www.snailspacenarrowboatholidays.com).

ii Bluebell Canal Holidays (07854 596989/597185; http://www.bluebellnarrowboat.co.uk).

iii Pintail Boats (07980 607070/07582 252262; www.pintailboats.co.uk).

iv Duck Island Boat Company (07925 236621; www.lancastercanalboathire.com).

v Barge and Boat Hire (01995 640833; www.LCCruises.co.uk).

vi Bumbles Boat Hire (01772 691010; www.repairhub.co.uk/e/28079/bumbles-boat-hire).

vii Water Gem – Day Boat Hire (07412 835115/07492 430020; www.facebook.com/pages/category/Boat-Rental/Watergem-day-boat-hire-655279061288956).

● Bilsborrow

Lancs. PO, tel, stores, fish & chips, off-licence, garage. A village which straggles along the A6. The church of St Hilda, built 1926-7, is set apart, up on a hill; there are three pubs very close to the canal.

The Flower Bowl Entertainment Centre Garstang Road, Bilsborrow PR3 0BT (01995 676210; www.theflowerbowl.uk). Multi-facetted amusement location that embraces bowling, curling, a cinema, golf simulator, a coffee shop, crazy golf, a garden centre and, when it all gets too much, a restaurant and a hotel! Open *daily 09.30-22.30*. For Satnav use PR3 0RB.

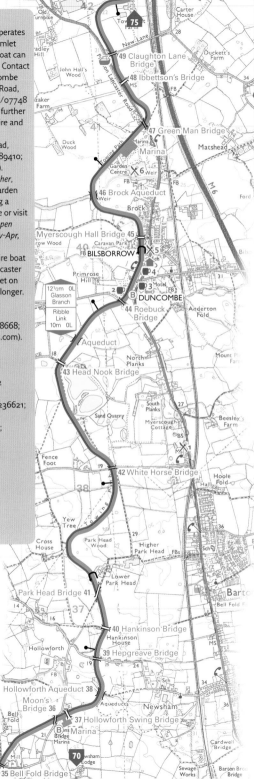

Garstang

There is a flurry of canal
interest around the Calder Aqueduct
and Catterall Basin, and those who moor
here and walk up the hills to the east of Bridge 54
(where there is a useful coal merchant – 01995 602150)
will also be rewarded with splendid views over Cockerham Sands
and the Fylde. The canal then temporarily moves away from the hills and the
remains of Greenhalgh Castle to cross the River Wyre on a fine stone aqueduct, 110ft long
and 34ft high, attributed to John Rennie. There are steps down if you wish to have a better
look at it. The attractive town of Garstang is soon reached; the area around Garstang Basin is a
popular *mooring* for pleasure boats. The town lies to the north east as the canal passes a marina
and continues to wind through countryside that is as green and pleasant as ever, but which is
now overlooked by the steep slopes of the Pennines.

Boatyards

Ⓑ **Bridgehouse Marina** Nateby Crossing Lane,
Nateby, Garstang PR3 0JJ (01995 603207;
www.bridgehousemarina.co.uk). Between bridges
64 and 66. 🛢🚽⚓ Gas, winter storage, slipway,
crane, chandlery, boat sales, boat and engine
repairs, day hire, toilets, solid fuel, toilets, showers,
telephone. DIY facilities. Also caravan park.

Pubs and Restaurants

⬤✕ **1 The Kenlis Arms Hotel** Ray Lane, Barnacre, Preston PR3 1GD (01995 603307; www.kenlisarms. co.uk). A handsome red-brick pub Serving real ale and food *Thu-Sun 12.30-20.00 (Sun 18.00).* Dog- and child-friendly, garden with play area. Real fires. B&B. *Open Mon-Wed 17.00-23.00 & Thu-Sun 10.30-23.00.*

⬤✕ **2 Th'Owd Tithebarn** The Wharf, Church Street, Garstang, Preston PR3 1PA(01995 604486; www.tithebarngarstang.co.uk). A uniquely old-fashioned establishment overlooking the canal basin. Real ale is served together with food *Mon-Fri L and E & Sat-Sun all day 12.00-20.00).* Dog- and child-friendly. Traditional pub games, occasional live music and real fires. *Open Mon-Sat 11.30-23.00 (Sat 00.00) & Sun 12.00-23.00.*

⬤✕ **3 The Royal Hotel** Market Place, Garstang, Preston PR3 1ZA (01995 603318). A coaching inn, dating from the 1670s but with parts surviving from 1480. Real ale is served and food is available *Mon-Sat L and E & Sun 12.00-20.30.* Dog-friendly and garden. Traditional pub games. Camping nearby. B&B. *Open Mon-Sat 11.00-00.00 (Sat 01.00) & Sun 12.00-00.00.*

⬤ **4 The Farmers Arms** 18 Church Street, Garstang PR3 1PA (01995 602101). Family pub serving real ales. Patio. Traditional pub games and sports TV. *Open daily 11.00-00.00.*

⬤ **5 The Crown** 34-37 High Street, Garstang, Preston PR3 1EF (01995 471198; www.crowngarstang.co.uk). Serving real ales and food *L and E.* Children welcome and there is outside seating. Traditional pub games and sports TV. *Open 12.00-00.00 (Fri-Sat 01.00).*

⬤ **6 The Kings Arms** High Street, Garstang, Preston PR3 1EA (01995 601531). A sport-orientated pub, serving real ale, with outside seating. Traditional pub games, sports TV and Wi-Fi. *Open Mon-Sat 09.00-00.00 (Fri-Sat 01.00) & Sun 10.00-00.00.*

✕⬤ **7 Pipers Restaurant** 46 High Street, Garstang, Preston PR3 1EA (01995 606665; www.pipersrestaurant. co.uk). Set in a quaint, 18th-C building, this restaurant serves modern English cuisine in the form of bistro-style *lunches* and an à la carte *dinner* menu. Open *Tue-Wed E; Thu-Sat L and E and Sun 12.00-20.00.*

⬤ **8 The Wheatsheaf** 1 Park Hill Road, Garstang, Preston PR3 1EL (01995 603398). Once a farm house, this Grade II listed hostelry now dispenses real ale and serves *breakfast, lunch and supper.* Dog-friendly and garden. Live music *Fri-Sat.* Traditional pub games and sports TV. Camping nearby. *Open Mon-Sat 10.00-00.00 (Fri-Sat 01.00) & Sun 10.00-00.00.*

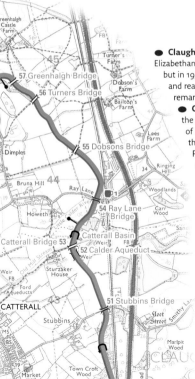

⬤ **Claughton Hall** 1/4 mile east of the canal. This hall was originally an Elizabethan mansion built next to the village church for the Croft family, but in 1932-5 the whole house, except for one wing, was dismantled and reassembled on top of the moor north of the village. It was quite a remarkable undertaking and still stands in defiant isolation.

⬤ **Greenhalgh Castle** Just north of the canal on a grassy knoll are the modest ruins of Greenhalgh Castle. It was built in 1490 by the Earl of Derby, who placed Richard III's crown on Henry Tudor's head after the victory at Bosworth Field. In the 17th C it was destroyed by the Roundheads during the Civil War, when the Royalists made a final stand there. Ask at the adjacent farm to visit the ruins.

⬤ **Garstang**
Lancs. PO, tel, stores, banks, chemist, fishmonger, baker, butcher, delicatessen, hardware, off-licence, fish & chips, takeaways, library, garage. A friendly place, referred to as 'Cherstanc' in the Domesday Book, lying north east of the canal, which retains the atmosphere of a small market town. In the 18th C Garstang was a popular stopping point for coaches en route from London to Edinburgh and the traditional market which still takes place every Thursday dates back to 1310, in the time of Edward II. Near the canal is the 18th-C church of St Thomas, surrounded by a tidy churchyard. Opposite the cobbled market place is an interesting town hall with diminutive bell-tower. Built 1755-64 to acknowledge the town's promotion by the king to borough status, it was rebuilt in 1939. The market cross, erected in 1754, is an elegant column topped by a ball. There was at one time a dozen ale houses in the town; a surprising number still remain!

Visit Garstang Centre 1 Cherestanc Square, Garstang PR3 1EF (01995 602125; www.wyre.gov.uk/info/200361/tourist_ information_centres/225/visit_garstang_centre). *Open Mon-Sat 10.30-15.30 (closed 13.00-13.30 for lunch).*

Potters Brook

Continuing northwards through quiet, modest and unspoilt pasture land, the canal passes countryside which is empty of villages but full of farms and houses which are dotted about the landscape. The absence of any locks certainly makes this an ideal waterway for restful cruising, while the wildlife and the generously proportioned stone-arched bridges always supply interest along the way. From Potters Brook Bridge (81) a lane across the A6 leads to a *pub* beside what used to Bay Horse Station. Just north of Potters Brook is the Ellel Grange estate with its remarkable spired church, ornamental canal bridge and the Grange itself, shrouded by tall trees; unfortunately the estate is private.

Ellel Grange Bay Horse, Ellel, Lancaster LA2 0HN (01524 751651; www. ellelministries.org). On the banks of the canal. A very fine Italianate villa built for William Preston, a merchant, in 1857–9. It is a large mansion with two broad towers that compete in vain with the graceful spire of the charming little church of St Mary, built in 1873 at a cost of £7000, which stands in the grounds of the house. It was also built by William Preston. Purchased in 1986 by the Ellel Ministries, it was the first of their centres to be established and it still remains the international headquarters of the work. As well as holding Healing Retreats and Training Courses, Ellel Grange accommodates the Special Ministries Unit which provides longer-term help for those in need.

Pubs and Restaurants

▶✕**The Bay Horse Inn** Bay Horse, Ellel LA2 0HR (01524 791204; www.bayhorseinn.com). North east of bridge 81, across the A6. Real ale is served in this friendly and cosy country pub, which has an open fire *during the winter*. Restaurant and bar meals are available *Wed-Sun L and E*. Children are welcome if you are eating, and there is a garden. *Open Wed-Sun L and E*.

BIRD LIFE

The *Grey Heron* is a familiar large, long-legged wetland bird. The adult has a dagger-like, yellow bill and a black crest of feathers. The head, neck and underparts are otherwise whitish except for black streaks on the front of the neck and breast. The back and wings are blue-grey. In flight, the wings are broad and rounded with black flight feathers; the heron employs a slow, flapping wingbeat and holds its neck folded in a hunched 's' shape close to its body. The juvenile is similar to the adult but the markings are less distinct and the plumage more grubby in appearance. The heron is often seen standing motionless for hours on end on long, yellow legs, sometimes with its neck hunched up. It will occasionally actively stalk prey which comprise mainly amphibians and fish, especially eels. The call is a harsh and distinctive 'frank'. The heron nests in loose colonies mainly in trees but sometimes seen on coasts in winter.

The *Green Woodpecker*, despite its size and bright, colourful plumage, can be surprisingly difficult to see. It is usually rather wary and often prefers to hide behind tree trunks rather than show itself. Sometimes it is seen feeding on lawns or areas of short grass when the green back, greenish buff underparts and red and black facial markings can be seen. It uses its long tongue to collect ants. If disturbed the green woodpecker flies off revealing a bright yellow-green rump. The spiky tail gives support when climbing tree trunks. Its presence is often detected by a loud and distinctive yaffling call. The stout, dagger-like bill is used to excavate wood for insect larvae and to create nest holes. It favours open, deciduous woodland.

WALKING AND CYCLING

The 260-mile Lancashire Cycleway (Routes 90/91) comprises two circular routes, which meet in the historic village of Whalley in the Ribble Valley. In places the Cycleway intersects with the canal, while following minor roads wherever possible. It takes you through a host of different landscapes from the rugged Bowland Hills and West Pennine Moors, to the rich pastures of the Fylde Plain and the outstanding coastal scenery at Silverdale. Part of the Cycleway at Rivington was used in the 2001 Commonwealth Games.

The northern loop explores the remote Bowland Fells, the rich Fylde Plain and the lush valleys of the Lune and Ribble,

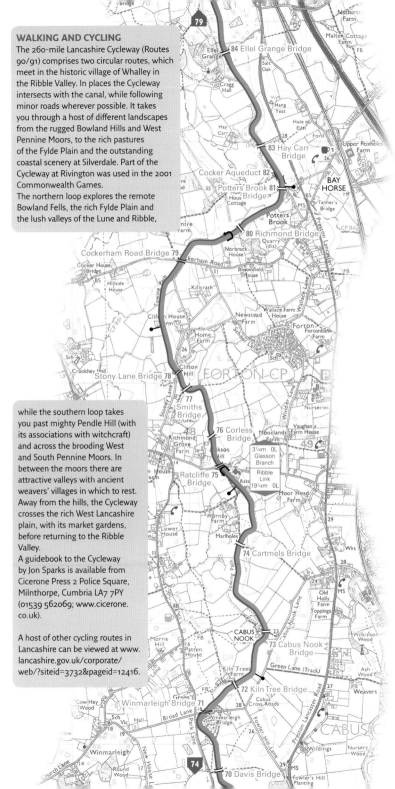

while the southern loop takes you past mighty Pendle Hill (with its associations with witchcraft) and across the brooding West and South Pennine Moors. In between the moors there are attractive valleys with ancient weavers' villages in which to rest. Away from the hills, the Cycleway crosses the rich West Lancashire plain, with its market gardens, before returning to the Ribble Valley.

A guidebook to the Cycleway by Jon Sparks is available from Cicerone Press 2 Police Square, Milnthorpe, Cumbria LA7 7PY (01539 562069; www.cicerone.co.uk).

A host of other cycling routes in Lancashire can be viewed at www.lancashire.gov.uk/corporate/web/?siteid=3732&pageid=12416.

The Glasson Branch

Double Bridge marks the end of a rocky cutting and the junction with the Glasson Branch. Just around the corner on the main line is Galgate and a large *boatyard and mooring site*. The extremely attractive Glasson Branch leads off down to the west to connect the Lancaster Canal with the Lune estuary via Glasson Dock. The branch was finished in 1826, long after the main line of the canal was completed, and provided the canal with its only direct link with the sea. There are six wide locks whose bottom gates feature the same excellent type of sliding paddles seen on the Leeds & Liverpool Canal (*see* Navigational Note 2). Gates must be locked after use, and the locks left *empty*, even when going up. The arm falls through the Conder Valley, a pleasant, quiet stretch of countryside whose proximity to the sea is betrayed by the many seagulls cruising around. After the bottom lock, the canal runs in a straight line through saltings and marshland to Glasson Basin, where there is a large *boatyard*, mainly for seagoing yachts and *moorings*.

The main line of the canal continues northwards through beautiful undulating green countryside, then passes through an unusually long wooded cutting, marked by Deep Cutting Bridge, and ends in the outskirts of Lancaster.

NAVIGATIONAL NOTES

1 Glasson Basin Lock 7 will take boats up to 87' 10" x 26' 3" with 11' 9" draught. Anyone wishing to use this lock *(for which 24hrs notice is required)* should contact the Canal & River Trust 0303 040 4040; www.canalrivertrust.org.uk/contact-us/ways-to-contact-us. The dock links to a sea lock which operates from *2hrs* before high water and is under the jurisdiction of Lancaster Ports Commission (01524 751724). You must give them at least *24hrs notice during winter months* while *summer opening* is arranged around the times of high water.

2 The locks on the Glasson Branch will take boats up to 67' 6" x 16' with 3' 10" draught. You will need a Watermate key to operate them. Gates must be locked after use, and the locks left *empty*, even when going up.

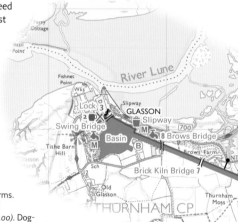

Pubs and Restaurants

🍺✕ **1 The Mill Inn** Mill Lane, Conder Green LA2 0BD (01524 752852; themillatcondergreen.co.uk). Near Sixth Lock. Real ale and food served *Mon-Fri L and E & Sat-Sun 12.00-21.30* in a sympathetically restored, 17th-C grain mill. Gardens, with moorings close by. Dog-friendly; Wi-Fi. B&B. *Open daily 12.00-23.00.*

🍺 **2 The Dalton Arms** Ten Row, West Quay, Glasson Dock, Lancaster LA2 0BZ (01524 753007; www.daltonarms.info). Traditional family-run country pub. Real ale. Food available *Tue-Fri L and E & Sat-Sun 12.00-20.00 (Sun 19.00).* Dog-friendly, patio. Quiz *Thu*. Newspapers and real fires. *Open Mon-Fri L and E (not Mon-Tue L) & Sat-Sun 12.00-23.00 (Sun 19.00).*

✕🍷 **3 Lantern O'er the Lune Café** West Quay, Glasson Dock, Lancaster LA2 0BY (01524 752323; www.lanternoerlune.co.uk). Overlooking the basin, this friendly café serves main meals along with cakes, tea and coffee. Outdoor seating. *Open Wed-Sun 10.00-15.00 (Sun 09.30).* Bistro *open Fri-Sat 18.00-21.00.*

🍺✕ **4 The Stork** Corricks Lane, Conder Green, Lancaster LA2 0AN (01524 751234; www.thestorkinn.com). Delightful country pub serving real ale and food *Mon-Thu L and E & Fri-Sun 12.00-21.00 (Sun 20.00).* Dog- and family-friendly, garden with play area. Sports TV and Wi-Fi. Camping. B&B. *Open 12.00-23.00 (Fri-Sat 00.00).*

🍺 **5 The Plough Inn** Main Road, Galgate LA2 0LQ (01524 751337; www.plough-galgate.co.uk). Real ale and food *Mon-Fri L and E & Sat-Sun 12.00-21.00 (Sun 20.00)* is dispensed in this 16th-C coaching inn. Garden, open fires and Wi-Fi. Sports TV and traditional pub games. Dogs welcome. *Open daily 12.00-23.00.*

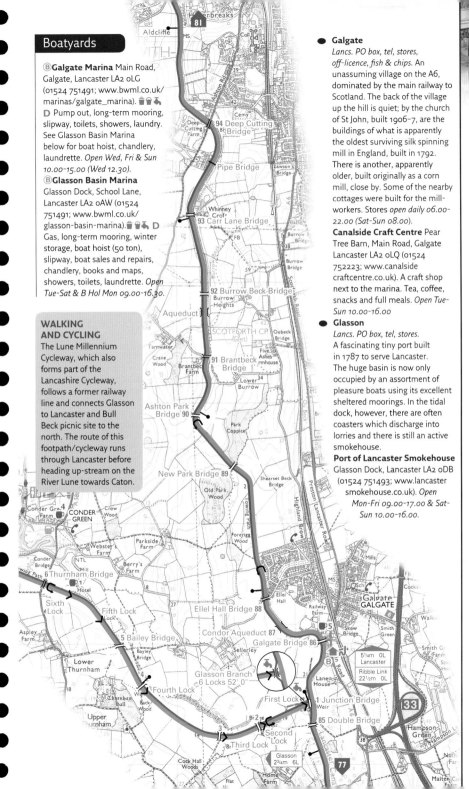

Boatyards

ⓑGalgate Marina Main Road, Galgate, Lancaster LA2 0LG (01524 751491; www.bwml.co.uk/marinas/galgate_marina). 🛉🛉🛠 D Pump out, long-term mooring, slipway, toilets, showers, laundry. See Glasson Basin Marina below for boat hoist, chandlery, laundrette. *Open Wed, Fri & Sun 10.00-15.00 (Wed 12.30).*

ⓑGlasson Basin Marina Glasson Dock, School Lane, Lancaster LA2 0AW (01524 751491; www.bwml.co.uk/glasson-basin-marina). 🛉🛉🛠 D Gas, long-term mooring, winter storage, boat hoist (50 ton), slipway, boat sales and repairs, chandlery, books and maps, showers, toilets, laundrette. *Open Tue-Sat & B Hol Mon 09.00-16.30.*

WALKING AND CYCLING

The Lune Millennium Cycleway, which also forms part of the Lancashire Cycleway, follows a former railway line and connects Glasson to Lancaster and Bull Beck picnic site to the north. The route of this footpath/cycleway runs through Lancaster before heading up-stream on the River Lune towards Caton.

● **Galgate**
Lancs. PO box, tel, stores, off-licence, fish & chips. An unassuming village on the A6, dominated by the main railway to Scotland. The back of the village up the hill is quiet; by the church of St John, built 1906-7, are the buildings of what is apparently the oldest surviving silk spinning mill in England, built in 1792. There is another, apparently older, built originally as a corn mill, close by. Some of the nearby cottages were built for the mill-workers. Stores *open daily 06.00-22.00 (Sat-Sun 08.00).*

Canalside Craft Centre Pear Tree Barn, Main Road, Galgate Lancaster LA2 0LQ (01524 752223; www.canalside craftcentre.co.uk). A craft shop next to the marina. Tea, coffee, snacks and full meals. *Open Tue-Sun 10.00-16.00*

● **Glasson**
Lancs. PO box, tel, stores. A fascinating tiny port built in 1787 to serve Lancaster. The huge basin is now only occupied by an assortment of pleasure boats using its excellent sheltered moorings. In the tidal dock, however, there are often coasters which discharge into lorries and there is still an active smokehouse.

Port of Lancaster Smokehouse Glasson Dock, Lancaster LA2 0DB (01524 751493; www.lancaster smokehouse.co.uk). *Open Mon-Fri 09.00-17.00 & Sat-Sun 10.00-16.00.*

Lancaster Canal

The Glasson Branch

79

Lancaster

The canal now enters Lancaster, losing its rural identity as buildings close in. There is a *fish & chip shop* just west of Bridge 98. At Bridge 100 the towpath returns to the west side of the canal, where it stays for the rest of the journey northwards. The canal passes through the heart of Lancaster, passing well-restored mills, including Moor Lane with its conspicuous red-brick water tower and now the home of Reebok UK, and continues north, passing an old dry dock by Bridge 103, to cross an aqueduct, built in 1961, over the A683. The imposing aqueduct which carries the canal over the River Lune quickly follows, affording fine views along the Lune valley. The canal then rejoins the side of the valley, turning west, then north again to head towards the sea at Hest Bank. There is a useful *shop* just south of Bridge 110, open daily *07.30–22.30*.

Lancaster

Lancs. All services. Today Lancaster's quay, once a great shipping port handling more cargo than Liverpool, is a quiet backwater, with pleasant walks. There are some fine canalside buildings.

Lancaster Castle Castle Parade, Lancaster LA1 1YJ (01524 64998; www.lancastercastle.com). On the site of Roman fortifications, this is a mainly 13th-C and 14th-C construction, except for the Norman keep, which is surmounted by a beacon tower. *Open daily 09.30–17.00.* Guided tours (Court sittings permitting) from *10.30–16.00.* Charge. Gift shop.

Cottage Museum 15 Castle Hill, Lancaster LA1 1YS (01524 64637; www.lancashire.gov.uk/leisure-and-culture/museums/the-cottage-museum). Opposite the castle, this is part of a 1739 house containing the artifacts of an artisan, c. 1820. Activities. *Open 13.00–16.00.* Charge.

Lancaster Priory & Parish Church Castle Hill , Lancaster LA1 1YZ (01524 65338; www.lancasterpriory. org). There has been a church on this site since AD 630. The present building is an attractive 15th-C church in late Perpendicular style, with an original Saxon western doorway. Church *open all year round 09.30–17.00.* Free. Guided tours *on request.* Refectory *open Easter–Oct, 10.00–16.00.* Interesting book stall. Nearby are the excavated remains of a Roman bath house.

Lancaster City Museum Old Town Hall, Market Square, Lancaster LA1 1HT (01524 64637; www.lancashire. gov.uk/leisure-and-culture/museums/lancaster-city-museum). Lancashire's past, the King's Own Regiment Museum, portraits and landscapes, changing exhibitions, events and activities. *Open Mon–Sat 10.00–17.00.* Free.

Ashton Memorial Williamson Park, Quernmore Road, Lancaster LA1 1UX (01524 33318; www.lancaster.gov.uk/sites/williamson-park/ashton-memorial). Dominated by the Ashton Memorial folly, which contains an exhibition gallery. Also tropical butterfly house and over 50 acres of parkland including landscaped gardens, children's playground and an ornamental lake. Shop and café. *Open Apr–Sep 10.00–17.00 & Oct–Mar 10.00–16.00.* Charge.

Maritime Museum Old Customs House, St George's Quay, Lancaster LA1 1RB (01524 382264; www. lancashire.gov.uk/leisure-and-culture/museums/lancaster-maritime-museum). Walk towards the river from bridge 99, turning left into Damside. Lifeboats, fine models and artefacts from Glasson Dock. Gift shop. *Open daily 10.00–16.00.* Charge. The riverside path to the west connects with Glasson Dock about 5 miles away.

Visitor Information Centre The Storey, Meeting House Lane, Lancaster LA1 1TH (01524 582394; www. visitlancaster.org.uk). *Open Mon–Sat 10.00–16.00.*

Lune Aqueduct

This splendid edifice carries the navigation for some 600ft across the River Lune, which is 60ft below. Designed by John Rennie, it was built between 1794–7 by Alexander Stevens, a Scotsman who died before it was completed. The bottom of the channel is apparently 7 or 8ft deep, containing a layer of puddled clay about 3ft thick. There is said to be a plug which can be pulled to drain the structure into the River Lune below. Its total cost was £48,320 18s 6d.

Hest Bank

Lancs. PO box, tel, takeaway, fish & chips. The seashore is only a couple of hundred yards from the navigation, and at low water miles of sandy beach are uncovered.

Pubs and Restaurants

▶✕ 1 **The Water Witch** Aldcliffe Lane, Lancaster LA1 1SU (01524 63828; www.waterwitchlancaster.co.uk). Warm and friendly, with a stone floor and a good variety of freshly-cooked food available *daily 12.00–21.00 (Sun 20.00).* Real ale is served together with real cider *in summer.* Outside seating, moorings, open fires and Wi-Fi. Quiz *Thu. Open daily11.00–00.00.*

▶✕ 2 **The White Cross** Quarry Road, Lancaster LA1 4XT (01524 33999; www.thewhitecross.co.uk). Canalside at bridge 100. Real cider, real ales and food *daily 12.00–21.00.* Children welcome, patio and moorings. Large-screen TV, traditional pub games and Wi-Fi. Newspapers and quiz *Tue. Open Mon–Sat 11.30–23.00 (Fri–Sat 00.15) & Sun 12.00–23.00.*

▶ 3 **The Waggon & Horses** 27 St George's Quay, Lancaster LA1 1RD (01524 846094; www.wagonandhorseslancaster. co.uk). Worth a look in if you are visiting the Maritime Museum, this pub serves real ale, and food *Mon–Fri L and E & Sat-Sun 12.00-21.00. Wed* quiz. Dog-friendly, courtyard seating. Occasional live music, sports TV and Wi-Fi. B&B. *Open daily 12.00–01.00.*

▶✕ 4 **Hest Bank** 2 Hest Bank Lane, Lancaster LA2 6DN (01524 824339; www.thehestbankinn.co.uk). You can still see the window for the guiding light, which once showed the way across the sands. Now this old coaching inn, which dates from 1554, is justly popular and you can share the shelter it once offered to abbots and monks, soldiers and highwaymen, the Duke of Devonshire and Prince Frederick of Prussia. Real ale and fresh local food, and seafood *Tue–Fri L and E & Sat-Sun 12.00-20.30 (Sun 19.30).* Dog- and child-friendly, impressive garden. Newspapers, real fires and Wi-Fi. Quiz *Wed.* Mooring. *Open daily 12.00-23.00.*

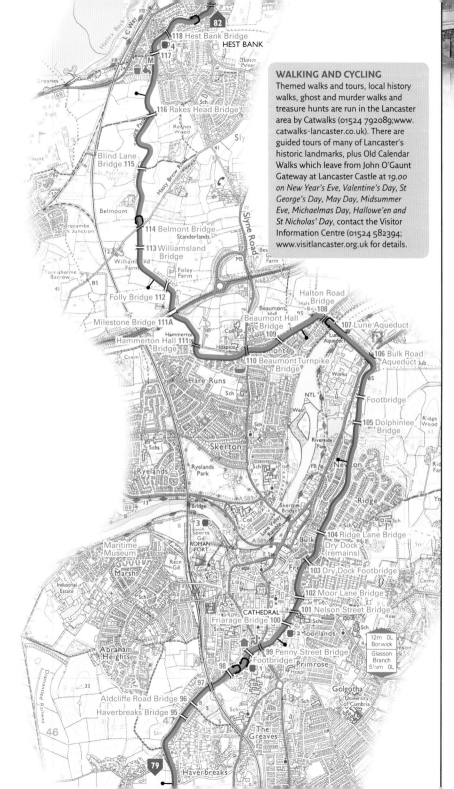

WALKING AND CYCLING

Themed walks and tours, local history walks, ghost and murder walks and treasure hunts are run in the Lancaster area by Catwalks (01524 792089;www.catwalks-lancaster.co.uk). There are guided tours of many of Lancaster's historic landmarks, plus Old Calendar Walks which leave from John O'Gaunt Gateway at Lancaster Castle at *19.00 on New Year's Eve, Valentine's Day, St George's Day, May Day, Midsummer Eve, Michaelmas Day, Hallowe'en and St Nicholas' Day*, contact the Visitor Information Centre (01524 582394; www.visitlancaster.org.uk for details.

118 Hest Bank Bridge
HEST BANK

116 Rakes Head Bridge

Blind Lane
Bridge 115

114 Belmont Bridge
Standerlands
113 Williamsland
Bridge

Folly Bridge 112

Milestone Bridge 111A
Hammerton Hall 111
Bridge

110 Beaumont Turnpike
Bridge

Hare Runs

Halton Road
Bridge 108

Beaumont
Hall
Bridge 109

107 Lune Aqueduct

106 Bulk Road
Aqueduct

Footbridge

105 Dolphinlee
Bridge

Skerton

Ryelands
Park

Newton

Ridge

104 Ridge Lane Bridge
Dry Dock
(remains)

103 Dry Dock Footbridge

102 Moor Lane Bridge

101 Nelson Street Bridge

Maritime
Museum

ROMAN
FORT

CATHEDRAL
Friarage Bridge 100

2 Moorlands

99 Penny Street Bridge
Footbridge
Primrose

Abraham
Heights

98

Aldcliffe Road Bridge 96
Haverbreaks Bridge 95

97

1

Golgotha
University
of Cumbria

The
Greaves

| 12m 0L Borwick |
| Glasson Branch 5¼m 0L |

79 Haverbreaks

81

Carnforth

The canal now passes Hest Bank and Bolton-le-Sands, with the sea never far away to the west and the A6 beside and below. As the waterway comes into Carnforth, it often affords grand views over Morecambe Bay before sneaking quite inconspicuously through the town, mostly in a cutting, passing a *sanitary station, pump out and showers*. Carnforth railway station offers an excellent jumping off point to explore the attractions of the Lake District coast and the train journey to Carlisle, via Barrow-in-Furness, is an excitement in itself, much of the track being virtually on the beach! Indeed three suggested visits, within easy reach of the line, are listed on page 83. Carnforth is also the starting point for possibly the ultimate 'railway ring' – one that can be comfortably accomplished in a day. Travelling in an anti-clockwise direction: take the train to Hellifield, thence north up the extraordinary Settle-Carlisle line; returning via the aforementioned Cumbrian coast railway. Soon after leaving Carnforth the navigation dives under the motorway spur road and finds itself diverted along a new channel for several hundred yards before going under the main line of the M6: this diversion was presumably cheaper to build than a long, finely-angled skew motorway bridge over the navigation. Beyond the motorway lies peaceful green countryside backed, unmistakably, by the foothills of the Lake District. At Capernwray the canal crosses the River Keer on a minor aqueduct built by John Rennie in 1797; the nearby railway, which goes to Leeds, also crosses the Keer, on a very impressive viaduct.

● **Bolton-le-Sands**
Lancs. PO, tel, stores, off-licence, butcher, chemist, takeaways, fish & chips, garage. A pleasant village of narrow streets, with a pub at each end and the shops strung out over more than a mile.

● **Carnforth**
Lancs. PO, tel, stores, banks, chemists, takeaways, off-licence, hardware, baker, library, station. Not particularly attractive but useful for supplies, especially the superb selection of pies at Madisons in Market Street, 01524 732021, and of interest as an important railway junction. It is possible to catch trains not only north–south but east over the beautiful green hills to Skipton and Leeds, west to Barrow and right round the coast to Carlisle. Carnforth was the last town in the country to lose its regular British Rail steam locomotive service in 1968: it is now a centre for steam-hauled railtours over the national railway system. The Tearooms, as featured in the film *Brief Encounter*, have been restored (as has the famous clock) and there is a small museum.

Leighton Moss Nature Reserve Storrs Lane, Silverdale, Carnforth LA5 0SW (01524 701601; www.rspb.org.uk/reserves/guide/l/leightonmoss). ¼-mile south of Silverdale railway station – just one stop away from Carnforth. Leighton Moss is the largest reed bed in north west England, and home to rare birds such as breeding bitterns, bearded tits and marsh harriers. Also deer and a wide

There are two useful cycle shops in Carnforth: Dyno Start

WALKING AND CYCLING
There are two useful cycle shops in Carnforth: Dyno Start 1-3 Scotland Road, Carnforth LA5 9JY (01524 732089; www.dynostart.com) *open Mon-Fri 09.00-17.00* and Vanilla Bikes 9-11 New Street, Carnforth LA5 9BX (01524 734300; www.vanillabikes.com *open Mon-Fri 09.00-16.00*.

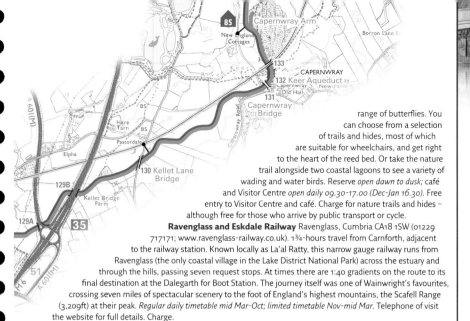

range of butterflies. You can choose from a selection of trails and hides, most of which are suitable for wheelchairs, and get right to the heart of the reed bed. Or take the nature trail alongside two coastal lagoons to see a variety of wading and water birds. Reserve *open dawn to dusk;* café and Visitor Centre *open daily 09.30-17.00 (Dec-Jan 16.30).* Free entry to Visitor Centre and café. Charge for nature trails and hides – although free for those who arrive by public transport or cycle.

Ravenglass and Eskdale Railway Ravenglass, Cumbria CA18 1SW (01229 717171; www.ravenglass-railway.co.uk). 1¾-hours travel from Carnforth, adjacent to the railway station. Known locally as La'al Ratty, this narrow gauge railway runs from Ravenglass (the only coastal village in the Lake District National Park) across the estuary and through the hills, passing seven request stops. At times there are 1:40 gradients on the route to its final destination at the Dalegarth for Boot Station. The journey itself was one of Wainwright's favourites, crossing seven miles of spectacular scenery to the foot of England's highest mountains, the Scafell Range (3,209ft) at their peak. *Regular daily timetable mid Mar-Oct; limited timetable Nov-mid Mar.* Telephone of visit the website for full details. Charge.

The Lake District Coast Aquarium South Quay, Maryport CA15 8AB (01900 817760; www.coastaquarium. co.uk). 2¾-hours travel from Carnforth and worth it for the journey alone! This is the point where the coastal line heads inland for Carlisle so a good place to de-train and enjoy the fascinations of this aquarium. It houses over 55 themed tanks containing a variety of the marine life found around the Cumbrian coastline, from fish to crustaceans, as well as a purpose built tropical marine community reef tank. A must for all those fascinated by everything that goes on under the water! Friendly café and gift shop. *Open daily 10.00-17.00.* Charge.

Pubs and Restaurants

✕♀ 1 **Miaitalia** Bye-Pass Rd, Bolton-le-Sands, Carnforth LA5 8JA (01524 823323; www.miaitalia. co.uk). The real flavour of Italy with all the excellent food freshly prepared. Proper Italian ice creams contrast with a warm, friendly welcome, especially to children, who are provided with entertainment. Real coffee and pastries. *Open Tue-Sun 16.30-21.00 (Sat 21.30) & Mon during school holidays.*

🍺 2 **The Royal Hotel** Main Road, Bolton-le-Sands, Carnforth LA5 8DQ (01524 732057; www.royalhotelbls. co.uk). A choice of real ale, plus a good range of excellent food *daily 12.00-21.00 (Sun 20.00).* Dart board, pool table and sports TV. Children welcome. Garden, quiz *Thu.* Wi-Fi and camping. B&B. *Open daily 12.00-23.00 (Fri-Sat 00.00)*

🍺✕ 3 **The Canal Turn** Lancaster Road, Carnforth LA5 9EA (01524 734750; www.thecanalturn.co.uk). A very attractive canalside pub in cottages once known as 'Pig & Piano Row', and which housed workers from nearby iron and gas works. Meals are served *Mon-Sat L and E & Sun 12.00-20.00.* Dogs welcome, patio. Traditional pub games and Wi-Fi. Mooring. *Open daily 11.00-23.00 (Sun 22.30).*

🍺 4 **The Shovel Inn** 68 North Road, Carnforth LA5 9NA (01524 733402). West of bridge 128. A friendly pub serving real ale and food *L.* Dog-friendly, courtyard seating. Traditional pub games, real fires, sports TV and Wi-Fi. *Open Mon-Fri 16.00-23.00 (Fri 00.00) & Sun 12.00-00.00).*

🍺✕ 5 **The Royal Station Hotel** Market Street, Carnforth LA5 9BT (01524 733636; www.royalstation. co.uk). Bang in the centre of town, this handsome establishment played host to Trevor Howard, Celia Johnson and Stanley Holloway in the Noel Coward film 'Brief Encounter', which was filmed around Carnforth Station. Queen Victoria is also reputed to have stayed here. They offer real ale, plus food *Mon-Sat 12.00-20.00 (Thu-Sat 21.00) & Sun 12.00-19.30.* Breakfast *09.00-11.30.* Dog- and child-friendly. Beer garden, sports TV, traditional pub games, newspapers and Wi-Fi. Live music *Fri-Sat.* B&B. *Open from 12.00 (Sat-Sun 09.00).*

🍺 6 **The Snug** Unit 6, Carnforth Gateway Building, Carnforth LA5 9TR (07927 396861; www. thesnugmicropub.blogspot.com). Minimalist micro-pub in the old station buildings serving real ales, real ciders and an excellent selection of quality gins. Snacks, conversation and the whoosh of passing trains greet the visitor, as does the striking floor to ceiling, glazed wooden drinks cabinet. Traditional pub games and newspapers. Platform seating, dogs welcome. *Open Mon-Tue 17.00-21.00; Wed-Fri L and E; Sat 12.00-21.00 & Sun 13.00-16.30.*

▌Borwick

Beyond Keer Aqueduct and the railway viaduct is the Capernwray Arm, a short branch to a worked-out quarry, and now offering some attractive sheltered moorings. The canal then winds around the hillside to end abruptly just beyond Borwick and right beside the M6: only the very hard of hearing will be able to enjoy a sojourn here! The abandoned Tewitfield locks begin across the road from the present terminus and the walker and cyclist can continue towards Kendal by following the towpath under the A6070 bridge. The locks are in surprisingly good condition and it is only on reaching the top of the flight you realise that, during the 1960's construction of the motorway, scant regard was paid to accommodating any future navigation along the northern reaches of the then derelict Lancaster Canal. There is no bridge – and insufficient clearance to construct one. At Tewitfield, where there are the usual *boater services*, including *toilets and showers, a pump out and recycling facilities*, the Lancaster Canal Trust (www.lctrust.co.uk) has established a volunteer base in the redundant Methodist chapel.

● **Borwick**
Lancs. PO box, tel. A small, old and attractive village, spread around a green. Overlooking the canal is Borwick Hall, a large and sombre Elizabethan manor house, built around a high 15th-C tower and with extensive gardens.
Capernwray Dive Centre Jackdaw Quarry, Capernwray Road, Over Kellet, Carnforth LA6 1AD (01524 735132; www.dive-site.co.uk). ¼-mile south west of Capernwray Bridge 131. Large flooded former quarry, now operated as an inland scuba diving site. Equipment hire and tuition. Café and accommodation. *Open Tue-Fri 10.00-17.00 & Sat-Sun 09.00-17.00.* Charge. Advanced booking recommended.
Greenlands Farm Village Tewitfield, Carnforth LA6 1JH (01524 784184; www.greenlandsfarmvillage.co.uk). A short walk north east from the terminus, along A6070. Family fun from an amalgam of soft play, an open farm, donkey rides, artisan village, picnic area,

go-karting, straw barn frolicking, climbing wall – to name but a few. Café. *Open daily 10.00-17.00.* Charge.
Old School Brewery Holly Bank Barn, Crag Road, Warton LA5 9PL (01524 740888; www. oldschoolbrewery.co.uk). Founded in 2012, as something of a hobby, the brewery now delivers to a huge variety of pubs and bars across the Cumbria and Lancashire area and is producing more beer than they could ever have imagined! Shop *open Mon-Fri 09.00-17.00* selling a range of their bottled beers and merchandise.
● **Warton**
Lancs. PO, tel, stores, brewery. A village steeped in history, with the earliest recorded reference in the Doomsday Book. The parish church of St Oswald stands on the site of a former dedication, believed to date from before the Norman Conquest, while the south wall of the present building dates from 14th C. Nearby are the ruins of the rectory, reputed to have been built around 1267.

▌Pubs and Restaurants

● 1 **The Malt Shovel** 66 Main Street, Warton, Carnforth LA5 9PG (01524 874149; www.facebook. com/wartonmaltshovel). Dating back to the 1700s, this pub still dispenses real ale and food *daily 12.00-19.30*. Garden and live music *alternate Fri*. Traditional pub games, real fires, sports TV and Wi-Fi. *Open 12.00-23.30 (Fri-Sat 01.00)*.
● ✕ 2 **The George Washington** Main Street, Warton, Carnforth LA5 9PJ (01524 732865; www. georgewashingtonwarton.co.uk). Reflecting the village's distant connection with the first American president, this 18th-C hostelry serves real ale and food *Tue-Sat L and E & Sun 12.00-18.00*. Dog-friendly, garden. Traditional pub games, real fires and Wi-Fi. B&B. *Open Mon-Sat 12.00-22.30 (Mon-Tue 16.00) & Sun 12.00-22.00*.
● 3 **The Nib** 9 Mill Lane, Millhead, Carnforth LA5 9HN (01524 733734). Diminutive, Victorian pub – a true locals local – serving real ale. Traditional pub games and sports TV. B&B. Entrance through the back door!

● ✕ 4 **Longlands Hotel** Tewitfield Locks, Tewitfield, Carnforth LA6 1JH (01524 781256; www. longlandshotel.co.uk). Just north east of the canal terminus. This popular country pub serves real ale and home-made bar and restaurant meals *daily L and E*. Pizzas available *Mon-Sat 12.00-21.00 & Sun 17.00-20.00*. Breakfast is also available. Dog- and family-friendly, garden. Traditional pub games, newspapers, real fires, sports TV and Wi-Fi. *Occasional* live music. Camping. B&B. *Open all day*.
● ✕ 5 **The New Inn** 40 Yealand Road, Yealand Conyers, Carnforth LA5 9SJ (01524 805037; www. thenewinnyealand.co.uk). Featuring a 17th-C fireplace, complete with ornamental plasterwork breast, this pub serves real ale and excellent food *daily 12.00-21.00*. Dog- and child-friendly, garden. Newspapers, real fires and Wi-Fi. B&B. *Open 11.00-23.00*.

Boatyards

⑧Tewitfield Marina Chapel Lane, Tewitfield, Carnforth LA6 1JH (01524 782092; www.tewitfieldmarina.co.uk). 🚽🛁🛒 Long- and short-term moorings, showers, toilets, laundry, holiday accommodation.

WALKING AND CYCLING

The remaining 14½ miles of the Northern Reaches of the Lancaster Canal, through to its terminus at Kendal, is well waymarked with its distinctive finger posts, guiding both walker and cyclist alike through the relatively few deviations from the original line of the waterway. For the walker, the going is easy, while a confident cyclist will enjoy both the towpath and the occasional off-piste sections. The enjoyment of both will be greatly enhanced by investing in the excellent guide to the waterway, published by the Lancaster Canal Trust (www.lctrust.co.uk) and now in its sixth edition.

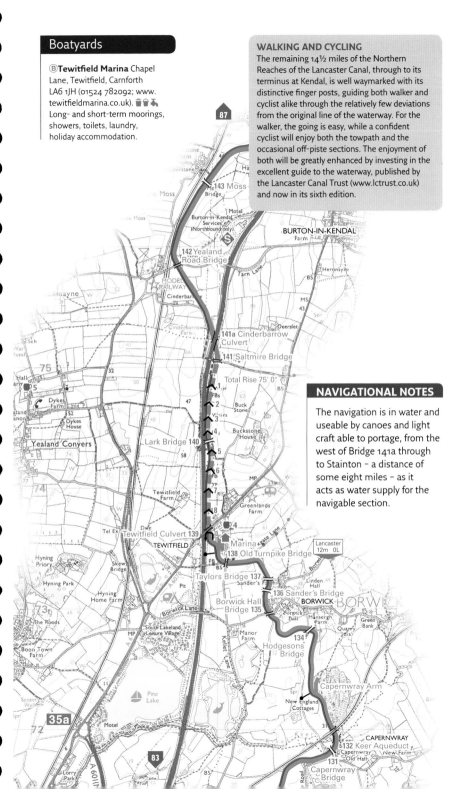

NAVIGATIONAL NOTES

The navigation is in water and useable by canoes and light craft able to portage, from the west of Bridge 141a through to Stainton – a distance of some eight miles – as it acts as water supply for the navigable section.

85

Burton-in-Kendal

There is no getting away from the fact that where ever you are on this stretch of the waterway, the M6 motorway is now by far and away the dominant transport link – both in terms of its size and the volume of its traffic. Notwithstanding this double entendre, there is cause to linger and explore the surrounding area, both for its geology (in the form of Limestone Pavement) and the richness of its built environment, of which many of the local pubs are excellent exemplars. As a continuing supply for the southern reaches of the navigation, the canal is very much in water, and intact, while it is impossible not to view the short-sightedness of the road builders of the 60s – when the motorcar was viewed as king – in a very dim light indeed. Better, instead, to gaze upwards, both east and west and enjoy the beauty of the fells and the promise of a diversion, together with more rewarding perambulation.

● **Beetham**
Cumbria. PO box, tel. Records of the area pre-date the Norman Conquest while today paper manufacture predominates, with the Billerud factory producing specialist wrapping for the food and medical industries. The village is the start of the Fairy Steps, leading out onto Beetham Fell and so called – as legend has it – because if you climb the steps, without touching the limestone sides of the narrow gully, the fairies will grant your wish!

● **Burton-in-Kendal**
Cumbria. PO, tel, stores, butcher. A name recognisable to north-bound travellers on the M6 due to the eponymous service station nearby. Sitting astride what was once one of the main routes into Scotland, the village was important as a staging post and somewhere for travellers to seek sustenance for themselves and their packhorses.
Cinderbarrow Miniature Railway Tarn Lane, Yealand Redmayne, Carnforth LA5 9RX (01524 781767; www.lmmes.co.uk). A charming little pint-sized railway running around the picnic site at Cinderbarrow with 'carriages' hauled by a wide variety of tiny steam locomotives brought along by members of the Lancaster and Morecombe Model Engineering Society. *Open Apr-Sep, Sun & B Hol Mon. Trains run 10.30-12.30 & 13.15-15.45.* Charge.

● **Holme**
Cumbria. PO, tel, stores. Sandwiched between the West Coast Main Line railway, the M6 and the canal, the village is not short of transport links! With the completion of the Lancaster Canal in 1819 (some 20 years after the more southerly stretch began operation) the waterway provided ready transport for the 19th-C Jute Mill.

● **Kirby Lonsdale**
Cumbria. PO, tel, stores, chemist, banks, bakers, off-licence, butcher, takeaways, fish & chips, brewery, library, garage. The town developed close to a crossing point of the River Lune, at the convergence of several drovers' roads and packhorse routes. St Mary's Church is of Norman origin, with three doorways and the inner northern arcade dating from the early 12th C. The southern arcade and the base of the tower date from later in the same century. Immediately to the south east of the town are two listed river crossings: the original Devil's Bridge (dating from around 1370) and its 1930s successor, both well worth a visit.
Leighton Hall Storrs Lane, Carnforth LA5 9ST (01524 734474; www.leightonhall.co.uk). Very much a lived-in family home, rather than a museum, with all the rooms still in daily use by the Gillow family. Outside there is a fertile 19th-C walled garden with herb patch and ornamental vegetable plot, a woodland walk and Caterpillar Maze. A bird of prey demonstration is included at 15.30, weather permitting. Tea room, gift shop and plant sales. *Open May-Sep, Tue-Fri 14.00-17.00 & Sun in Aug.* Charge.
Limestone Pavements
(www.morecambebaynature.org.uk/limestone-pavement). Somewhat different to other geological forms and habitats scattered around the head of Morecombe Bay, these continuous layers of limestone – formed by a quirky glacial process – have been shaped into a pattern of 'clints' (blocks) and 'grikes' (gaps) supporting a rich diversity of common and specialist botanical species. An excellent example is Farleton Fell – *see* www.tgomagazine.co.uk/walk/farleton-knott for further details.
The Hawk Garden Storrs Lane, Carnforth LA5 9ST (01524 734474; www.thehawkgarden.co.uk). Based at Leighton Hall, these are the birds you will see flying during an afternoon's visit. However, if you want hands-on experience it is possible to book a session independently and fly these birds of prey in beautiful surroundings. Visit the website for details.

WALKING AND CYCLING
Just as the brief diversion around the first M6 culvert is well waymarked, so the walk across the field, parallel with the motorway at the second culvert, is also well sign posted.
Warton Crag makes an interesting walk and a route that takes in Leighton Moss (see page 83) can be viewed at www.walkingenglishman.com/lancashire05.html). An alternative walk is detailed at www.lancashirewalks.com/wartoncragarchive.pdf.
The unique Limestone Pavement is prevalent in this area (*see* above) and well worth a deviation from the canal to explore. For further details visit www.where2walk.co.uk/walks/yorkshire_dales/farleton-fell-hutton-roof).

Pubs and Restaurants

1 The Kings Arms Main Street, Burton-in-Kendal LA6 1LR (01524 781409; www.kingsarmsburton.co.uk). Spacious village pub serving real ale and locally-sourced (very in the case of the veg!) food *Mon-Tue L and E & Wed-Sun 12.00-21.00*. Dog- and family-friendly, garden. Real fires. B&B. *Open Mon-Tue L and E & Wed-Sun 11.00-23.00*.

2 The Smithy Inn Milnthorpe Road, Holme LA6 1PS (01524 781302). Large, friendly, village-centre pub serving real ale and food *L and E*. Dogs and children welcome, garden. Real fires. *Open Mon-Fri L and E; Sat 11.45-23.00 & Sun 11.00-22.30*.

X 3 The Wheatsheaf Stanley Street, Beetham LA7 7AL. 01539 562123; www.wheatsheafbeetham.com). Cosy, 15th-C hostelry, serving real ale and excellent food *daily 12.00-21.00* (tea and scones *from 11.00*). Dogs, children and muddy boots welcome, garden. Real fires. B&B. *Open 11.00-23.00 (Sun 22.30)*.

4 The Plough Cow Brow, Lupton LA6 1PJ (01539 567700; www.theploughatlupton.co.uk). Roadside pub serving real ale and food *daily 12.00-21.00*. Dog- and child-friendly, garden. Real fires and Wi-Fi. Camping. B&B. *Open 11.00-23.00 (Sun 22.30)*.

5 The Kings Arms 7 Market Street, Kirkby Lonsdale LA6 2AU (01524 271220; https://www.facebook.com/kingsarmshotelkirkbylonsdale). The oldest pub in the town, this 16th-C gem dispenses a good selection of real ale. Dog- and family-friendly, outside seating. Newspapers, real fires and Wi-Fi. B&B. *Open 12.00-23.00 (Sun 23.00)*.

X 6 Avanti Bar & Restaurant 57 Main Street, Kirkby Lonsdale, Carnforth LA6 2AH (01524 273500; www.avantirestaurant.co.uk). Rustic Mediterranean cuisine with Spanish and Italian influence in a stylish restaurant. Coffee available *from 10.00; Lunch 12.00-14.00 (Fri-Sun 14.30) &* main menu served *18.00-20.30 (Fri-Sun 21.00)*. Walled garden for al fresco dining.

7 The Red Dragon Inn 59-61 Main Street, Kirkby Lonsdale LA6 2AH (01524 271205; www.facebook.com/reddragonkirkby). Traditional pub serving real ale and food *L and E*. Dog- and child-friendly, outside seating. Real fires and Wi-Fi. B&B. *Open 10.00-23.00*.

8 The Royal Barn New Road, Kirkby Lonsdale LA6 2AB (01524 271918; www.kirkbylonsdalebrewery.com). Proud to be putting the 'ale' in Lonsdale, this brewery tap dispenses a wide range of real ales and real cider, together with snacks and pies for beer lovers and cakes for coffee lovers. Dog- and family-friendly. *Fortnightly* live music. Newspapers, real fires and Wi-Fi. *Open 10.00-23.00 (Mon-Wed 21.30)*.

X 9 The Crossing Point Café 7 Market Square, Kirkby Lonsdale, Carnforth LA6 2AN (01524 298050; www.crossingpointcafe.co.uk). An eatery that is all about local, in-season produce and fresh food, with cakes, scones and treats baked *daily*, catering for foodies and ramblers alike. *Open Wed-Mon 10.00-16.00*; breakfast served *until 12.00*.

X 10 The Snooty Fox 33 Main Street, Kirkby Lonsdale LA6 2AH (01524 297298). Close to the town square, this pub dispenses real ale from an impressive oak-panelled bar, together with food *all day*. Dog- and child-friendly, outside seating. Traditional pub games, newspapers, real fires, sports TV and Wi-Fi. B&B. *Open Mon-Sat 11.00-23.00 & Sun 12.00-22.30*.

Crooklands

It is with some relief that the third (and final) crossing of the canal, performed by the motorway, is now in view accompanied by the promise of a more peaceful journey to come into the south Lakeland scenery, already undulating into less distant horizons. Here Crooklands meets the waterway with the slipway more than hinting at navigation, which in fact extends westwards to Stainton as the Lancaster Canal Trust's trip boat bears further witness. The garage beside Millness Bridge 164 provides sustenance as well as fuel. Beyond the village is the County Showground (a concert venue as well as a focus for rural pursuits) as the canal meanders off into lush pasture, passing scattered farmsteads. Stainton Aqueduct, recently restored at a cost of £2m after extensive damage by Storm Desmond in December 2015, is the first engineering pièce de résistance to be met along this waterway's Northern Reaches, quickly followed by Hincaster Tunnel. Although both relatively diminutive in scale compared with some of their more southerly cousins, they are nonetheless most pleasing in terms of their execution and quality of construction. This attention to detail being further echoed in the construction of the bridges spanning the horse-path over the Tunnel itself. Indeed, it is hard not to be struck by the condition of the masonry on nearly all the structures along this waterway looking, as they do, as if they were completed two years ago, rather than two hundred.

Crooklands
Cumbria. PO box, tel, stores, off-licence, takeaway, garage. Home to the Westmoreland County Agricultural Society's annual show, in existence for exactly 20 years longer than the Lancaster Canal's Northern Reaches, this agricultural community is overlooked by St Patrick's Church perched on the hillside and approached by little more than a cart track. The original building dates from the 16th C but a drastic re-modelling in 1852 incorporates only the odd niche and window from the original.

Heversham
Cumbria. PO box, tel. A haunt of William Wordsworth and reputed to be the inspiration for his poem "The World is too Much with us." At times it is hard not to consider the poem's subsequent lines in relation to the invasive trunk road system of the area.

Hincaster
Cumbria. PO box. Best known as the site of the only tunnel on the canal – 378yds in length. Each portal is faced with local limestone and the bore is lined with approximately four million bricks – a commodity in short supply in this locality owing to a dearth of clay. They were in fact made from material dug at Mosside Farm, close to Milness Bridge 164, just outside Crooklands. The claypits and bricks works were resurrected some

30 years later to supply the Lancaster and Carlisle Railway Company.

Lakeland Maze Farm Park Raines Hall, Sedgwick, Kendal LA8 0JH (01539 561760; www.lakelandmaze. co.uk). Twice winner of the Maize Maze of the year, this attraction offers small (and not so small) people the chance to get lost (and found), enjoy tractor rides and feed farm animals. Camping. *Open Easter-Aug daily & weekends in Sep 10.00-18.00. Charge.*

Levens
Cumbria. PO box, tel, stores, off-licence. There are traces of settlement dating from the Bronze Age around this pretty village, lying in the Lyth Valley, between the Rivers Kent and Gilpin and famed for its damson trees.

Levens Hall and Gardens Kendal LA8 0PD (01539 560321; www.levenshall.co.uk). An imposing building, occupied since around 1350, with an Elizabethan interior featuring fine oak panelling and ornate plasterwork. This has always been a family residence and a visit allows one to trace their stories, see the building as it is lived in and examine its fascinating contents. The topiary is recognised by the Guinness Book of Records as being the oldest in the world. House, gardens, gift shop, plant centre and Buttery restaurant. *Open May-Sep, Sun-Thu 10.00-17.00. Charge.*

● **Milnthorpe**

Cumbria. PO, tel, stores, chemist, bank, butcher, takeaways, library, garage. Originally a thriving centre of business, stimulated by its port on the River Bela which is, in turn, a tributary of the River Kent. Today this is only navigable as far inland as Arnside, well to the south of the village. In 1886, John Dobson established a comb-making business in Bela Mill, using horn as his raw material. Today this material has been superseded by injection moulding and the company continues to enjoy world-wide sales. There is a *Friday* market in the square, its origins dating back to an ancient charter of 1334.

● **Sedgwick**

Cumbria. PO box, tel. The village came into being as a Roman fording place on the River Kent, its name of Norse origins from the word Sigg, meaning a dairy farm. Much of its subsequent development, towards the end of the 18th C, can be attributed to

John Wakefield – a banker and businessman – who opened a gunpowder works powered by the river. Additional factories grew up locally until, by the middle of 19th C, 50 people were employed. Gunpowder manufacture finally ceased in 1935. John Wakefield's son, William, went on to build the Grade II listed, Victorian Gothic Sedgwick House, now turned into 21 apartments.

Sizergh Castle Sizergh, Kendal LA8 8DZ (01539 560951; https://www.nationaltrust.org.uk/ sizergh). Fortified with a stout pele tower (in common with many Cumbrian country houses) to resist marauding Scottish cattle rustlers, this has been home to the Strickland family since 13th C. Acquired by the National Trust in 1950 – together with its gardens, parkland and estate – the original owners are still in residence. There are oak-panelled interiors and, in the Inlaid Chamber, the panelling displays floral and geometric marquetry patterns in contrasting dark bog-oak and light poplar. Café and shop. *Opening times vary throughout the season* so visit the website for details.

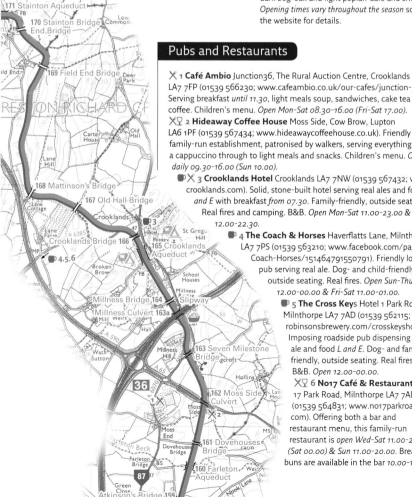

Pubs and Restaurants

✕ 1 **Café Ambio** Junction36, The Rural Auction Centre, Crooklands LA7 7FP (01539 566230; www.cafeambio.co.uk/our-cafes/junction-36). Serving breakfast *until 11.30*, light meals soup, sandwiches, cake tea and coffee. Children's menu. *Open Mon-Sat 08.30-16.00 (Fri-Sat 17.00).*

✕♀ 2 **Hideaway Coffee House** Moss Side, Cow Brow, Lupton LA6 1PF (01539 567434; www.hideawaycoffeehouse.co.uk). Friendly family-run establishment, patronised by walkers, serving everything from a cappuccino through to light meals and snacks. Children's menu. *Open daily 09.30-16.00 (Sun 10.00).*

◗✕ 3 **Crooklands Hotel** Crooklands LA7 7NW (01539 567432; www. crooklands.com). Solid, stone-built hotel serving real ales and food *L and E* with breakfast *from 07.30*. Family-friendly, outside seating. Real fires and camping. B&B. *Open Mon-Sat 11.00-23.00 & Sun 12.00-22.30.*

◗ 4 **The Coach & Horses** Haverflatts Lane, Milnthorpe LA7 7PS (01539 563210; www.facebook.com/pages/ Coach-Horses/151464791550791). Friendly locals' pub serving real ale. Dog- and child-friendly, outside seating. Real fires. *Open Sun-Thu 12.00-00.00 & Fri-Sat 11.00-01.00.*

◗ 5 **The Cross Key**s Hotel 1 Park Road, Milnthorpe LA7 7AD (01539 562115; www. robinsonsbrewery.com/crosskeyshotel). Imposing roadside pub dispensing real ale and food *L and E*. Dog- and family-friendly, outside seating. Real fires. B&B. *Open 12.00-00.00.*

✕♀ 6 **No17 Café & Restaurant** 17 Park Road, Milnthorpe LA7 7AD (01539 564831; www.no17parkroad. com). Offering both a bar and restaurant menu, this family-run restaurant is *open Wed-Sat 11.00-23.00 (Sat 00.00) & Sun 11.00-20.00.* Breakfast buns are available in the bar *10.00-12.00.*

♿✕ **7 The Strickland Arms** Nannypie Lane, Sizergh LA8 8DZ (01539 561010; www.thestricklandarms.com). Set on the approach to Sizergh Castle, in a peaceful location, this solid stone-built hostelry dispenses real ale (several from Cumbrian microbreweries) and food *Mon-Fri L and E & Sat-un 12.00-21,00 (Sun 20.30)*. Dog- and family-friendly, outside seating. Quiz *Wed*. Real fires. Takeaway fish & chips *Fri E*. *Open 12.00-23.00 (Sun 22.30)*.

♿✕ **8 Hare & Hounds** Levens, Kendal LA8 8PN (01539 560004; www.hareandhoundslevens.co.uk). Dating from 1724, this thriving village local serves real ales and excellent food *daily 12.00-21.00*. Dog- and

family-friendly, garden. Real fires and Wi-Fi. B&B. *Open 12.00-23.00*.

♿ **9 Gilpin Bridge Inn** Levens, Kendal LA8 8EP (01539 552206; www.robinsonsbrewery.com/gilpinbridgeinn). Large country pub, best known for its food, serving real ale and meals *L and E*. Dog- and child-friendly, garden. Real fires. B&B. *Open Mon-Fri L and E and Sat-Sun 12.00-23.00 (Sun 20.30)*.

♿ **10 The Punch Bowl** Barrows Green, Natland LA8 0AA (01539 560267). Complete with piano and pool table, this pub serves real ale and food *L and E*. Dog- and Family-friendly, garden. Real fires. *Open Mon-Sat L and E (not Mon L) & Sun 12.00-22.30*.

WALKING AND CYCLING

Once past the third M6 crossing the excellent towpath is followed through to a point ¼ mile north of Hincaster Tunnel where the route briefly leaves the navigation, using a minor road alongside, to cross the A590. Immediately north of the dual carriageway bridge you will see a waymarked finger post on your right pointing uphill to re-join the line of the navigation, temporarily subsumed by a couple of fields.

The Hincaster Trailway (01539 561243; www.hincastertrailway.co.uk) provides a safe, largely off-road route and an interesting 2½-mile diversion for towpath walkers.

An interesting walks leaflet, entitled Sedgwick's Drumlins and Panoramas, is available from the Old Smithy – immediately above the aqueduct on the right. Modest charge.

NAVIGATIONAL NOTES

The slipway between Bridges 163a and 164 is available to small, trailable, licensed craft. Canal & River Trust (0303 040 4040; www.canalrivertrust.org.uk/contact-us/ways-to-contact-us) *require 24hrs notice of intended use.*

BOAT TRIPS

nb Waterwitch operates *40-minute* boat trips, along the Northern Reaches of the Lancaster canal, from Crooklands Bridge LA7 7NW – *May-Sep* – on *Sun & B Hol Mon at 11.00 & 16.00*. For more information visit www.lctrust.co.uk or telephone 07504 710351. Available for charter.

Entrance to the Hincaster Tunnel

Kendal

Leaving the solid charm of Sedgwick, its sturdy buildings echoed by the aqueduct spanning the main street, the infilled line of the canal can be picked up crossing a couple of fields to re-appear in woodland beyond. Standing incongruous and forlorn, framed by hawthorn, is Horse Park Bridge waiting patiently for a ribbon of water to return: a 'sentiment' echoed by a couple more bridges between here and Kendal, all in a perfect state of repair, bearing superb testament to the calibre of Rennie's engineering and its execution by the craftsmen on the ground. The manner in which the navigation snakes its way towards Kendal, the River Kent never far away, is truly charming: sometimes in a side cutting, whilst at others sharing open pasture with somnolent, cud-chewing cows. With the town visible in the distance, trunk roads begin to close in and soon the line of the canal – depicted by a succession of bridges, including the superb Changeline Bridge – is winding its way through the suburbs, its route passing a mix of allotments and light industry. Canal Head is marked by an eclectic mix of substantial stone buildings, warehouses in the main and most dating from the arrival of the canal, giving a clear indication of the significant impact that the navigation would have made on the town.

● **Kendal**
Cumbria. All services. It would be nigh on impossible to find fault with this quintessential, Cumbrian town: neat, tidy, solid, set off to perfection by the fast-flowing River Kent running through its midst. Known for such diverse manufacture as mint cake and snuff, Kendal was once home to John Cunliffe and the locations for his most famous creation, Postman Pat, were inspired by the town and its surrounding villages. It's locally-quarried, grey limestone buildings might have earned it the nickname Auld Grey Town but its recorded history, dating back to the Domesday Book has been colourful nonetheless. There is a useful cycle shop Giant Cycles, The Old Brewery, Wildman St, Kendal LA9 6EN (01539 728057; www.giant-kendal.co.uk/gb) *open Mon-Sat 09.00-17.30.*

Abbot Hall Art Gallery Kirkland, Kendal LA9 5AL (01539 722464; www.abbothall.org.uk). Housed in a Grade I listed Georgian villa, the gallery has an enviable reputation for its exhibitions of work by national and international artists. Substantial redevelopment is planned as part of the Lake District's recent designation as a UNESCO World Heritage Site. Shop and café. *Open Mon-Sat 10.30-17.00 (Nov-Feb 16.00).* Charge.

Kendal Castle Castle Hill, Kendal LA9 7BJ. Lying immediately to the west of the line of the canal, the ruined remains of this 12th-C building are best understood through the exhibition in Kendal Museum. Originally home to the Barons of Kendal, the most famous members being the Parr family with Katherine Parr becoming the sixth and final wife of Henry VIII. The castle fell into ruin during Tudor times and has remained so ever since.

Kendal Museum Station Road, Kendal LA9 6BT (01539 815597; www.kendalmuseum.org.uk). One of the oldest museums in the country and as such it retains possibly the largest taxidermy collection in Europe. Artefacts in the collection represent geology, archaeology, social and natural history on both a local and global scale. Café and shop. *Open Tue-Thu 10.00-16.00. Charge.*

Lakeland Climbing Centre Lake District Business Park, Kendal LA9 6HN (01539 721766; www.kendalwall. co.uk). Claiming to have the craziest climbs, the tallest wall and to be the source of skyline indoor aerial adventure, this establishment offers an enclosed diversion for the brave and fearless during inclement weather. Wi-Fi, showers and changing areas. *Open 10.00-22.00 (Sat-Sun & B Hol 18.00).* Charge.

The Box Theatre Beezon Road, Kendal LA9 6EL (01539 814729/814700; www.kendal.ac.uk/about-us/facilities/the-box). Situated on Kendal College's Arts & Media campus, close to the railway station, this striking performance venue is renown for its 'twisted cube', slate construction and is used for everything from live theatre through to cinema screenings. For the cinema programme visit www. londonnet.co.uk/cinema/kendal-thebox.html.

The Brewery Arts Centre 122a Highgate, Kendal LA9 4HE (01539 725133; www.breweryarts. co.uk). Opened in 1972, converted from the old Vaux Brewery premises, the Arts Centre has subsequently hosted a wide range of events and has become one of the North West's most important arts education centres. The Brewery gardens represent a living example of this town house amenity, long since disappeared. Bar, café, restaurant and gallery. Box office *open daily 12.00-20.00.* One of the eateries are *open daily from 10.00 (Sun 12.00).* Visit the website for further details.

Tourist Information Centre C48a Branthaite Brow, Kendal LA9 4TX (01539 735891; www. madeincumbria.co.uk/contactus.asp). Kendal Town Council publish a series of free guides to local amenities, culture, and walking trails available here. *Open Mon-Sat 09.00-17.00.*

Travelling Local buses are largely operating by Stagecoach Beezon Road, Kendal LA9 6BW (01539 722143; www.stagecoachbus.com). Traveline 0871 200 22 33. National Rail (03457 48 49 50; www.ojp.nationalrail.co.uk/service/planjourney/ search). For the cheaper ticket alternative visit https://www.trainsplit.com.

● **Natland**
Cumbria. PO, tel. There are signs, in the form

91

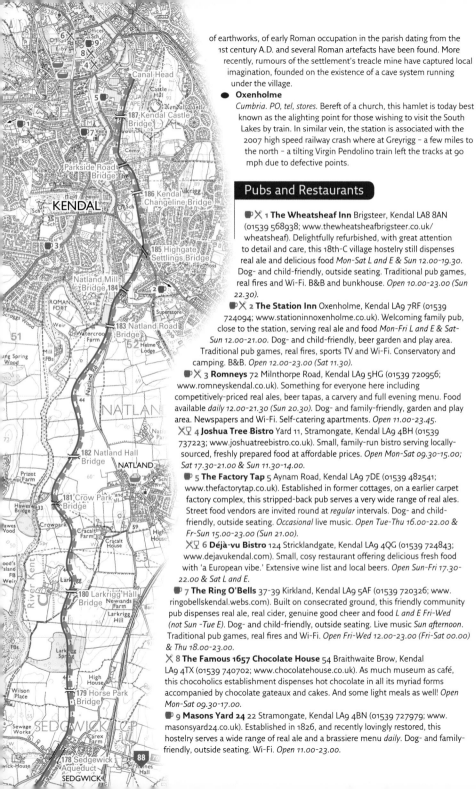

of earthworks, of early Roman occupation in the parish dating from the 1st century A.D. and several Roman artefacts have been found. More recently, rumours of the settlement's treacle mine have captured local imagination, founded on the existence of a cave system running under the village.

● **Oxenholme**
Cumbria. PO, tel, stores. Bereft of a church, this hamlet is today best known as the alighting point for those wishing to visit the South Lakes by train. In similar vein, the station is associated with the 2007 high speed railway crash where at Greyrigg – a few miles to the north – a tilting Virgin Pendolino train left the tracks at 90 mph due to defective points.

Pubs and Restaurants

●✗ **1 The Wheatsheaf Inn** Brigsteer, Kendal LA8 8AN (01539 568938; www.thewheatsheafbrigsteer.co.uk/wheatsheaf). Delightfully refurbished, with great attention to detail and care, this 18th-C village hostelry still dispenses real ale and delicious food *Mon-Sat L and E & Sun 12.00-19.30.* Dog- and child-friendly, outside seating. Traditional pub games, real fires and Wi-Fi. B&B and bunkhouse. *Open 10.00-23.00 (Sun 22.30).*

●✗ **2 The Station Inn** Oxenholme, Kendal LA9 7RF (01539 724094; www.stationinnoxenholme.co.uk). Welcoming family pub, close to the station, serving real ale and food *Mon-Fri L and E & Sat-Sun 12.00-21.00.* Dog- and child-friendly, beer garden and play area. Traditional pub games, real fires, sports TV and Wi-Fi. Conservatory and camping. B&B. *Open 12.00-23.00 (Sat 11.30).*

●✗ **3 Romneys** 72 Milnthorpe Road, Kendal LA9 5HG (01539 720956; www.romneyskendal.co.uk). Something for everyone here including competitively-priced real ales, beer tapas, a carvery and full evening menu. Food available *daily 12.00-21.30 (Sun 20.30).* Dog- and family-friendly, garden and play area. Newspapers and Wi-Fi. Self-catering apartments. *Open 11.00-23.45.*

✗♟ **4 Joshua Tree Bistro** Yard 11, Stramongate, Kendal LA9 4BH (01539 737223; www.joshuatreebistro.co.uk). Small, family-run bistro serving locally-sourced, freshly prepared food at affordable prices. *Open Mon-Sat 09.30-15.00; Sat 17.30-21.00 & Sun 11.30-14.00.*

● **5 The Factory Tap** 5 Aynam Road, Kendal LA9 7DE (01539 482541; www.thefactorytap.co.uk). Established in former cottages, on a earlier carpet factory complex, this stripped-back pub serves a very wide range of real ales. Street food vendors are invited round at *regular* intervals. Dog- and child-friendly, outside seating. *Occasional* live music. *Open Tue-Thu 16.00-22.00 & Fr-Sun 15.00-23.00 (Sun 21.00).*

✗♟ **6 Déjà-vu Bistro** 124 Stricklandgate, Kendal LA9 4QG (01539 724843; www.dejavukendal.com). Small, cosy restaurant offering delicious fresh food with 'a European vibe.' Extensive wine list and local beers. *Open Sun-Fri 17.30-22.00 & Sat L and E.*

● **7 The Ring O'Bells** 37-39 Kirkland, Kendal LA9 5AF (01539 720326; www.ringobellskendal.webs.com). Built on consecrated ground, this friendly community pub dispenses real ale, real cider, genuine good cheer and food *L and E Fri-Wed (not Sun -Tue E).* Dog- and child-friendly, outside seating. Live music *Sun afternoon.* Traditional pub games, real fires and Wi-Fi. *Open Fri-Wed 12.00-23.00 (Fri-Sat 00.00) & Thu 18.00-23.00.*

✗ **8 The Famous 1657 Chocolate House** 54 Braithwaite Brow, Kendal LA9 4TX (01539 740702; www.chocolatehouse.co.uk). As much museum as café, this chocoholics establishment dispenses hot chocolate in all its myriad forms accompanied by chocolate gateaux and cakes. And some light meals as well! *Open Mon-Sat 09.30-17.00.*

● **9 Masons Yard 24** 22 Stramongate, Kendal LA9 4BN (01539 727979; www.masonsyard24.co.uk). Established in 1826, and recently lovingly restored, this hostelry serves a wide range of real ale and a brasserie menu *daily.* Dog- and family-friendly, outside seating. Wi-Fi. *Open 11.00-23.00.*

LEEDS & LIVERPOOL CANAL

MAXIMUM DIMENSIONS

Liverpool to Wigan, and Leigh Branch
Length: 72' 0"
Beam: 14' 3"
Headroom: 8' 0"

Wigan to Leeds
Length: 60' 0"
Beam: 14' 3"
Headroom: 8' 0"

Rufford Branch
Length: 62' 0"
Beam: 14' 3"
Headroom: 8' 0"

MANAGER

0303 040 4040
www.canalrivertrust.org.uk/contact-us/ways-to-contact-us

MILEAGE

LIVERPOOL. Canal terminus to Burscough, junction with Rufford Branch: 24½ miles
Wigan, junction with Leigh Branch: 35 miles
Johnson's Hill Locks: 47¼ miles
Blackburn, Top Lock: 56 miles
Burnley: 72½ miles
Skipton: 98 miles
Bingley Five Rise: 110¾ miles
Apperley Bridge: 118 miles
LEEDS, River Lock: 127¾ miles
Locks: 91
Leigh Branch: 7¼ miles, 2 locks
Rufford Branch: 7¼ miles, 8 locks

With a length of 127¼ miles excluding branches, the Leeds & Liverpool Canal is the longest single canal in Britain built by a single company. The canal has its beginnings in the River Douglas, a little river made navigable by 1740 from Wigan to Parbold, Tarleton and the Ribble estuary. Several ambitious trans-Pennine canal schemes had been mooted; one for a canal from Liverpool to Leeds, to connect with the head of the Aire & Calder Navigation. The Leeds & Liverpool Canal was authorised in 1770, and construction began at once, with John Longbotham as engineer. The first (lock-free) section from Bingley to Skipton was opened within three years; by 1777 two long sections were open from the Aire & Calder at Leeds to Gargrave (incorporating many new staircase locks) and from Wigan to Liverpool. The L & L bought out the River Douglas navigation at an early stage to gain control of its valuable water supply. It was replaced by a proper canal branch to Rufford and Tarleton, where it joined the (tidal) River Douglas. In 1790 work began again, with Robert Whitworth as the company's engineer; but after 1792 and the outbreak of war with France, investment in canals declined steadily. The whole of the main line from Leeds to Liverpool was finished by 1816 actually *sharing* the channel of the Lancaster Canal for 10 miles from Wigan Top Lock to Johnson's Hill Bottom Lock. The Lancaster used to branch off up what became the Walton Summit Branch. In 1820 a branch was opened to join the Bridgewater Canal at Leigh. A short branch (the Springs Branch) was also made to rock quarries at Skipton and an important 3-mile-long canal from Shipley to Bradford. The cut down into the Liverpool Docks was made in 1846. The prosperity of the company after 1820 was not, at first, greatly affected by the advent of railways. The scale of the navigation (the locks were built as broad locks 62ft by 14ft, allowing big payloads to be carried along the canal) contributed to the high dividends paid to shareholders for several years. Water supply was, however, a problem and in spite of the building of copious reservoirs, the canal had to be closed for months on end during dry summers, driving carriers' custom away to the railways. Use of the navigation for freight declined throughout the last century; the hard winter of 1962/63 finished off many traders. Today this canal offers boaters, walkers and cyclists an exhilarating link between two superb cities.

93

Liverpool

The Liverpool Canal Link was officially opened to boaters on 20 April 2009. It runs from the bottom of the existing Stanley Locks and linking Stanley Dock to Canning Dock, via the old West Waterloo Dock; Princes Dock and an underground section near Pier Head, in front of the Royal Liver Building. Canning Dock in turn provides a link into the revitalised Albert Dock which will, for the first Time in its history play host to a regular influx of narrowboats.

Navigation now begins just north of Vauxhall Bridge B. It runs north from the city centre for about 6 miles, parallel and close to Liverpool Docks, before turning east to Aintree, Wigan and the Pennines. Liverpool, while at one time not an attractive place from the canal, is slowly changing and although some factories still have their backs to the waterway, considerable effort has been made to improve the access to the towpath which is alive with walkers, fishermen and cyclists. The water, however, is surprisingly clear. Eldonian Village forms an attractive backdrop to the moorings in the terminus basin. There is a *PO* beside bridge 2A together with a very comprehensive range of *shops*.

NAVIGATIONAL NOTES

1 Just north of the terminus is the Stanley Dock Branch, until recently used only by intrepid navigators as a useful link into the tidal River Mersey. Today this compact flight of locks gives access to the Liverpool Canal Link, leading across the historic Pier Head, in front of the Royal Liver Building and ultimately into Salthouse Dock. There are four locks on this branch leading down into Stanley Dock and passage can be booked at www.canalrivertrust.org.uk/enjoy-the-waterways/boating/planning-your-boat-trip/booking-your-passage-online).

2 There are unlimited boat movements during allocated windows *Wed-Mon 08:00-09:30* travelling out of Liverpool and *13.00-16.00* travelling into Liverpool.

3 Pontoon moorings in Salthouse Dock can also be booked via the website.

4 Levels within the old docks – traversed as part of the Liverpool Link – can vary, with the partially infilled West Waterloo Dock providing as little as 2' 6" draught.

5 Navigators wishing to enter the Mersey should contact the Mersey Docks and Harbour Company (0151 949 6000) – the lock is operated *24hrs a day*.

6 Those navigating the Leeds & Liverpool Canal will need, as well as a windlass, a Canal & River Trust handcuff lock key and a Watermate key.

7 Mooring at unrecognised sites in the city centre is not recommended.

● **Liverpool**
Merseyside. All services. In the first century AD it was 'lifrugpool', a settlement next to a muddy creek; now it is one of Britain's largest ports. Famous worldwide as the place where the Beatles began their march to fame, and equally well known for the exploits of Liverpool Football Club. Club. There is much to be seen in this ancient port. The Anglican Cathedral, begun in 1904 and finished in 1978, is the largest in the world; the Roman Catholic Cathedral has stained glass by John Piper and Patrick Reyntiens. On the pierhead is a memorial to the engineers lost on the *Titanic*, which sank in 1912. The superb Albert Dock development and Liverpool Tate and The Walker Art

Pubs and Restaurants

There are many to be found here.

Galleries, together with a wide range of theatres and museums, are attracting an ever increasing number of tourists. As a city it has more Georgian buildings than Bath, a UNESCO World Heritage waterfront and has convincingly re-established itself upon a reputation as a cultural and leisure centre which was recognised with the award of City of Culture 2008.

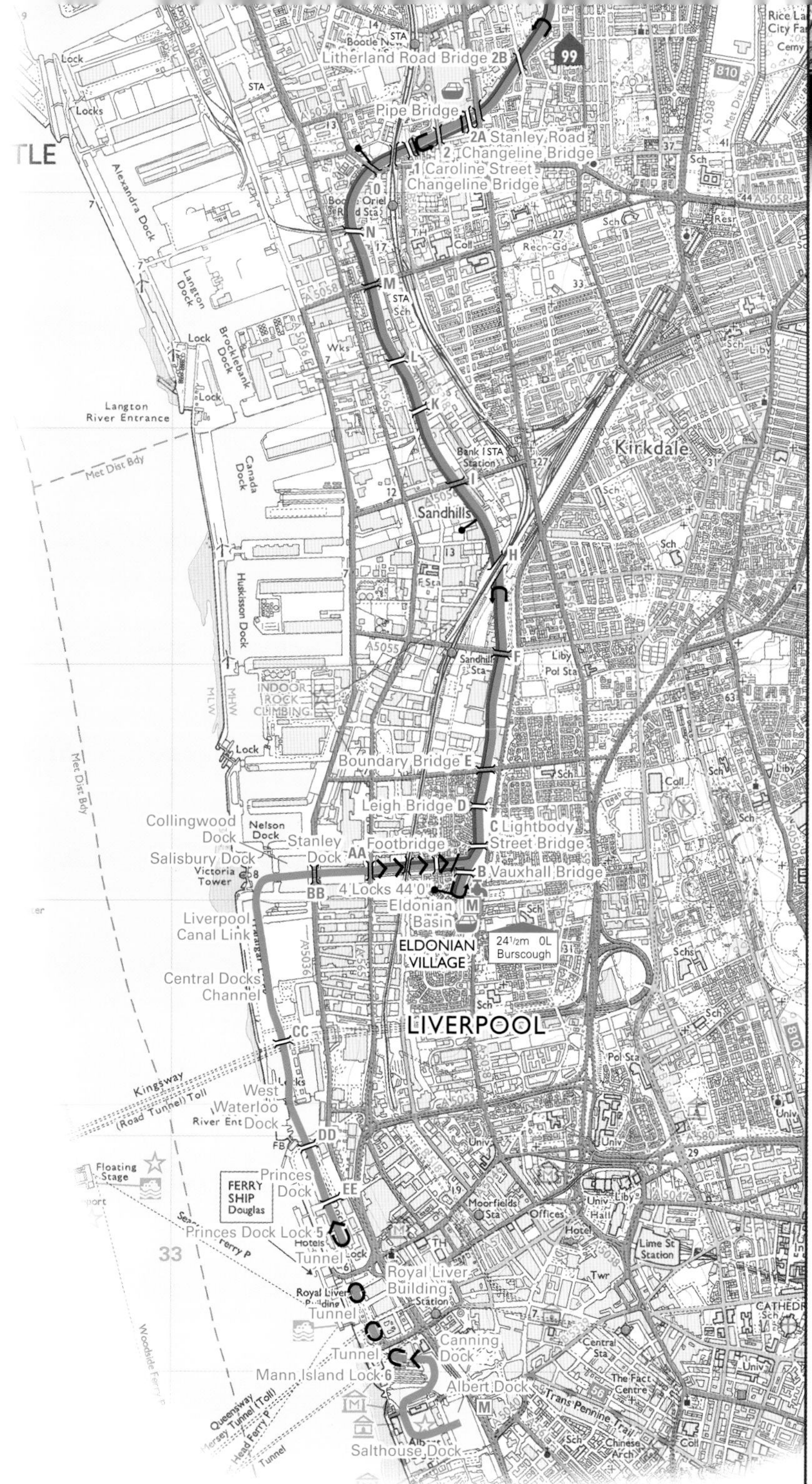

Litherland Road Bridge 2B
99
Pipe Bridge
2A Stanley Road
2 Changeline Bridge
1 Caroline Street
Changeline Bridge
Oriel
d Sta
N
M
STA
Sch
Wks
L
K
Bank I STA
Station
Sandhills
13
H
Sandhill
Sta
F
Liby
Pol Stn
Boundary Bridge E
Leigh Bridge D
C Lightbody
Footbridge   Street Bridge
Stanley   AA
Dock
B Vauxhall Bridge
BB   4 Locks 44'0"
M
Eldonian
Basin
ELDONIAN
VILLAGE
24½m 0L
Burscough
LIVERPOOL
Collingwood
Dock   Nelson
Dock
Salisbury Dock
Victoria
Tower
Liverpool
Canal Link
Central Docks
Channel
CC
Kingsway
(Road Tunnel) Toll
West
Waterloo
River Ent   Dock
FB
DD
Princes
Dock
EE
FERRY
SHIP
Douglas
Princes Dock Lock 5
Hotels
Tunnel
Royal Liver
Building
Royal Liver
Building
Tunnel
Mann Island Lock 6
Tunnel
Canning
Dock
Albert Dock
Queensway
Tunnel (Toll)
Head Fact P
Tunnel
Salthouse Dock

Kirkdale

INDOOR
ROCK
CLIMBING

Lock

Alexandra Dock
Locks
Lock
Langton
Dock
Brocklebank
Dock
Lock
Canada
Dock
Langton
River Entrance
Met Dist Bdy
Huskisson Dock

Floating
Stage

Moorfields
Sta

Lime St
Station

CATHEDRAL

Trans Pennine Trail

Chinese
Arch

Albert Dock The Colonnades, Albert Dock, Liverpool L3 4AF (0151 707 0729; www.albertdock.com). The largest grouping of Grade I listed buildings in England–opened in 1846 as warehousing for a range of precious cargo from around the world, these buildings have been transformed into an award-winning tourist destination including shops, cafés, restaurants, galleries and museums.

Beatles Story Britannia Vaults, Kings Dock Street, Liverpool L3 4AD (0151 709 1963; www.beatlesstory.com). The title says it all. *Open daily 09.00-18.00.*

Bluecoat Arts Centre Bluecoat Chambers, School Lane, Liverpool L1 3BX (0151 702 5324; www.thebluecoat.org.uk). A striking 18th-C building housing a varied selection of visual and performing arts. Also educational programmes, artists' studios, shops and a café. *Open daily 09.00-18.00. (Sun 10.00).*

Bluecoat Display Centre College Lane, Liverpool L1 3BZ (0151 709 4014; www.bluecoatdisplaycentre.com). Craft and design centre in an adjacent street. *Open Mon-Sat 10.00-17.30, Sun 12.00-17.00.*

British Music Experience Cunard Building, Pier Head, Liverpool L3 1DS (0151 519 0915; www.britishmusicexperience.com). Tells the story of British music through costumes, instruments, performance and memorabilia from the Beatles to Bowie through to Adele, Oasis and the X Factor. *Open daily 09.00-18.00. Charge. Café open 09.00-17.30.*

Chinese Arch Berry Street, Liverpool. The largest outside China from where it was originally shipped, the arch stands 15m high and spans Nelson Street complete with its five roofs and 200 ornate dragons.

Croxteth Hall & Country Park Muirhead Avenue East, Liverpool L11 1EH (0151 233 3020; www.liverpoolcityhalls.co.uk/croxteth-hall). Once the ancestral home of the Molyneux family, the Earls of Sefton, the estate now offers the opportunity to visit the historic Hall, the 500- acre Country Park, the Walled Garden and the Home Farm. Only the Country Park is free. *Open Easter-Sep 10.30-17.00* and farm, café and shop *open weekends Oct-Easter.*

Empire Theatre Lime Street, Liverpool L1 1JE (0844 871 3017; www.liverpooltheatres.com/empire.htm). A popular theatre with a diverse programme of in-house productions and touring shows.

Fact 88 Wood Street, Liverpool L1 4DQ (0151 707 4444; www.fact.co.uk). Exciting, purpose-built arts centre, completed in 2003, housing a range of galleries, a café, restaurant and bar. *Open Sun–Fri 12.00–18.00, Sat from 11.00. Free.*

Liverpool Cathedral St James Mount , Liverpool L1 7AZ (0151 709 6271; www.liverpoolcathedral.org.uk). The largest Anglican cathedral in Britain, resplendent in red sandstone, built to the design of Sir Giles Gilbert Scott and begun in 1904. The 331ft tower extends the full width of the building and is home to the heaviest ringing peal of bells in the world–all 30 tons of them. Inside there are soaring gothic arches, a massive organ and together with worship there are regular recitals and concerts. Refectory and shop. *Open daily 08.00-18.00 (attractions 10.00-17.00). Free-donations. Charge for Tower and Embroidery Gallery.*

Liverpool City Sights 9 Glegg Street, Liverpool L3 7DX (0151 298 1253; www.liverpoolcitysights.co.uk). Hop on hop off service, on open-top buses, operating *daily throughout the year.* First tour from Pier Head, Canada Boulevard L3 1BY *at 09.50 and last 16.50.* Tickets can be purchased for *24hrs or 48hrs.* Charge. Also **Maghull Coaches** (0151 933 2324; www.cityexplorerliverpool.co.uk) operate a similar service *daily* with the first tour departing from Pier Head at *10.00 and the last at 16.30.*

Liverpool City Walks Canada Boulevard, Liverpool L3 1BY (www.liverpoolcitywalks.com). Provides a structured approach to explore Liverpool's unique historical and architectural features. The Heritage Walk comprises 75 gunmetal markers set in footways and pedestrian areas throughout the city centre. Themed sub-trails within the heritage walk provide an opportunity to focus on three specific areas of the city's rich architectural legacy: 1) Maritime and Commerce; 2) Arts and Heritage and 3) Learning and Religion. Contact the TIC for further details.

Martin Mere Fish Lane, Ormskirk L40 0TA (01704 895181; www.wwt.org.uk/wetland-centres/martin-mere). A major Wildlife & Wetlands Trust site approaching 600 acres that in winter hosts thousands of migratory wetland birds. There is plenty to do and see at all times of the year and it makes a worthwhile visit either from the city (Merseyrail train to Ormskirk and then a No 3 bus) or as you follow the canal east through Burscough. Café, shop and picnic area. Children's activities. *Open Apr-Oct 09.30-18.00 & Nov-Mar 09.30-16.30.* Charge.

Mendips & 20 Forthlin Road 251 Menlove Avenue, Liverpool L25 7SA (0151 427 7231; www.nationaltrust.org.uk/beatles-childhood-homes). Where Sir Paul McCartney lived with his parents and John Lennon grew up with his aunt and uncle. Both homes have been sensitively restored and can be visited on a tour commencing either in the city centre or from Speke Hall. Booking essential–no direct access to either property. For tours visit the online booking service at www.live.advancedticketing.co.uk//k?ntbeatles).

Mersey Ferries Pier Head, Georges Parade, Liverpool L3 1DP (0151 330 1003; www.merseyferries.co.uk). Long ago made redundant by road and rail tunnels under the Mersey, these fine vessels now offer a variety of River Explorer Cruises and regular trips along the Manchester Ship Canal. Telephone or visit the website for details. *Open 08.00-20.00.*

Merseyside Maritime Museum Albert Dock, Liverpool L3 4AQ (0151 478 4499; www.liverpoolmuseums.org.uk/maritime/). The chance to discover Liverpool's maritime heritage from tales of the Titanic to the transatlantic slavery trade. Shop and restaurant. *Open daily 10.00-17.00. Free.*

MerseyTravel PO Box 1976 Liverpool L69 3HN (0151 330 1000; www.merseytravel.gov.uk). Also National Rail Enquiries 08457 48 49 50 *(24hrs)*. Offers a journey planner, bus train and ferry timetables and regular promotions. *Open daily 7.00-20.00 (Sat-Sun 08.00).*

Metropolitan Cathedral Mount Pleasant, Liverpool L3 5TQ (0151 709 9222; www.liverpoolmetrocathedral.org.uk). Standing on the site once occupied by the Poor Law Institute, today's striking building, with its interior lantern tower of multi-coloured glass, has had a somewhat chequered career. Of the original design by Sir Edwin Lutyens, dating from 1933, only the Crypt was built and after the war inflation had raised the estimated cost of completion to £27m. Sir Frederick Gibberd produced a design that met the new brief, namely, that the cathedral should be completed within five years, incorporate the original crypt and cost no more than £1m. Building recommenced in 1962 and the finished cathedral–known locally as 'Paddy's Wigwam" – was consecrated in May 1967. Café bar and gift shop. *Open daily 07.30-18.00.* Lutyens Crypt *Open Mon-Sat 10.00-16.00.* Free – donations welcome.

Mr Hardman's Photographic Studio 59 Rodney Street, Liverpool L1 9EX (0151 709 6261; www.nationaltrust.org.uk). The complete studio, housed in an elegant Georgian terrace, where one of the city's best known portrait and landscape photographers lived and worked. *Open mid Mar-Oct, Wed-Sun 10.00-15.30.* Charge for timed ticket and guided tour which must be pre-booked by telephone.

Museum of Liverpool Pier Head, Liverpool L3 1DG (0151 478 4545; www.liverpoolmuseums.org. uk/mol/). An opportunity to explore the richness of Liverpool's cultural diversity in a striking new building rearing up over the Liverpool Link. *Open daily 10.00-17.00.* Shop and café. Free.

Prince's Road Synagogue Synagogue Chambers, Prince's Avenue, Liverpool L8 1TG (0151 709 3431; www.princesroad.org). Arguably Europe's finest example of Saracenic or Moorish revival style of synagogue in a Grade II listed building. Pre-booked guided tours are available *Mon-Thu 09.30-15.30.*

Radio City Tower St John's Beacon, 1 Houghton Street, Liverpool L1 1RL (0151 472 6800; www.radiocity.co.uk). Stunning views over the city and the Mersey estuary from the top of the 440ft Radio City Tower. *Open daily 10.15-17.15.* Charge. Refreshments and Wi-Fi.

Rice Lane City Farm Rawcliffe Road, Walton, Liverpool L9 1AW (0151 530 1066; www. ricelanecityfarm.org.uk). 224 acres of countryside–11 of which are woodland. There is a variety of rare breeds of farm animals together with ponies, goats and poultry. *Open daily 10.00-15.30.* Free – donations welcome.

Royal Court 36 Hope Street, Liverpool L1 1HL (0151 709 4321; www.royalcourtliverpool.co.uk). An impressive, 1500-seat Grade II listed building presenting a major events programme including drama, opera, comedy and popular music gigs.

Royal Liverpool Philharmonic Hall Hope Street, Liverpool L1 9BP (0151 709 3789; www.liverpoolphil.com). Art Deco building opened in 1939 to replace the original which was destroyed by fire and now home to the Royal Liverpool Philharmonic Orchestra. The hall hosts around 60 orchestral concerts a year together with drama, film and other arts.

St George's Hall St George's Place, Liverpool L1 1JJ (0151 225 6909; www.stgeorgesliverpool.co. uk). A stunning reflection of the City's prosperity in the 19th C, built in the neo-classical style to house the law courts and as a music venue. One of the first buildings to greet the visitor arriving at Liverpool Lime Street Station. Heritage Centre and Tourist Information *(open daily 10.00-17.00)* and Café *open daily 08.30-16.30 (Sun 16.00).* Hall *open to visitors 10.00-16.00.* Free.

Sefton Park Palm House Sefton Park, Liverpool L17 1AP (0151 726 2415; www.palmhouse.org.uk). An octagonal, three-tiered, Grade II listed Victorian glasshouse housing Liverpool's botanical collection. Inside and outside the palm house are beds of formal bedding and statues. Regular events which may *curtail opening. Open daily Mar-Oct 10.00-17.00 & Nov-Feb 10.00-16.00. Later summer opening.* For Satnav use L17 1AL.

Seized Albert Dock, Liverpool L3 4AQ (0151 478 4466; www.liverpoolmuseums.org.uk/ maritime/visit/floor-plan/seized/index.aspx). The museum tells the exciting story of smugglers and duty men, from the 1700s to the present day. Shop and café. *Open daily 10.00-17.00, last admission 16.00.* Free.

Speke Hall The Walk, Liverpool L24 1XD (0844 800 4799; www.nationaltrust.org.uk/ speke-hall-garden-and-estate). Black and white, half- timbered house dating back to 1490 complete with priest hole, fine Jacobean plasterwork, a Great Hall, Victorian kitchen and servants' hall. Restaurant and children's play area. Charge. *Open Wed-Sun, Apr-Oct & Nov-Mar weekends Nov, Dec, Feb and Mar:* Estate & Gardens *10.30-17.00;* Hall *12.30-17.00 and* Hall *tours 10.30-12.30.*

Sudley House Mossley Hill Road, Liverpool L18 8BX (0151 478 4016; www.liverpoolmuseums. org.uk/sudley/). Take the train to either Airburth or Mossley Hill stations. Victorian interior decoration and craftsmanship together with fine examples of 18th- and 19th-C art – the art collection of a Victorian merchant in its original setting. *Open daily 10.00-17.00.* Free. Tearoom *open daily 12.00-15.45.* Wi-Fi.

Tate Liverpool Albert Dock, Liverpool L3 4BB (0151 702 7400; www.tate.org.uk/visit/tate-liverpool). One of the largest galleries of contemporary and modern art outside London housed in part of the splendidly converted Grade I listed warehouses surrounding Albert Dock. Shop and Café. *Open daily 10.00-17.50.* Free. Charge for touring exhibitions

The Walker Art Gallery William Brown Street, Liverpool L3 8EL (0151 478 4199; www.liverpoolmuseums.org.uk/walker). One of Europe's foremost art galleries with outstanding collections from 1300 to the present day. *Open daily 10.00-17.00.* Shop and Café. Free.

Victoria Gallery and Museum University of Liverpool, Ashton Street, Liverpool L69 7ZX (0151 794 5927; www.vgm.liverpool.ac.uk). Collection of modern and classical art with works by Epstein, Audubon and Freud. *Open Tue-Sat 10.00-17.00.* Café *open Mon-Sat 09.00-16.00 (Sat 10.00) closed B Hols.*

Western Approaches - Liverpool War Museum 1-3 Rumford Street, Liverpool L2 8SZ (0151 227 2008; www.liverpoolwarmuseum.co.uk). Re-creation of the underground centre that orchestrated the Battle of the Atlantic during World War II. Shop. *Open daily 10.00-17.00. Last admission 16.00.* Charge.

Williamson Tunnels Heritage Centre The Old Stableyard, Smithdown Lane, Liverpool L7 3EE (0151 709 6868; www.williamsontunnels.co.uk). A unique labyrinth of tunnels under Edge Hill created by 19th-C philanthropist Joseph Williamson- 'The Mole of Edge Hill.' The Visitor Centre offers an insight into the life and underground world of one of Liverpool's most eccentric characters. Also 45-minute guided tours through a small section of the tunnel system. *Open Tue-Sun 10.00-17.00 (Thu-Sun in winter).* Charge.

World Museum William Brown Street, Liverpool L3 8EN (0151 478 4393; www.liverpoolmuseums. org.uk/wml). Thousands of exhibits, including an exploration of the Earth and cosmos, with themes ranging from the oceans to the stars-much very hands-on and interactive. A wide ranging and ever changing programme of events for all the family. Shop and Café. *Open daily 10.00-17.00.* Free.

Tourist Information Centres Liverpool Central Library, William Brown Street, Liverpool L3 8EW (0151 233 3069; www.visitliverpool.com/plan-your-visit/ visitor-centres) *open daily 09.30-17.00 (closed B Hols)* and British Music Experience Cunard Building, Pier Head, Liverpool L3 1DS (0151 233 0090; www. visitliverpool.com/plan-your-visit/visitor-centres) *open daily 09.30-17.30.*

Albert Dock, Liverpool

Litherland

North of Litherland the canal turns east to Aintree. Soon the first of many swing bridges is encountered; for the first few miles these bridges have to be locked to combat vandalism. All navigators should ensure that they have both a Watermate and a Handcuff key before reaching these bridges.

● **Bootle**
Merseyside. All services. Now a busy suburb of Liverpool, this settlement was described in early Victorian times as 'containing, with the township of Linacre, 808 inhabitants. The village comprises several good houses and is very much resorted to during summer for the benefit of sea-bathing.'

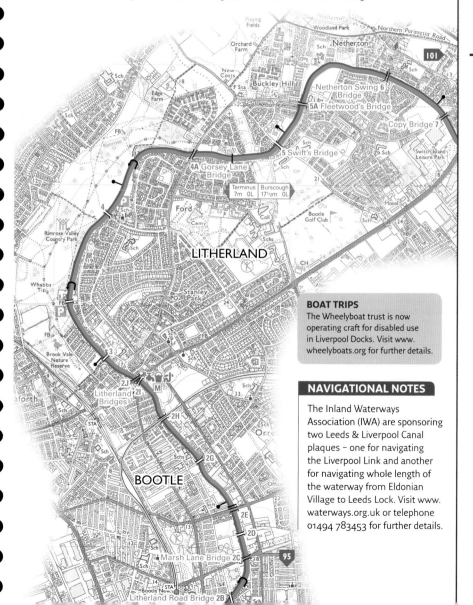

BOAT TRIPS
The Wheelyboat trust is now operating craft for disabled use in Liverpool Docks. Visit www.wheelyboats.org for further details.

NAVIGATIONAL NOTES

The Inland Waterways Association (IWA) are sponsoring two Leeds & Liverpool Canal plaques – one for navigating the Liverpool Link and another for navigating whole length of the waterway from Eldonian Village to Leeds Lock. Visit www.waterways.org.uk or telephone 01494 783453 for further details.

Maghull

Aintree marks the limit of Liverpool's outskirts and here is of course the Aintree Race Course. At the east end of the racecourse is another swing bridge; this carries a main road and traffic lights are installed, but boat crews operate the bridge themselves. The canal turns north again and emerges into open countryside, although Maghull soon interrupts this with a series of swing bridges. On the offside, between bridges 13 and 14, there is a *PO, a bank and a variety of restaurants and takeaways.*

● **Melling**
Merseyside. Tel. The village stands on an isolated hillock at a safe distance from the big city. The church is a landmark in the area; it was built in the 15th C with rock from an adjacent quarry.

● **Maghull**
Merseyside. All services. A small town astride the canal, convenient for supplies.

St Andrew's Church Damfield Lane, Maghull, Liverpool L31 6DD. Just north of bridge 12A. Though separated from the rest of the town by a dual carriageway, it is well worth a visit. It was built in the late 19th C, but its style is in imitation of that of the 13th C to accord with the tiny 700-year-old chapel, known as Old St Andrew's, which sits in its grounds. To the west of 11B Drapers Bridge, close to the railway station, there is a pub and a useful parade of shops including a late closing store.

Pubs and Restaurants

◗✕ 1 **The Bootle Arms** Rock Lane, Melling, Liverpool L31 1EN (0151 526 2886; www. bootlearmspub.co.uk). Family-friendly pub serving real ale and food *daily 12.00-22.00 (Sun 21.00)*. Beer garden and children's play area. *Open 12.00-23.00 (Sun 22.00).*

◗ 2 **The Hare & Hounds** 53 Liverpool Road North, Maghull, Liverpool L31 2HP (0151 526 1447; www. emberinns.co.uk/the-hare-and-hounds-maghull). Near bridge 14. Real ales and traditional bar meals are available *daily 11.30-22.00* in this open-plan, roadside pub. Patio seating area, children welcome and Wi-Fi. *Open 11.30-00.00.*

◗ 3 **The Frank Hornby** 38 Eastway, Maghull L31 6BR (0151 520 4010; www.jdwetherspoon.com/pubs/all-pubs/england/merseyside/the-frank-hornby-liverpool). Named after the famous inventor

of Meccano and the Hornby model trains (and not totally devoid of examples of his work!) this suburban pub serves a good selection of real ales and food *08.00-23.00*. Family-friendly, patio. Real fires and Wi-Fi. *Open daily 08.00-23.30 (Fri-Sat 01.00).*

◗ 4 **Maghull Cask Café** 43 Liverpool Road South, Maghull, Liverpool L31 7BN (0151 526 3877). Micro-pub dispensing real ales, real cider, a range of bottled Continental beers and wine. Dog-friendly. Wi-Fi. *Open Thu-Sat 16.00-21.00 & Sun 12.00-21.00).*

◗ 5 **The Alt Park Hotel** Northway, Maghull, Liverpool L31 5JA (0151 526 4257; www.sizzlingpubs.co.uk/findapub/eastandwestmidlands/thealtparkhotelmaghull). With an emphasis on steaks, this family-oriented pub serves real ale and food all day. Sports TV. *Open 12.00-23.00 (Fri-Sat 00.00).*

NAVIGATIONAL NOTES

1 For those boaters heading into Liverpool, it is now possible to self-book passage onto and along the Liverpool Canal Link. *See* Navigational Notes on page 86.

2 All moveable bridges between Eldonian Village and Maghull are now boater-operated and assisted passage is no longer necessary or available.

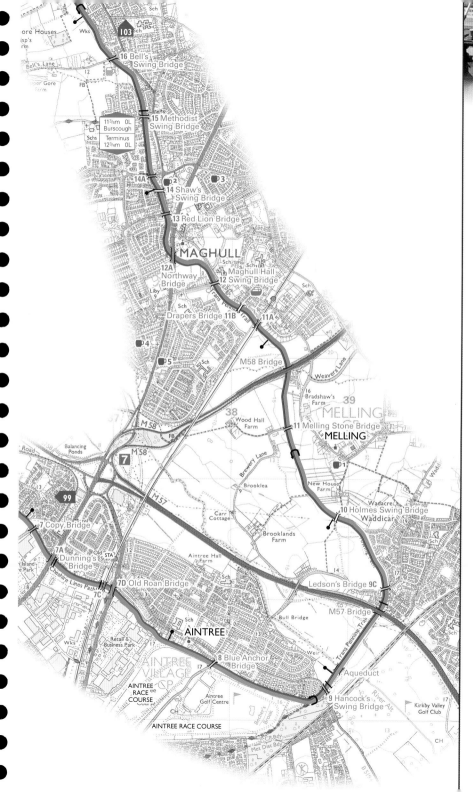

103

16 Bell's Swing Bridge

15 Methodist Swing Bridge

11³/₄m 0L
Burscough
Schs   Terminus
12³/₄m 0L

14A
14 Shaw's Swing Bridge

2

3

13 Red Lion Bridge

MAGHULL

12A Northway Bridge

Maghull Hall

12 Swing Bridge

Drapers Bridge 11B

11A

4

5

M58 Bridge

Bradshaw's Farm

39

MELLING

38   Wood Hall Farm

11 Melling Stone Bridge

MELLING

M58

7

M58

Brewery Lane

1

99

Brookrea

New House Farm

10 Holmes Swing Bridge

Wadacre

Waddicar

7 Copy Bridge

Carr Cottage

Brooklands Farm

7A Dunning's Bridge

7D Old Roan Bridge

7C

Ledson's Bridge 9C

M57 Bridge

AINTREE

8 Blue Anchor Bridge

Bull Bridge

Aqueduct

AINTREE VILLAGE CP

AINTREE RACE COURSE

Aintree Golf Centre

Weir

9 Hancock's Swing Bridge

Kirkby Valley Golf Club

AINTREE RACE COURSE

Haskayne

The canal now enters continuous open countryside, which soon establishes itself as extremely flat and intensively cultivated lowlands: indeed it is more akin to Cambridgeshire or Lincolnshire than to the rest of Lancashire. However, it is pleasant enough and the canal forms one of its more important features – a view which is borne out by the large number of people usually to be seen walking and boating upon it, as well as the hundreds of anglers enjoying their sport in this well-stocked length of canal. As if in compensation for the unexciting landscape, the traveller is offered a truly astonishing number (and variety) of pubs on or near the canal, all the way from Lydiate to Wigan. The digging of the canal is reputed to have commenced in the low cutting between bridges 24 and 25, and this clearly provided an excellent source of stone for local bridges.

Haskayne
Lancs. PO box. There are just two pretty houses here: the old post office and a thatched cottage opposite. The remainder of the village sprawls away from the navigation but there is no sign of a church. Within the village, several buildings date from 17th C, including a cruck-framed cottage. Clad in a mix of brick and stone, with a thatched roof, parts of the four crucks are visible in the interior walls. Look out for two original cast iron 'milestones' – triangular in section – along this section of the towpath.

FERTILE RELIEF

This was once an area of low lying marshland, much of it below sea level and, consequently, thinly populated. The original course of the River Douglas ran close by, joining the sea near Southport. At some point its course was blocked – possibly by giant sand dunes thrown up by a great storm – and it found a new, northern mouth in the Ribble estuary, leaving behind the area known today as Martin Mere. This once extended to 15 square miles but in 1787 Thomas Eccleston of Scarisbrick Hall, with the help of John Gilbert, set about draining it for agricultural use (it was Gilbert who, as agent to the Duke of Bridgewater, enlisted James Brindley's help in constructing Britain's first major canal). Once drained the mere required vast quantities of manure to raise its fertility for crop production. 'Night soil' was shipped in along the canal from the large conurbations of Liverpool and Wigan and off-loaded at a series of small wharfs, some still visible today. Part of the mere remains undrained, a haven for migrating geese.

Pubs and Restaurants

1 The Scotch Piper Southport Road, Lydiate, Liverpool L31 4HD (0151 526 2207). An attractive old world, thatched pub dispensing real ales and good conversation in generous measure. No large (or small) screen TV, fruit machines or juke boxes. Dog- and family-friendly, outside seating. Traditional pub games, newspapers, real fires and Wi-Fi. *Open 12.00-00.00.*

2 The King's Arms Hotel 1 Delph Lane, Haskayne (01704 840033). Friendly, heritage pub – with a real community feel – serving a rotating range of real ales. Dog- and child-friendly, outside seating. *Open daily 14.00-00.00 (Sat-Sun 12.00).*

3 The Ship 6 Rosemary Lane, Haskayne, Ormskirk L39 7JP (01704 840077; www.theshipinnhaskayne.com). A well-known canal pub with a garden and waterside terrace serving real ale. Excellent fresh food served in a homely, dark-beamed bar tastefully decorated with horse brasses available – including seafood, steaks and pasta – *daily 12.00-20.00.* Children welcome. Reputed to be the first pub on the canal, which was started in the adjacent cutting. *Regular* live music, traditional pub games garden and play area. Dog-friendly and open fires. Wi-Fi. *Open 12.00-23.00.*

4 The Saracen's Head 100 Summerwood Lane, Halsall, Ormskirk L39 8RH (01704 840204; www.thesaracensheadhalsall.co.uk). Real ales together with a wide range of food served *Mon-Sat L and E & Sun 12.00-19.45.* Family-friendly, garden. Newspapers and Wi-Fi. B&B. *Open 11.30-00.00.*

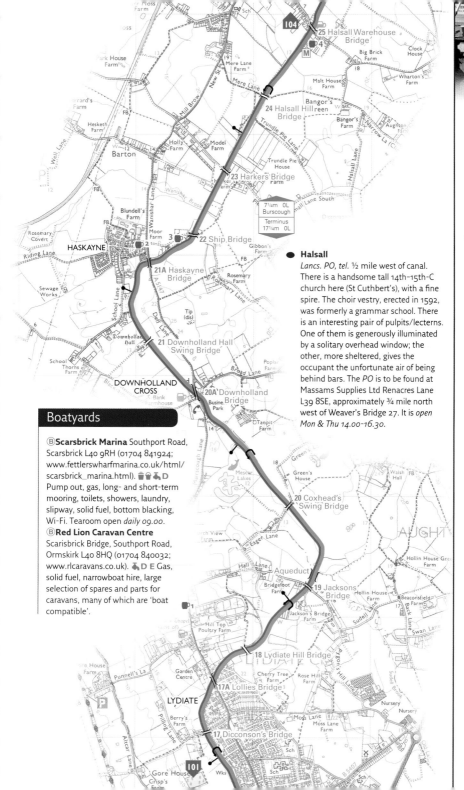

104
25 Halsall Warehouse Bridge
M **4**
Big Brick Farm
Clock House
Wharton's Farm
Malt House Farm
Bangor's Farm
24 Halsall Hillreen Bridge
Bangor's Farm
Narrow La (Clo
Aughton

Mere Lane Farm
New St
Mere Lane
Mill Brow

Trundle Pie Lane
Trundle Pie House
23 Harkers Bridge Farm

7¼m 0L
Burscough
Terminus
17¼m 0L

Gibbon's Farm
FB

22 Ship Bridge

Model Farm
Holly Farm
Barton
Moor Farm
3 **22** Ship Bridge
Blundell's Farm
2
21A Haskayne Bridge
HASKAYNE
Rosemary Lane
Rosemary Farm

Riding Lane
Sewage Works
Downholland Hall
21 Downholland Hall Swing Bridge
Tip (dis)
Dell Lane

School Thorns Farm
DOWNHOLLAND CROSS
Poplar Farm
Broad Lane
Bank Farmhouse
20A Downholland Bridge
Busine Park
Tanpit Farm

Boatyards

Ⓑ**Scarsbrick Marina** Southport Road, Scarsbrick L40 9RH (01704 841924; www.fettlerswharfmarina.co.uk/html/scarsbrick_marina.html). 🚽🚿⚓D Pump out, gas, long- and short-term mooring, toilets, showers, laundry, slipway, solid fuel, bottom blacking, Wi-Fi. Tearoom open *daily 09.00*.

Ⓑ**Red Lion Caravan Centre** Scarisbrick Bridge, Southport Road, Ormskirk L40 8HQ (01704 840032; www.rlcaravans.co.uk). ⚓D E Gas, solid fuel, narrowboat hire, large selection of spares and parts for caravans, many of which are 'boat compatible'.

● **Halsall**
Lancs. PO, tel. ½ mile west of canal. There is a handsome tall 14th-15th-C church here (St Cuthbert's), with a fine spire. The choir vestry, erected in 1592, was formerly a grammar school. There is an interesting pair of pulpits/lecterns. One of them is generously illuminated by a solitary overhead window; the other, more sheltered, gives the occupant the unfortunate air of being behind bars. The *PO* is to be found at Massams Supplies Ltd Renacres Lane L39 8SE, approximately ¾ mile north west of Weaver's Bridge 27. It is open *Mon & Thu 14.00-16.30.*

Mescar Lakes
Green's House
Green's House
Walsh Hall
FB

20 Coxhead's Swing Bridge
Hollin House Green Farm
AUGHT

Eager Lane
Hall Lane
Aqueduct
Bridgefoot Farm
19 Jacksons Bridge
Hollin House Farm
Beaconsfield Farm
Sudell Lane
Back Lane
Swan Lane
Jackson's Bridge Farm
1
Hill Top Poultry Farm

18 Lydiate Hill Bridge
LYDIATE
Ⓟ
Cherry Tree Farm
Rose Hill Farm
Nursery
Nursery
Garden Centre
Punnell's La
17A Lollies Bridge
Berry's Farm
LYDIATE
Pilling Lane
Moss Lane Farm
Moss Lane Farm
Sch

17 Dicconson's Bridge
Altcar Lane
Gore House
Crisp's
101
Wks
Sch
Sch

Burscough

On now past a massive caravan site on one side and attractive woods containing the private Scarisbrick Hall on the other; then out again into the open flatlands. An attractively produced information board, at the north end of bridge 27A, offers a fascinating insight into the history of the parish and the past habitation of the hall. The Southport–Manchester line converges from the north west; it runs near the canal all the way into Wigan, and has some wonderfully remote stations. A flurry of swing bridges brings the canal into Burscough; just beyond is the junction with the Rufford Branch.

● **Burscough**
Lancs. PO, tel, stores, chemist, bank, hardware, tool hire, fish & chips, takeaways, off-licence, library, garage, stations. Formerly a canal village and a staging post on the one-time Wigan-Liverpool 'packet boat' run, this place attaches more significance nowadays to the benefits of road and rail transport. It still boasts two stations (one is on the Preston-Liverpool line) and suffers from heavy through traffic. A very convenient place for taking on provisions. Recent developments around the old wharf have added a range of amenities and generally brought an area of redundant buildings back to life – an initiative that should be applauded. They include craft and food emporiums, an arts centre and a music school. There is a useful cycle shop just north of Bridge 32A – Jack Parker Cycles 62-64 Liverpool Road North, Burscough L40 4BY (01704 892442 www.jackparkercycles.org.uk). *Open Mon-Sat 09.00-17.30 (not Wed).*

Boatyards

Ⓑ**Lathom Marina** The Workshop, Crabtree Lane, Burscough, Ormskirk L40 0RW (01704 894782). Winter storage, slipway, chandlery, boat and engine sales and repairs, salvage, canopy manufacture and repairs.
Ⓑ**The Burscough Boat Trading Ltd** Unit 5, Osprey Place, Guys Industrial Estate North, Burscough L40 8TG (01704 891675/897762; www.burscoughboats.com). Boat building and fitting out, self-drive boat hire and a variety of cruises from Bridge 32A.

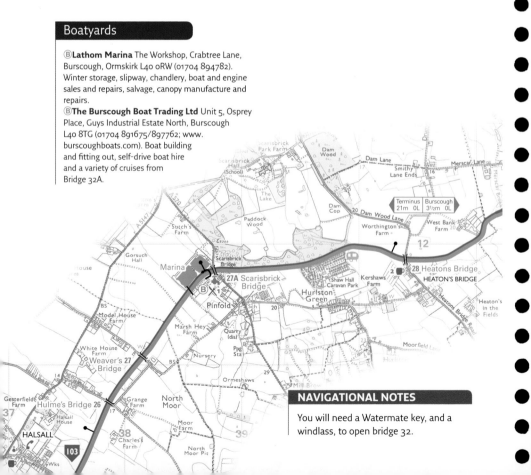

NAVIGATIONAL NOTES

You will need a Watermate key, and a windlass, to open bridge 32.

Pubs and Restaurants

X⚲ 1 Nellie Indian Restaurant 540 Southport Road, Scarisbrick L40 8HQ (01704 841222/941333; www.nellieonline.co.uk/restaurant). Formerly the Red Lion, now turned into a good, reasonably priced Indian restaurant. *Open 17.30-23.00 (Sat-Sun 16.00).*

▶X⚲ 2 Heatons Bridge Inn 2 Heatons Bridge Road, Scarisbrick L40 8JG (01704 840549). Friendly unspoilt canalside pub, at bridge 28. Real ales together with inexpensive, traditional pub food served *Wed-Sat L and E & Sun-Mon 12.00-16.00.* Dog- and child-friendly, garden. Quiz and bingo *Tue.* Traditional pub games, newspapers and Wi-Fi. Camping. *Open 12.00-00.00.*

▶X 3 The Farmers Arms 36 New Lane, Burscough L40 8JA (01704 896021; www.farmersarmsburscough. co.uk). A bright, friendly pub of great character with an open fire, serving real ale. Full à la carte menu together with a wide and interesting range of bar food *Tue-Sun 12.00-20.00 (Fri-Sat 20.30)* served in nicely furnished surroundings. Child- and dog-friendly. Open fires, large-screen TV, traditional pub games and Wi-Fi. Moorings and quiz *Wed. Open 12.00-00.00*

▶ 4 The Slipway 48 Crabtree Lane, Burscough L40 0RN (01704 895000). Attractive canalside setting (beside bridge 32) for this pub serving real ales and food *daily Mon-Fri L and E & Sat-Sun 12.00-20.00 (Sun 19.00).* Dog- and child-friendly, large garden. Live music *Sat.* Real fires, sports TV and Wi-Fi. Camping. *Open daily 12.00-23.00 (Fri-Sat 00.00).*

▶ 5 The Bridge 73 Liverpool Road North, Burscough L40 0SA (01704 891541). Traditional village pub serving real ale and bar snacks. Children welcome, outside seating area. Traditional pub games and sports TV. *Regular* live music. *Open Mon-Thu 16.00-23.00 & Fri-Sun 12.00-02.00 (Sun 23.00).*

▶X 6 The Old Packet House 29 Liverpool Road North, Burscough L40 5TN (01704 807330; www. oldpackethouse.com). Complete with a series of old prints of Burscough, this pub dispenses real ale and food *Mon-Fri L and E & Sat-Sun 12.00-20.00 (Sun 19.00).* Dog- and family-friendly, canalside garden. *Occasional* live music and quiz *Thu.* Wi-Fi. *Open Mon-Sat 12.00-23.00 (Fri-Sat 00.00) & Sun 12.00-22.30.*

▶X 7 The Hop Vine Liverpool Road North, Burscough L40 4BY (01704 893799; www. thehopvinepub.co.uk). Popular brew-pub serving its own real ales and guests, together with appetising food *Mon-Sat L and E and all day Sun.* Children welcome, outside seating area and open fires. Quiz *Tue. Occasional* live music. *Open Mon-Sat 10.30-00.00 (Fri-Sat 00.30) & Sun 10.30-23.00.*

X 8 The New Ponderosa Café 3 Mart Lane Burscough L40 0SD (07968 688156). Unpretentious and inexpensive café serving breakfasts, snacks, tea, coffee and sandwiches. *Open Mon-Sat 07.00-13.00.*

X 9 Infusions Café Bistro 2-4 Orrell, Burscough L40 0SQ (01704 893356; www.infusionscafebistro. com). Family-run coffee shop serving a tasty range of paninis, jacket potatoes, sandwiches, wraps, cakes, coffees, teas, smoothies and milk shakes. Recently a tasty selection of home-cooked meals, including

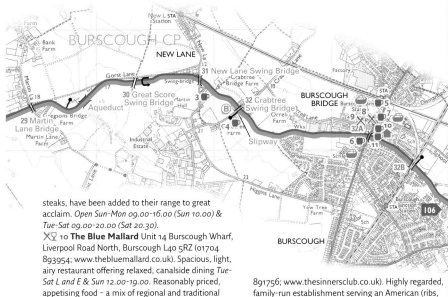

steaks, have been added to their range to great acclaim. *Open Sun-Mon 09.00-16.00 (Sun 10.00) & Tue-Sat 09.00-20.00 (Sat 20.30).*

X⚲ 10 The Blue Mallard Unit 14 Burscough Wharf, Liverpool Road North, Burscough L40 5RZ (01704 893954; www.thebluemallard.co.uk). Spacious, light, airy restaurant offering relaxed, canalside dining *Tue-Sat L and E & Sun 12.00-19.00.* Reasonably priced, appetising food – a mix of regional and traditional dishes – served by friendly staff. Visit website for details of special evenings.

X⚲ 11 The Sinners Club Burscough Wharf, Liverpool Road North, Burscough L40 5RZ (01704 891756; www.thesinnersclub.co.uk). Highly regarded, family-run establishment serving an American (ribs, fries and burgers – to name but a few dishes) menu *Tue-Fri 16.30-21.00 & Sat-Sun 12.00-21.15 (Sun 19.45).* Friendly staff, cool blues and mellow rock. *Open Tue-Fri 16.30 'til late & Sat-Sun 12.00 'til late.*

105

Parbold and Rufford

The Rufford Branch leaves the Leeds & Liverpool main line just east of Burscough, through an imposing arched bridge dated 1816. A canal settlement, now a conservation area, surrounds the top lock and the roomy dry dock here (also *showers* and the usual *facilities*). The locks come thick and fast to begin with, as the canal falls through the fertile and gently sloping farmland towards the distant Ribble estuary and a connection with the Lancaster Canal. The country is generally quiet, flat and unspectacular. At times the busy A59 intrudes noisily. There is a useful *farm shop* (01704 892599) on this road just west of Bridge 5A *open daily 09.00-18.00 (Sat-Sun 17.00)*. East of the junction with the Rufford Branch, the canal meanders through the flat countryside to the village of Parbold with its ancient sail-less windmill. Here the canal crosses the River Douglas and then joins the Douglas Valley, a pretty, narrow wooded valley which the canal shares with the railway. Appley Lock is reached: there are two locks alongside, now semi-derelict and therefore only the lock on the main line is in operation. The shallower locks were once used as a navigable sidepond for boats passing in opposite directions. **As with all subsequent locks, the gates should be closed and the paddles lowered and padlocked after use to combat vandalism and wastage of water.**

NAVIGATIONAL NOTES

You will need a Watermate key to open bridges 33 and 36 and a windlass and Watermate key to operate Lock 1 and Bridge 1 on the Rufford Branch.

Map labels

109
Marina
Marina 7 Rufford Lock
Holland Meadow
6 Marsh Meadow Swing Bridge
Marsh Moss Bridge
Kiln Farm
Sluice Lane
Towing Path
Causeway Farm
Marsh Moss
NTL
5A Canal Bridge
White Dial Farm
Springwell Farm
Low Meadow
FB
Prescott's Farm
Autocross Circuit
FB
5 Prescott Bridge
Anchor Farm
Chicken Lock 6
Wham Bridge
4 Baldwins Bridge
Saulthouse Farm
Lathom's Farm
3 German's Bridge
5 German's Lock
6
cough idge
Black Brook
Warper's Moss
Eller Brook
Wham Ditch
Hoscar Moss
Meadow Lane
Ws
New Sutch House Farm
Old Sutch House
4 Moss Lock
Sutch Lane
Bleak Hall Farm
Bleak Lane
2A
6¾m 8L Tarleton
105
3 Runnel Brow Lock
HOSCAR
Hoscar Moss Road
Frog Lane
STA
2 Runnel Brow Bridge
1 Bridge
1 Lathom Locks
Henry's Farm
1 Junction Bridge
Carr Lane Farm
33 Glovers Swing Bridge
Towing Path
5209
Terminus 24½m 0L   Wigan 10½m 6L
Ring-o'-Bells Bridge 34
Ring o'Bells Moss Bridge 35
Briars Hall Farm
45
Duttons Farm
Lowry Hill
Taylor's Farm
46
Round Thorn
Aqueduct 35A
Moss Bridge
Hollowford Lane
47
36 Spencer's Swing Bridge
Course Lane
37
Sewage Works
Rigby's Farm
37A
Deans La
Back Lane
Newburgh
PO
Nursery
Lawrensons
Cross (restored) FB
Giant's Hall
STA
48
37B
5
Parbold Bridge 37D
37C
6
Boundary Farm
Doug Far
32

Parbold

Lancs. PO, tel, stores, chemist, bank, butcher, hardware, delicatessen, takeaways, fish & chips, greengrocer, off-licence, library, garage, station. Parbold is prettiest near the canal bridge, where the brick tower of the old windmill is complemented by an equally attractive pub. Unfortunately the rest of the village is being engulfed by acres of new housing. Local landmarks are the tall spires of Parbold's two churches, and Ashurst's Beacon high on a hill to the south. The latter was built in 1798 by Sir William Ashurst in anticipation of an invasion by the French. The beacon was intended as a local warning sign.

Douglas Navigation

The little River Douglas, or Asland, was made navigable in the first half of the 17th C, well before the great spate of canal construction. It provided the Wigan coalfield with a useful outlet to the tidal River Ribble, from which the cargoes could be shipped over to Preston or along the coast. When the Leeds & Liverpool Canal was built, the old river navigation became superfluous. The new company constructed their own branch to the Ribble estuary (the Rufford Branch). Between Parbold and Gathurst it is possible to find many traces of the old navigation, including several locks.

Pubs and Restaurants

♣✕ 1 **The Ship Inn** 4 Wheat Lane, Lathom L40 4BX (01704 893117; www.shipatlathom.co.uk). Near second lock down, on Rufford Branch. An old canal pub formerly known as the 'Blood Tub' – black puddings were once made here, and a bucket of pig's blood could be exchanged for a pint of beer. Busy, welcoming, comfortable with real ales and excellent food served *daily 12.00-21.00 (Sun 20.00)*. Family-friendly, garden, open fires and Wi-Fi. *Open daily 12.00-00.00 (Sun 23.30).*

♣✕ 2 **The Ring O'Bells** Ring O'Bells Lane, Lathom L40 5TF (01704 893157; www.ainscoughs.co.uk/ The-Ring-O-Bells/welcome-to-the-ringo-bells.html). Canalside at bridge 34. Tastefully modernised country pub serving an interesting variety of bar meals *daily Mon-Fri L and E & Sat-Sun 12.00-21.00 (Sun 20.00)*. Dog- and child-friendly, garden. Wi-Fi. Quiz *Thu*. *Open daily 11.00-23.00 (Fri-Sat 00.00).*

✕ 3 **Yours is the Earth** 2 Mill Lane, Parbold WN8 7NW (01257 462999; www.yoursistheearth.co.uk). Canalside, bridge 37. Traditional chintzy tearoom serving coffee, lunch and tea. Tasty ice creams. All food home-made including soups and cakes. *Open Mon-Sat 10.00-17.00 (Sat 10.30) & Sun 10.30-16.30.*

♣✕ 4 **The Windmill Hotel** 3 Mill Lane, Parbold WN8 7NW (01257 462935; www.thewindmillparbold.co.uk). Old village local dispensing real ale, and an imaginative selection of traditional, home-cooked food *Mon-Fri L and E & Sat-Sun 12.00-21.00 (Sun 20.00)*. Dog- and family-friendly, outside seating. The pub is the brewery tap for the nearby Windmill Brewery. *Open Mon-Sat 12.00-23.00 (Fri-Sat 23.30) & Sun 12.00-22.30.*

♣ 5 **The Railway Hotel** 1 Station Road, Parbold WN8 7NU (01257 462917; www.railwayhotelparbold.co.uk). Friendlyy, welcoming pub, serving real ales together with hot pies and mugs of tea and coffee. Dog-, boater-, rambler- and family-friendly, outside seating. Traditional pub games, newspapers, real fires, sports TV and Wi-Fi. *Occasional* live music. *Open Mon-Thu 17.00-23.00 & Fri-Sun 12.00-23.30 (Sun 22.30).*

♣✕ 6 **The Stocks Tavern** 16 Alder Lane, Parbold WN8 7NN (01257 462874; www.thestockstavern. co.uk). Fine, traditional country pub, dating from 1810 and recently refurbished, serving real ales and generous portions of food *Mon-Fri L and E & Sat-Sun 12.00-21.00 (Sun 20.00)*. Family friendly, garden. *Open 12.00-23.00 (Sun 22.30).*

♣✕ 7 **The Wayfarer** 1–3 Alder Lane, Parbold WN8 7NL (01257 464600; www.wayfarerparbold.co.uk). Dating back to before 1668 this cosy pub-cum-restaurant serves real ales (at least one from its own brewhouse) and food *Mon-Fri L and E & Sat-Sun 12.00-21.30 (Sun 20.30)*. Dog- and family-friendly, garden. Wi-Fi. *Open Mon-Fri L and E & Sat-Sun 12.00-22.00.*

♣✕ 8 **The Boathouse** Mill Lane, Appley Bridge WN6 9DA (01257 252456; www.appleybridgeboathouse. com). Modern, waterside pub serving real ale and food *Tue-Sat L and E & Sun 12.00-19.00*. Dog- and child-friendly, garden. Moorings. *Open Tue-Sat 11.30-22.30 (Fri-Sat 23.30) & Sun 12.00-22.00.*

♣ 9 **The Wheatsheaf** 287 Miles Lane, Appley Bridge WN6 9DQ (01257 252299). Village pub serving real ales and bar snacks (including homemade pizzas). Dog- and family-friendly, garden. Quiz *Tue. Occasional* weekend live music. Wi-Fi. *Open Mon-Fri 15.00-23.00 & Sat-Sun 12.00-23.00 (Sun 22.30).*

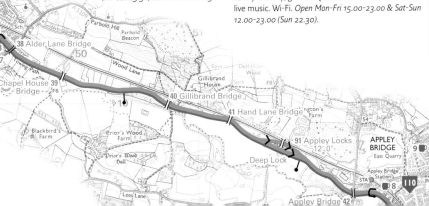

▌Tarleton

A line of trees and the spire of Rufford church are followed by the beautiful Rufford Old Hall, on the west bank. Then the waterway leads back out into open, flat and fairly featureless countryside, with the River Douglas never far away but initially out of sight. Beside Spark Bridge 8A there are *facilities including a pump out, showers and a toilet.* At Sollom there used to be a lock, but now it is no more. This is where the canal turns into the old course of the River Douglas, and it twists and turns as though to prove it. The 'new' course of the Douglas (which was once navigable from the sea right up to Wigan) comes alongside the canal at the busy road bridge near Bank Hall, a house hidden by trees. From here it is only a short distance to the final swing bridge and Tarleton Lock, where the canal connects with the tidal River Douglas – which in turn flows into the River Ribble near Preston forming the newly opened Ribble Link with the Lancaster Canal.

NAVIGATIONAL NOTES

1 Navigators entering the Rufford Branch canal from the sea should remember that they will need Watermate key – as well as a windlass – to open the locks up the branch. Both available from James Mayor's boatyard. See page 101.

2 Those who wish to navigate the Ribble Link should visit www.canalrivertrust.org.uk/enjoy-the-waterways/boating/planning-your-boat-trip/booking-your-passage-online to book a passage and download the relevant information. Bookings can also be made (and the guidance notes obtained) by telephoning 0303 040 4040. *Passage can be booked up some time ahead, for this popular waterway, so advanced planning is necessary. Passage is free to CRT long term licence holders. Operating times are dictated by tides in the Ribble estuary, but a journey can be made Easter–Oct during daylight hours, Nov–Easter on request.* The staircase and sea lock are manned, and the link will operate one way each day. There is no mooring on the Link. As the River Ribble is tidal, boats should carry, *as a minimum*: anchor, chain and warp, VHF radio or mobile phone, lifejackets for all on board, fire fighting equipment, coastal flares. Your engine must be sufficiently powerful to cope with tidal conditions, and be sure to check that your boat insurance covers tidal waters.

3 If you need help or advice while on the River Ribble, call Preston Riversway Control on VHF channel 16 (working on channel 14), or telephone 01772 726871.

4 If you wish to visit Preston Marina they can be contacted on 01772 733585, VHF channels 80 & 37. For detailed visiting information see www.prestonmarina.co.uk where you can download pilotage, berthing and locking details.

5 *At least 24hrs notice of a booking cancellation must be given to CRT or a fee will be charged.*

Rufford

Lancs. PO box, tel, chemist, stores, garage, station. The church is a small Italianate Victorian building containing many monuments to the Heskeths who owned Rufford Hall for several centuries; obviously a prolific family, judging by one large sculpture depicting a brood of 11 children, dated c.1458. The family now resides in Northamptonshire. *Gas and coal* are available in the garage where there is a very small *stores*.

Rufford Old Hall NT 200 Liverpool Road, Rufford L40 1SG (01704 821254; www.nationaltrust.org.uk). On the west bank of the canal. A medieval timber-framed mansion with Jacobean extensions given to the National Trust in 1936. The interior is magnificently decorated and furnished in period style, especially the great hall with its hammerbeam roof and 15th-C intricately carved movable screen – one of the few still intact in England. The Hall also houses a folk museum and an exhibition. Gardens and tearoom. *House open daily mid Mar–Oct 11.00– 17.00 (except Thu and Fri). Gardens as per house.* Charge.

Note: although the Hall is beside the waterway, it is not possible to enter the grounds directly from the canal. Navigators should therefore tie up near bridge 8, walk up to the village and turn left at the main road. The entrance is a few hundred yards along the wall on the left.

Tarleton

Lancs. PO, tel, stores, butcher, baker, chemist, delicatessen, hardware, takeaways, off-licence, fish & chips, library, garage. A large village luckily avoided by the A59 road. There are some useful *shops* in the village centre and along the road south past the Cock & Bottle.

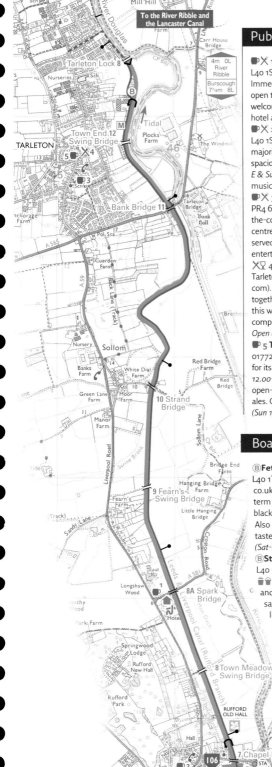

Pubs and Restaurants

◗▶╳ 1 **The Rufford Arms** 380 Liverpool Road, Rufford L40 1SQ (01704 822040; www.ruffordarms.com). Immediately west of bridge 8A. Restaurant with a bar open to diners serving reasonably priced food. Children welcome. *Open L and E and all day Sat and Sun*. Private hotel accommodation – bookings via the website. Wi-Fi.

◗▶╳ 2 **The Hesketh Arms** 81 Liverpool Road, Rufford L40 1SB (01704 821002). In the centre of the village, majoring on beers from local microbreweries, this spacious hostelry serves real ale and food *Mon-Sat L and E & Sun 12.00-20.00*. Family-friendly, garden. *Monthly* live music and quiz *Tue*. *Open 12.00-23.00 (Fri-Sat 00.00)*.

◗▶╳ 3 **The Cock & Bottle** 70 Church Road, Tarleton PR4 6UP (01772 812518; www.thwaitespubs.co.uk/the-cock-and-bottle-tarleton). West of bridge 12. Village-centre pub dispensing real ale. Bar snacks and meals served *daily L and E*. Garden, sports TV and *regular* live entertainment. *Open 12.00*.

╳♀ 4 **Whittles Farm Restaurant** 94 Church Road, Tarleton PR4 6UP (01772 817435; www.whittlesfarm.com). Light bites, à la carte and table d'hôte menus, together with *Sun* specials are all within the repertoire of this welcoming restaurant, set in an upmarket shopping complex. Booking recommended. Limited *Mon* menu. *Open daily 10.00-16.30 (Sun 11.00)*.

◗▶ 5 **The Village Inn** Mark Square, Tarleton PR4 6TU 01772 815959; www.villageinntarleton.co.uk). Known for its excellent food – *available Mon-Sat L and E & Sun 12.00-19.00* – served in generous portions, this modern, open-plan pub (also known as the Lord Lilford) serves real ales. Open fire and courtyard seating. *Open 12.00-23.00 (Sun 19.00)*.

Boatyards

Ⓑ**Fettlers Wharf Marina** 20 Station Road, Rufford L40 1TB (01704 821197; www.fettlerswharfmarina.co.uk). 🚿🛒🛢D Pump out, gas, long- and short-term mooring, boat sales, slipway, bottom blacking, solid fuel, toilets, showers, laundry, Wi-Fi. Also ╳ **Tastebuds Café** (01704 822888; www.tastebudsatthewharf.co.uk) *open daily 09.00-16.30 (Sat-Sun 17.00)*

Ⓑ**St Mary's Marina** Diamond Jubilee Road, Rufford L40 1TD (01704 823697; www.stmarysmarina.co.uk). 🚿🛒🛢D Pump out, slipway, hard standing, repairs and servicing, long- and short-term mooring, boat sales, boat painting, toilets and showers, laundrette, library service and visiting PO *Tue 10.00-15.00*. Also ╳ **The Boathouse Brasserie** (01704 822458; www.theboathouserufford.co.uk) *open daily 09.30-17.00*.

Ⓑ**James Mayor** The Boatyard, Tarleton PR4 6HD (01704 812250/07885 762347; www. tarletonboatyard.com). 🛢 D E Overnight mooring, long-term mooring, winter storage, slipway up to 65 feet, 3-ton crane, boat transportation, boat and engine sales, engine repairs, showers, toilets.

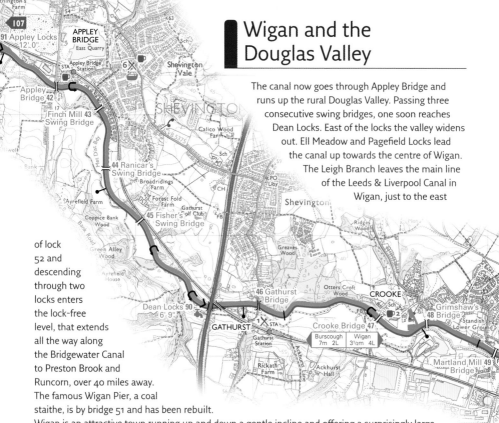

Wigan and the Douglas Valley

The canal now goes through Appley Bridge and runs up the rural Douglas Valley. Passing three consecutive swing bridges, one soon reaches Dean Locks. East of the locks the valley widens out. Ell Meadow and Pagefield Locks lead the canal up towards the centre of Wigan. The Leigh Branch leaves the main line of the Leeds & Liverpool Canal in Wigan, just to the east of lock 52 and descending through two locks enters the lock-free level, that extends all the way along the Bridgewater Canal to Preston Brook and Runcorn, over 40 miles away. The famous Wigan Pier, a coal staithe, is by bridge 51 and has been rebuilt.

Wigan is an attractive town running up and down a gentle incline and offering a surprisingly large range of shops within a short walk of the waterway. There are several shopping arcades, both old and new, and all the well-known retail outlets are represented. Many of the older buildings employ a deep red, terracotta brick and the municipal buildings, particularly the town hall, speak of a past industrial prosperity. The two railway stations (one on the West Coast Mainline) and conveniently placed within 50 yards of one another, offer easy access to all parts of the country.

Pubs and Restaurants

✕🍷 1 **The Baby Elephant** 162 Gathurst Lane, Gathurst, Shevington WN6 8HZ (01257 251155; www. babarelephant.co.uk/shevington.html). Formerly the Navigation Inn, now a restaurant serving contemporary Asian cuisine and tapas. Takeaway service. *Open daily 17.30-23.00 (Sat-Sun 15.00).*

🍺 2 **The Crooke Hall Inn** Crooke, Standish Lower Ground, Wigan WN6 8LR (01942 236088; www. allgatesbrewery.com/pubs/crooke-hall-inn). Cosy village pub, with friendly atmosphere, in the pretty Douglas Valley serving a large selection of real ales and real cider. Food is available *daily 12.00-20.00 (Mon-Tue 15.00 during winter)*. Dog- and child-friendly *(until 21.00)* garden. *Occasional* live music. Traditional pub games, newspapers, sports TV and Wi-Fi. *Open 12.00-23.00 (Fri 00.00).*

🍺 3 **The Moon Under Water** 5-7a Market Place, Wigan WN1 1PE (01942 323437; www.jdwetherspoon. co.uk/home/pubs/the-moon-under-water-wigan).

Real ale dispensed in a busy, town centre, ex-building society premises. Food available *daily from 08.00*. Children welcome, large-screen TV and Wi-Fi. *Open daily 08.00-00.00 (Fri-Sat 01.00).*

🍺 4 **Wigan Central Arch** No. 1 & 2, Queen Street, Wigan WN3 4DY (01942 246425; www.wigancentral.bar/ index.html). Award-winning pub dispensing a wide range of British and Continental bottled beers, real ales and a selection of rotating draught ciders: delightful and cosy. Bar snacks available. Dog-friendly. Quiz *Mon & Sun* live music. Wi-Fi. *Open Mon-Thu 12.00-23.00; Fri-Sat 12.00-00.00 (Sat 11.00) & Sun 12.00-22.30.*

🍺 5 **The Anvil** Dorning Street, Wigan WN1 1ND (01942 239444; www.allgatesbrewery.com/pubs/the-anvil). Popular town-centre hostelry serving an excellent range of real ales together with real cider. Also draught and bottled continental beers. Sports TV and outside seating area – no children. *Open Mon-Sat 11.00-23.00 & Sun 12.00-22.30.*

● **Appley Bridge**
Lancs. PO, tel, stores, station. Affluent, canalside hamlet with an attractive coffee shop – ✕ 6 **My Coffee** 272c Miles Lane WN6 9JA (07447 009491) *open Wed-Sun 08.30-15.30.*

● **Wigan**
Gt Manchester. All services. A large, heavily industrialised town whose skyline is now a mixture of industrial chimneys and towering concrete blocks of offices and flats. There is a covered market hall in the traditional mould, and an Olympic-size swimming pool.
All Saints Church 192 Atherton Road, Hindley, Wigan WN2 3XA (www.wiganparishchurch.org). A very large and impressive parish church surrounded by beautiful rose gardens. There are several fine stained-glass windows, including a charming William Morris example depicting St Christopher.
Museum of Wigan Life 41 Library Street, Wigan WN1 1NU (01942 828128; www.wigan.gov.uk/ Resident/Museums-archives/Museum-of-Wigan-Life/visiting-the-museum.aspx). Lively displays depicting everything from sport to World Wars. *Open Mon-Wed & Sat 10.00-14.00 & Thu-Fri 12.00-17.00.*
Trencherfield Mill Heritage Way, Wigan WN3 4EF

(01942 828128/777566.; www.wigan.gov.uk/ Resident/Museums-archives/Trencherfield-Mill-Engine.aspx). Although converted to apartments, the engine shed – home to probably the largest working steam-powered mill in Europe, installed in 1907 when the mill was constructed – has been retained. The engine is in beautifully restored condition; its operators are very knowledgeable and there is an audio-visual presentation linked to some clever lighting that shows off the engine to its best. There is also a range of working cotton spinning machinery which is used to demonstrate the processes that were carried out at this mill. This is a marvellous opportunity to get to grips with what made this area such a hub of the industrial revolution: a revolution whose successful was, to a large extent, dependant upon the presence of the Leeds and Liverpool Canal. *Open Sun 11.00* for tours and the engine is in steam *alternate Sun* – visit website for details. Charge.
Tourist Information Wigan Library, The Wiend, Wigan WN1 1NH (01942 828128; www.wigan.gov. uk/Resident/Libraries/Wigan-Library.aspx). Helpful library staff will try to assist with any enquiries. *Open Mon-Sat 09.00-17.00 (Sat 14.00).*

NAVIGATIONAL NOTES

1 You will need a Watermate key to open Bridge 43; however Bridges 43-45 are usually left open.
2 The locks (nos 85-1) between Wigan and Leeds are 60ft long and cannot accommodate a full-length narrowboat.

3 You will require a Canal & River Trust handcuff key.
4 CRT have a dry dock for hire in Wigan. Contact 0303 040 4040; www. canalrivertrust.org.uk/contact-us/ways-to-contact-us for further details.
5 *See* Navigational Notes on page 113

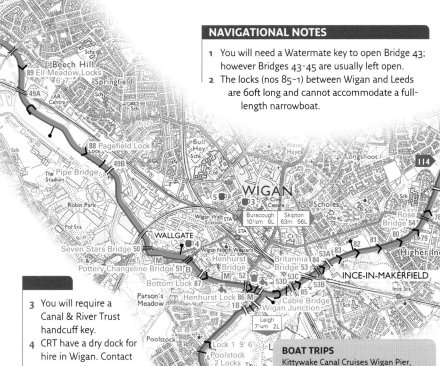

BOAT TRIPS

Kittywake Canal Cruises Wigan Pier, Wallgate, Wigan WN3 4EU (01942 836885/07850 562043; www.kittywake. co.uk) operate public and charter trips from No1 Terminal Building, near Wigan Pier. Visit their website or telephone for further details.

Plank Lane

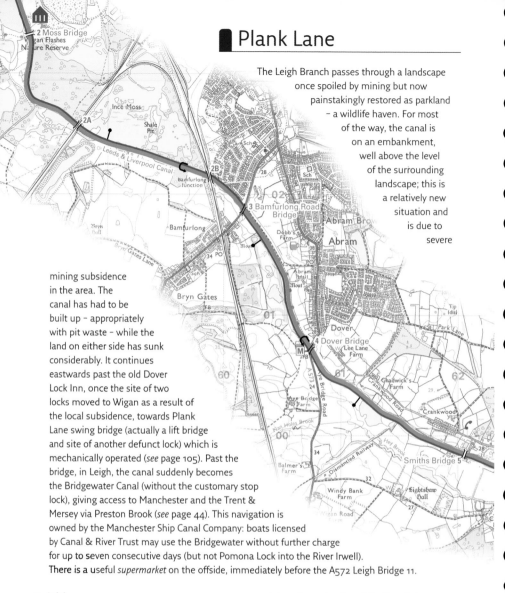

The Leigh Branch passes through a landscape once spoiled by mining but now painstakingly restored as parkland – a wildlife haven. For most of the way, the canal is on an embankment, well above the level of the surrounding landscape; this is a relatively new situation and is due to severe mining subsidence in the area. The canal has had to be built up – appropriately with pit waste – while the land on either side has sunk considerably. It continues eastwards past the old Dover Lock Inn, once the site of two locks moved to Wigan as a result of the local subsidence, towards Plank Lane swing bridge (actually a lift bridge and site of another defunct lock) which is mechanically operated (*see* page 105). Past the bridge, in Leigh, the canal suddenly becomes the Bridgewater Canal (without the customary stop lock), giving access to Manchester and the Trent & Mersey via Preston Brook (*see* page 44). This navigation is owned by the Manchester Ship Canal Company: boats licensed by Canal & River Trust may use the Bridgewater without further charge for up to seven consecutive days (but not Pomona Lock into the River Irwell).

There is a useful *supermarket* on the offside, immediately before the A572 Leigh Bridge 11.

Leigh
Gt Manchester. All services. Once the archetypal mill town, most of the tall buildings and chimneys have now been demolished. In the market place you can see the fine Edwardian baroque town hall, built 1904–7, facing the battlemented church of St Mary. This church was originally built in 1516 but was extensively rebuilt in the late 19th C and is the burial place of Thomas Tyldesley, killed at the battle of Wigan Lane.
Pennington Flash Country Park off St Helen's Road, Leigh WN7 3PA (01942 489007; www.wigan.gov.uk/ Resident/Leisure/Greenheart/Pennington-Flash.aspx). 1100-acre park centred on the flash or lake. Walks, birdwatching, sailing, fishing, golf, picnic areas and

information centre. *Open daily 08.30–dusk.*
Three Sisters Recreation Area Three Sisters Road, Bryn, Ashton-in-Makerfield WN4 8DD (01942 720453; www.wigan.gov.uk/Resident/Leisure/Greenheart/ Three-Sisters.aspx). Site of the Wigan Alps: three colliery spoil tips now landscaped to provide an international karting circuit (01942 270230), racing circuit, boating lake, picnic area and visitor centre. Telephone for details or visit their website.
Turnpike Gallery Civic Square, Leigh WN7 1EB (01942 404469; www.wlct.org). Home to major touring arts exhibitions. *Open Tue-Fri 10.00-17.00 & Sat 10.30-15.30.*

Pubs and Restaurants

🍺 1 **The Spinning Jenny** 33 King Street, Leigh WN7 4LP (01942 608218; www.greatukpubs.co.uk/spinningjennyleigh). Busy, town-centre pub with a leaning towards sports, dispensing real ale and food *all day, every day*. Family-friendly *(until early evening)* outside seating. Traditional pub games, sports TV and Wi-Fi. *Open Mon-Thu 10.00-23.00 (Mon 11.00); Fri-Sat 10.00-01.00 & Sun 12.00-01.00.*

🍺 2 **The Boars Head** 2 Market Place, Leigh WN7 1EG (01942 673036). A grand wooden staircase dominates the bar area of this historic pub serving real ale. Family-friendly, outside seating. Traditional pub games, occasional live music and sports TV. *Open Mon-Sat 10.30-23.00 (Sat 00.00) & Sun 12.00-22.30.*

🍺 3 **The Waterside Inn** Twist Lane, Leigh WN7 4DB (01942 605005; www.greeneking-pubs.co.uk/pubs/lancashire/waterside-inn). This pub is contained within very handsome grade II listed canalside buildings, one a two-storey stone warehouse dated 1821, the other a brick warehouse dated 1894. A distinctive wooden tower adjoins. Real ale is served, and food is available *daily 11.00-21.00.*

Open fires, a garden, moorings and family-friendly. *Weekend* discos *'til late*. Wi-Fi. *Open 11.00-23.00 (Fri-Sat 01.00).*

🍺 4 **The White Lion** 6A Leigh Road, Leigh WN7 1QL (07713 863835; www.allgatesbrewery.com/pubs/the-white-lion). Situated opposite Leigh's historic parish church, this friendly All Gates Brewery pub serves a range of their own (and guest) real ales. Over 18s only, beer garden. Traditional pub games, newspapers, real fires, sports TV and Wi-Fi. *Open Mon-Fri 14.00-23.00 & Sat-Sun 12.00-23.00 (Sun 13.00).*

🍺 5 **The Thomas Burke** 20A Leigh Road, Leigh WN7 1QR (01942 685640; www.jdwetherspoon.com/pubs/all-pubs/england/lancashire/the-thomas-burke-leigh). Named in honour of a famous local tenor – the 'Lancashire Caruso' – this striking pub serves a large range of real ales and food *daily 08.00-00.00*. Large screen TV and Wi-Fi. Children welcome and outside drinking area. *Open 08.00-00.00 (Fri-Sat 01.00).*

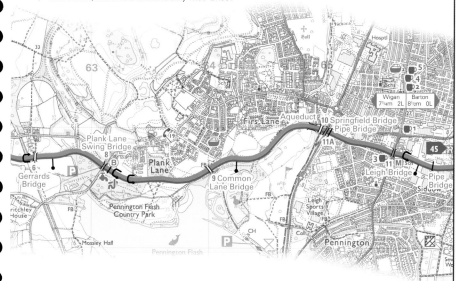

Boatyards

Ⓑ **Pennington Wharf Marina**
Plank Lane, Leigh WN7 4QD (01257 481054; www.bwml.co.uk/pennington-wharf-marina). RSW Pump out, short- and long-term moorings, toilets, showers, laundry

NAVIGATIONAL NOTES

1 Poolstock locks, Pagefield lock and Ell Meadow lock will be locked overnight from *20.00 until 08.00.*

2 Plank Lane Swing Bridge 8 is now boater operated and requires a Watermate Key. It is available for use at all times outside the periods *Mon-Fri 08.00-09.30 & 16.00-18.00*. Any difficulties contact CRT (0303 040 4040; www.canalrivertrust.org.uk/contact-us/ways-to-contact-us).

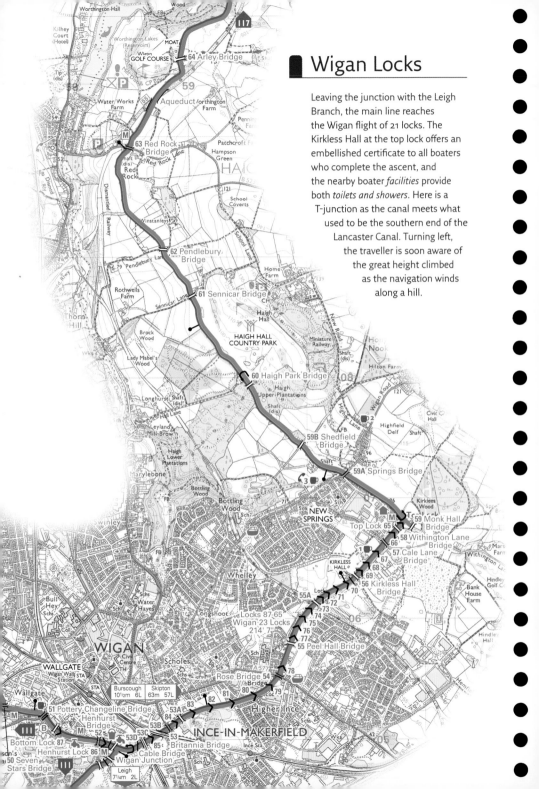

Wigan Locks

Leaving the junction with the Leigh Branch, the main line reaches the Wigan flight of 21 locks. The Kirkless Hall at the top lock offers an embellished certificate to all boaters who complete the ascent, and the nearby boater *facilities* provide both *toilets and showers*. Here is a T-junction as the canal meets what used to be the southern end of the Lancaster Canal. Turning left, the traveller is soon aware of the great height climbed as the navigation winds along a hill.

New Springs

Gt Manchester. PO box, tel, stores, off-licence, takeaway. Once an industrial hub with collieries and ironworks lining the canal as it struggled up the 21 locks to the summit. The acres of partially landscaped waste ground today belie the past activity of Rose Bridge Colliery (near bridge 54) and Ince Hall Coal and Cannel Company higher up (cannel is a dull coal that burns with a smoky, luminous flame). Hardest of all to imagine is the massive operation of Wigan Coal and Iron Co. who, at the turn of the century, employed 10,000 people at their works beside the top nine locks of the flight. Then one of the largest ironworks in the country, it mined 2 million tons of coal to produce 125,000 tons of iron annually. The skyline here was dominated by 10 blast furnaces, 675 coking ovens and a 339ft high chimney. It must have been an impressive sight on the night skyline, viewed from the streets of Wigan. Stores *open daily 06.00-23.00.*

Haigh Hall Copperas Lane, Haigh, Wigan WN2 1PE (01942 828280; www.wigan.gov.uk/ Resident/Leisure/Greenheart/Haigh-Hall-and-Country-Park.aspx). On east bank of the canal.

The pre-Tudor mansion was rebuilt by its owner, the 23rd Earl of Crawford, between 1830 and 1849. The reconstruction was designed and directed by the Earl, and all the stone, timber and iron used on the job came from the estate. The Hall is now owned by Wigan Corporation, who allow the citizens to use it for private wedding receptions, etc. There is little to see in the house and it is not normally open to the public. The park and grounds around the hall are *open daily all year, except 25-26 Dec and 1 Jan* and contain much that caters for the family: there are children's amusements, gardens and woodlands, a nature trail and selection of waymarked walks, miniature railway, a model village, crazy golf course, shop and cafeteria. Entry to the park is free but there is a charge for the amusements which are *open May-Sep.* Audio trail for the blind and partially sighted using a braille map and tape player.

Haigh Stables Gallery Haigh Country Park, Copperas Lane, Haigh, Wigan WN2 1PE (01942 831831; www.facebook.com/HaighStablesGallery). Daily art and craft workshops for groups and individuals. Hands-on creativity painting, batik, stencilling, clay, canal art for adults and children. *Open Tue-Sun 11.00-16.00.*

Pubs and Restaurants

🍺 1 **The Kirkless Hall Inn** 2 Canal Bank, Top Lock, Wigan WN2 1JW (01942 355805; www.facebook.com/kirklesshallinn/?rf=162326530451576). Distinctive black and white building housing spacious and comfortable bars. A wide range of excellent food is offered *L and E daily.* Dogs welcome together with children until *20.30. Regular* live music, garden, real fires and sports TV. Traditional pub games and newspapers. *Open Mon-Sat 12.00-22.30 (Fri-Sat 23.30) & Sun 12.00-23.00, but may close Mon & open later in winter.*

🍺 2 **The Colliers Arms** 192 Wigan Road, Wigan WN2 1DU (01942 833318; www.facebook.com/colliersarmswigan). Real ale dispensed in a charming 17th-C listed hostelry overlooking the canal. Bar snacks *usually available.* Dog- and child-friendly, garden. Traditional pub games, newspapers, real fires, sports TV and Wi-Fi. *Open Mon-Thu 15.00-23.00; Fri-Sat 14.00-23.30 (Sat 12.30) & Sun 14.00-23.00.*

🍺 3 **The Crown Hotel** 106 Wigan Road, Aspull, Wigan WN2 1DP (01942 242539; www.facebook.com/The-Crown-Hotel-New-Springs-Aspull-113069139361149). A community pub, well worth a visit, serving real ale and bar snacks L. Dog- and family-friendly, beer garden. Live entertainment Fri-Sat. Traditional pub games, newspapers, real fires and Wi-Fi. *Open Mon-Fri 19.00-00.00; Sat 14.00-01.00 & Sun 12.00-23.00, but may close Mon & Wed in winter.*

NAVIGATIONAL NOTES

1 The locks between Wigan and Leeds (nos 85–1) are 60ft long and, therefore, cannot accommodate a full-length narrowboat.

2 The Wigan Flight, extending from Bottom Lock 85 to Top Lock 65, is open daily during the season as follows: 08.00-09.00 for entry into the flight; 12.00-13.00 for entry and exit onto/off the flight and 17.00-18.00 to exit the flight.

3 Roving lock keepers will attend the flight to oversee passage and ensure that water levels are maintained. This is not primarily for the provision of assisted passage but staff will help customers when needed.

4 You will require a Canal & River Trust handcuff key.

Adlington

The canal continues to run as a 9-mile lock-free pound – known as the Lancaster Pool – along the side of the valley from which the industries surrounding Wigan can be viewed in the distance. It enjoys a pleasant and quiet isolation in this lightly wooded area. Already the navigation is well over 300ft above the sea, and the bleak hills up to the east give a hint of the Pennines that are soon to be crossed. The conspicuous tower east of Adlington stands on a hill that is over 1500ft high. Wandering northwards, beyond the village, the waterway remains hemmed in for much of the way by woodland and is undisturbed by the railway and main roads that for a while follow it closely. Soon the greenery gives way to views of Chorley's rows of rooftops across the valley. The canal crosses this valley, but shuns the town. There is a *slipway* just to the north of Cowling Bridge 75A, on the towpath side.

Pubs and Restaurants

● X 1 **The Bridge** 11 Park Road, Adlington PR7 4HZ (01257 480507). Beside Bridge 69. Welcoming, family- and dog-friendly establishment serving real ale. Moorings, a garden and *regular* live music. Sports TV, traditional pub games and Wi-Fi. *Open Mon-Thu 14.00-00.00 (Tue & Thu 15.00) & Fri-Sun 12.00-00.00.* There is a *greengrocer* further west, along Park Road.

● 2 **The Cardwell Arms** Chorley Road, Adlington PR6 9LH (01257 480319; www.facebook.com/The-Cardwell-Arms-185200778640313). Welcoming locals' bar, with a large games room, dispensing real ale and food *Mon-Fri 15.00-20.00 & Sat-Sun 12.00-20.00 (Sun 18.00).* Quiz *Thu* and live music *Sat*. Dog- and family-friendly, outdoor seating. Traditional pub games, sports TV and Wi-Fi. *Open Mon-Thu 14.00-23.30 (Mon 16.00) & Fri-Sun 12.00-00.45 (Sun 23.30).*

● X 3 **The Marina Café** Park Road, Adlington PR7 4HZ (01257 485641; www.brothersofcharity.org.uk/What-We-Do/Social-Enterprises/The-Marina-Caf%C3%A9.aspx). East of bridge 69, beside the marina. Friendly establishment managed by the Brothers of Charity, serving hearty meals, snacks and daily specials. *Open Mon-Sat 09.30-15.30.*

● 4 **The (Bottom) Spinners Arms** 23 Church Street, Adlington PR7 4EX (01257 483331). One of two pubs in the village with the same name, this hostelry serves the 'Bottom Enders' of Lower Adlington – close to the canal – dispensing real ale and tasty bar meals *Wed-Sun L.* No intrusive pub games, an open log fire, sports TV and Wi-Fi. Dog- and child-friendly, outside seating. Quiz *Tue* and Bingo *Wed. Open daily 12.00-00.00 (Fri-Sat 01.00).*

● 5 **The (Top) Spinners Arms** 105 Railway Road, Adlington PR6 9QZ (01257 483025). Despite its quirky bar (with a sloping floor) this pub still manages to serve a full pint of real ale! Child- and dog-friendly, outdoor patio seating (on the level), sports TV and traditional pub games. Wi-Fi and real fires. *Open Mon-Fri 16.30-00.00 (Fri 16.00) & Sat-Sun 13.00-00.00.*

● 6 **The Elephant & Castle** 1 Bolton Road, Adlington PR6 9NH (01257 474799). Pleasant, open-plan pub serving real ales and food *Mon-Fri 17.00-20.00 (not Wed) & Sat-Sun 12.00-18.00.* Dog- and child-friendly, garden. Traditional pub games, real fires, sports TV and Wi-Fi. *Open Mon-Fri 14.00-00.00 (Wed 16.00) & Sat-Sun 12.00-01.00 (Sun 00.00).*

● X 7 **The White Horse** 32 Chorley Road, Heath Charnock PR6 9JS (01257 481766). Traditional two-roomed family pub (complete with small play area) serving real ale. Dog- and family-friendly, garden. *Weekend* live music and *Sun* music quiz. Traditional pub games, sports TV and Wi-Fi. *Open 15.00-00.00 (Sat-Sun 12.00).*

X 8 **The Boatyard Bus Café** Ellerbeck Narrowboats, Rawlinson Lane, Heath Charnock, PR7 4DE (01257 480825; www.ellerbecknarrowboats.co.uk). Established in one of the last Leyland Olympian double-decker buses to be built (just up the road) and once operated by Pilkingtons in Accrington. Today, in café-guise, the bus dispenses excellent barista coffee, breakfast, snacks, paninis, baked potatoes, tea and cake. *Open Wed-Sun 08.30-15.00 (Sun 09.30).*

● 9 **The Prince of Wales** 9-11 Cowling Brow, Chorley PR6 0QE (01257 260815; www.facebook.com/Prince-of-Wales-Cowling-Brow-Chorley-508827712510514). Friendly local serving a wide range of real ales, real cider and sandwiches and pies *L. Weekend* live music. Dog- and child-friendly, outside seating. Newspapers, real fires and Wi-Fi. *Open 12.00-23.00.*

Boatyards

Ⓑ**White Bear Marina** Park Road, Adlington PR7 4HZ (01257 481054; www.bwml.co.uk/white-bear-marina). 🚿🚿♨D Pump out, slipway, gas, overnight mooring, long-term mooring, winter storage, laundrette, showers, toilets, solid fuel, waterway guides, café (next door). *Open Tue, Thu-Fri 09.15-16.30 (Fri-16.00) Wed 13.30-16.30 & Sat 09.15-14.30.*

Ⓑ X**Ellerbeck Narrowboats** Rawlinson Lane, Heath Charnock, PR7 4DE (01257 480825; www.ellerbecknarrowboats.co.uk). D Pump out, gas & coal, daily and evening narrowboat hire, long-term moorings, toilets, boaters bathroom and laundrette, chandlery, café. *Open Mon-Sat 09.00-19.00.*

Ⓑ**P B Mechanical Services** Rawlinson Lane, Heath Charnock PR7 4DE (01257 474422; www.pbmechanical.co.uk). New, second hand and vintage engine sales, engine servicing, repairs and overhauls, electrical and plumbing work, chandlery. *Open Mon-Sat 10.00-18.00.*

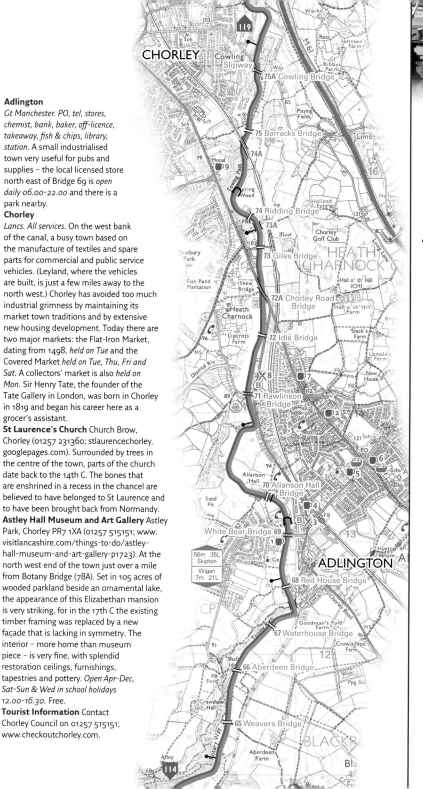

● **Adlington**
Gt Manchester. PO, tel, stores, chemist, bank, baker, off-licence, takeaway, fish & chips, library, station. A small industrialised town very useful for pubs and supplies – the local licensed store north east of Bridge 69 is *open daily 06.00-22.00* and there is a park nearby.

● **Chorley**
Lancs. All services. On the west bank of the canal, a busy town based on the manufacture of textiles and spare parts for commercial and public service vehicles. (Leyland, where the vehicles are built, is just a few miles away to the north west.) Chorley has avoided too much industrial grimness by maintaining its market town traditions and by extensive new housing development. Today there are two major markets: the Flat-Iron Market, dating from 1498, *held on Tue* and the Covered Market *held on Tue, Thu, Fri and Sat.* A collectors' market is also *held on Mon.* Sir Henry Tate, the founder of the Tate Gallery in London, was born in Chorley in 1819 and began his career here as a grocer's assistant.

St Laurence's Church Church Brow, Chorley (01257 231360; stlaurencechorley. googlepages.com). Surrounded by trees in the centre of the town, parts of the church date back to the 14th C. The bones that are enshrined in a recess in the chancel are believed to have belonged to St Laurence and to have been brought back from Normandy.

Astley Hall Museum and Art Gallery Astley Park, Chorley PR7 1XA (01257 515151; www. visitlancashire.com/things-to-do/astley-hall-museum-and-art-gallery-p1723). At the north west end of the town just over a mile from Botany Bridge (78A). Set in 105 acres of wooded parkland beside an ornamental lake, the appearance of this Elizabethan mansion is very striking, for in the 17th C the existing timber framing was replaced by a new façade that is lacking in symmetry. The interior – more home than museum piece – is very fine, with splendid restoration ceilings, furnishings, tapestries and pottery. *Open Apr-Dec, Sat-Sun & Wed in school holidays 12.00-16.30.* Free.

Tourist Information Contact Chorley Council on 01257 515151; www.checkoutchorley.com.

Withnell Fold

The canal sidesteps Chorley to the east, passing instead some large and resplendent outlying textile mills. There is a *slipway* just to the north of the M61 bridge, on the off-side. Now the boater enters a most delightful stretch of waterway. The junction with the old Walton Summit Branch features a canal cottage and the bottom lock in the Johnson's Hill flight. A short but energetic spell of windlass-wielding is required here, for the seven locks are very close together. It is rewarding work, for the steep countryside yields good views, and the locks are tidily maintained and painted. Near the middle lock is an old toll house and a *telephone*, while at the top lock there is a pub, a boatyard and, together with the usual facilities, *showers, toilets and a self-operated pump out*. The canal now changes course to north east and flows along a beautifully secluded and often wooded valley at a height of over 350ft above sea level. Even the old paper mills at Withnell Fold, which once brought a glimpse of industry, have been converted into small, discreet, industrial units. There is an excellent nature reserve developed in the old filter beds and sludge lagoons opposite which, derelict for many years, gradually infilled with silt and reedswamp to provide natural plant and animal habitats.

Pubs and Restaurants (pages 111)

🍺 1 **Malt 'n' Hops** 50-52 Friday Street, Chorley PR6 0AA (01257 260074). Guest real ales that change on a daily basis are dispensed in the congenial surroundings of this displaced antique dealer! Also real cider. Dog- and child-friendly *(until 20.00)* garden. *Sun* live music. Newspapers, real fires and Wi-Fi. *Open Mon-Fri 12.00-23.00 (Mon 15.00) & Sat-Sun 12.00-00.00.*

🍺✕ 2 **Malthouse Farm** Moss Lane, Whittle-Le-Woods, Chorley PR6 8AB (01257 232889; www.chefandbrewer.com/pubs/lancashire/malthouse-farm). A listed farm house converted to an upmarket pub and restaurant. Open fires and exposed beams. Real ales are available together with an extensive range of home-cooked food served *daily 12.00-22.00 (Sun 21.00)*. Children welcome, dogs outside only. Garden and moorings. Newspapers and Wi-Fi. B&B. *Open 12.00-23.00 (Sun 21.00).*

🍺 3 **The Red Lion** 196 Blackburn Road, Wheelton, Chorley PR6 8EU (01254 659890; www.facebook.com/LowerWheelton/?rf=270972499684136). A changing selection of real ales served in a popular village pub which serves food *daily 12.00-21.00* (tea and coffee *from 10.00*). Quiz *Mon* and live music *Thu*. Real fires and Wi-Fi. *Open Sun-Thu 11.00-23.00 (Wed-Thu 23.30) & Fri-Sat 00.30.*

✕♣ 4 **The Village Tearoom** 202 Blackburn Road, Wheelton PR6 8EY (01254 830160; www.thevillagetearoomatwheelton.co.uk). Cakes, pastries, biscuits and desserts all freshly prepared on a *daily* basis, compliment breakfast, soup, sandwiches and salads. Also an appetising range of hot snacks, afternoon tea and a takeaway service which includes picnic hampers. Gifts. *Open Tue-Sun 09.00-16.30 (Sun 10.00).*

🍺✕ 5 **The Red Cat** 114 Blackburn Road, Heapey PR6 8LL (01257 263966; www.theredcatrestaurant. co.uk). Now a gastro-pub, this establishment serves real ale and food *Mon-Thu 12.00-21.30 (Mon 18.00) & Fri-Sun 12.00-22.00 (Sun 21.00)*. Conservatory for casual drinkers, *open as per restaurant times.*

🍺 6 **The Top Lock** Copthurst Lane, Heapey, Chorley PR6 8LT (01257 263328; http://thetoplockchorley. co.uk). Well placed to slake the toiling boaters' thirst, this pub serves reasonably-priced, traditional pub food *daily 11.00-21.00 (Sun 20.30)* together with a good selection of real ales. Vegan options available. Quiz *Wed* and live music *Thu*. Extremely dog-friendly, children welcome and outside seating. Wi-Fi. *Open 11.00-23.00.*

🍺✕ 7 **The Dressers Arms** 9 Briers Brow, Wheelton, Chorley PR6 8HD (01254 830041; www.dressersarms. co.uk). This superb pub, completely rebuilt following a major fire in 2014, still dispenses a wide range of real ales and serves food *daily 12.00-21.00 (Sun 20.00)*. Dog- and child-friendly, garden. Quiz *Tue* and live music *Thu*. Newspapers, real fires and Wi-Fi. *Open 11.00-23.00.*

✕♣ 8 **Wan's Cantonese Restaurant** Briers Brow, Wheelton, Chorley PR6 8HD (01254 830171; www.heapeyandwheelton.org/business/fullpage/wans.htm). Above the Dressers Arms, serving authentic Chinese food. *Open Mon-Sat 18.00-23.00 & Sun 13.00-20.00.*

🍺 9 **The Golden Lion** 398 Blackburn Road, Higher Wheelton, Chorley PR6 8HP (01254 832681; www.facebook.com/thegoldenlionhigherwheelton). A pleasant walk up the footpath south of bridge 86. Real ales in a small, welcoming main road pub. Food available *Mon-Fri L and E & Sat-Sun 12.00-20.30 (Sun 19.00)*. Quiz *Wed*. Dog- and family-friendly, garden. Traditional pub games, newspapers, real fires, sports TV and Wi-Fi. *Open Mon-Sat 11.30-23.30 & Sun 12.00-22.00.*

Boatyards

Ⓑ **Botany Bay Boatyard** 7 Botany Bay, Chorley PR6 9AE (07967 380464/07770 576288; www.botanybayboatyard.co.uk). Next to Bridge 78A. ⚓ Boat sales and repairs, engine sales and repairs, boat fitting out, hard standing and winter storage, bottom blacking, DIY facilities, painting and sign writing, short-term moorings, boat transport, cranage.

Wheelton

Lancs. Tel, stores, off-licence, laundrette, garage. The village is best accessed by walking east from Bridge 82. Once dominated by its cotton mill, the narrow steeply-sloping streets are still bounded by terraces of solid weavers' cottages with the war memorial clock tower visible from most points.

Walton Summit Branch

The short branch used to be part of the Lancaster Canal, originally projected to run south from Preston to the Bridgewater Canal. The Lancaster Canal Company, after arranging with the Leeds & Liverpool Company to share a common course between Johnson's Hill Locks and Wigan Top Lock, was daunted by the prospect of constructing an expensive aqueduct over the River Ribble in Preston. A 'temporary' tramroad was built to connect the two lengths of canal between Preston and Walton Summit. The tramway, which opened in 1803, featured a short tunnel and a light trestle bridge over the Ribble. The tramroad was never replaced by a canal; indeed the whole line was closed by 1880. However in 2002, more than 200 years after the truncated Lancaster Canal was completed, the navigation has finally been connected into the rest of the waterways system with the opening of the Ribble Link, using the tidal rivers Douglas and Ribble. Most of the canal branch has been severed by the building of a motorway, although plenty of it still remains in an unnavigable state.

Botany Bay Village Botany Bay, Chorley PR6 9AF (01257 261220; www.botanybay.co.uk). Canalside near bridge 78A. Themed shopping centre in a converted mill together with restaurants and children's play area.

Withnell Fold

Lancs. A remarkable, small estate village, built to house workers at the canalside paper mills which are now demolished. Grouped around three sides of a spacious square, the terraced cottages present an intimately united front which is almost unnerving to the casual visitor – especially as on the fourth side of the square is an old set of wooden stocks.

Blackburn

Passing under the M65, the canal curls round a steep and thickly wooded valley, crossing it on a high embankment before entering the outskirts of Blackburn. Close to bridge 95 the delightfully named suburb of Cherry Tree provides *a range of shops, including a stores, fish & chips, takeaways, laundrette and station*. It seems to take a long time to get through this large town, as there is a flight of six locks here, raising the canal's level to a height of over 400ft above sea level, affording excellent views. Careful thought should be given to choosing a mooring site in Blackburn, especially if staying more than a few hours. There are *showers and toilets* beside Bridge 100 and a good towpath exists throughout the city.

Pubs and Restaurants

🍺✕ **1 The Royal Oak** Blackburn Old Road, Riley Green PR5 0SL (01254 201445; www.royaloak-rileygreen.co.uk). An oak-beamed pub dating from 1620 which serves real ale and real cider. Food is available *Mon-Fri L and E & Sat-Sun 12.00-21.00 (Sun 20.00)*. Dog- and child-friendly, beer garden. Real fires and Wi-Fi. *Open Mon-Sat 11.30-23.00 & Sun 12.00-22.30.*

🍺 **2 The Station** 391 Preston Old Rd, Blackburn BB2 5LW (01254 201643). An excellent place to sample the full range of local brewer, Thwaites, range of real ales. Outdoor drinking area, large-screen TV and traditional pub games. *Open Sun-Thu 15.00-00.30 (Sun 11.00) & Fri-Sat 11.00-01.30.*

🍺 **3 The Postal Order** 15-19 Darwen Street, Blackburn BB2 2BH (01254 676400; www.jdwetherspoon.com/pubs/all-pubs/england/lancashire/the-postal-order-blackburn). Once the general post office, now serving real ales and real ciders over the longest bar in town, together with food *daily 08.00-22.00*. Family-friendly, outside seating. Large screen TV and Wi-Fi. *Open 08.00-00.00 (Fri-Sat 00.30).*

🍺 **4 The Drummers Arms** 65 King William Street, Blackburn BB1 7DT (07446 010313; www.facebook.com/DrummersArms). Single-roomed pub, walls adorned with old pub signs and brewery memorabilia, serving locally-brewed real ales and real cider. Music-oriented, with *regular Sun* sessions, juxtaposed with classic tracks from an eclectic jukebox. Small terrace. *Open daily 12.00-20.00 (Fri-Sat 23.00).*

🍺 **5 The Lemon Tree** 29 Blakey Moor, Blackburn BB2 1LL (0254 51761). Known for decades as The Jubilee, this town-centre hostelry serves three changing ales and food *L. Occasional* live music. *Open daily 12.00-20.00 (Fri-Sat 00.00).*

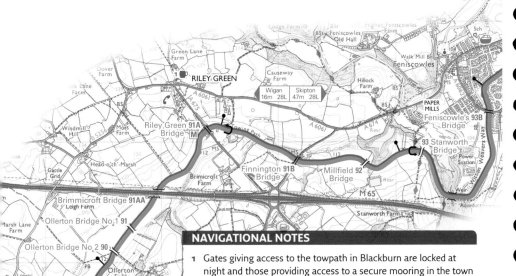

NAVIGATIONAL NOTES

1 Gates giving access to the towpath in Blackburn are locked at night and those providing access to a secure mooring in the town can be opened with a CRT Handcuff Key. For suitable moorings consult the lock keeper.

2 There is the usual range of services, together with *showers and toilets* beside Bridge 100.

3 Locks 57-52 require a Handcuff Key.

● **Blackburn**

Lancs. All services. Few of the Pennine towns which sprang up with the Industrial Revolution can be described as beautiful. In an attempt to rectify this, Blackburn has taken drastic steps in recent years to construct a new town centre. Nevertheless the most impressive features of the town are still the old cotton mills.

Blackburn Cathedral Cathedral Close, Blackburn BB1 5AA (01254 503090; www.blackburncathedral. com). Dating from 1820-6, the parish church was raised to cathedral status in 1926. Extensive renovations have been made inside. Very striking 13ft sculpture of 'Christ the Worker' in aluminium and black iron by John Hayward. Large churchyard.

King George's Hall Northgate, Blackburn BB2 1AA (01254 582579; www.kinggeorgeshall.com). Entertainment complex promoting a wide-ranging programme of music and theatre. Charge.

Museum & Art Gallery Museum Street, Blackburn BB1 7AJ (01254 667130; www.blackburn.gov.uk). Exhibits include natural history, pottery, early manuscripts and a large collection of English, Greek and Roman coins. In the art gallery are over 1200 beautiful Japanese prints, as well as English watercolours of the 18th C–20th C. Also incorporated is the Lewis Textile Museum: a series of period rooms demonstrating the development of the textile industry from the 18th C by means of full-size working models, including Hargreaves' Spinning Jenny. *Open Wed-Sat 12.00-16.45; closed B Hols.* Free.

Waves Water Fun Centre Nab Lane, Blackburn BB2 1LN (01254 268800; www.blackburn. gov.uk). The town's own tropical paradise. Cafeteria. Full disabled access. Technical tours by arrangement. Charge.

Witton Country Park Preston Old Road, Blackburn BB2 2TP (01254 666976; www.blackburn.gov.uk/Pages/ Witton-Country-Park-.aspx). Nearly 500 acres of magnificent parkland, including the beautiful landmark, Billinge Hill. Tree and nature trails; wayfaring course; picnic sites and children's play area. *Open Mon-Fri 06.30-21.00 & Sat-Sun 09.00-16.00. Reduced opening hours in winter.*

Blackburn Visitor Centre Blackburn Market, Church Street, Blackburn BB1 5AF (01254 688040; www.visitblackburn.co.uk/visitor-centre). *Open Mon-Sat 09.00-17.00 (Sat 16.00).*

Hoghton Tower Hoghton, Nr Blackburn PR5 0SH (01254 852986; www.hoghtontower.co.uk). Past the Royal Oak at bridge 91A. So enjoyable was a joint of beef devoured during a visit, that James I knighted the remains 'Sir Loin'. More recently this 16th-C fortified hilltop mansion is visited for its dungeons, doll's houses, picturesque gardens, as well as for the magnificent banqueting hall. Tearoom. *Open Apr-Oct, Sun-Thu 10.00-16.00.* Charge.

Rishton

Of particular interest to those on the canal are the fine canopied wharves of the Depot at Eanam Wharf, now converted for business use. The canal leaves Blackburn and embarks upon a course of twists and turns that emphasise the hilliness of the countryside. The scenery varies all the time between heavy industrial development (and its effects) and – just around a corner – green fields, farms and distant views of wild moorlands. The Calder Valley motorway (M65) follows the line of the canal to Burnley. Of interest is the fine L-shaped wharf building with a large central arch at Simpson's Bridge, now in a serious state of dereliction. Beyond Church, the first of four swing bridges appears (nos. 113, 114 and 115 require a handcuff key and a windlass): they are the only ones between Wigan and Gargrave.

● Rishton
Lancs. PO, tel, stores, chemist, butcher, baker, takeaways, DIY shop, fish & chips, off-licence, library, garage, station. A small grey town that grew up around the cotton mills in the 19th C by courtesy of the Petre family of the Dunkenhalgh Estate, who used to be lords of the manor and are still local landowners. For more about the industrial archaeology and general history of the Rishton area visit www.facebook.com/ RishtonWebsite.

● Church
Lancs. PO box, tel,, stores fish & chips, takeaways, bakery, garage, station. An industrial community which was originally based on calico printing, established on the canal bank by the family of the famous statesman Sir Robert Peel. The row of terraced houses is characteristic of so many of the towns in this industrial area. The parish church of St James is right on the banks of the canal; only the tower and font remain from the original 15th-C building. There are two delightful windows designed by Edward Burne Jones. To arrange a visit telephone 01254 725450. The canal is close by and there are excellent moorings at this, the central point of the Leeds and Liverpool Canal, which is depicted by a sculpture. **Dunkenhalgh Hall** Clayton-le-Moors. Standing in 16 acres of gardens and woodland, it is a beautiful Elizabethan mansion, extensively altered in the 19th C. Its name is said to be derived from a Scottish raider named Duncan, who chose to settle there. The hall is now used as a hotel.

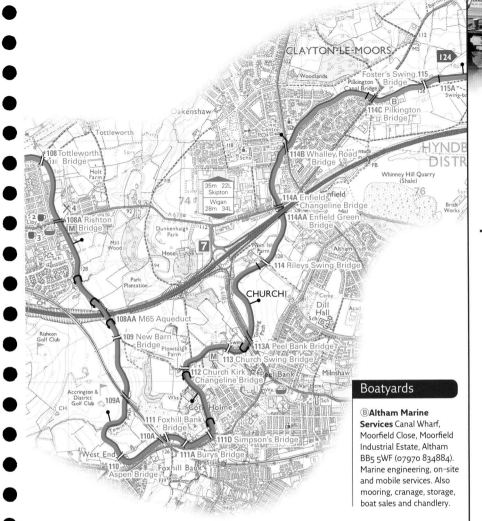

Boatyards

Ⓑ Altham Marine Services Canal Wharf, Moorfield Close, Moorfield Industrial Estate, Altham BB5 5WF (07970 834884). Marine engineering, on-site and mobile services. Also mooring, cranage, storage, boat sales and chandlery.

Pubs and Restaurants

⬤ 1 The Rishton Arms Station Road, Rishton BB1 4HF (01254 886396; www.thwaitespubs.co.uk/rishton-arms-rishton). Worth the walk for the friendly welcome in this comfortable local beside the railway station. A traditional pub with two rooms serving a range of ales (including a mild) from local brewer Thwaites. Dogs welcome, outside seating. Sports TV, *regular* live music and traditional pub games. *Open Mon-Fri 17.00-00.00 (Fri 14.00) & Sat-Sun 12.00-00.00.*

⬤ 2 The Walmsley Arms 51 High Street, Rishton BB1 4LD (01254 602004; www.thwaitespubs.co.uk/walmsley-arms-rishton). Welcoming pub serving real ale. Child- and dog-friendly. Beer garden. *Open Mon-Fri 12.00-00.00 & Sat-Sun 12.00-01.00.*

⬤ 3 The Roebuck Inn High Street, Rishton BB1 4JZ (0254 883714). Imposing village pub serving real ales. *Open daily 12.00-23.00.*

✕ 4 Canal View Café 2-4 Hermitage Street, Rishton BB1 4NL (07951 365497). Friendly, welcoming café serving everything from breakfast to a range of tasty hot meals, tea and coffee. Children welcome. Canalside seating. Takeaway service. *Open Sat-Thu 09.00-16.00.*

123

Hapton

The navigation continues to wind eastwards along the side of what turns out to be the Calder Valley with the M65 motorway to the south. High ground rises on each side of the valley, and in the distance the summit of Pendle Hill (1831ft high) can be clearly seen when it is not obscured by cloud. This is an attractive length of canal, unspoilt by industry and greatly enhanced by the ever-changing views from the side of the hill along which the canal is cut, although the motorway is uncomfortably close throughout. Soon the distant mass of dwellings is recognisable as the suburbs of Burnley and the canal ducks through Gannow Tunnel (559yds long) to swing sharply over the M65. At Rose Grove there are *moorings* together with *a pump out, showers and toilets* with full disabled access

WALKING AND CYCLING

To rejoin the canal beyond Gannow Tunnel leave the towpath and follow the subway under the motorway. Bear round to the right under the A67 and take the path leading uphill to the right of the Derby Hotel. Cross the road and go up the steps and then follow the straight path leading steadily downhill to the eastern tunnel portal. The town of Accrington lies a little to the south of the waterway but is the centre for the Hyndburn District which covers Rishton, Church and Clayton-le-Moors.

There is a beautifully produced range of walking and cycling guides to this area which can be obtained (for the most part free) from Accrington Information Centre at the Town Hall (01254 388111; www.hyndburnbc.gov. uk/contact-us). *Open Mon-Fri 09.00-16.00.*

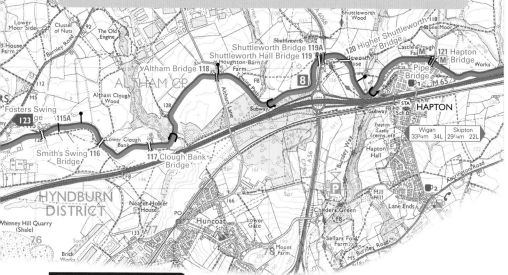

Pubs and Restaurants

🍺 **1 The Railway Inn** 17 Manchester Road, Hapton, Burnley BB12 7LF (01282 773719). Traditional local's drinking pub. Pool, darts, sports TV and Wi-Fi.

🍺✕ **2 The Hapton Inn** Accrington Road, Hapton BB11 5QL (01282 771152). ¾ mile south of Hapton Bridge 121, past the station. Popular eatery serving real ale and food *Mon-Fri L and E and all day Sat, Sun & B Hols.* Outside seating and children welcome. *Mon-Thu L and E; Fri-Sat 11.30-23.30 & Sun 12.00-23.00.*

🍺 **3 Gannow Wharf** 168-170 Gannow Lane, Burnley BB12 6QH (07855 315498). Six constantly rotating real ales are served in this friendly, canalside pub. Children welcome until 18.00. *Occasional weekend live*

music. Traditional pub games and sports TV. Secure moorings. *Open Mon-Thu 17.30-23.30; Fri 17.00-00.00 & Sat-Sun 15.00-00.00.*

🍺 **4 The Dugdale Arms** Dugdale Road, Burnley BB12 6DW (01282 423909; www.thwaites.co.uk/pubs-and-pub-finder/pubs/padiham/dugdale-arms). Approached from western end of Gannow Tunnel. Thwaites beers served in a large, modern suburban pub. Children allowed and good disabled access. Sports TV, beer garden and traditional pub games. Live entertainment at weekends. *Open Mon-Thu 15.00-00.00 & Fri-Sun 12.00-00.00.*

Boatyards

ⓑ**Knott's Bridge Moorings** 13 Water Street, Hapton BB12 7DW (07791 785158). 🛏️🚿 E Pump out, overnight mooring, long-term mooring (24/7 security), DIY facilities, engine repairs.

● **Hapton**
Lancs. PO box, tel, stores, takeaway, fish & chips, station. A small and unmistakably northern village, with regular streets of terraced houses.

Weavers' Triangle, Burnley

Burnley

This is an industrial stretch where the canal was once a main artery for the town and its industries. The area around bridge 130, known as the Weavers' Triangle, has been recognised to be of great interest – fine warehouses, tall chimneys and loading bays flank the canal here. At Burnley Wharf there is a museum in the old toll house and wharf master's house. The huge Burnley Embankment carries the navigation across part of the town – called 'the straight mile' it is 3/4 mile long, but no less dramatic for that; 60ft high, it incorporates an aqueduct over a main road. The whole area of the embankment has been tidied up and the towpath opened up offering excellent access to a wealth of pedestrianised shopping, together with good *moorings*. The town is within easy reach and the attractive Thompson Park (good play area and boating lake) can be found north of the aqueduct after bridge 130H. Now the canal negotiates a landscape which alternates between open country, towns and semi-towns, with the massive distant bulk of Pendle Hill in the background. Cobbled streets of terraced houses run down to the canal and old wharves, some disused and overgrown, are under renovation for offices and housing. There is excellent *mooring* immediately south of bridge 140 on the offside, together with an attractive children's playground opposite.

● **Burnley**
Lancs. All services. A large industrial northern town, which has worked hard to improve its appearance. It was once the world centre for cotton weaving. The excellent shopping centre is only 10 minutes' walk from Finsley Gate Bridge.
Burnley Mechanics Theatre Manchester Road, Burnley BB11 1BH (01282 664400; www. burnleymechanics.co.uk). Built in 1854 and converted into a theatre in 1979, this Grade II* listed building now houses a thriving arts centre and real ale bar. *Regular* performances and events – visit the website or telephone for details.
Pendle Village Mill Hollin Bank, Brierfield BB9 5NG (01282 442424; www.pendlevillage.co.uk). Just south of Bridge 139. A mill shop selling fabrics, clothes, crafts and gifts. Tearoom – see **Pubs and Restaurants** page 121. *Open Mon-Sat 10.00-17.30 (B Hols 17.00) & Sun 10.30-16.30.*
Queen Street Mill Textile Museum Harle Syke, Burnley BB10 2HX (01282 412555; www.lancashire.gov. uk/leisure-and-culture/museums/queen-street-mill-textile-museum). North east of Burnley Embankment, along Eastern Avenue and Briercliffe Road from the football ground. This is Britain's only working 19th-C weaving mill: 300 looms powered by the 500hp steam engine 'Peace'. Virtually unchanged until it closed in 1982, the mill has now found a new lease of life, with some of the former employees back again to work the looms. Mill shop and café. Due to the 115ft mill chimney requiring strengthening work, access to the museum is currently limited, so telephone or visit the website for further details. Charge.

Reel Cinema Hollywood Park, Manchester Road, Burnley BB11 2EJ (01282 416329; www.reelcinemas. co.uk/burnley/now). Multi-screen cinema not far from the canal.
Towneley Hall Museum Towneley Park, Burnley BB11 3RQ (01282 477130; www.towneley.org.uk). On the southern outskirts of Burnley, 1¼ miles south east of the CRT yard. Set in extensive parkland with two golf courses (one 9-hole and the other 18-hole) and play area, the grandiose, battlemented house dating from the 14th C was the home of the Towneley family until 1902. It is now an art gallery and museum with rooms lavishly furnished in period style. Gift shop. *Open Sat-Thu 12.00-17.00.* Charge.
Weavers' Triangle 85 Manchester Road, Burnley BB11 1JZ (01282 452403; www.weaverstriangle.co.uk). The area between bridges 129B and 130B is one of the best-preserved 19th-C industrial districts in the country – there are weaving sheds with 'north light' roofs, engine houses, spinning mills and well-preserved terraces of 19th-C houses. An explanatory leaflet and town trail guide are available from: the Tourist Information Centre or the **Visitor Centre**, Burnley Wharf, 85 Manchester Road, Burnley BB11 1JZ (01282 452403; www.weaverstriangle. co.uk). *Open Easter–Sep, Sat-Tue 14.00-16.00 & Oct, Sat-Sun 14.00-16.00.* Free – donations welcome.

● **Brierfield**
Lancs. PO, tel, stores, chemist, baker, hardware, off-licence, takeaways, fish & chips, butcher, greengrocer, library, garage, station. A small industrial town merging into Burnley at one end and into Nelson at the other. The parish church of St Luke in Colne Road is a Victorian building with an unusually designed clock tower culminating in a steep pyramid roof.

Pubs and Restaurants

🍺 1 **The Swan** 44 St James Street, Burnley BB11 1NQ (01282 424035; www.thwaitespubs.co.uk/the-swan-hotel-burnley). Established in one of the town's oldest buildings – variously a farmhouse, prison and a morgue – this busy hostelry serves real ale. Sheltered beer garden. Traditional pub games, *occasional* live

music and sports TV. *Open daily 10.00-00.00.*
🍺 2 **The Mechanics Theatre** Mechanics Institute, Manchester Road, Burnley BB11 1BH (01282 664400; www.burnleymechanics.co.uk). Town centre. Bistro *open Mon-Fri 11.00-15.00 & Sat 11.30-14.00.* Pre-theatre meals on performance nights when the bar will *stay open until late.*

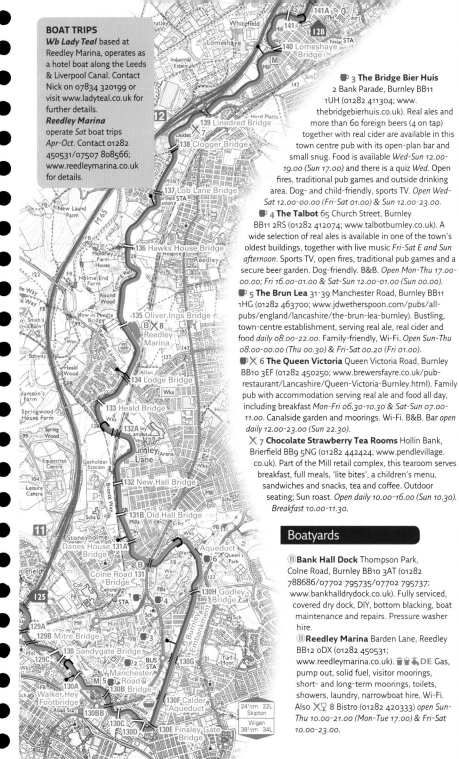

BOAT TRIPS

Wb Lady Teal based at Reedley Marina, operates as a hotel boat along the Leeds & Liverpool Canal. Contact Nick on 07834 320199 or visit www.ladyteal.co.uk for further details.

Reedley Marina operate *Sat* boat trips *Apr-Oct*. Contact 01282 450531/07507 808566; www.reedleymarina.co.uk for details.

3 The Bridge Bier Huis 2 Bank Parade, Burnley BB11 1UH (01282 411304; www. thebridgebierhuis.co.uk). Real ales and more than 60 foreign beers (4 on tap) together with real cider are available in this town centre pub with its open-plan bar and small snug. Food is available *Wed-Sun 12.00-19.00 (Sun 17.00)* and there is a quiz *Wed*. Open fires, traditional pub games and outside drinking area. Dog- and child-friendly, sports TV. *Open Wed-Sat 12.00-00.00 (Fri-Sat 01.00) & Sun 12.00-23.00.*

4 The Talbot 65 Church Street, Burnley BB11 2RS (01282 412074; www.talbotburnley.co.uk). A wide selection of real ales is available in one of the town's oldest buildings, together with live music *Fri-Sat E and Sun afternoon*. Sports TV, open fires, traditional pub games and a secure beer garden. Dog-friendly. B&B. *Open Mon-Thu 17.00-00.00; Fri 16.00-01.00 & Sat-Sun 12.00-01.00 (Sun 00.00).*

5 The Brun Lea 31-39 Manchester Road, Burnley BB11 1HG (01282 463700; www.jdwetherspoon.com/pubs/all-pubs/england/lancashire/the-brun-lea-burnley). Bustling, town-centre establishment, serving real ale, real cider and food *daily 08.00-22.00*. Family-friendly, Wi-Fi. *Open Sun-Thu 08.00-00.00 (Thu 00.30) & Fri-Sat 00.20 (Fri 01.00).*

6 The Queen Victoria Queen Victoria Road, Burnley BB10 3EF (01282 450250; www.brewersfayre.co.uk/pub-restaurant/Lancashire/Queen-Victoria-Burnley.html). Family pub with accommodation serving real ale and food all day, including breakfast *Mon-Fri 06.30-10.30 & Sat-Sun 07.00-11.00*. Canalside garden and moorings. Wi-Fi. B&B. Bar *open daily 12.00-23.00 (Sun 22.30).*

7 Chocolate Strawberry Tea Rooms Hollin Bank, Brierfield BB9 5NG (01282 442424; www.pendlevillage.co.uk). Part of the Mill retail complex, this tearoom serves breakfast, full meals, 'lite bites', a children's menu, sandwiches and snacks, tea and coffee. Outdoor seating; Sun roast. *Open daily 10.00-16.00 (Sun 10.30). Breakfast 10.00-11.30.*

Boatyards

Bank Hall Dock Thompson Park, Colne Road, Burnley BB10 3AT (01282 788686/07702 795735/07702 795737; www.bankhalldrydock.co.uk). Fully serviced, covered dry dock, DIY, bottom blacking, boat maintenance and repairs. Pressure washer hire.

Reedley Marina Barden Lane, Reedley BB12 0DX (01282 450531; www.reedleymarina.co.uk). DE Gas, pump out, solid fuel, visitor moorings, short- and long-term moorings, toilets, showers, laundry, narrowboat hire, Wi-Fi. Also 8 Bistro (01282 420333) *open Sun-Thu 10.00-21.00 (Mon-Tue 17.00) & Fri-Sat 10.00-23.00.*

Foulridge

The navigation winds as it follows the hillside; but this ceases at Nelson, where it crosses the valley on a minor aqueduct and begins to climb the pretty Barrowford Locks, having finally seen off the motorway. Immediately to the north of Bridge 141C, on the offside, there is a *canal users recycling point*, complete with its own *mooring*. This is a refreshing stretch, in which the canal leaves the succession of industrial towns. It rises through the seven Barrowford Locks, passing Barrowford Reservoir (in which the summit level's surplus water is stored), and at the beautifully kept top lock reaches the summit level of the whole canal. Soon various feeder streams can be seen, continuously pouring vital water supplies into the navigation. Meanwhile, distant mountainous country frames beautiful old stone farms nearer at hand. Before long everything is blotted out by Foulridge Tunnel; at the other end there is an old wharf (*café, toilets and showers*) where it is possible to moor to visit the village.

WALKING AND CYCLING

To rejoin the canal beyond Foulridge Tunnel follow the waymarked route along minor roads and footpaths, skirting one of the navigation's extensive water supply reservoirs. Further afield, there is a selection of walks leaflets featuring a variety of treks (from 5 to 45 miles) around Pendle Moors whilst 'Bowland by Bike' is a selection of 10 on- and off-road rides around the area. Available from TICs. National Cycle Route 68 uses this section of the towpath.

● **Nelson**
Lancs. All services. Nelson is a conglomerate of a number of small villages that combined in the 19th C to form one industrial town. The centre has been redeveloped with a large covered shopping precinct. One of Nelson's more valuable assets is the easy access to the beautiful Moors and Forest of Pendle, behind which looms Pendle Hill.

● **Barrowford**
Lancs. PO, tel, stores, chemist, butcher, off-licence, greengrocer, takeaways, fish & chips. There are still some attractive terraces of stone cottages in this village, which lie a short walk to the west of the locks. The Toll House, the last intact survivor from the old Marsden (Nelson) to Long Preston turnpike road, together with the 17th-C Park Hill (the birthplace of Roger Bannister, the first 'four minute miler') now houses:
Pendle Heritage Centre Colne Road, Barrowford, Nelson BB9 6JQ (01282 677150; www.htnw.co.uk). *Open daily 10.00–17.00 (Dec-Feb 10.00–16.00 except Xmas).* Exhibition on Pendle Witches; 18th-C walled garden and woodland walk; cruck barn with animals; parlour shop and tearoom-cum-restaurant. Also Pendle Arts Gallery. Charge. John Wesley preached from the packhorse bridge in the 1770s; there is a fine park by the river containing traces of a mill dating from 1311.
Tourist Information Centre – details as per Pendle Heritage Centre.

● **Foulridge**
Lancs. PO box, tel, fish & chips, butcher. Attractive around the green, where alleys festooned with washing lines give the place a homely air. In the surrounding countryside are scattered the reservoirs that feed the summit level of the canal. There is a reception centre housing a small museum in the old warehouse on the wharf.

● **Foulridge Tunnel**
1640yds long, with no towpath, this tunnel is, not surprisingly, barred to unapproved boats. The hole in the hill sprang to fame in 1912 when a cow fell into the canal near the tunnel mouth and for some reason decided to struggle through to the other end of the tunnel. The gallant but weary swimmer was revived with alcohol at the Foulridge end. The tunnel roof drips liberally.

NAVIGATIONAL NOTES

Entrance to Foulridge Tunnel is restricted and controlled by lights. Please obey signs giving instructions.

BOAT TRIPS
M.V. Marton Emperor operates canal trips *May–Oct Sun 14.30* from Foulridge Wharf, just north of the tunnel. Also trips through the tunnel to Barrowford run on *selected Sun May–Sep 11.00* – see website. Private charters available throughout year in centrally heated boat. For further details telephone 01282 844033 or visit www.boattrips.info.co.uk.

Pubs and Restaurants

🍽 1 **The George & Dragon** 217 Gisburn Road, Barrowford BB9 6JD (01282 618710; www.facebook.com/barrowforddragon). Popular local dispensing real ale and food *L and E*. Dog-friendly, patio. Quiz *Wed*, live music *Sat*. Sports TV. *Open daily 12.00–23.00 (Sun 22.30).*

✕🍷 2 **Zio Italian Restaurant** Gisburn Road, Barrowford BB9 6DT (01282 601999; www.baccirestaurants.co.uk/italian_restaurant/restaurants/Zio). Friendly restaurant serving classic Italian regional dishes together with traditional Lancashire cuisine. Children welcome. *Open Mon-Fri L and E; Sat 17.30–23.00 & Sun 17.00–22.00.*

✕🍷 3 **Bombay Lounge** 117B Gisburn Road, Barrowford BB9 6EW (01282 616006; www.bombayloungebarrowford.co.uk). Well-respected Indian restaurant, with attentive staff, that also offers a free delivery on £10+ orders within a 5-mile radius. *Open Mon-Sat 17.00–23.00 (Sat 00.00) & Sun 17.00–22.00.*

🍽 4 **The New Inn** Skipton Old Road, Foulridge, Colne BB8 7PD (01282 543316; www.facebook.com/foulridge). A popular village pub serving good food and real ales. Traditional home-cooking *L and E*. Dog- and child-friendly, outside seating. Real fires. *Open daily 12.00–23.00 (Sun 22.30).*

🍽 5 **The Hare & Hounds** Skipton Old Road, Foulridge BB8 7PD (01282 864235). Majoring on food, this village-centre pub serves real ale and meals *L and E*. Dog- and family-friendly, outside seating. Real fires. *Open daily 12.00–23.00 (Sun 22.30).*

✕🍷 6 **Café Cargo** Warehouse Lane, Foulridge BB8 7PP (01282 865069; www.cafecargo.org.uk). Canalside at the wharf, this establishment serves breakfast, lunch and teas and becomes a bistro at night. Children welcome. Canalside seating. *Open daily 08.30–20.30.*

Barnoldswick

Meanwhile the navigation continues northward through this very fine countryside to Salterforth, crossing over the little 'County Brook' between bridges 149 and 150. This is one of the more remote sections of the whole canal and probably the most beautiful. There is also much canal interest, for just south of bridge 153 was the junction, now disappeared, of the Rain Hall Rock Branch, essentially a linear quarry where the limestone was loaded directly from the rock face onto the boats. Walk up the road from the bridge (east) and turn right at the top where it will come into view, straddled by a tall three-arched viaduct. A mile further along one rounds a corner and is confronted by Greenberfield Top Lock (*showers, toilet, camping and an attractive picnic area with refreshments – Mar-Oct, daily 10.30-17.00*) which introduces the beginning of the long descent towards Leeds – the feeder from the distant Winterburn Reservoir enters the canal at the top lock. The three locks here were built in 1820 to replace the original flight (the old dry bed of the earlier route can be seen on the towpath side) and are set in beautiful uplands – for the next few miles the canal winds through scenery that is composed of countless individual hillocks, some topped by clumps of trees. Beyond are distant mountains.

Boatyards

Ⓑ**Lower Park Marina** Kelbrook Road, Barnoldswick BB18 5TB (01282 815883; www.lowerparkmarina.com). 🛶D Pump out, gas, overnight mooring, long-term mooring, day boat hire, boat sales, winter storage, cranage, DIY facilities, wet dock, solid fuel, boat repairs, chandlery, gifts, books and maps, hot drinks and fresh milk.

● **Salterforth**
Lancs. PO box, tel. A small village of narrow streets and terraced houses in an upland setting. Children will enjoy the playground north of bridge 151.

● **Barnoldswick**
Lancs. PO, tel, stores, banks, chemist, butcher, baker, hardware, takeaways, off-licence, fish & chips, library, garage. Set back from the canal, the mainstay of this town's existence is the Rolls Royce factory, where experimental work is done on aero engines. The centre of the town is compact and dominated by the modern Holy Trinity Church completed in 1960.
Bancroft Mill Engine Trust Gillians Lane, Barnoldswick BB8 5QR (01695 424166; www.bancroftmill.org.uk). A 600 hp steam engine and its two boilers, once powering the looms of Bancroft Mill, saved for preservation. *Regular* steaming and weaving demonstrations. Cafeteria and shop. *Open every Sat 11.00-15.00* for static viewing. Free. Visit website for details of steaming days when the engine runs at *intervals between 13.00 and 15.45*. Charge.
Tourist Information Centre Post Office Buildings, Fernlea Avenue, Barnoldswick BB18 5DL (01282 666704; www.visitbarnoldswick.co.uk). *Open Mon, Wed, Thu-Fri 09.00-16.00 (closed 13.00-13.30)*.
Pennine Way The Pennine Way is a walking route covering 268 miles of Pennine highland from Edale in the south to Kirk Yetholm in the north. Because of the nature of the route much of the Way is rough, hard walking, but it gives a superb view from the mountains. At East Marton the Pennine Way shares the canal towpath for a short distance – you will notice that the stones here abound with fossils.

Pubs and Restaurants

🍺✕ 1 **The Anchor Inn** Salterforth Lane, Salterforth, Barnoldswick BB18 5TT (01282 850055; www.theanchorinnsalterforth.co.uk). An historic village canalside pub serving real ales, where a second building was built on top of the first – hence where you now drink was once the bedrooms. Real ale and wide range of good, traditional pub food served *all day from 12.00*. Built beside the old packhorse road, the downstairs room (and now the cellar) hosts a spectacular display of stalactites. Dog- and child-friendly, garden. Moorings and camping. Traditional pub games, real fires, sports TV and Wi-Fi. *Open 12.00-23.00*.
🍺✕ 2 **McCullogh's Bar** 18-22 Rainhall Road, Barnoldswick BB18 5AF (01282 813374; www.barnoldswickmusicandartscentre.com/mcculloughs-bar). Welcoming, relaxing pub with quirky décor and friendly staff, serving real ale. Food is available in the Bernulfsuuic Restaurant which offers an interesting Sun roast. *Open Wed 10.00-15.00; Thu-Sat 09.00-00.00 & Sun 10.00-22.00*.

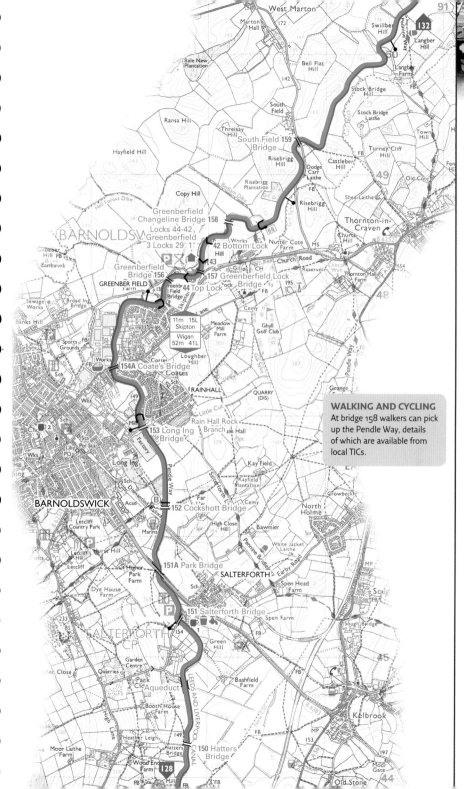

West Marton

Marton Hall

Swillber Hill

Langber Hill

132

Bale New Plantation

Bell Flat Hill

Langber Farm

Ransa Hill

South Field

Stock Bridge Hill

Stock Bridge Laithe

Threlsay Hill

South Field 159 Bridge

Town Hill

Hayfield Hill

Risebrigg Hill

Dodge Carr Laithe

Turney Cliff Hill

Castleber Hill

49

Old Cote

Copy Hill

Risebrigg Plantation

Risebrigg Hill

Shed Laithe

Thornton-in-Craven

Church Hill

Greenberfield Changeline Bridge **158**
Locks 44-42
Greenberfield
3 Locks 29' 1"

BARNOLDSW

42 Bottom Lock
Hill

Nutter Cote Farm

Church Road

MS

Church Well

Thornton Hall Farm

48

Gilleber Hill FB
Earthwork

Greenberfield Bridge **156**

GREENBER FIELD

Greenber Field Farm

Skipton

157 Greenberfield Lock Bridge

Reservoir

Sewage Works

Broad Ing Bridge

44 Top Lock

FB

Banks Hill

11m 15L
Skipton

Wigan
52m 41L

Meadow Mill Farm

Cemy

Ghyll Golf Club

Sports Grounds

FB Works

Loughber Hill

154A Coate's Bridge
Coates

Sch

RAINHALL

QUARRY
(DIS)

Grange

Little Cut

Rain Hall Rock

WALKING AND CYCLING
At bridge 158 walkers can pick up the Pendle Way, details of which are available from local TICs.

153 Long Ing Bridge

Branch ain Hall

Kay Field

Kayfield Plantation

Crowbeck

Long Ing

BARNOLDSWICK

Dismantled Railway

Pendle Way

Far Cemy

North Holme

152 Cockshott Bridge

High Close Hill

Bawmier

Pennine Bridge

White Jacket Laithe

Letcliff Country Park

Hurst Hill

151A Park Bridge

SALTERFORTH

Earby Road

Spen Head Farm

Higher Park Farm

Sch

Spen Farm

Sough Bridge

Dye House Farm

151 Salterforth Bridge

Spen Farm

45

SALTERFORTH CP

154

Green Hill

Garden Centre

Quarries

Bashfield Farm

Park Clo
Aqueduct

LEEDS AND LIVERPOOL CANAL

Kelbrook

Booth House Farm

Moor Laithe Farm

High Lane

Heather Leigh

150 Hatters Bridge

Wood End Farm

128

Hatters Bridge

MP

Moor Gate

44

Old Stone

Gargrave

Around East Marton, after skirting the isolated church, the surroundings change briefly: the navigation enters a cutting, passes under a double-arched main road bridge and enters a sheltered fold housing a farm, *a pub* and some *moorings*. A steep wooded cutting leads the canal back into the rugged moorlands. There is a useful *shop* and *restaurant* at Wilkinsons Farm, together with *B&B* and *camping*, by bridge 162, which can also be reached via a lane to the side of the Cross Keys. This is another outstanding stretch, in which the navigation continues to snake extravagantly around the splendid green and humpy hills that fill the landscape. The six Bank Newton Locks lower the canal into Upper Airedale, yielding excellent views across the valley to the hills and moors beyond. The River Aire flows in from the north, accompanied by the railway line to Skipton and Leeds from Morecambe, Settle and distant Carlisle. The canal crosses the river

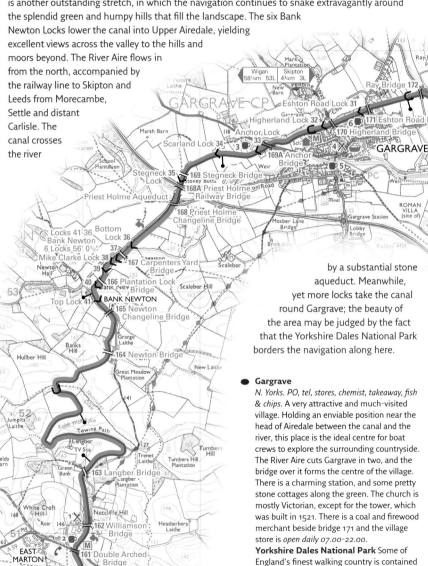

by a substantial stone aqueduct. Meanwhile, yet more locks take the canal round Gargrave; the beauty of the area may be judged by the fact that the Yorkshire Dales National Park borders the navigation along here.

● **Gargrave**
N. Yorks. PO, tel, stores, chemist, takeaway, fish & chips. A very attractive and much-visited village. Holding an enviable position near the head of Airedale between the canal and the river, this place is the ideal centre for boat crews to explore the surrounding countryside. The River Aire cuts Gargrave in two, and the bridge over it forms the centre of the village. There is a charming station, and some pretty stone cottages along the green. The church is mostly Victorian, except for the tower, which was built in 1521. There is a coal and firewood merchant beside bridge 171 and the village store is *open daily 07.00–22.00.*

Yorkshire Dales National Park Some of England's finest walking country is contained in this area of fine views, deep valleys, open moorland and rugged hills. Designated as a National Park in 1954 the Dales, covering 680 sq miles, are hardly scarred by habitation.

Pubs and Restaurants

✕🍷 1 **Abbot's Harbour Restaurant** Sawley House, East Marton, Skipton BD23 3LP (01282 843207; www.facebook.com/pages/Abbots-Harbour/1475073889377638). Charming canalside restaurant set in a 12th-C building constructed by Cistercian monks who worked the land and provided shelter to travellers between abbeys. Traditional English home-cooked food available *Fri–Wed 10.00–17.00 (Sun 09.00)*. Children, walkers, cyclists and boaters most welcome. Outside seating.

🍺✕ 2 **The Cross Keys East** East Marton, Skipton BD23 3LP (01282 844326; www.thecrosskeys.uk.com). Traditional 16th-C inn, overlooking the canal. A range of real ales is available together with a modern English menu served *Tue–Fri L and E; Sat 11.30–21.00 & Sun 12.00–20.00*. Dog- and family-friendly, garden. Newspapers, real fires and Wi-Fi. *Open Tue–Sat 11.30–21.00 (or later) & Sun 12.00–20.00*.

🍺✕ 3 **The Anchor Inn** Hellifield Road, Gargrave, Skipton BD23 3NB (01756 749666; www.brewersfayre.co.uk/pub-restaurant/Yorkshire/Anchor-Inn-Skipton.html). Usual Brewers Fayre pub serving food *daily 11.30–21.45 (Sun 12.00)*. Breakfast available *from 06.30 (Sat–Sun 07.00)*. Large garden with children's play area. B&B. Wi-Fi. *Open daily 12.00–23.00 (Sun 22.30)*.

✕ 4 **The Dalesman** 45 High Street, Gargrave, Skipton BD23 3LX (01756 749250). 500 yards from Higherlands Lock and bridge 170. A one-room replica of a boater's cabin. Home made meals and 200 varieties of old-fashioned sweets. Dogs and children welcome. *Open Tue–Sun 09.00–16.30 (Wed & Sun 10.00)*

🍺 5 **The Mason's Arms** Marton Road, Gargrave, Skipton BD23 3NL (01756 749304; www.masonsarmsgargrave.co.uk). An attractive old local pub with a bowling green at the rear dispensing real ales and food *daily 12.00–20.30*. Dog- and child-friendly, garden. Traditional pub games, newspapers, real fires, sports TV and Wi-Fi. Quiz *Sun (in winter)*. Camping and B&B. *Open 12.00–00.00 (Wed 23.00)*

🍺✕ 6 **The Old Swan** 20 High Street, Gargrave, Skipton BD23 3RB (01756 749232; www.old-swan-inn.co.uk). Imposing village centre pub and restaurant serving real ales and traditional home-cooked food *daily L and E*. Dog- and child-friendly, garden. Traditional pub games, real fires, sports TV and Wi-Fi. Camping and B&B. *Open 12.00–23.00*.

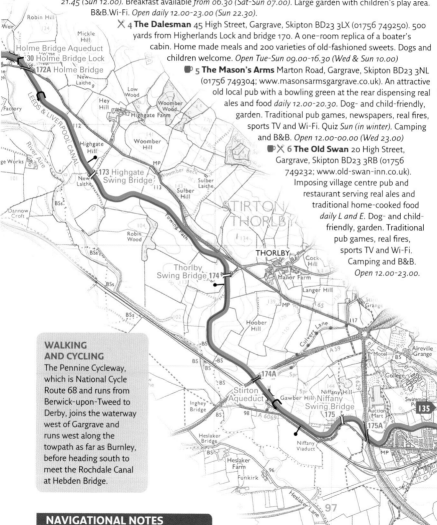

WALKING AND CYCLING

The Pennine Cycleway, which is National Cycle Route 68 and runs from Berwick-upon-Tweed to Derby, joins the waterway west of Gargrave and runs west along the towpath as far as Burnley, before heading south to meet the Rochdale Canal at Hebden Bridge.

NAVIGATIONAL NOTES

Locks 41–30 require a Handcuff Key.

Skipton

The canal now turns south east and proceeds down Airedale, a valley which contains it from here right through to Leeds. Upper Airedale is a flat, wide valley defined by tall steep hills. The countryside is open, unploughed and very inviting to walkers, especially with the moorlands stretching away over the top of the hills. In this robust landscape the navigation hugs the hillsides just above the valley floor, enjoying a lock-free pound that is 17 miles long – although the navigator's relief at the absence of locks may be tempered by the abundance of swing bridges. Entering Skipton, which is usually bristling with pleasure boats, the navigator will see the Springs Branch, a little arm packed with moored craft, that leads off past the town centre and soon finds itself in what is virtually a ravine, overlooked by the castle more than 100ft above. (Navigation is limited – see Navigational Note, see page 136.) At the junction is a boatyard: next door is a restored canal warehouse. On leaving Skipton the canal continues along the hillside down the valley of the River Aire, with the main road just beside and below the navigation. Excellent views are offered up and down this splendid valley and the surrounding countryside. The village of Bradley has an attractive waterfront and the pub is well worth the 1/4 mile uphill walk (take the first turning on the right over the lift bridge). *Visitor moorings are on the towpath side only.*

Pubs and Restaurants

There is a wide choice of pubs in Skipton. This is just a selection within reach of the canal:

🍺✕ 1 **Herriots Hotel** Broughton Road, Skipton BD23 1RT (01756 792781; www.herriotsforleisure. co.uk). Home-made food to suit all tastes is on offer *L and E* in this bar and in à la carte restaurant, together with real ales. Dog- and child-friendly, outside seating. Newspapers and Wi-Fi. B&B. *Open 11.00-23.30.*

🍺 2 **The Yorkshire Rose** 10 Coach Street, Skipton BD23 1LH (01756 793884;www.yorkshireroseskipton. com). Real ale is served in this town-centre pub, together with food *10.30-20.00* Dog- and family-friendly, outside seating. Newspapers, sports TV and Wi-Fi. *Open Mon-Sat 10.30-23.00 (Fri-Sat 00.00) & Sun 10.30-22.30.*

🍺 3 **The Royal Shepherd Inn** Canal Street, Skipton BD23 1LB (01756 797507) Friendly, welcoming family-run pub (overlooking the Springs Branch) offering home-cooked food *L* and real ale. Dogs welcome, outside seating. Traditional pub games, real fires and Wi-Fi. *Open 12.00-23.00.*

🍺✕ 4 **Bistro des Amis** 1 Jerry Croft, Skipton BD23 1DX (01756 797919; www.lebistrodesamis. co.uk). Everyone (including children) is made welcome in this French bistro with a modern twist, whether visiting for a special meal, a pint of real ale or just a coffee. The relaxed, homely atmosphere is highly inductive to enjoying the quality food, fine wines and the sounds of the recorded chansons, jazz or blues. Food available *Mon & Wed-Sat L and E & Sun 12.00-20.00. Wi-Fi. Open Mon & Wed-Fri L and E & Sat-Sun 10.00-23.00 (Sun 22.00).*

✕ 5 **Bean Love** 17 Otley Street, Skipton BD23 1DY (01756 791534; www.beanloved.co.uk). Coffee bar offering wide range of coffees, homemade bread, soup and sandwiches, sit-in and takeaway. *Open Mon-Sat 07.30-17.00 (Sat 08.00) & Sun 09.00-17.00.*

🍺 6 **The Cock & Bottle** 30 Swadford Street, Skipton BD23 1RD (01756 794734). Exposed stone walls and beamed ceilings make this 18th-C coaching inn a congenial pub in which to enjoy a good selection of real ales. Food is available *Mon-Sat 11.00-21.00 (Sat 17.00) & Sun 12.00-17.00.* Dog- and child-friendly, outside seating. Traditional pub games, newspapers, real fires and Wi-Fi. *Open Mon-Sat 11.00-23.00 (Fri-Sat 00.00) & Sun 12.00-23.00.*

🍺 7 **The Narrow Boat** 36-38 Victoria Street, Skipton BD23 1JE (01756 797922; www.markettowntaverns. co.uk/pub-and-bar-finder/yorkshire/the-narrow-boat). A lively real ale drinkers pub that pays homage to the traditional brewery and to the canal. Furnished with old pews, this hostelry dispenses at least six ever-changing cask ales and a variety of Belgian and German bottled beers, together with real cider. Food available *Mon-Fri L and E & Sat-Sun 12.00-20.30 (Sun 18.00).* Dog- and family-friendly, outside seating. Newspapers and Wi-Fi. *Open 12.00-23.00.*

🍺✕ 8 **The Woolly Sheep** 38 Sheep Street, Skipton BD23 1HY (01756 700966; www.woollysheepinn. co.uk). With its cobbled courtyard and stone-flagged floors, this 18th-C hostelry dispenses real ales and food *Mon-Sat 11.30-21.00 & Sun 12.00-20.00.* Family-friendly, outside seating. Newspapers, real fires and Wi-Fi. B&B. *Open Mon-Thu 10.00-23.00 (Thu 00.00) Fri-Sat 10.00-01.00 & Sun 12.00-23.00.*

🍺 9 **The Slaters Arms** Crag Lane, Bradley BD20 9DE (01535 632179; www.theslatersarms.co.uk). Cosy, 18th-C local, with a warm welcome,inglenook fireplace and log fires in *winter.* Well kept real ales together with an appetizing range of homemade food is available *Tue-Sat L and E (not Tue E) & Sun 12.00-19.30.* Dogs and children welcome (*'early doors'* or if eating) garden. Traditional pub games and newspapers. *Open Mon-Sat L and E & Sun 12.00-22.30.*

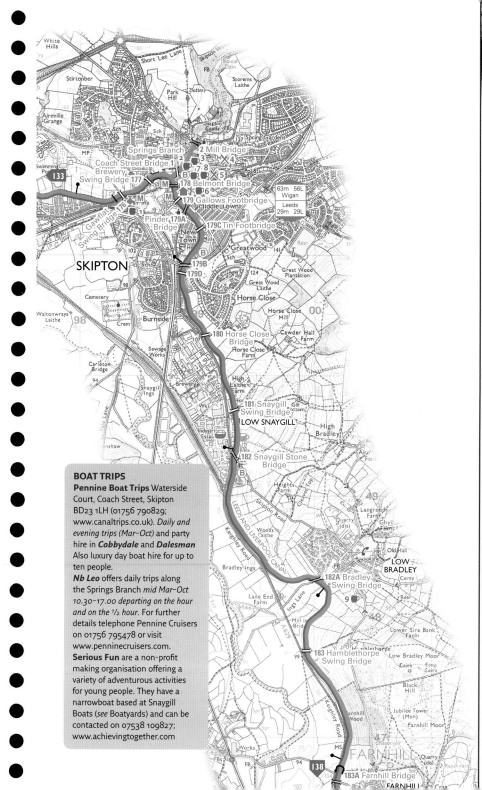

BOAT TRIPS

Pennine Boat Trips Waterside
Court, Coach Street, Skipton
BD23 1LH (01756 790829;
www.canaltrips.co.uk). *Daily and
evening trips (Mar–Oct)* and party
hire in *Cobbydale* and *Dalesman*
Also luxury day boat hire for up to
ten people.

Nb Leo offers daily trips along
the Springs Branch *mid Mar–Oct
10.30–17.00 departing on the hour
and on the ½ hour*. For further
details telephone Pennine Cruisers
on 01756 795478 or visit
www.penninecruisers.com.

Serious Fun are a non-profit
making organisation offering a
variety of adventurous activities
for young people. They have a
narrowboat based at Snaygill
Boats (*see* Boatyards) and can be
contacted on 07538 109827;
www.achievingtogether.com

Brewery Swing Bridge, Skipton

NAVIGATIONAL NOTES

1 Bridges 173–176, 181, 183–185 and 188–191 require a handcuff key. Bridges 177, 182A and 187 require a Watermate Key. *See* Navigational Notes on pages 144 for keys required for structures closer to Leeds.
2 Turning in the Springs Branch is restricted and craft over 35ft should be confident that they can reverse out avoiding moored craft. Craft less than 35ft may still have to reverse to find a turning area.

Boatyards

ⓑ**Pennine Cruisers** The Boat Shop, 19 Coach Street, Skipton BD23 1LH (01756 795478; www.penninecruisers.com). At junction with Springs Branch. ⚓ D E Pump out, gas, narrowboat hire, day-hire craft, overnight mooring, long-term mooring, winter storage, dry dock, boat building, boat sales, chandlery, books, maps and gifts, engine repairs, covered wet dock, solid fuel. *Open Mar-Oct, daily 09.00-17.00.*

ⓑ**Snaygill Boats** Skipton Road, Bradley, Nr Skipton BD20 9HA (01756 795150; www.snaygillboats. co.uk). At bridge 182. 🛒 🎁 D E Pump out, gas, narrowboat hire, overnight mooring, long-term mooring, chandlery, dry docks for narrow and wide beam boats, books, maps and gifts, engine repairs, toilet, Shower. *Open 09.00-17.00* during season.

● **Skipton**

N. Yorks. All services. Skipton is probably the most handsome town along the whole Leeds & Liverpool Canal. It is an excellent place for visiting from the canal, for one can moor snugly and safely about one minute's walk away from the centre. It still maintains its importance as a market town, which is referred to in its name: Saxon 'Scip-tun' means sheep-town. The wide High Street is very attractive, lined with mostly Georgian houses, and headed at the northern end by the splendid castle and the well-kept graveyard of the parish church. There is an interesting water mill beside the Springs Branch.

Church of the Holy Trinity High Street, Skipton BD23 1NJ (www.holytrinityskipton.org. uk) Standing opposite the castle, it is a long battlemented church, encircled by large lawns and flourishing gardens. It is in Perpendicular style dating from the 14th C, though it was greatly renovated after suffering serious damage during the Civil War. It has a fine oak roof and a beautifully carved Jacobean font cover.

Craven Museum & Gallery Town Hall, High Street, Skipton BD23 3RA (01756 706407; www. cravenmuseum.org). Outstanding local geology and archaeology collection together with a colourful insight into life in the Craven Dales. *Open Mon & Wed-Sat 10.00-16.00.* Free.

Cycle Hire Dave Ferguson Cycles Albion Yard, 3 Rope Walk, Otley Street, Skipton BD23 1ED (01756 795367; www.davefergusoncycles.com). Spares, repairs, sales and bike hire. *Open Mon & Wed-Sat 09.30-17.30 (Mon 10.00).*

● **Springs Branch**

A short (770yds) but very unusual branch that leaves the Leeds & Liverpool Canal, passes the centre of Skipton and soon finds itself in what is virtually a ravine, overlooked by the castle that towers 100ft above. The branch is navigable by small craft, and makes an interesting diversion by boat or foot. (The towpath continues past the arm, into Skipton Woods.) It was built by the Earl of Thanet, the owner of Skipton Castle, to carry limestone away from his nearby quarry. It was extended by 240yds in 1797 from the water-mill bridge through the deep rock cutting, and 120ft-chutes were constructed at the new terminus to drop the rock into the boats from the horse tramway that was laid from the quarry to the castle. The quarry still flourishes, but the canal and tramway have not been used since 1946. Trains and lorries have replaced them. Now a picturesque backwater the Springs Branch acted for many years as a feeder to the Leeds & Liverpool Canal, taking water from Eller Beck, which runs beside it.

Skipton Castle Skipton BD23 1AW (01756 792442; www.skiptoncastle.co.uk). A magnificent Norman castle, with 17th C additions, that dominates Skipton High Street. After a three-year siege during the Civil War, Cromwell's men allowed the restoration of the castle, but ensured that the building could never again be used as a stronghold. The six massive round towers have survived from the 14th C and other notable features are the 50ft-long banqueting hall, a kitchen with roasting and baking hearths, a dungeon and the 'Shell Room', the walls of which are decorated with sea shells. Picnic area, licensed tearooms and shop. *Open Apr-Sep daily 10.00-17.00 & Oct-Mar 10.00-16.00 (Sun 11.00 throughout year).*

Tourist Information Centre Town Hall, High Street, Skipton BD23 1AH (01756 792809; www. yorkshire.com/view/attractions/skipton/skipton-tourist-information-centre-1164928). *Open Mon-Sat 09.30-16.00.*

Skipton Woods Fine woods leading up the little narrow valley from the Springs Branch. For access, just keep on walking up the towpath of the branch.

Embsay and Bolton Abbey Steam Railway Bolton Abbey Station, Skipton BD23 6AF (01756 710614; www.embsayboltonabbeyrailway.org.uk). Talking timetable (01756 795189). 1 mile north of Skipton off the A59/65 bypass. Bus service from Skipton. A 4-mile round-trip either steam or diesel-hauled. Bookshop, café and picnic site (at all stations). Disabled access at Bolton Abbey Station. *Services throughout year.* Visit website or telephone the talking timetable (01756 795189) for details of upcoming events.

THE SETTLE-CARLISLE RAILWAY

O.S. Nock, the well-known railway writer, described this line (accessible from Skipton station) as 'the only mountain railway in the world built for express trains'. Completed in 1876, at a cost of almost £3.5 million; 72 miles long – including 20 large viaducts, 14 tunnels and no sharp curves and, in common with so many canal projects, some 50% over budget, it very nearly fell to the neo-Beeching axe. It was both one of the most awesome feats of Victorian railway engineering and one of the most fiercely contested closure battles. It is, therefore, fortunate that in the light of today's burgeoning rail freight flows, common sense finally prevailed, saving the line for a rapidly growing commercial traffic – and our wonder and enjoyment. A regular service connecting the isolated communities along the line (swelled by tourist traffic in the summer months) together with ever-increasing pressure on the West Coast Main Line, will undoubtedly ensure the future of this route.

Silsden

There is a fine wooded stretch north of Kildwick; then one curves sharply round the outcrop on which crouches Farnhill Hall, a mellow stone building. The intriguing village of Kildwick has some well-restored canalside buildings now used as private residences. There are good *moorings* here prior to quieter country: the main road and the railway cut the valley corner while the canal takes the longer route round to Silsden. Overlooking Airedale, the green hills are very steep and beautifully wooded in places. The distant rows of chimneys, factories and terraced houses across the valley comprise Keighley; most of its industrial and suburban tentacles are quickly passed by the canal, although the constant succession of little swing bridges regularly impedes a boat's progress. This type of swing bridge is prone to intermittent stiffness due to the elements, and all require a handcuff key. There is a *stores and fish & chips* to be found south of Bridge 197, and an attractive *mooring* by woods, to the east of bridge 195.

Pubs and Restaurants

🍺 1 **The White Lion** Priestbank Road, Kildwick BD20 9BH (01535 632265; www.thewhitelionkildwick. co.uk). 17th-C coaching Inn, close to the canal, serving real ales and *food Mon-Sat L and E & Sun 12.00-16.00.* Garden with views over the Aire Valley; dog- and child-friendly. Traditional pub games and Wi-Fi. B&B. *Open Mon-Sat 12.00-23.00 (Fri-Sat 00.00) & Sun 12.00-22.30.*

🍺 2 **The Robin Hood** 19 Kirkgate, Silsden BD20 0AJ (01535 643997; www.robinhoodsilsden.com/index). Decorated with pictures of old Silsden, this pub serves real ales and food *daily 12.00-21.00 (Sun 16.00).* Dog-friendly, outside seating. Traditional pub games, real fires, sports TV and Wi-Fi. *Open Mon-Sat 11.00-23.00 (Fri-Sat 00.00) & Sun 12.00-23.00.*

🍺 3 **The Red Lion** 47 Kirkgate, Silsden BD20 0AQ (01535 930884; www.facebook.com/redlion.silsden). Three-roomed, locals' pub serving real ales. Dog- and child-friendly, outside seating. Traditional pub games, real fires, sports TV and Wi-Fi. Poker *Tue. Open 11.30-23.30 (Fri-Sat 01.00).*

🍺 4 **The Punch Bowl Inn** Bridge Road, Silsden BD20 9ND (01535 657807; www.punchbowlsilsden. co.uk/index). Comfortable, two-roomed pub, to the west of the canal, serving real ales and food *Tue-Sun L.*

Dog- and family-friendly, outside seating. Quiz *Tue* and live music *Wed.* Traditional pub games and Wi-Fi. *Open 12.00-23.00.*

🍺 5 **The King's Arms** Bolton Road, Silsden BD20 0JY (01535 653216). Friendly, welcoming pub serving an excellent selection of real akes and real cider. Music *Tue & Thu,* Quiz *Wed* and bingo *Sun.* Dog-friendly, outside seating. Traditional pub games, real fires and Wi-Fi. *Open 12.00-00.00 (Mon 23.00).*

🍺 6 **The Boltmaker's Arms** 117 East Parade, Keighley BD21 5HX (07428 726668; www.boltmakersarms.co.uk). Intimate, one-roomed pub – the de facto Timothy Taylor tap – dispensing real ales, real cider and at least 50 single malt whiskies. Dogs welcome and children *until 20.00,* outside seating. Traditional pub games, newspapers, real fires, sports TV and Wi-Fi. *Open Mon-Sat 11.00-23.00 (Fri-Sat 00.00) & Sun 12.00-22.30.*

There are plenty of other pubs in Keighley.

Boatyards

Ⓑ**Silsden Boats** Canal Wharf, Elliot Street, Silsden, nr Keighley BD20 0DE (01535 653675; www.silsdenboats.co.uk). 🛒♿D Pump out, gas, narrowboat and wide-beam boat hire, boat sales, slipway, books maps and gifts, toilets. *Open Mon-Fri 09.00-16.00.*

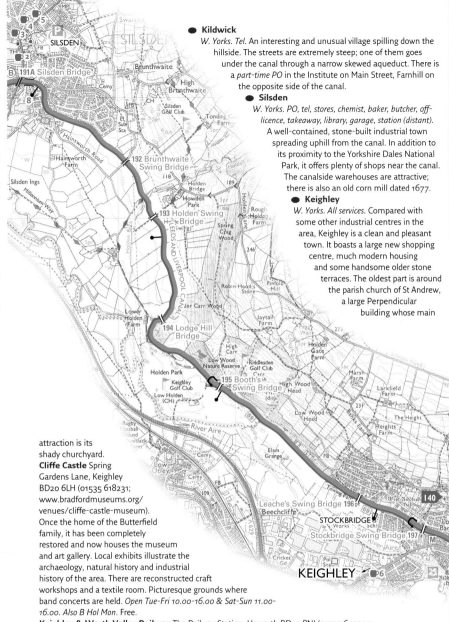

● **Kildwick**

W. Yorks. Tel. An interesting and unusual village spilling down the hillside. The streets are extremely steep; one of them goes under the canal through a narrow skewed aqueduct. There is a *part-time PO* in the Institute on Main Street, Farnhill on the opposite side of the canal.

● **Silsden**

W. Yorks. PO, tel, stores, chemist, baker, butcher, off-licence, takeaway, library, garage, station (distant). A well-contained, stone-built industrial town spreading uphill from the canal. In addition to its proximity to the Yorkshire Dales National Park, it offers plenty of shops near the canal. The canalside warehouses are attractive; there is also an old corn mill dated 1677.

● **Keighley**

W. Yorks. All services. Compared with some other industrial centres in the area, Keighley is a clean and pleasant town. It boasts a large new shopping centre, much modern housing and some handsome older stone terraces. The oldest part is around the parish church of St Andrew, a large Perpendicular building whose main attraction is its shady churchyard.

Cliffe Castle Spring Gardens Lane, Keighley BD20 6LH (01535 618231; www.bradfordmuseums.org/venues/cliffe-castle-museum). Once the home of the Butterfield family, it has been completely restored and now houses the museum and art gallery. Local exhibits illustrate the archaeology, natural history and industrial history of the area. There are reconstructed craft workshops and a textile room. Picturesque grounds where band concerts are held. *Open Tue-Fri 10.00-16.00 & Sat-Sun 11.00-16.00. Also B Hol Mon.* Free.

Keighley & Worth Valley Railway The Railway Station, Haworth BD22 8NJ (01535 645214; www.kwvr.co.uk). Privately preserved by volunteers of the Keighley & Worth Valley Railway Preservation Society, the line runs for 5 miles from the British Rail station at Keighley up to Haworth, the home of the Brontë family, and Oxenhope. British Railways closed the line in 1961, but the Society eventually succeeded in reopening it in 1968 with a regular service of steam trains. In the mornings, the service is operated by diesel railbuses, but in the afternoons magnificent steam engines puff their way along the track. In the goods yard at Haworth the Society has a splendid collection of steam engines and carriages, mostly ancient. The line was made famous by the film *The Railway Children. Open every weekend, most school holidays and throughout the summer.*

Tourist Information Centre 2/4 West Lane, Howarth BD22 8EF (01535 642329; www.haworth-village.org.uk/visitors/visiting-bronte-country/visitor-information.asp). *Open Apr-Sep 10.00-17.00 & Oct-Mar 10.00-16.00 (Wed 10.30).*

139

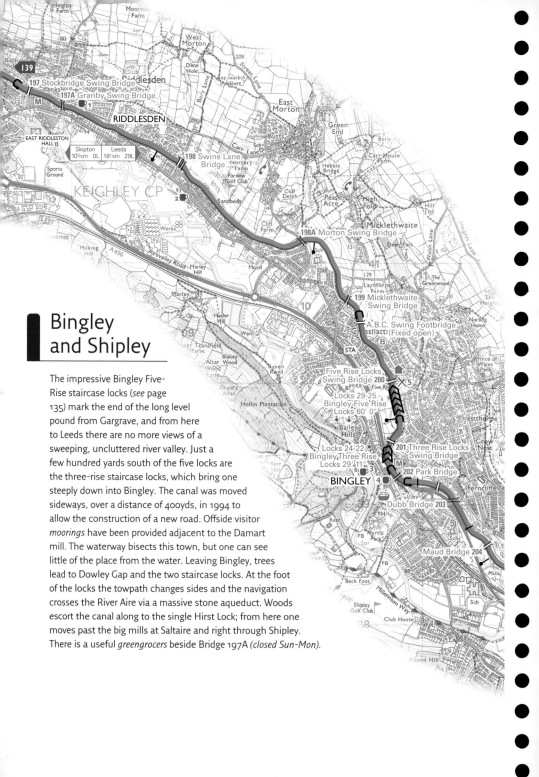

Bingley and Shipley

The impressive Bingley Five-Rise staircase locks (*see page 135*) mark the end of the long level pound from Gargrave, and from here to Leeds there are no more views of a sweeping, uncluttered river valley. Just a few hundred yards south of the five locks are the three-rise staircase locks, which bring one steeply down into Bingley. The canal was moved sideways, over a distance of 400yds, in 1994 to allow the construction of a new road. Offside visitor *moorings* have been provided adjacent to the Damart mill. The waterway bisects this town, but one can see little of the place from the water. Leaving Bingley, trees lead to Dowley Gap and the two staircase locks. At the foot of the locks the towpath changes sides and the navigation crosses the River Aire via a massive stone aqueduct. Woods escort the canal along to the single Hirst Lock; from here one moves past the big mills at Saltaire and right through Shipley. There is a useful *greengrocers* beside Bridge 197A (*closed Sun-Mon*).

Pubs and Restaurants

🍺 **1 The Marquis of Granby** 1 Hospital Road, Riddlesden BD20 5EP (01535 607164). Real ale is served in this bright and cheerful canalside pub, together with food *L and E*. Quiz *Thu*. Family- and dog-friendly, outside seating. Real fires, sports TV and Wi-Fi. Coffee and bacon butties available *from 10.00*. Bar *opens 12.00-00.00 (Mon-Thu 23.00)*.

🍺 **2 The Airedale Heifer** Bradford Road, Sandbeds, Keighley BD20 5LY (01274 515870; www.theairedaleheifer.co.uk). Brewery tap to the Bridgehouse Brewery (the brewery is situated behind the pub) this solid, stone-built establishment dispenses real ale and excellent quality food *Mon-Fri L and E & Sat-Sun 12.00-21.00*. Dog- and child-friendly, garden. Real fires and Wi-Fi. *Open daily 10.30-23.00 (or later)*.

🍺 **3 The Brown Cow** Ireland Bridge, Bingley BD16 2QX (01274 564345; www.browncowbingley.com). An excellent selection of real ales and good quality home-cooked food is served *Mon-Fri L and E & Sat-Sun 12.00-21.00 (Sun 20.00)* in this riverside pub. Dog- and child-friendly, garden. Quiz *Tue* and live music *Sat*. Real fires and Wi-Fi. *Open 11.30-23.00 (Fri-Sat 00.00)*.

🍺 **4 Chip N Ern** 73 Main Street, Bingley BD16 2JA (01274 985501). Friendly micro-pub, with a wood-panelled ground floor bar, serving real ales and real cider downstairs and gin upstairs. Musician's jam night *Tue*. Dog- and family-friendly. Wi-Fi. *Open Mon-Fri 16.00-00.00 & Sat-Sun 12.00-23.00 (Sat 00.00)*

✗ **5 Five Rise Locks - Café & Store** 2 Beck Lane, Bingley BD16 4DS (01274 569664; www.fiveriselockscafe.co.uk). An inexpensive selection of hot and cold, freshly made sandwiches, paninis, jacket potatoes, full English breakfasts, homemade cakes, tea, coffee and a children's menu. Dogs, babies and children welcome. *Open Apr-Oct, Tue-Fri 10.00-17.00 (& Jul-Aug Mon) & Sat-Sun 09.30-17.30; Nov-Mar, Tue-Sun 10.00-16.00*.

🍺 **6 The Fishermen's Inn** Wagon Lane, Bingley BD16 1TS (01274 510479; www.thefishermansinn.com). A comfortable pub serving real ales and home-made food *Mon-Fri L and E & Sat-Sun 12.00-21.00 (Sun 20.00)*. Dog- and family-friendly, garden. Real fires and Wi-Fi. *Open 12.00-23.30*.

🍺✗ **7 The Boathouse Inn** Victoria Road, Saltaire BD18 3LA (01274 585690; www.theboathouseinn.co.uk). Flying in the face of a century and a quarter of local tradition this is the first licensed premises in Saltaire, and it dispenses real ale and food *daily 12.00-22.30 (Sat-Sun 10.00)*. Dog- and child-friendly (*until 21.00)*. Real fires, sports TV and Wi-Fi. *Open Mon-Thu 11.00-22.30 & Fri-Sun 10.00-23.30 (Sun 22.30)*.

🍺 **8 The Ring o' Bells** 3 Bradford Road, Shipley BD18 3PR (01274 584386). A traditional and homely pub, serving real ale and food *daily 12.00-21.00 (Fri-Sun 19.00)*. Dog-friendly, patio. Occasional live music. Traditional pub games, sports TV and Wi-Fi. *Open Mon-Sat 11.00-00.00 & Sun 12.00-23.00*.

✗♀ **9 The Waterside Bistro & Bar** 7 Wharf Street, Shipley BD17 7DW (01274 594444; www.watersideshipley.com). Well-thought off, small and intimate candle-lit restaurant serving a modern British menu. Canalside seating *in summer*. *Open Tue-Sat L and E*.

🍺 **10 The Sir Norman Rae** Victoria House, Market Square, Shipley BD18 3QB (01274 535290; www.jdwetherspoon.com/pubs/all-pubs/england/west-yorkshire/the-sir-norman-rae-shipley). Named after a local benefactor, mill owner and politician, this popular pub serves a wide range of real ale and food *08.00-23.00*. Family-friendly, sports TV and Wi-Fi. *Open daily 08.00-23.00*.

Also try: 🍺 **11 The Salt Cellar** 192 Saltaire Road, Shipley BD18 3PR (01274 584286) and 🍺 **12 Fanny's Ale & Cider House** 63 Saltaire Road, Saltaire BD18 3JN (01274 591419).

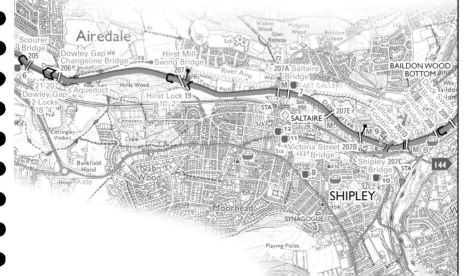

Bingley Five-Rise Locks

● **Baildon**
W. Yorks. All services. 1¹/₂ miles north of Shipley.
A very old industrial town huddled on a hilltop on
the edge of Baildon Moor. Stretching from Baildon
to Bingley is the Glen, a wooded valley that curves
below the heights of the moor. A splendid scenic
tramway carrying two tramcars connects the coach
road to the higher parts of Baildon Moor – *in summer
a frequent service operates, but in winter it is arranged
only to suit the needs of residents at the upper level*.
East Riddlesden Hall Bradford Road, Keightly BD20
5EL (01535 607075; www.nationaltrust.org.uk/east-
riddlesden-hall). Just south of swing bridge 197A. A
17th-C stone manor house complete with tithe barn.
Fine collection of Yorkshire oak furniture, textiles,
pewter, paintings and armour. The house is set in
mature grounds with beech trees, ducks and a pond
and the Starkie Wing provides a striking backdrop
to a garden planted with lavender, flowers and a

fragrant herb border. Also an orchard garden with
wild flowers, bulbs, perennials and, of course, apple
Blossom. Open times vary so telephone or visit the
website for details. Shop, picnic area and tearoom
(open as per house except 12.00 on Sat). Events.
Charge.

● **Bingley**
W. Yorks. All services. An industrial town now known
nationally as a centre for thermal underwear.
Standing at the south east end of the town, amidst
several old cottages, is the large parish church of
Holy Trinity, with its massive spire conspicuous from
the canal. *Stores open daily 07.00-23.00.*
Bingley Five-Rise Locks A very famous and
impressive feature of the canal system built in
1774 in 'staircase' formation. They are all joined
together rather than being separated by pounds of
'neutral' water. The top gates of the lowest lock are
the bottom gates of the lock above, and so on. This

means it is not possible to empty a lock unless the one below is itself empty. The rapid elevation thus resulting is quite daunting. The CRT Sanitary Station is housed in a handsome old stable, where towing horses were once rested.

● **Saltaire**

W. Yorks. PO, tel, stores, chemist, baker, off-licence, takeaways, fish & chips, butcher, garage, station. An estate village that owes its existence to the Utopian dream of Sir Titus Salt, a wealthy Victorian mill owner. He was so appalled by the working and living conditions of his workers in Bradford that he decided to build the ideal industrial settlement. This he did in 1850 on the banks of the canal and the River Aire – hence the name Saltaire. He provided every amenity including high standard housing, but no pub – for he was a great opponent of strong drink. The village has changed little since those days (save the recent addition of a pub!); everything is carefully laid out and the terraced houses are attractive in an orderly sort of way. There is an Italianate church near the canal, and a large park beside the river. Admirers of David Hockney's work should visit the art gallery. *Stores open daily 07.00-23.00.*

Salts Mill Victoria Road Saltaire BD18 3LA (01274 531163; www.saltsmill.org.uk). The 1853 Gallery showing David Hockney's work, further galleries and a local history exhibition; an inexpensive diner and a café, and three floors of shops. *Open Mon-Fri 10.00-17.30, and Sat,Sun 10.00-18.00 except Xmas.*

Tourist Information Centre Salt's Mill 2 Victoria Road, Saltaire BD18 3LA (01274 437942). *Open Apr-Sep, daily 10.00-17.00 & Oct-Mar daily 10.00-16.00.*

● **Shipley**

W. Yorks. PO, All services. A dark stone town built on a generous scale and based on textile and engineering industries. There are powerful-looking mills to be seen, as well as the town hall and a suitably battlemented Salvation Army citadel. Shipley is lucky enough to be on the edge of Baildon Moor and Shipley Glen. The 3-mile-long Bradford Canal used to join the Leeds & Liverpool in Shipley, by bridge 208, but this has all been filled in for years. There is a pub and restaurant beside bridge 207C together with a useful canalside supermarket between bridges 207D and 208 *(open Mon-Sat 08.00-22.00 & Sun 10.00-16.00).* There are public moorings at Ashley Lane – near bridge 207B – with town centre shopping a relaxed 5 minutes' walk away.

NAVIGATIONAL NOTES

1 Bridges 188–196 require a Handcuff key, although Bridges 189–91 are usually left open. Bridges 197, 197A, 198A and 199 need a Watermate key. Bridge 209 needs a Watermate key and a windlass.

2 Locks 29–14 and 12–4 require a Handcuff key. Locks 13 and 2 require a Handcuff key and are security locked outside opening hours – *see* note 3. Lock 1 requires a Watermate key.

3 Opening times for Bingley Five-Rise, Bingley Three-Rise and Field Locks: *mid Mar-Oct first passage commencing 08.00 & last passage commencing 17.00 (Oct 16.00).* They may be used only under the supervision of the lock keeper. To confirm times contact CRT 0303 040 4040; www.canalrivertrust.org.uk/contact-us/ways-to-contact-us.

4 *See* also Navigational Note on page 147.

Boatyards

Ⓑ**Hainsworth Boatyard** Fairfax Road, Bingley BD16 4DR (01274 565925/07736 120836; www.hainsworthsboatyard.co.uk). 🛢 Pump out, gas, overnight and long-term mooring, winter storage, slipway, chandlery, solid fuel, boat sales and repairs, engine repairs, toilets, Wi-Fi. International boat transporters. *24hr emergency call-out.*

Ⓑ**Gallows Bridge Moorings** Apperley Bridge, Bradford BD10 0UR (01274 616961; www.apperleybridgemarina.co.uk). In Shipley – just east of Gallows Footbridge 207D. Short- and long-term moorings.

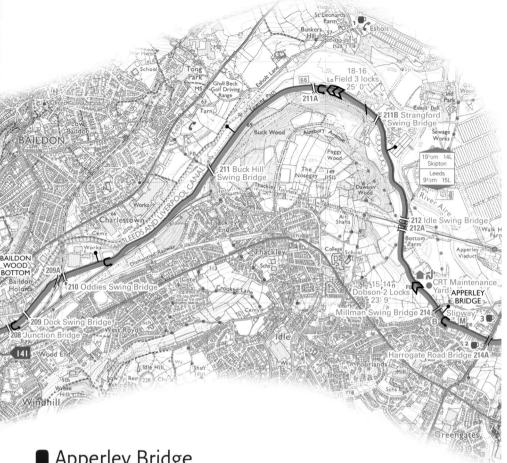

Apperley Bridge

This section sees the end of the wide open moorlands that frame the scenery further upstream: from now on, industry and housing begin to feature more as one approaches the outskirts of Leeds. The navigation, however, is thankfully sequestered from these intrusions into the landscape. Leaving Shipley, the adjacent railway cuts through a 500ft-high hill in two mile-long tunnels. The canal goes all the way round this delightfully wooded hill, tenaciously following the Aire Valley. Halfway round the long curve are Field Locks. Beyond the main railway bridge is a Canal & River Trust maintenance yard at the head of Dobson Locks and housed in a former canal warehouse. There are also *showers, toilets and a pump out* here. Temporarily traversing a built-up area, the navigation emerges yet again onto a wooded hillside overlooking the still rural and charming valley that contains the River Aire.

◾ NAVIGATIONAL NOTES

Bridge 214 needs a Watermate key. Bridges 215–219 require a Handcuff key. Bridge 215 is usually padlocked open to the canal.

● **Rodley**
W. Yorks. PO box, tel, takeaway, off-licence. Rodley has long been associated with the woollen industry with fulling mills and scribbling mills powered by the swift-flowing waters of the River Aire. It is still a useful village with two pubs, several shops and good visitor moorings.

Pubs and Restaurants

1 The Woolpack Main Street, Esholt, Shipley BD17 7QZ (01274 809495; www.thewoolpackesholt.com). As featured in the TV series *Emmerdale*. From bridge 211 follow the footpath north west to the main road, turn right, then take the turning to the right signposted Esholt. Real ale together with food *Wed–Sat 12.00–17.00 (Fri–Sat 19.00) & Sun 12.00–16.00*. Dog- and family-friendly, outside seating. Quiz *Thu*. Traditional pub games, real fires and Wi-Fi. *Open 12.00–22.00 (Thu–Sat 23.00).*

2 The Dog & Gun 1001 Harrogate Road, Apperley Bridge BD10 0LT (01274 611388). Just south of Bridge214A. Friendly local serving real ale and food *Wed–Fri E & Sat–Sun 12.00–20.30*. Beer garden, open fires, sports TV and Wi-Fi. *Open Mon–Thu 16.00–23.30 & Fri–Sun 12.00–00.00.*

3 The Stansfield Apperley Lane, Apperley Bridge BD10 0NP (0113 250 2659; www.thestansfieldarms.co.uk/taverns). A beautifully beamed pub, dating from 1543, serving real ales and food *daily 12.00–21.00 (Fri–Sat 22.00)*. Dog- and child-friendly, garden. *Occasional live music and real fires. Open 12.00–00.00 (Fri–Sat 01.00)*

4 The Railway Inn Calverley Bridge, Rodley LS13 1NR (0113 257 6603). Traditional canalside pub serving real ale and food *Wed–Sun L and E*. Child- and dog-friendly, outside seating. *Open 11.00–23.00.*

5 The Rodley Barge 182–184 Town Street, Rodley LS13 1HP (0113 257 4606). Unpretentious canalside pub by bridge 217 serving real ale and food *daily L*. All canal and towpath users are welcome – children *until 20.00*. Canalside garden, open fires, Wi-Fi and moorings. Quiz *Mon, Wed & Sun. Open 12.00–23.00.*

6 The Owl Inn I Rodley Lane, Rodley LS13 1LB (0113 345 5080). An attractive old pub serving real ales and food *daily 12.00–21.00*. Dog- and family-friendly, garden. Traditional pub games. *Open 12.00–23.00.*

7 Café Fraîche 33 Rodley Lane, Leeds LS13 1LB (0113 236 3520; www.cafefraiche.co.uk). *Open Mon–Sat 08.00–16.00 & Sun 08.30–14.30*, this friendly, family-run café serves an appetising selection of light meals, sandwiches, wraps, paninis, salads and specials together with an all day breakfast. Tea and coffee. Canal users most welcome.

Boatyards

ⒷApperley Bridge Marina Waterfront Mews, Apperley Bridge, Bradford BD10 0UR (01274 616961; www.apperleybridgemarina.co.uk) 🚻🚻♨ D Pump out, gas, short- and long-term mooring with *24hr* CCTV coverage, solid fuel, chandlery, toilets, showers. *Open Fri–Mon & Wed 09.30–15.00.* ✕ 8 Marina View Coffee Shop (07756 046753; www.marinaviewcoffeeshop.co.uk). *Open Fri–Mon 10.00–16.00.*

ⒷSwiftcraft The Boathouse, Parkin Lane, Apperley Bridge, Bradford BD10 0NF (01274 611786/07850 249449/07789 076314; www.swiftcraftboats.co.uk). Gas, overnight mooring, long-term mooring, DIY facilities, boat fitting out and repairs, boat sales, boat condition surveys, BSS surveys, Gas Safe registered.

ⒷRodley Boat Centre Canal Wharf, Canal Road, Rodley, Leeds LS13 1LP (0113 257 6132; www.rodleyboatcentre.com). By Bridge 217. 🚻🚻♨ D E Pump out, overnight mooring, long-term mooring, winter storage, slipway, chandlery, books and maps, marine engineers (inboard and outboard), generators and electrics. *24hr emergency call out. Open Mon–Fri 09.00–17.30 & Sat–Sun 10.00–16.00.*

145

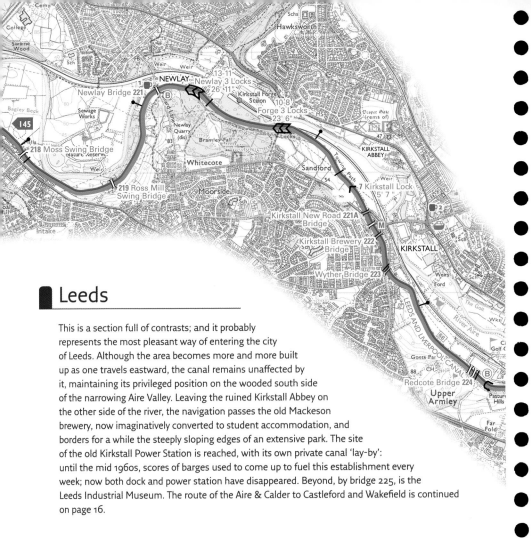

Leeds

This is a section full of contrasts; and it probably
represents the most pleasant way of entering the city
of Leeds. Although the area becomes more and more built
up as one travels eastward, the canal remains unaffected by
it, maintaining its privileged position on the wooded south side
of the narrowing Aire Valley. Leaving the ruined Kirkstall Abbey on
the other side of the river, the navigation passes the old Mackeson
brewery, now imaginatively converted to student accommodation, and
borders for a while the steeply sloping edges of an extensive park. The site
of the old Kirkstall Power Station is reached, with its own private canal 'lay-by':
until the mid 1960s, scores of barges used to come up to fuel this establishment every
week; now both dock and power station have disappeared. Beyond, by bridge 225, is the
Leeds Industrial Museum. The route of the Aire & Calder to Castleford and Wakefield is continued
on page 16.

Pubs and Restaurants

1 The Abbey Inn 99 Pollard Lane, Newlay,
Leeds LS13 1EQ (0113 258 1248; www.abbeyinn.
org). A small, friendly country pub – once used by
the nearby Abbey as a morgue – but now serving
real ales, real cider and excellent food *Thu-Sun
12.00-16.00 (Fri 19.00)*. Dog- and family-friendly,
garden. Quiz *Thu & Sun*. Traditional pub games,
regular live music, real fires and Wi-Fi. *Open
12.00-23.00.*

2 West End House 26 Abbey Road, Leeds LS5
3HS (0113 278 6332; www.westendleeds.co.uk).
Traditional, old, stone-built hostelry close to Kirkstall
Abbey, serving real ale, real cider and appetising food
Mon-Fri L and E; Sat 11.30-19.30 & Sun 12.00-18.00.
Dog-friendly, outside seating. Quiz *Tue & Thu*. Sports
TV and Wi-Fi. *Open Mon-Thu 11.30-23.00 (Thu 23.30)
Fri-Sat 11.30-00.00 & Sun 12.00-23.30.*

Leeds

W. Yorks. All services. See also page 18.

Leeds Industrial Museum Canal Road, Armley, Leeds LS12 2QF (0113 378 3173; www.leeds.gov.uk/museumsandgalleries/armleymills). There have been corn and fulling mills on this site since at least 1559, with the present building dating from 1805. When built it was the most advanced in the country and it now houses a superb range of real-life exhibits demonstrating the local textile, heavy engineering, tanning and printing trades. There are working cranes, locomotives and waterwheels, and a cinema of the 1920s. *Jack* the locomotive runs on 'steaming up' days. Shop and picnic area. Disabled access. The little stone bridge over the canal here dates from around 1770. *Open Tue-Say & B Hol Mon 10.00-17.00 and Sun 13.00-17.00. Charge.*

Kirkstall Abbey Abbey Road, Kirkstall LS5 3EH (0113 230 5492; www.leeds.gov.uk/museumsandgalleries/kirkstallabbey). The large elegant ruins of a Cistercian abbey founded in the 12th C. The remaining walls narrowly escaped demolition in the late 19th C, but are now carefully preserved, surrounded by a small, attractive park. *Open Tue-Sun 10.00-16.30 (Oct-Mar 16.00) & B Hol Mon 10.00-16.00. Free. Monthly weekend markets, Mar-Nov 12.00-15.00.*

Abbey House Museum Abbey Walk, Kirkstall LS5 3EH (0113 378 4079; www.leeds.gov.uk/museumsandgalleries/abbeyhouse). This splendid folk museum illustrates the life and work of the people of Yorkshire during the last 300 years. As well as exhibiting toys, costumes and pottery, it houses three streets of fully furnished 19th-C shops, cottages and workshops. *Open Tue-Fri & Sun 10.00-17.00; Sat 12.00-17.00 and B Hols 10.00-17.00. Charge.*

Tourist Information Centre Headrow, Leeds LS1 3AA (0113 378 6877; www.visitleeds.co.uk/maps-and-more/Tourist-Information-Centre.aspx‡). *Open Mon-Sat 10.00-17.00; Sun 11.00-15.00 & B Hol Mon 10.00-15.00.* Also Art Gallery Shop.

NAVIGATIONAL NOTES

In the interests of safety and water conservation Newlay, Forge and Kirkstall Locks cannot be operated outside the hours *08.15–18.00 mid-Mar-Oct* when CRT staff will be in attendance to provide assistance as required. However, please note that when travelling east the latest departure time from Newlay Top lock is *15.00* in order to arrive in Leeds Canal Basin by *18.00*. The latest departure time from Leeds, when travelling west, in order to clear Newlay Top Lock by *18.00*, is *15.00*. To confirm times and the availability of assistance contact CRT on 0303 040 4040; www.canalrivertrust.org.uk/contact-us/ways-to-contact-us. Uninterrupted passage between Granary Wharf and Newlay is advised.

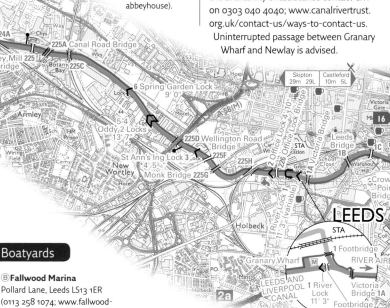

Boatyards

Ⓑ**Fallwood Marina**
Pollard Lane, Leeds LS13 1ER (0113 258 1074; www.fallwood-marina.co.uk). By bridge 221. 🛒🛎️⚓ Winter storage, crane, gas, paraffin, slipway, boat and engine repairs, showers, toilets. No dogs.

Ⓑ**Aire Valley Marina** Redcote Lane, Kirkstall, Leeds LS4 2AL (01575 560275; www.narrowboats.org/canal-service/15/aire+valley+marina). 🛒⚓E Gas, overnight mooring, long-term mooring, winter storage, slipway, DIY facilities, toilets, showers, laundrette.

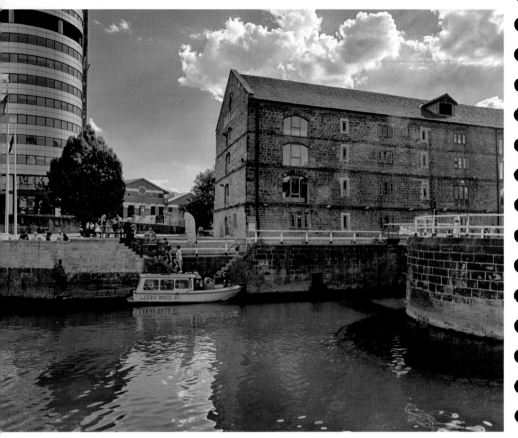

River Lock, Leeds

KEEPING THINGS ON THE LEVEL

The Macclesfield Canal adheres to a mainly level course, with all the locks (aside from the stop lock at Hall Green) in a single group at Bosley. Had the visionary scheme proposed by J. F Pownall, in his work *The Projected Grand Contour Canal to Connect with Estuaries and Canals in England* (1942), come to fruition, the Macclesfield would have formed a part of his grand plan:

'Through the heart of England there runs a *natural canal line*, as I shall term it. This is a line so naturally favourable for canal construction that a canal can follow it easily for miles at a time whilst remaining throughout at the same level. The old canal surveyors saw this line. . . A canal following this contour would therefore proceed right through the country solely on one level. . . it (also) proceeds in direct reaches for long-distances at a time. . . The natural canal line creates the remarkable possibility, never before known, of having a canal go through the length of the country and serve the great industrial areas without any variation from one level.

(There) are very great advantages. The Grand Contour Canal (would be) uniformly level at 310ft above sea level to serve London, Bristol, Southampton, Birmingham, Manchester, Leeds and Newcastle. All the existing canals would be branches from it. The waterway would be large enough to accommodate coastal vessels of a fair size. The Grand Contour Canal would become the primary water distributor of the country. Along the canal there will be formed a special layer in the bed. . . in this layer pipelines for the transport of commercial liquids and gases would be embedded.

Precisely because it expresses a natural feature, the Contour Canal will lie unobtrusively on the land and will have a characteristic scenery of its own.' *Precisely.*

MACCLESFIELD CANAL

MAXIMUM DIMENSIONS
Length: 70' 0"
Beam: 7' 0"
Headroom: 7' 0"

MILEAGE
HARDINGS WOOD JUNCTION
(Trent & Mersey Canal) *to:*
Congleton Wharf: 5¾ miles
Bosley Top Lock: 11½ miles
Macclesfield: 17 miles
Bollington: 20 miles

MARPLE JUNCTION
(Peak Forest Canal): 27¾ miles

Locks: 13

MANAGER
0303 040 4040;
www.canalrivertrust.org.uk/contact-us/
ways-to-contact-us

With the completion of the Trent & Mersey Canal in 1777, demand was created for an alternative canal link between the Midlands and Manchester, and a direct line through the manufacturing town of Macclesfield was an obvious choice. But it was not until 1825 that Thomas Telford was asked by promoters of the canal to survey a line linking the Peak Forest Canal and the Trent & Mersey Canal. The 28-mile line he suggested was the canal that was built, from Marple to just north of Kidsgrove, although Telford did not supervise the construction, leaving to go and build the Birmingham & Liverpool Junction Canal (now the Shropshire Union). William Crosley was the canal's engineer.

The canal, which runs along the side of a tall ridge of hills west of the Pennines, does, however, bear the distinctive hallmarks of Telford's engineering. Like the Shropshire Union, the Macclesfield is a 'cut and fill' canal, following as straight a course as possible, and featuring a many great cuttings and embankments. Apart from the stop lock at Hall Green, where a 1ft rise was insisted upon as a water preservation measure by the Trent & Mersey Canal Company – to whose Hall Green Branch the Macclesfield Canal connected at the stop lock, all the locks are grouped into one flight of 12 at Bosley. The canal is fed from nearby reservoirs, at Bosley and Sutton.

In spite of intense competition from neighbouring railways and the Trent & Mersey Canal, the Macclesfield carried a good trade for many years. Much of this was coal, along with cotton from the big mills established along its northern reaches. Following its purchase in 1846 by the Great Central Railway Company, the canal began a slow, but steady, decline. The Macclesfield Canal today is an extremely interesting cruising waterway, and forms part of the popular 100-mile Cheshire Ring canal circuit. Look out for the original, and very large, stone milestones showing distances from Hall Green stop lock (the original end of the canal) and Marple. These were removed during World War II in fear of helping invading forces. They have been lovingly restored to their former glory by the Macclesfield Canal Society.

Hardings Wood

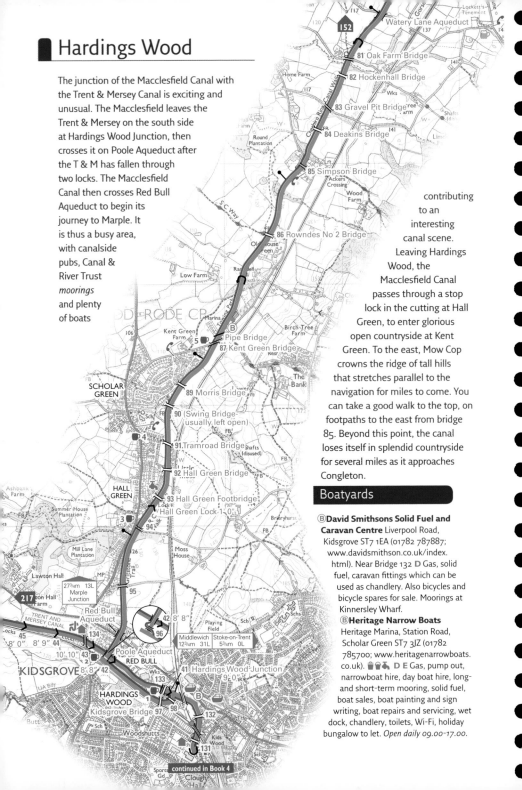

The junction of the Macclesfield Canal with the Trent & Mersey Canal is exciting and unusual. The Macclesfield leaves the Trent & Mersey on the south side at Hardings Wood Junction, then crosses it on Poole Aqueduct after the T & M has fallen through two locks. The Macclesfield Canal then crosses Red Bull Aqueduct to begin its journey to Marple. It is thus a busy area, with canalside pubs, Canal & River Trust *moorings* and plenty of boats contributing to an interesting canal scene. Leaving Hardings Wood, the Macclesfield Canal passes through a stop lock in the cutting at Hall Green, to enter glorious open countryside at Kent Green. To the east, Mow Cop crowns the ridge of tall hills that stretches parallel to the navigation for miles to come. You can take a good walk to the top, on footpaths to the east from bridge 85. Beyond this point, the canal loses itself in splendid countryside for several miles as it approaches Congleton.

Boatyards

Ⓑ**David Smithsons Solid Fuel and Caravan Centre** Liverpool Road, Kidsgrove ST7 1EA (01782 787887; www.davidsmithson.co.uk/index.html). Near Bridge 132 **D** Gas, solid fuel, caravan fittings which can be used as chandlery. Also bicycles and bicycle spares for sale. Moorings at Kinnersley Wharf.

Ⓑ**Heritage Narrow Boats** Heritage Marina, Station Road, Scholar Green ST7 3JZ (01782 785700; www.heritagenarrowboats.co.uk). ⛴🛁🚿 **D E** Gas, pump out, narrowboat hire, day boat hire, long- and short-term mooring, solid fuel, boat sales, boat painting and sign writing, boat repairs and servicing, wet dock, chandlery, toilets, Wi-Fi, holiday bungalow to let. *Open daily 09.00-17.00.*

Little Moreton Hall

Newcastle Road, Congleton, Cheshire CW12 4SD (01260 272018; www.nationaltrust.org. uk/little-moreton-hall). Just 3/4 mile west of the canal by footpath from bridge 86 (beware nettles and brambles!). This fabulous moated house is arguably the finest example of black and white timbered architecture in the UK, and is well worth the walk from the canal. It was built between 1559 and 1580 with carved gables and ornate windows, and has scarcely changed since. It contains a fine collection of oak furniture and pewter. Shop and tearoom. Opening times vary so visit website for full details. Charge.

Mow Cop

(www.mowcop.info). NT. Walk east from bridge 85. A hill nearly 1100ft above sea level, which gives a magnificent view across the Cheshire Plain, beyond Stoke and into Wales, which looks particularly good at night. On top of the hill is Mow Cop Castle, an imitation ruin built in 1754 by Randle Wilbraham, a local squire. It was on this spot that Hugh Bourne, a wheelwright, climbed to the summit to create the Primitive Methodists in 1807. Their first meeting lasted 14 hours, and was an endeavour to create a simpler form of religion. The memorial church was erected in 1862 on the site of this meeting. A hundred years later 70,000 disciples climbed to the top to worship on what had become, for them, a Holy Mountain. Bourne died at the age of 80, having seen over 5000 Methodist chapels founded. Coal from collieries to the east of Mow Cop was carried down to the canal by a tramway known as 'The Brake'.

Scholar Green

Cheshire. PO, tel, stores, off-licence. Bisected by the busy A34, the village is best known for the 18th-C Rode Hall, a Grade II* listed building that hosts a Farmers Market *on 1st Sat of the month.* The shop is *open late* and lies west of Bridge 90.

NAVIGATIONAL NOTES

The Macclesfield Canal is generally quite shallow, and mooring is usually only possible at recognised sites.

WALKING AND CYCLING

The towpath is in good condition throughout the length of this canal. Ambitious walkers will want to walk to the top of Mow Cop, which is best accessed from bridge 85. From the top you can follow a section of The Gritstone Trail north towards the Old Man of Mow, a 65ft-tall gritstone pillar left as the rock around it was quarried away. Just before a radio mast turn downhill as waymarked to pass through Roe Park Woods, then bear right to reach the lane leading to Ackers railway crossing and the canal. The Staffordshire Way leaves Mow Cop to head towards Kinver, on the Staffordshire & Worcestershire Canal.

Pubs and Restaurants

1 The Blue Bell 25 Hardingswood, Kidsgrove ST7 1EG (01782 774052; www.bluebellkidsgrove. co.uk). Canalside, at Hardings Wood Junction. Friendly, quiet, one-bar local, winnner of many CAMRA awards. Real ale, plus a range of specialist bottled beers, including many from Belgium, plus real cider and perry. No juke box, pool table or gaming machines. Note the trapdoor in the lounge ceiling. Well-behaved children welcome *until 21.00.* Dogs welcome. Snacks are available *at weekends. Open Tue–Fri 19.30–23.00; Sat 13.00–16.00, 19.30–23.00; Sun 12.00–22.30 (all day during summer). Closed Mon.*

✗ 2 The Red Bull Hotel Congleton Road South, Church Lawton ST7 3AJ (01782 782600; www.robinsonsbrewery.com/redbullchurchlawton) By Lock 43. Popular pub close to Hardings Wood Junction, serving real ale and bar meals, including fish dishes *Mon-Fri L and E & Sat-Sun 12.00-21.00 (Sun 20.00).* Family-friendly, garden. *Occasional* live music. Moorings. *Open daily 12.00-23.00 (Sun 22.30).*

✗ 3 The Bleeding Wolf Hotel 121 Congleton Road North, Scholar Green, Stoke-on-Trent ST7 3BQ (01782 782272; www.thebleedingwolf.co.uk). A large and lively thatched country pub with a conservatory, offering real ale and food (including a carvery *Sun 12.00-15.00) Mon-Fri L and E & Sat-Sun 12.00-21.30 (Sun 20.00).* Family-friendly, garden. *Occasional* live music, *regular* quiz nights. Real fires and Wi-Fi. *Open Mon-Thu L and E & Fri-Sun 12.00-00.00 (Sun 23.00).*

4 The Travellers Rest 175 Congleton Road North, Scholar Green, Stoke-on-Trent ST7 3HA (01782 782359; www.thetravs.com). Traditional country pub serving real ale, together with food *daily L and E (not Sun E).* Family-friendly, garden. Live music *Tue. Open Mon-Thu L and E & Fri-Sun 12.00-00.00 (Sun 22.30).*

5 The Rising Sun 112 Station Road, Scholar Green, Stoke-on-Trent ST7 3JT (01782 776235; www.facebook.com/RisingSunScholarGreen). A friendly and welcoming pub offering real ale, and excellent home-cooked food *Mon-Fri L and E & Sat-Sun 12.00-21.30 (Sun 20.00).* Dog- and family-friendly, garden. *Occasional* live music, real fires and Wi-Fi. *Open Mon-Thu L and E & Fri-Sun 12.00-00.00 (Fri 09.30).*

Congleton

The canal continues north east, crossing Watery Lane Aqueduct. To the east the ever-present range of hills is a reminder that the Pennine Chain lies just beyond. Passing a golf course, the embanked wharf which overlooks Congleton soon appears, with an aqueduct over the road that runs down into the town. The handsome warehouse at the wharf has now been converted into apartments. There is a useful *parade of shops (including a PO, stores, chemist, off-licence, takeaway, hardware, baker, fish & chips)*, just to the south east of Bridge 75. Beautifully elegant 'roving' bridges, 76 and 77, follow. These are known locally as 'snake bridges' and, in the days of horse-drawn boats, changed the towpath from one side to the other without having to un-hitch the horse. Past Congleton railway station, the canal is carried on a high embankment – a common feature of the Macclesfield – across a narrow valley, affording a good view westward of the tall and elegant railway viaduct crossing the same valley. Meanwhile the looming fell known as the Cloud, over 1000ft high and topped with remains of ancient earthworks, is given a wide berth as the navigation continues on its lonely lock-free course through this very fine landscape. There is a good walk to the top of the Cloud along footpaths east of bridge 71. The canal then continues its lonely course, turning east to cross the River Dane on an embankment – not very impressive from the boat, but superb when viewed from the river – and arrives at the foot of Bosley Locks, in a really delightful setting which is semi-wooded and semi-pastoral. There are good, quiet moorings here.

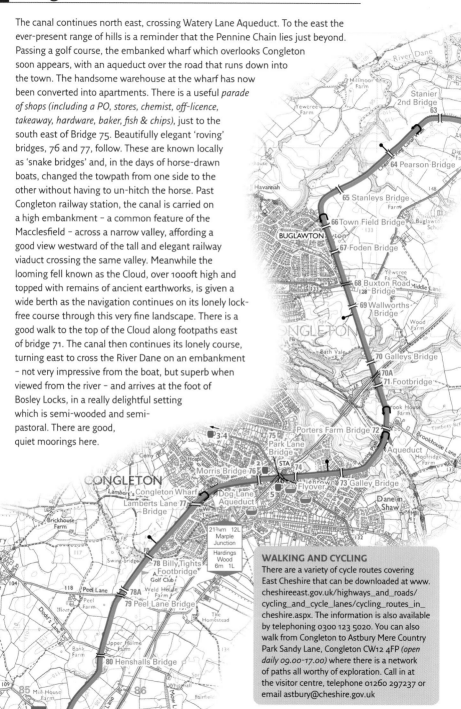

WALKING AND CYCLING
There are a variety of cycle routes covering East Cheshire that can be downloaded at www.cheshireeast.gov.uk/highways_and_roads/cycling_and_cycle_lanes/cycling_routes_in_cheshire.aspx. The information is also available by telephoning 0300 123 5020. You can also walk from Congleton to Astbury Mere Country Park Sandy Lane, Congleton CW12 4FP *(open daily 09.00-17.00)* where there is a network of paths all worthy of exploration. Call in at the visitor centre, telephone 01260 297237 or email astbury@cheshire.gov.uk

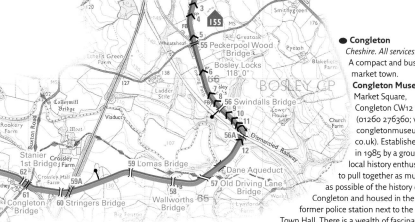

● **Congleton**
Cheshire. All services.
A compact and busy market town.

Congleton Museum Market Square, Congleton CW12 1ET (01260 276360; www. congletonmuseum. co.uk). Established in 1985 by a group of local history enthusiasts to pull together as much as possible of the history of Congleton and housed in the former police station next to the Town Hall. There is a wealth of fascinating artefacts on display, including an Anglo Saxon log boat, a burial urn from 1500 BC, two major coin hoards from the 17th C, together with numerous items of historical interest from more recent times. *Open Tue-Fri 10.30-16.15 & Sat-Sun 10.30-16.15 (Sun 12.00)*. Free. Donations welcome.

Tourist Information Centre Town Hall, High Street, Congleton CW12 1BN (01260 271095; www.congleton-tc.gov.uk/congleton-tourist-information-centre). *Open Mon-Fri 09.00-17.00 & Sat 09.30-14.30.*

● **Bosley Locks**
Effectively the only locks on all the 27 miles of the Macclesfield Canal, these handsome constructions are deep, raising the canal level by fully 118ft to well over 500ft above sea level. Each lock has a pair of mitred top gates instead of the more usual single one, and are a good example of Telford's practice of grouping locks together in flights; here there are 12 within just one mile.

● **Astbury**
Cheshire. PO box, tel, stores, delicatessen, butcher, baker, greengrocer. About 1 mile north west of bridges 79 and 80. A pretty village set just off the A34. St Mary's Church is amazing: its light interior and wide aisles are complemented by generous battlements along the roof and a tower standing quite separate from the body of the church. The *shops* are to be found at Glebe Farm.

Glebe Farm Peel Lane, Astbury Congleton CW12 4RQ (01260 273916; www.glebefarmastbury.co.uk). An interactive day out for children and an opportunity for some retail therapy for adults! An example of total farm diversification offering animal petting, tractor rides, indoor and outdoor play areas, craft shops, a coffee shop and a farm shop, delicatessen, butcher, baker and a visiting fish monger *Thu 10.45-16.45*. ✗ 6 Coffee Shop, and a farm *open Mon-Sat 08.30-16.30 (Sat 17.00) & Sun and B Hols 09.30-16.00*. Farm & Shop *open Mon-Sat 08.30-18.00 & Sun and B Hols 09.00-16.00*. Free entry.

Pubs and Restaurants

🍺✗ **1 The Egerton Arms** Astbury CW12 4RQ (01260 273946; www.egertonarms.co.uk). A handsome and justly popular village pub built c.1560 opposite the 11th-C church, serving real ale. Home-cooked food is available in both the bar and restaurant *L and E, daily*. Children, with well-behaved parents, are welcome *until 21.00*, and there is a large garden and play area. Wi-Fi and camping. Newspapers. B&B. *Open 11.30-23.00 (Sun 22.30)*.

🍺✗ **2 The Queen's Head** Park Lane, Congleton CW12 3DE (01260 272546; www.queensheadpub. org.uk). This welcoming pub serves real ales and food *Mon-Fri L and E & Sat-Sun 12.00-20.00 (Sun 16.00)*. Very dog-friendly, also children. Garden. Quiz *Mon* and sporadic live music. Traditional pub games, newspapers, real fires, sports TV and Wi-Fi. *Open 12.00-00.00 (Fri-Sat 01.00)*.

🍺 **3 The Beartown Tap** 18 Willow Street, Congleton CW12 1RL (07858 270775; www.facebook.com/beartown.tap). Main outlet for the Beartown Brewery, just across the road, this warm friendly pub serves a selection of their real ales, together with a good range of bottled beers. *Sun* Brunch *11.00-14.00*. There is a small library. Dog- and child-friendly *(until 20.30)* patio. *Sun* quiz and *regular* live music. Newspapers and real fires. *Open 16.00-23.00 (Fri-Sun 12.00)*.

🍺 **4 The Young Pretender** 30-34 Lawton Street, Congleton CW12 1RS (01260 273277; www. thebeerparlours.co.uk/the-young-pretender). Thriving town pub, established in a renovated toy shop, serving a range of local real ales and world beers. Bar food is available *daily 16.00-22.00 (Fri-Sun 12.00)*. Dog- and child-friendly *(until 20.00)* outside seating. Quiz *Sun*. Traditional pub games, newspapers, sports TV and Wi-Fi. *Open Mon-Thu 16.00-23.00 & Fri-Sun 12.00-01.00 (Sun 23.00)*.

🍺✗ **5 The Railway Inn** Biddulph Road; Congleton CW12 3JS (01260 272527; www. therailwayinncongleton.co.uk). A large family pub dispensing real ales and food *Mon-Fri L and E & Sat-Sun 12.00-21.00 (Sun 20.00)*. Dog- and family-friendly, play area and beer garden. Quiz *Thu*. Newspapers, real fires, sports TV and Wi-Fi. *Open 12.00-00.00 (Sun 23.00)*.

Oakgrove

The Macclesfield Canal completes the climb of Bosley Locks and resumes its lonely journey through open, attractive countryside. The facilities block beside Bridge 54 includes a *shower, toilets, a pump out and laundry*. Approaching Oakgrove the foothills and mountains of the Pennines, some over 1200ft high, spill right down to the canal. The swing bridge at Oakgrove was once a notorious obstacle on the canal, often requiring two very strong individuals to prise it open. Thankfully those days have long passed. The navigation now follows the contour of the land as it begins to swing around the hills, passing the large flat expanse of Danes Moss and approaching Macclesfield, now clearly visible to the north. If you choose to moor by Gurnett Aqueduct to visit the pubs nearby, take a look at the plaque on a cottage wall 25yds to the east. It commemorates the training here of James Brindley, the canal builder and civil engineer, between 1733–40 – he was apprenticed to Abraham Bennett. Just beyond the aqueduct, bridge 43 is a superb example of a typical 'snake bridge'.

- **Sutton Lane Ends**
Cheshire. PO, tel, stores. This village was the home of Charles Tunnicliffe, 1901–79, the bird artist.
- **Oakgrove** A delightful spot with a pub and a superb backcloth of tall, green hills which are ideal for energetic walks. The lane west of the bridge leads to Gawsworth. Sutton Reservoir is just north.
- **Gawsworth**
Cheshire. PO box, tel, community stores. Two miles west of Oakgrove. A refreshingly unspoilt village with several small lakes and a lovely 13th-C church, approached by a long avenue of elm trees. Facing the church is the old rectory, a half-timbered house built by Rector Baguley in 1470.
Gawsworth Hall Church Lane, Gawsworth, Macclesfield SK11 9RN (01260 223456; www.gawsworthhall.com). Close to the church, this is a beautiful black and white manor house, parts of which date from Norman times. It was once the home of Mary Fitton, possibly the Dark Lady of Shakespeare's sonnets. The park encloses a medieval jousting ground, and there is a *summer season* of open-air theatre. Tearoom and shop selling products. The Hall is *open mid-May–mid-Sep 14.00-17.00 & Jul-Aug Wed-Sat.* Charge. Regular events are also held at the Hall – *see* website.

Maggoty's Wood In this pleasant wood just outside the village is the grave of the eccentric fiddler and playwright, Maggoty Johnson. After being totally rejected by London critics he returned to Gawsworth where he died in 1773, having ordered that he should be buried far from the vulgar gentry who did not appreciate his genius.

- **Sutton Reservoir**
Close to the canal north of bridge 49, this reservoir holds up to 94 million gallons of water. The public are welcome to ramble and picnic here.

Pubs and Restaurants

🍴✕ 1 **Sutton Hall** Bullocks Lane, Macclesfield SK11 0HE (01260 253211; www.brunningandprice. co.uk/suttonhall). South of Bridge 44. A 16th-C manor house, family home of the Earls of Lucan (and subsequently a convent) now dispensing real ales and excellent food *daily 12.00-22.00 (Sun 21.30).* Dog- and child-friendly, patio, gardens and terraces. Newspapers, real fires and Wi-Fi. *Open 11.00-23.00 (Sun 22.30).*

🍴 2 **Church House Inn** Church Lane, Sutton Lane Ends SK11 0DS (01260 252436; www.churchhouse. pub). Well worth the ½ mile walk from Gurnett Aqueduct to enjoy this friendly and comfortable village local serving real ale, and good food *Mon-Fri L and E & Sat-Sun 12.00-21.00 (Sun 20.00).* Dog- and family-friendly, garden. Traditional pub games, newspapers, real fires and Wi-Fi. Camping. *Open 12.00-00.00.*

🍴✕ 3 **The Sutton Gamekeeper** 13 Hollin Lane, Sutton, Macclesfield SK11 0HL (01260 252000; www. thesuttongamekeeper.co.uk). Smart stone-built hostelry, serving real ale and food cooked from fresh, local ingredients *Tue-Fri L and E & Sat-Sun 12.00-21.30 (Sun 19.00).* Dog- and child-friendly, garden. Newspapers, real fires and Wi-Fi. *Open Tue-Sun & B Hol Mon 12.00-22.00.*

🍴 4 **Ye Old Kings Head** 30 Bradley Smithy, Byrons Lane, Gurnett SK11 0HD (01625 611444; www. facebook.com/yeoldekingsheadgurnett). A coaching house and smithy dating from 1695, which was visited by Bonnie Prince Charlie. This comfortable beamy pub serves real ales, and meals *Mon-Fri L and E & Sat-Sun 12.00-21.00.* Dog- and family-friendly, garden. *Occasional* live music, newspapers, real fires and Wi-Fi. *Open 12.00-23.00.*

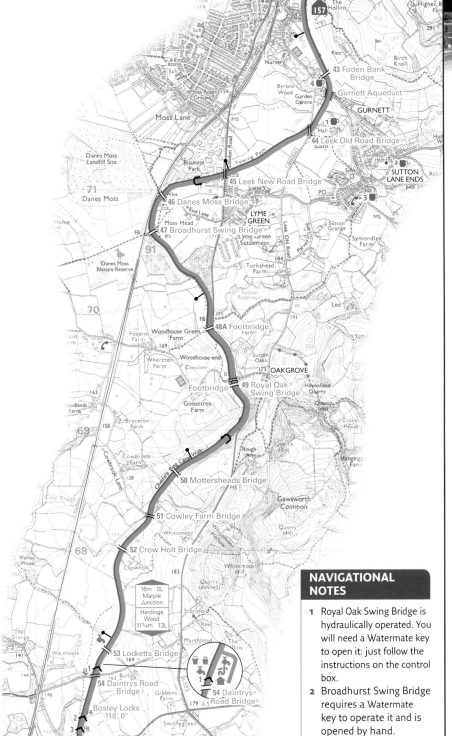

Macclesfield Canal Oakgrove

NAVIGATIONAL NOTES

1 Royal Oak Swing Bridge is hydraulically operated. You will need a Watermate key to open it: just follow the instructions on the control box.

2 Broadhurst Swing Bridge requires a Watermate key to operate it and is opened by hand.

155

Macclesfield

Leaving green and hilly countryside, the navigation enters the outskirts of Macclesfield, where some new housing incorporates a canal crane. A very wide stretch of water is overlooked by a vast and beautifully restored flour mill converted into up-market apartments, marking the site of the original Macclesfield Canal Company. This, the Hovis Mill, was built in the 1820s, and was the birthplace of the famous flour. The word Hovis is derived from the Latin 'hominisunvis' meaning 'power to the man'. Note the archway entrance off the canal, now blocked. The town itself is down the hill; the best place to moor is south of bridge 37, which is also handy for *shops – stores (open daily 07.00-22.00) off-licence, takeaway, fish & chips –* all to the east of the bridge. The tree-lined canal continues northwards to Bollington, passing through glorious open countryside with views of the hills all around, to the Adelphi Mill, once a silk mill and now converted into offices. A 60ft-high embankment and two aqueducts then carry the navigation across the valley towards the huge Clarence Mill, a textile mill now converted into thriving small manufacturing units. High on a hilltop to the south east of the town (directly east of Greens Bridge) is the White Nancy monument, recently renovated. This was erected by the Gaskell family in the 19th C at the northern end of the Kerridge Ridge, to commemorate the Battle of Waterloo, and was used by his family as a summerhouse.

Pubs and Restaurants

🍺 1 **The Dolphin Inn** 76 Windmill Street, Macclesfield SK11 7HS (01625 616179; www.robinsonsbrewery.com/thedolphin). A traditional, community local serving real ales. Child- and dog-friendly. Sports TV, beer garden, real fires, traditional pub games, newspapers and Wi-Fi. *Open Mon-Fri 17.00-01.00 & Sat-Sun 12.00-01.00 (Sun 22.30).*

🍺 2 **The Macc Bar** 1 Mill Green, Macclesfield SK11 7PE (01625 423704; www.maccbar.co.uk). This popular hostelry, dispensing a wide range of real ales, real cider, continental and American beers, bottled and craft ales, is a beer lovers paradise. Food is available *17.00-21.00 (Fri-Sun 12.00).* Dog- and child-friendly *(Until 19.00)* patio. Traditional pub games, real fires and Wi-Fi. *Open 12.00-23.00.*

🍺 3 **The Navigation** 161 Black Road, Macclesfield SK11 7LF (01625 422777). A Victorian local built for the original canal navvies. Real ale, a beer garden, sports TV and traditional pub games. Children and dogs welcome. Newspapers. *Open Mon-Thu 16.00-23.00 & Fri-Sun 12.00-00.00 (Sun 23.00).*

🍺 4 **The Puss in Boots** 198 Buxton Road, Macclesfield SK10 1NF (01625 263378; www.thepussinboots.co.uk). Canalside pub, with moorings, serving real ale and food *Mon-Fri 17.30-20.00 & Sat-Sun 12.00-20.00 (Sun 19.00).* Quiz *Thu.* Child-friendly, play area and canalside garden.

🍺 5 **The Wharf** 107 Brook Street, Macclesfield SK11 7AW (01625 261879; www.thewharfmacc.co.uk). Just west of the boatyard. Popular pub serving a wide range of real ales, real cider and bottled beers from around the world. *Regular* live music. Dog- and child-friendly, garden and open fires. Sports TV, traditional pub games and Wi-Fi. *Open Mon L and E; Tue-Thu 16.00-23.30; Fri 12.00-00.00 & Sat-Sun 15.00-00.00 (Sun 23.30).*

🍺 6 **The Treacle Tap** 43 Sunderland Street, Macclesfield SK11 6JL (01625 615938; www.thetreacletap.co.uk). A relaxed atmosphere pervades this former saddlery shop, which now dispenses real ale, bar meals and snacks *daily*, together with tea and coffee. Dog- and child-friendly *(until 20.00). Occasional* live music and quiz *Sun.* Newspapers and Wi-Fi. There is a fascinating range of events, far too varied to list. *Open Mon-Thu 16.00-23.00 & Fri-Sun 12.00-00.00 (Sun 23.00).*

🍺 7 **The Waters Green Tavern** 96 Waters Green, Macclesfield SK11 6LH (01625 422653; www.facebook.com/watersgreentavern). Run by the same landlord for more than 30 years (now with the assistance of his son) this welcoming pub serves a wide selection of rotating guest ales, together with real cider. *L* meals *Mon-Sat.* Dog- and child-friendly (daytime only) outside seating. Traditional pub games, real fires and Wi-Fi. *Open Mon-Fri L and E & Sat-Sun 12.00-23.00 (Sun 22.30).*

🍺 8 **The Three Crowns** 38 Rainow Road, Hurdsfield, Macclesfield SK10 2PF (01625 348237; www.threecrowns.robinsonsbrewery.com). A tiny Victorian stone terraced pub with a garden. Real ale is dispensed together with food *Mon-Fri 16.00-18.00 & Sat-Sun 12.00-17.00.* Dog- and family-friendly. Traditional pub games, newspapers, sports TV and Wi-Fi. *Open Mon-Fri 17.00-00.00 & Sat-Sun 12.00-00.00.*

🍺 9 **The Dog & Partridge** 97 Palmerston Street, Bollington SK10 5JX (01625 575979; www.dogpartridgebollington.robinsonsbrewery.com). A sociable village pub with an open fire. Real ale. There is a bridewell (prison), built in 1831, at the rear. Sandwiches available *L.* Dog- and family-friendly, garden, traditional pub games, sports TV, newspapers and Wi-Fi. *Open 12.00-00.00.*

🍺 10 **The Vale Inn** 29-31 Adlington Road, Bollington, Macclesfield SK10 5JT (01625 575147; www.valeinn.co.uk). Community focused pub, with its own microbrewery, dispensing real ales and real cider. Appetising, homemade food is available *Mon-Fri L and E & Sat-Sun 12.00-21.30 (Sun 20.30).* Dog- and child-friendly, garden. Newspapers, real fires and Wi-Fi. *Open Mon-Thu L and E & Fri-Sun 12.00-23.00 (Sun 22.30).*

WALKING AND CYCLING

The White Nancy Monument can be reached by walking south from Kerridge Bridge (27) and following the path. It was a folly constructed in 1817 by John Gaskell – whose ancestral home was the nearby Ingersley Hall – to commemorate the victory at the Battle of Waterloo. It was probably named after one of his daughters, although another theory has it that it bears the name of the lead horse that hauled all the building materials to the top of the ridge. Once at the top you will find it an excellent spot for a picnic, and you can walk along the Saddle of Kerridge, enjoying extensive views. For a refreshing pint and a meal there is a handy pub ⬤╳ 11 **The Bulls Head** 2 Oakhouse, Kerridge SK10 5BD (01625 575522; www. thebullsheadsk10.co.uk) nearby.

The Middlewood Way follows the line of the former Macclesfield, Bollington and Marple Railway and is a well surfaced, 10-mile route suitable for walkers, cyclists, pushchairs and wheelchairs. In conjunction with the canal towpath it can be used to form a circular walk with starting/finishing points at Bollington, Poynton and Marple. A PDF detailing the trail is downloadable from the website (01625 383700; www.cheshireeast.gov.uk/leisure,_culture_and_tourism/ranger_service/countryside_sites/middlewood_way.aspx). *See* also **WALKING AND CYCLING** page 159.

11m	0L
Marple Junction	
Hardings Wood	
16¾m	13L

Ⓑ**Freedom Boats** Swettenham Wharf, Brook Street, Macclesfield SK11 7AW (01625 420042; www. freedomboats.co.uk). 🚽 D Pump out, gas, day-hire craft, overnight mooring, long-term mooring, winter storage, slipway, boat and engine sales and repairs, toilets, books and maps, solid fuel, well-stocked chandlery. *Open daily 10.00-17.00.*

Ⓑ**Peak Forest Cruisers** The Wharf, Buxton Road, Macclesfield SK11 1LZ (01625 424172). Long-term mooring. *Nearby* 🛁 either side of bridge 37.

Ⓑ**Bollington Wharf** Grimshaw Lane, Bollington

SK10 5JB (01625 575811/07828 763885; www. bollington-wharf.com). 🛁🛁🛁 D Pump out, gas, overnight and long-term mooring, day boat hire, cycle hire, boat repair and maintenance, solid fuel. Craft courses – *see* website for details. *Emergency call-out. Open daily 08.00-18.00.*

Ⓑ**Kerridge Dry Dock** The Barn, Oaklands Farm, Kerridge SK10 5AP (01625 574287). Between bridges 28 and 29. Long-term mooring, winter storage, dry dock, boat and engine repairs, bottom blacking, marine engineering. *Call out during daylight hours.*

● **Macclesfield**
Cheshire. All services. Earliest records of a settlement are to be found in the Domesday Book, when the area was detailed as part of the land of Earl Edwin of Mercia. The town grew rapidly until it became the most important town in east Cheshire, being recognised as a borough in 1220. At that time it was the administrative centre for the Macclesfield Forest, and was granted its charter in 1261. Following set-backs resulting from the Battle of Flodden Field in 1513, the town was granted a new charter in 1595, and this was replaced by yet another, granted by Charles II, in 1684. Now the town is an interesting combination of modern industry and old market town, with cobbled streets and a picturesque medieval Market Place, encircled by busy modern roads. There are several fine classical buildings, making the most of the local stone, and detailed in the fine Town Trail leaflet available at the Tourist Information Centre. In the 18th C the town was one of the leading silk producing centres, but now there are only two small manufacturers left. One interesting feature of the town is the Unitarian Chapel in King Edward Street, approached through a narrow passage and guarded by a lovely wrought-iron gate: it is dated 1689 and is 'for William and Mary's subjects dissenting from the Church of England'.
St Michael's Church Market Place, Macclesfield SK10 1HW (01625 421984; www.stmichaels-macclesfield.com). Very little remains of the original structure founded in 1278 by Queen Eleanor and then known as All Hallows, although the Savage Chapel, the oldest stone building in the town, survives. The church still contains many fine monuments.
Silk Museum & Paradise Mill Park Lane, Macclesfield SK11 6TJ (01625 612045; www. macclesfieldmuseums.co.uk/venues/the-silk-museum). Built 1820 – 60, this handloom silk-weaving mill finally closed down in 1981. Here you can see Jacquard handlooms in action, authentic room settings and an exhibition of a whole wealth

of material connected with one of Macclesfield's major industries. *Open Mon-Sat 10.00-16.00.* The guided Mill Tours are a must and give a fascinating insight into a time-warp method of silk-production used in the manufacture of gentleman's ties. The looms are just as they were left when the final shift walked out of the building with the knowledgeable guide bringing it all back to life again. Tours take place *11.45, 13.00 & 14.15.* Charge.
West Park Museum Prestbury Road, Macclesfield SK10 3BJ (01625 665010; www.macclesfieldmuseums. co.uk/venues/west-park-museum). Opened in 1898, and situated in a park containing the largest bowling green in Europe, the collections include fine and decorative art, local history and Egyptian antiquities, plus a section devoted to Charles Tunnicliffe (1901–79), the famous bird artist. *Open Sat-Sun 10.00-16.00.* Free.
Macclesfield Leisure Centre Priory Lane, Macclesfield SK10 4AF (01625 383981; www. everybody.org.uk/locations/macclesfield). Three swimming pools, six squash courts and a host of other facilities. *Open Mon-Fri 06.00-22.30 & Sat-Sun 08.00-21.00 (Sat 19.00).* Charge.
Tourist Information Centre Town Hall, Market Place, Macclesfield SK10 1DX (01625 378123; www.visitmacclesfield.co.uk/macclesfield-visitor-information-centre). *Open Mon-Sat 10.00-16.00 (Sat 15.00)*

● **Bollington**
Cheshire. PO, tel, stores, chemist, takeaway, fish & chips. There is a good view of this stone-built town from the huge canal embankment which cuts across it. From here it is only 1 mile to the boundary of the Peak District National Park. The white tower on the ridge south of the town is called White Nancy (*see* **Walking and Cycling** page 169). Stores are *open daily 07.00-22.00.*
Bollington Leisure Centre 5 Heath Road, Bollington SK10 5EX (01625 574774; www.bollingtonleisure. co.uk). Squash courts, a swimming pool and other facilities. *Open Mon-Fri 06.30-22.00 (Fri 20.00) & Sat-Sun 07.45-18.00.* Charge.

WALKING AND CYCLING

There are many stimulating walks available throughout Cheshire, several in the Macclesfield area that are within reach of this waterway. You will find details at www.bootsandpaws.co.uk/acheshire.html). The Middlewood Way (see also www.macclesfield.gov.uk) is a level 10-mile footpath and cycleway (part of Route 55 of the National Cycle Network) along the course of the old Macclesfield, Bollington and Marple Railway. It runs between Macclesfield and Marple. For much of its length it closely follows the Macclesfield Canal and there are several options for circular walks. The railway was opened for passenger traffic in 1869, just 38 years after the Macclesfield Canal was completed, and for goods on 1 March 1870. Cotton, silk, coal and passengers were carried, but the railway always struggled to make a profit. It was finally closed in January 1970 and converted for recreational use in 1985. Dr David Bellamy performed the opening ceremony and then, having proclaimed it 'tewiffic', removed his socks and shoes and waded into a nearby pond.

BIRD LIFE

The *Great Tit* is a common woodland and garden species, appreciably larger than the blue tit alongside which it is often seen at bird feeders. The great tit has bold black and white markings on its head and a black bib forming a line running down its chest, broader in the male than the female. The underparts are otherwise yellow and upperparts mainly greenish. Juveniles have sombre plumage with no white on the head. Their song is extremely variable but a striking 'teecha teecha teecha' is rendered by most males. In summer the birds feed mainly on insects.

Marple Junction

Macclesfield Canal

Macclesfield

Higher Poynton

This isolated stretch is typical of the Macclesfield Canal and in its beautifully quiet, rural isolation it represents much of the charm that most canals possess. Winding northwards along the summit level at over 500ft above the sea, the navigation generally follows the contours of this upland country, but crosses several valleys on embankments with fine aqueducts. There is a pleasant *picnic area* south of Hag Footbridge 16, good *moorings* by the Miners Arms, bridge 18, and between bridges 20 and 19, and a fine shady, wooded section between bridges 22 and 21. There are few centres of population near the canal, just the odd pub here or there, and the countryside is quite unspoilt. Around Higher Poynton the canal becomes wider, the result of ancient subsidence from a coal mine, which necessitated the continual raising of the canal banks and bridges to hold the water in the sinking canal. Be sure to adhere to the main channel here. An old branch near bridge 15 used to lead to the mine; now it is used by a boatyard.

Higher Poynton
Cheshire. PO box, tel. Considered by some to be the most pleasant moorings on the canal, where the wide water supports large families of ducks, geese and swans. There is a recreation field adjacent, and a handy *pub*. Poynton itself, with its wide selection of facilities, is 1½ miles west of Brownhills Bridge 15.
Anson Engine Museum Anson Road, Poynton SK12 1TD (01625 874426; www.enginemuseum.org). A working display of early internal-combustion engines, with emphasis on those made in the Manchester area. Tearoom and shop. *Open Apr-Oct, Fri & Sun 10.00-16.00.* Charge.
Lyme Park Disley, Stockport SK12 2NR (01663 762023; www.nationaltrust.org.uk/lyme-park). Two miles east of Higher Poynton. Pedestrian entrance at West Parkgate, ¼ mile south east of bridge 17 or footpath from bridge 15.

In the centre of a 1400-acre park containing deer is this magnificent Italianate palace which was transformed from a Tudor house by the Venetian architect Leoni. Some of the original Elizabethan interiors can still be seen. There are Mortlake tapestries, a large collection of English clocks, Grinling Gibbons wood carvings, countless works of art, and four Chippendale chairs claimed to be covered with material from a cloak worn by King Charles I at his execution. The Victorian garden has a sunken parterre, an Edwardian rose garden, a reflection lake, a ravine garden, a Wyatt conservatory and an 18th-C hunting tower. The house featured in a BBC adaptation of *Pride and Prejudice* as 'Pemberley'. Children's playground. Restaurant, café, tearoom and shop. The garden, park, shop and café are open *daily throughout the year* while the house and restaurant *opening times vary.* Check the website for details. Charge.

Pubs and Restaurants

⬤✕ 1 **The Windmill** Holehouse Lane, Whiteley Green SK10 5SJ (01625 574222; www.thewindmill.info). Dating from the 15th C, when it was recorded as a farm house, it became a pub in 1674. Real ale is served, along with food available *Mon-Fri L and E & Sat-Sun 12.00-21.30 (Sun 20.00).* Child- and dog-friendly, open fires and a garden. Newspapers and Wi-Fi. *Open 12.00.*
⬤✕ 2 **The Miners Arms** Wood Lane North, Four Lane Ends, Adlington SK10 4PF (01625 872731; www. facebook.com/minersarmsadlington). A big, bustling, lively and thriving country pub which is pleasantly family orientated, having extensive gardens and amusements for children. Real ale is served, along with a good choice of food and a children's menu *Mon-Thu L and E & Sat-Sun 12.00-21.30 (Sun 19.00).* Dog- and child-friendly. *Regular* music nights. Newspapers, real

fires and Wi-Fi. *Open daily 12.00-23.00 (Sun 22.30).*
⬤ 3 **The Boar's Head** 2 Shrigley Road North, Higher Poynton SK12 1TE (01625 876676; www. boarsheadpub.com). An imposing, ivy-clad, red-brick pub serving real ale and food *daily.* Popular with walkers and cyclists, garden. Traditional pub games, real fires, sports TV and Wi-Fi. *Open Mon-Fri L and E & Sat-Sun 12.00-00.00.*
⬤✕ 4 **The Farmers Arms** 90 Park Lane, Poynton SK12 1RE (01625 875858; www.farmersarms.pub). Smart, up-market pub majoring on food, dispensing real ale and serving meals daily *11.00-22.00 (Sun 21.00).* Family-friendly. *Occasional* live music, newspapers, sports TV and Wi-Fi. *Open Mon-Sat 11.00-23.00 (Fri-Sat 00.00) & Sun 11.00-21.00.*

WALKING AND CYCLING
The Gritstone Trail passes through Lyme Park and continues up onto the moors, passing White Nancy (*see* page 156). The Middlewood Way (*see* page 159) continues to to the west of the canal. Jacksons' Brickworks (01625 383700; www.cheshireeast.gov.uk/leisure,_culture_and_tourism/ranger_service/countryside_sites/ jacksons_brickworks_lnr.aspx) in Higher Poynton, reclaimed by nature after its industrial interlude, is now a valuable wildlife resource. The 22-acre site is managed as a mosaic of different habitats including Wetland, Grassland, Semi-natural Woodland and scrub. It is especially important for the great crested newt. It is accessible from Bullocks Bridge 13.

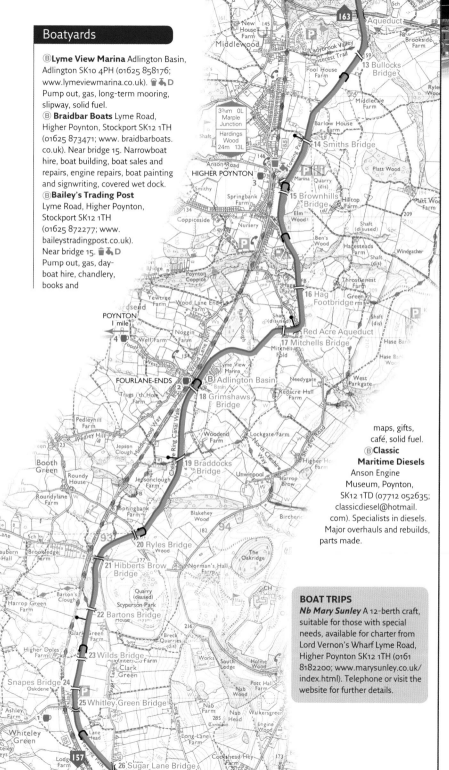

Boatyards

Ⓑ**Lyme View Marina** Adlington Basin, Adlington SK10 4PH (01625 858176; www.lymeviewmarina.co.uk). ♒♨D Pump out, gas, long-term mooring, slipway, solid fuel.

Ⓑ **Braidbar Boats** Lyme Road, Higher Poynton, Stockport SK12 1TH (01625 873471; www. braidbarboats. co.uk). Near bridge 15. Narrowboat hire, boat building, boat sales and repairs, engine repairs, boat painting and signwriting, covered wet dock.

Ⓑ**Bailey's Trading Post** Lyme Road, Higher Poynton, Stockport SK12 1TH (01625 872277; www. baileystradingpost.co.uk). Near bridge 15. ♒♨D Pump out, gas, day-boat hire, chandlery, books and

maps, gifts, café, solid fuel.

Ⓑ**Classic Maritime Diesels** Anson Engine Museum, Poynton, SK12 1TD (07712 052635; classicdiesel@hotmail. com). Specialists in diesels. Major overhauls and rebuilds, parts made.

BOAT TRIPS

Nb Mary Sunley A 12-berth craft, suitable for those with special needs, available for charter from Lord Vernon's Wharf Lyme Road, Higher Poynton SK12 1TH (0161 8182200; www.marysunley.co.uk/ index.html). Telephone or visit the website for further details.

Marple Junction

Another massive embankment and a tall aqueduct, this time over a railway, are crossed on the way into High Lane. The canal proceeds northwards in a cutting through High Lane, passing the junction with the short High Lane Arm – well protected and now used as a club mooring site – and a children's play park. There are *moorings* between the arm and bridge 11, with *shops* close by. Beyond the town is a restored mill; then open country intervenes, offering views westward of Stockport and the southern outskirts of Manchester. There is a useful *little shop* down the hill from Bridge 6. At Bridge 3 there is a *takeaway, fish & chips and a laundrette*. Goyt Mill appears, thankfully restored and now housing workshops, heralding the start of Marple, a busy boating centre much enjoyed by the citizens of Manchester. The area of the junction with the Peak Forest Canal is delightful: an old turnover bridge, mellow wharf buildings and the nearby flight of Marple Locks are framed by the distant mountainous country across the Goyt Valley. The canal here is 500ft above sea level.

Boatyards

(B)**Canal & River Trust Marple Yard** Marple Junction, on the Macclesfield Canal (0303 040 4040; enquiries.manchesterpennine@canalrivertrust.org.uk). 🚿🛟⚓ Overnight mooring.

● **High Lane**
Gt Manchester. PO, tel, stores, chemist, off-licence, takeaway, fish & chips, delicatessen, library, station. More of a spread than a village, but there are good moorings and it is useful for supplies. High Lane is effectively at the south east corner of the Manchester conurbation, and is quite indistinguishable from its neighbours. The very long Disley Railway Tunnel passes deep underneath.

● **Marple**
Gt Manchester. All services. A typical residential town, serving as a dormitory base for Stockport and Manchester. Elements of the old village can still be seen, buried amongst the suburbia, but much the most attractive part is by the canal. The rugged Ludworth Moor is not far away, where 'Robin Hood's Picking Rods' still stand, the supposed remains of a Celtic Druid's temple.

● **Marple Locks**
The 16 locks at Marple were not built until 1804,

four years after the rest of the Peak Forest canal was opened. The 1-mile gap thus left was bridged by a tramway, while the Canal Company sought the cash to pay for the construction of a flight of locks. This was obviously a most unsatisfactory state of affairs, since limestone from Doveholes had to be shifted from wagon to boat at Buxworth Basin, from boat to wagon at Marple Junction, and back into boat again at the bottom of the tramway. Not surprisingly, a container system was developed – using iron boxes with a 2-ton payload – to ease the triple transshipment. However, this was no long-term solution, and when the necessary £27,000 was forthcoming the company authorised construction of the flight of locks. Today they stand comparison with any flight on the network. Note especially Samuel Oldknow's superb warehouse by lock 9, opposite the lock keeper's house, now tastefully converted to offices.

Pubs and Restaurants

✗ 1 **Blueberries** 37 Buxton Road, High Lane SK6 8DR (01663 766900; www.blueberriescafe.co.uk/index.html). Freshly made, appetising food is served in this friendly welcoming café, majoring on breakfast, lunch and homemade cake. Tea and coffee. Takeaway service. *Open Tue-Sat 08.00-15.00 & Sun 10.00-14.00.*

🍺 2 **The Horseshoe Inn** 1 Buxton Road, High Lane SK6 8AA (01663 762487; www.robinsonsbrewery.com/horseshoehighlane). Traditional village local serving real ale and food *Wed-Sun L and E.* Family-friendly, garden. Traditional pub games. *Open Mon-Thu 14.00-23.30 (Wed-Thu & Sun 12.00) & Fri 12.00-00.00.*

🍺 3 **The Royal Oak** Buxton Road, High Lane SK6 8AY (01663 766827). Friendly establishment serving

real ale and food *Mon-Fri L and E & Sat-Sun 12.00-18.00.* Dog- and child-friendly. Garden, open fires and traditional pub games. *Open 12.00-00.00.*

🍺✗ 4 **The Ring O'Bells** 130 Church Lane, Marple SK6 7AY (0161 427 2300; www.robinsonsbrewery.com/ringobells). An award-winning, comfortable and friendly traditional pub serving food *Mon-Fri L and E & Sat-Sun 12.00-19.45.* Dog- and family-friendly, garden. *Weekend* brass band music in *summer.* Real fires. B&B. *Open 12.00-00.00.*

Also try: 🍺✗ 5 **The Red Lion** 112 Buxton Road, High Lane SK6 8ED (01663 765227; www.facebook.com/redlionhighlane) and 🍺✗ 6 **The Dog & Partridge** 88 Buxton Road, High Lane SK6 8HJ (01663 762413; www.crowncarveries.co.uk/nationalsearch/northwest/thedogandpartridgestockport).

See also **Pubs and Restaurants** on page 181.

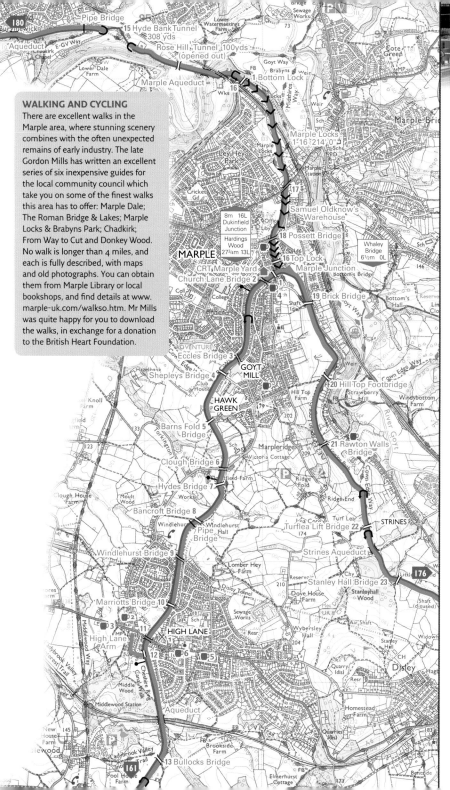

WALKING AND CYCLING

There are excellent walks in the Marple area, where stunning scenery combines with the often unexpected remains of early industry. The late Gordon Mills has written an excellent series of six inexpensive guides for the local community council which take you on some of the finest walks this area has to offer: Marple Dale; The Roman Bridge & Lakes; Marple Locks & Brabyns Park; Chadkirk; From Way to Cut and Donkey Wood. No walk is longer than 4 miles, and each is fully described, with maps and old photographs. You can obtain them from Marple Library or local bookshops, and find details at www. marple-uk.com/walkso.htm. Mr Mills was quite happy for you to download the walks, in exchange for a donation to the British Heart Foundation.

MANCHESTER BOLTON & BURY CANAL

MAXIMUM DIMENSIONS
Length: 68' 0"
Beam: 14' 2"
Headroom: 6'
Draught: 3' 6"

MANAGER
Canal & River Trust (0303 040 4040;
www.canalrivertrust.org.uk/contact-us/ways-
to-contact-us

**MANCHESTER BOLTON &
BURY CANAL SOCIETY**
Meadowbank, Ringley Road, Radcliffe,
Manchester M26 1FW
manchesterboltonandburycs@waterways.org.uk
www.mbbcs.org.uk

MILEAGE
SALFORD junction with the River Irwell to:
Park House Bridge 22: 2½ miles
Clifton Aqueduct: 4¾ miles
Giants Seat: 6¼ miles
Nob End: 8 miles

BOLTON: 11 miles
NOB END junction with the Bolton Branch to:
Radcliffe: 2½ miles
Elton reservoir: 3¾ miles
BURY canal terminus: 5 miles

Note: With the exception of approximately two
miles through Salford, and a slightly lesser distance
approaching Bolton, it is possible to follow most
of the original line of the canal, although not all
of it is in water. However, the Manchester Bolton
& Bury Canal Society has produced an excellent
towpath guide, packed with fascinating historical
detail, available through their website above. This
forms an essential companion to this guide.
**Most bridges (and all the locks) shown on
the mapping date from the time before the
canal was abandoned.** However, many have
since vanished. Missing bridge numbers, within the
sequence, will usually relate to structures spanning
culverts, arms or sluices and have been omitted for
clarity. A second bridge number shown in brackets
denotes a spurious number recently applied to the
bridge by the then, British Waterways.

The initiative for the construction of this navigation stemmed, in 1790, from a group of Bolton men who commissioned Matthew Fletcher (of Wet Earth Colliery and a man with close links to the Mersey & Irwell Navigation) to make an initial survey and prepare an estimate. His finding were largely supported by a second survey, carried out a year later by Hugh Henshall – builder of the Trent & Mersey and Chesterfield Canals – and an Act was passed for its construction in the autumn of 1791.

The first engineer was Charles Roberts, who was succeeded by John Nightingale (Matthew Fletcher's nephew) in 1793, for failing to discharge his duties with proper discretion and 'oeconomy.'

The canal was to be for narrowboats and by the time meetings took place with the Leeds & Liverpool Company, with a view to a possible junction with their broad-beam waterway at Red Moss (4½-miles west of Bolton) a five-mile section – between Oldfield Road, Salford and Rhodes Lock – had already been built. Consequently plans were amended and the offending stretch re-modelled.

The first tolls were taken in 1795 and the length to Rhodes Lock was opened mid-1796. The Bury Arm remained navigable for narrowboats only until a year later and the final connection with the Irwell was ultimately completed in December 1808. The total cost was put at £115,500 and included the impressive Prestolee Locks: two staircases, of three locks each.

The navigation was subsequently worked by both wide-beam craft and 68ft narrowboats which predominated, each one carrying nine boxes containing between 35cwt and 2 tons of coal: an early and efficient form of containerisation.

In 1809 the proprietors of the MB&B Canal heard of the Leeds & Liverpool's intention to build a branch from Wigan to Worsley (connecting with the Bridgewater Canal) thereby scotching any likelihood of a Red Moss extension.

Traffic, although steady, was modest with coal from the Clifton area up to Bolton and Bury and down to Manchester being the staple. In 1835 this amounted to 120,000 tons and was accompanied by building and road stone, flagstones and limestone, groceries and various sundries.

Passenger-carrying flyboats were popular, initially between Bolton and Manchester and, from 1810, from Bolton to Bury. Passengers taking the former service changed at Prestolee Locks, transferring via a covered walkway to save the wait while six locks were worked.

In the 1830's the canal company morphed into a railway and canal company with a view to constructing a Manchester to Bolton line 'upon or near the Line of the ... Canal.' In the event the line was built – but quite separately from the navigation.

Over its lifetime the waterway remained a coal-carrying canal, although it suffered from subsidence, especially along lengths bordering the River Irwell and during the 1880's many miles of retaining walls were constructed, along with re-puddling of the bed.

In 1905 the annual tonnage included bricks, salt, manure, pulp and cotton while, in 1941, a seven-mile section was initially abandoned by Act of Parliament, with the final stretch – between Ladyshore Colliery and Bury – remaining operational until 1951. The final Act of Abandonment came exactly a decade later.

The Meccano Bridge, Nob End

Salford

From Oldfield Road, the canal – its original course somewhat displaced by the arrival of the Manchester & Bolton Railway – ducks under the line and more or less shadows the trackbed (immediately to the east), until it finally becomes fully visible again, immediately beyond the Lafarge Tarmac works. Here it is reassuringly complete, in water and boldly delineated by the robust masonry of the towpath coping stones. In summer months the water is populated by a riot of colourful plants, while this surprisingly tranquil environment (for an area so close to the city centre) is disturbed only by the regular passing of trains. Most of the original bridges are intact and evidence of past industry is not difficult to detect. At Clifton the River Irwell appears on the right, emphasising just how perilously close the two water courses run – both here and at many other points along this navigation's length.

Salford

Gt Manchester. All services. Although now merged with Manchester, Salford was granted its charter in 1230, 71 years before that of its now larger neighbour. It has a fine new University, dating from 1967 and a Roman Catholic cathedral consecrated in 1848. It is, however, most widely known as being the subject of many paintings by the artist L S Lowry (1887-1976). What is less widely known is that he gained his inspiration by walking the streets of Salford for many years as a rent collector, only painting in the evenings and at weekends – a fact to which he would never willingly admit. His work is exhibited at The Lowry, Salford Quays (see below).

Clifton Country Park Clifton Hose Road, Swinton M27 6NG (0161 793 4219; www.visitsalford.info/wetearthcolliery.htm). Amongst other things, the Park features the industrial remains of Wet Earth Colliery. Established around 1740, the colliery was one of the first deep mines to be sunk in the Irwell Valley and is important on at least three counts: the first application of steam winding in the area, its very long working life (1740-1928), and because of its association with James Brindley and his ingenious hydraulic pumping scheme – in continuous use from 1756 to 1924. Visit the website to download PDFs giving further, fascinating insight.

The Lowry Pier 8, The Quays, Salford M50 3AZ (0843 208 6000; www.thelowry.com). Rising up from the regenerated docklands, this glass and metallic building (opened in 2000) houses two main theatres and studio space for performing arts, presenting a full range of drama, opera, ballet, dance, musicals, children's shows, popular music, jazz, folk and comedy, together with gallery space. It also shows the work of L S Lowry alongside contemporary exhibitions. Restaurant, café, bars and shops. Gallery *open daily 11.00-17.00 (Sat 10.00).* Free.

Ordsall Hall 322 Ordsall Lane, Salford M5 3AN (0161 872 0251; www.salfordcommunityleisure.co.uk/culture/ordsall-hall). The Hall is a Grade I listed Tudor manor house, was first recorded in 1177. Since then, it has been home to medieval gentry, Tudor nobility, Catholics loyal to the crown, butchers, farmers, an Earl, an artist, priests, scout troops, mill workers, cows and several ghosts! Today it is an engaging heritage site, surrounded by landscaped grounds. Café and shop. *Open Sun-Thu 10.00-16.00 (Sun 13.00).* Charge.

Salford Museum & Art Gallery Peel Park, The Crescent, Salford M5 4WU (0161 778 0800; www.salfordcommunityleisure.co.uk/culture/locations/salford-museum). In the centre of Salford University campus. Stroll down a Victorian street, admire the Landau carriages and discover a Victorian heritage.

WALKING AND CYCLING

This is a rewarding navigation for the walker, while the experienced cyclist will also find it possible to follow the waterway throughout, using a suitable machine. The most realistic starting point is Salford Crescent Station, although the canal can be followed from its junction with the River Irwell, the first quarter of a mile having been restored. However, this stretch is scheduled for development and it may, therefore, be necessary to start from Ordsall Lane or from Oldfield Road, where it intersects the Salford Crescent to Salford Central railway line.

From Oldfield Road turn left down Upper Wharf Street, right up Back Hulme Street and left along Hulme Street to intersect The Crescent dual carriageway, turning left.

After 300yds turn left into Old Fire Station Square, exiting right along Christchurch Avenue into University Road West, which becomes University Road beside Salford Crescent Station.

Follow this until approximately 100yds after it turns sharply to the right, taking the path on your left through the trees. Take the next path on your left, through a passageway between the houses to join Strawberry Hill. Turn left and then 1st right down Lissadel Street. Cross Fredrick Street and continue to the junction with Broughton Road, turning right. Take the 1st left along Langley Road South and follow this for approximately 1 mile to the Lafarge Tarmac plant on the left. Turn left up Park House Bridge Road to join the line of the canal, (now in water), which can be followed to Clifton Aqueduct. *(continued on page 169)*

Test your strength or listen to the Victorian Top 20. Experience the sight and sounds of Victorian Salford with original shop fronts and fascinating interiors. Victorian gallery with paintings, pottery and fine art. Temporary exhibition programme, from hands-on activities to modern art. Coffee shop. *Open Tue-Fri 09.30-16.30 & Sat-Sun 11.30-16.00. Free.*

Working Class Movement Library 51 The Crescent, Salford M5 4WX (0161 736 3601; www.wcml.org.uk). The Working Class Movement Library records over 200 years of organising and campaigning by ordinary men and women. The collection provides a rich insight into working people's daily lives as well as their thoughts, hopes, fears and the roles they played in the significant events of their time. Bookshop and gallery. *Open Tue-Fri 10.00-17.00 & 3rd Sat in month 10.00-16.00. Closed B Hols. Free.*

Travel Information Traveline 0871 200 22 33; www.raildar.co.uk/radar.html or www.tfgm.com.

Tourist Information Salford no longer has its own, staffed Information Centre, so see page 38 for details of the Manchester Centre or visit www.visitsalford.info.

For Manchester attractions see page 182.

NAVIGATIONAL NOTES

1 See page 39 for details of the Manchester Ship Canal transit and using the Pomona Lock connection between the River Irwell and the Bridgewater Canal in Manchester.

2 Contact Canal & River Trust (0303 040 4040; www.canalrivertrust.org.uk/contact-us/ways-to-contact-us) for details on accessing the first ¼ mile of the navigation from the River Irwell.

Pubs and Restaurants

1 **The Old Pint Pot** 2 Adelphi Street, Salford M3 6EN (0161 839 7958; www.facebook.com/pintpotsalford). Large, split-level, riverside pub, dispensing real ale, real cider and food *L and E*. Dog-friendly, terrace. Traditional pub games, sports TV and Wi-Fi. *Open 11.00-23.00.*

2 **The New Oxford** 11 Bexley Square, Salford M3 6DB (0161 832 7082; www.thenewoxford.com). Friendly, welcoming pub serving a superb selection of real ales, continental draught lagers, real cider and over 100 bottled continental beers. Appetising, freshly cooked bar meals are available *Mon-Sat 12.00-16.00).* Dog-friendly, outside seating. Sports TV and Wi-Fi. *Open daily 12.00-00.00.*

3 **The Kings Arms** 11 Bloom Street, Salford M3 6AN (0161 832 3605; www.kingsarmssalford.com). An eclectic mix of beer, food, film, music and the performing arts, this Grade II listed pub serves real ale and homemade food *daily – Sun* roasts *13.00-17.00*. Downstairs lies the pub part, whilst upstairs is devoted to the community-led Studio Salford. Beer garden. Knitting club *Mon. Quiz Wed. Open 12.00-23.00.*

4 **The Eagle Inn** 18 Collier Street, Salford M3 7DW (0161 819 5002; www.eagleinn.info). Traditional, back street local, known to its regulars as the Lamp Oil, serving real ale and real cider in its unadulterated, Grade II listed, 1903 interior. The attached cottage has been converted to a live music venue. Patio, traditional pub games and Wi-Fi. Dog-friendly. *Open Mon-Fri 15.00-23.00 (Fri 01.00) & Sat-Sun 13.00-01.00 (Sun 23.00).*

For **Pubs and Restaurants** in Manchester *see* page 189.

Manchester Bolton & Bury Canal Salford

Ringley

By any standards the Clifton Aqueduct is an impressive structure and serves as a foretaste of the engineering glories that this waterway has yet to disclose. The motorway represents the first real obstacle to restoration but the broad track under its Irwell flyover suggests at least one immediate solution. To the north three electricity pylons are planted squarely in the navigation's bed which, together with Rhodes Lock, is firmly fenced off making it a somewhat forbidding proposition. However, the tantalising views of the river, some 40-feet below, glimpsed through the boughs of the ensuing sylvan glade, are more than compensation.

● Clifton Junction
Gt Manchester PO box, tel, station (limited service). As its name suggests, this was the point where the now defunct Manchester, Bury & Rossendale Railway met the Manchester & Bolton Railway. The former crossed the River Irwell on the Clifton Viaduct, just downstream of the aqueduct and known locally as the Thirteen Arches. Battery and pottery manufacture are also to be found in the district, although there is little to mark its centre.
Fletcher's Canal This early navigation ran north, for approximately one mile, along the west bank of the River Irwell, from its intersection with the Manchester Bolton & Bury Canal beside the Clifton Aqueduct, serving Wet Earth Colliery (www.salford.gov.uk/parks-and-open-spaces/salford-parks/clifton-country-park/wet-earth-colliery). Little evidence of its existence remains today.

● Stoneclough
Gt Manchester. PO box, tel, station (Kearsley). Once home to a power station, a cotton mill and a paper mill, Stoneclough is effectively a suburban area of Kearsley and embraces Prestolee and Ringley. St Saviour's Church, with its detached tower, sits in a field between the Horseshoe pub and the Irwell, overlooking Ringley Old Bridge. The original church was erected in 1625, rebuilt in 1820 and totally replaced in 1854 with the current edifice, which contains the Rococo chancel rails, communion table and some stained glass from the original. The tower dates from the 17th-C structure.

● Farnworth
Gt Manchester. PO, tel, stores, chemist, delicatessen, baker, butcher, greengrocer, hardware, banks, off-licence, takeaways, fish & chips, station. The town lies on the northern limits of the Duke of Bridgewater's Worsley Navigable Levels: the 46-mile interconnected, underground arrangement of canals linking a series of coal mines with the Bridgewater Canal at Worsley Delph. Commenced in 1757, this system employed a complex series of inclined planes and narrow, wooden craft known as 'starvationers'. Iron foundries and cotton and paper mills were also established in the area.
Farnworth Little Theatre Cross Street, Farnworth, Bolton BL4 7AJ (0845 643 0808; www.farnworthlittletheatre. weebly.com). Long standing, amateur theatrical company who put on approximately five productions per year to great acclaim. Telephone or visit the website for further details.
Farnworth Market King Street, Farnworth BL4 9DL (01204 336840; www.bolton.gov.uk/website/Pages/FarnworthMarket.aspx). A well-established, traditional street market selling everything from fruit and vegetables to meat clothing and toys. *Open Mon & Fri-Sat 09.00-17.00.* Flea market *Sat 07.00-14.00.*

● Moses Gate
Gt Manchester. PO box, tel, stores, chemist, hardware, takeaways, fish & chips, off-licence, garage, station. A corruption of the words Moss – a boggy place – and the old English 'gata' meaning a road. The Industrial Revolution brought chemical works, paper mills and a bleach works, all since demolished.
Moses Gate Country Park Hall Lane, Farnworth BL4 3DN (01204 334343). A 750-acre site situated at Moses Gate in the Croal and Irwell Valleys, part of which is also known as Crompton Lodges. *Open dawn to dusk.*

WALKING AND CYCLING

Clifton to Ringley: Cross the river on the Clifton Aqueduct and head north towards the M60, taking the path that runs between the lagoons and the Irwell – negotiating the motorway through the Irwell flyover – picking up the towpath and line of the navigation (now protected by a chain link fence) just beyond the electricity pylon.

Follow the towpath, running between the river and canal bed, to its intersection with Red Rock Lane, at Giant's Seat. Beyond the garden centre, and just before the sewerage works, take the path leading uphill to the right to regain the towpath and follow the line of the waterway running above the works boundary fence to its junction with Ringley Road – crossing Fold Road beside the Horseshoe pub. (continued on *page 164*).

Pubs and Restaurants

X **1 The Horseshoe** 395 Fold Road, Ringley, Stoneclough M26 1FT (01204 571714; www. thehorseshoeringleyvillage.co.uk). Beside Bridge 41, and opposite the old Packhorse Bridge crossing the River Irwell, this popular pub serves real ale and food *Mon-Sat L and E (Not Mon E) and Sun 12.00-20.00.* Dog- and child-friendly, garden. Real fires and Wi-Fi. *Open Sun-Thu 12.00-22.30 (Tue-Thu 23.00) & Fri-Sat 12.00-00.00.*

X **2 La Roma** Ringley Hall Road, Stoneclough M26 1GT (01204 707932; www.laromarestaurant.co.uk). Situated in the old Lord Nelson pub, overlooking the Irwell, this restaurant serves all the Italian classic dishes *Mon-Fri L and E &Sat-Sun 12.00-22.00 (Sun 21.00).* Children welcome, outside seating.

3 The Grapes 47 Market Street, Stoneclough M26 1HF (01204 572360/07809 484271; www.facebook. com/TheGrapesHotel). Friendly local, in the village centre, serving real ale and food *Tue-Sun 12.00-20.00.* Dog- and child-friendly, garden. Live music *Fri.* Traditional pub games, sports TV and Wi-Fi. B&B. Takeaway service (07890 427992). *Open 12.00-00.00 (Fri-Sun 01.00).*

4 The Market Street Tavern 131 Market Street, Stoneclough M26 1HF (01204 572985). Compact local serving a rotating range of real ale. Dogs and children Welcome; *monthly* live music and sports TV. Outside seating, traditional pub games and Wi-Fi. *Open Mon-Fri 14.00-23.00 (Fri 01.00) & Sat-Sun 12.00-01.00 (Sun 23.00).*

5 The Britannia Inn 32-34 King Street, Farnworth BL4 7AF (01204 572538; www.britanniainnfarnworth.co.uk). Friendly local serving real ale and food *daily 11.00-16.00. Weekend* live music. Outside seating, traditional pub games, sports TV and Wi-Fi. *Mon-Sat 11.00-23.00 (Wed, Fri & Sat 00.00) & Sun 12.00-00.00.*

6 The Wellington Inn 56 Market Street, Farnworth BL4 7NY (01204 862180; www.facebook.com/pages/Wellington/11854361 8200819?rf=1699601540320913). Bearing a name that is often abbreviated locally to an item of waterproof footwear, this community pub dispenses well-kept real ale and good conversation, together with food *L. Regular* live music, sports TV, traditional pub games and Wi-Fi. *Open 11.30-00.30 (Fri-Sat 02.30).*

7 The Railway Inn Egerton Street, Moses Gate BL4 7JZ (01204 791410; www.joseph-holt.com/pubs/view/railway-hotel). Imposing, two-roomed pub serving real ale. Dog-friendly, *occasional weekend* live music. Traditional pub games, sports TV and Wi-Fi. *Open 13.00-23.00 (Thu-Sat 00.00).*

Bolton

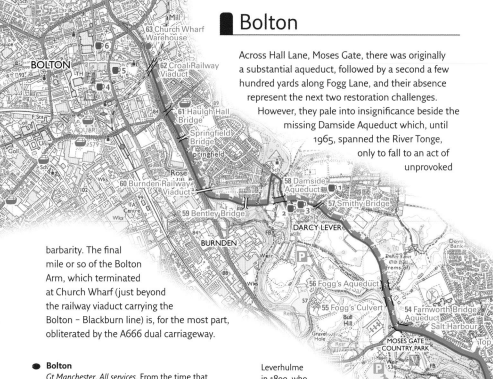

Across Hall Lane, Moses Gate, there was originally a substantial aqueduct, followed by a second a few hundred yards along Fogg Lane, and their absence represent the next two restoration challenges. However, they pale into insignificance beside the missing Damside Aqueduct which, until 1965, spanned the River Tonge, only to fall to an act of unprovoked

barbarity. The final mile or so of the Bolton Arm, which terminated at Church Wharf (just beyond the railway viaduct carrying the Bolton – Blackburn line) is, for the most part, obliterated by the A666 dual carriageway.

Bolton

Gt Manchester. All services. From the time that Flemish weavers first settled in the area during 14th C, Bolton has been a focus for textile production which, with the invention of Arkwright's Spinning Jenny and Carding Machine, together with Crompton's Spinning Mule, saw the town rise to become one of the world's largest centres of cotton spinning during the 1920's. By 1930 there were 216 cotton mills and 29 dyeing and bleaching works, yet just 50 years later production had virtually come to a standstill. At the turn of the 20th C, Bolton was heralded as the third largest engineering centre in Lancashire (after Manchester and Oldham) producing everything from railway locomotives to wrought iron, yet today there is, again, but scant evidence of this industry. However, gracious buildings and wide-open leafy squares still testify to the town's past glories and the swathes of generous, pedestrianized streets make walking through the centre a positive delight. The 700 listed buildings and 26 conservation areas remain as a lasting witness to the prosperity brought about through previous endeavour.

Aquarium Le Mans Crescent, Bolton BL1 1SE (01204 332853; www.boltonmuseums.org.uk/aquarium). An extensive collection, containing a wide range of fresh water fish from all over the world. *Open Mon-Sat 09.00-17.00 (Wed 09.30) & Sun 10.00-16.00.* Free.

Hall i' th' Wood Green Way, off Crompton Way, Bolton BL1 8UA (01204 332377/332853; www.boltonmuseums.org.uk/historic-halls). Originally a late medieval yeoman farmer's house, later inhabited by Samuel Crompton and finally purchased by Lord Leverhulme in 1899, who restored the building and donated it to Bolton Corporation in 1902. *Open Tue 10.00-16.00 & Sun 12.00-16.00.* Free.

Market Ashburner Street, Bolton BL1 1TJ (01204 336825; www.bolton.gov.uk/website/Pages/BoltonMarket.aspx). This award-winning market has a growing reputation as the premier food market in the North West. *Open Tue & Thu-Sat 09.00-17.00.*

Museum and Art Gallery Le Mans Crescent, Bolton BL1 1SE (01204 332211; www.boltonmuseums.org.uk/museum). Fine and decorative art; botany; local history and Egyptology. Family-friendly events and exhibitions all the year round. *Open as per Aquarium.* Free.

Smithills Hall Smithills Dean Road, Bolton BL1 7NP (01204 332377/332853; www.boltonmuseums.org.uk/historic-halls). Grade I listed building, containing fine examples of architecture through the ages, from medieval and Tudor right through to Victorian times. The hall is set in formal gardens overlooking the west Pennine moors. *Open Wed-Fri 10.00-16.00 & Sun 12.00-16.00.* Free.

Tourist Information Centre Central Library, Le Mans Crescent, Bolton BL1 1SE (01204 334321; www.visitbolton.com). *Open Mon, Tue & Thu 09.00-19.30; Wed 09.30-17.30 & Fri-Sat 09.00-17.30 (Sat 17.00).*

WALKING AND CYCLING

Moses Gate to Bolton: At the light controlled, equestrian crossing over A6053 (Hall Lane) head north into the woods, along Fogg Lane (in reality just a path!) until, after approximately 1/3rd mile, two paths appear, heading uphill on the right. Take the second one that runs at approximately 45° to Fogg Lane to re-join the line of the towpath, distinguished (as in so many places along this waterway) by the row of substantial coping stones.

Beyond Smithy Bridge 57 a tarmac path leads to the start of the demolished Damside Aqueduct, which can be negotiated by taking the path into Crossen Street and turning right beside No 5, descending the steps onto Radcliffe Road and again turning right. Follow the road over the River Tonge and turn immediately left into Chapel Place, along a track (beside the Lever Bridge pub) signposted Restricted Byway. At the brick wall take the path up to the right where evidence of the canal again becomes visible amongst the trees.

By the time A666 St Peter's Way strikes in from the left, there is little left to do save more or less follow its course along grassy, meandering pathways, first walking under the redundant Burden Railway Viaduct. After approximately ¼ mile, having passed behind a housing estate, the path joins Hilden Street, which can be followed to its junction with A579, Bradford Street. Turn left and, having crossed the road, take the path right, through trees, again paralleling St Peter's Way to its intersection with the railway viaduct, picking up the underpass and a path leading up Church Bank, into the town. Sadly, the last mile or so of waterway now lies beneath the pounding wheels and tarmac of the busy A666.

Lock 1 and Margaret Fletcher Tunnel

Pubs and Restaurants

1 The Levers Arms 3 Top O'th Lane, Darcy Lever, Bolton BL3 1SS (01204 392486). 200yds north west of 59 Bentley Bridge. Friendly, welcoming community pub serving real ale and real cider. Dogs welcome. Garden, sports TV and traditional pub games. Quiz *Thu. Open Mon-Fri 15.00-23.00 (Sat 00.00) & Sat-Sun 12.00-00.00 (Sun 23.00).*

2 The Volunteer 276 Radcliffe Road, Bolton BL3 1RS (01204 524271; www.facebook.com/thevollydarcy). On the Crossen Street towpath diversion. Lively, community local serving real ale. Garden, traditional pub games and sports TV. Dog-friendly. *Open 13.00-00.00 (Sat-Sun 12.00).*

3 The Farmers Arms 357 Radcliffe Road, Bolton BL3 1RU (01204 524106; www.facebook.com/TheFarmersArmsBolton/?ref=py_c). Comfortable, rambling hostelry, serving real ale and food *daily 12.00-19.00.* Family-friendly, outside seating. Traditional pub games and *occasional* live music. *Open 12.00-00.00.*

4 The Spinning Mule Nelson Square, Bolton BL1 1JT (01204 533339; www.jdwetherspoon.com/pubs/all-pubs/england/greater-manchester/the-spinning-mule-bolton). Named after the invention which revolutionised the cotton industry (giving Bolton world-wide fame) this pub now serves real ale, real cider and food *daily 08.00-23.00.* Children welcome. Sports TV and Wi-Fi. *Open 08.00-00.00 (Fri-Sat 01.00).*

5 The Dragonfly 60-62 Bradshawgate, Nelson Square, Bolton BL1 1DP (01204 533708; www.facebook.com/dragonflybolton). Landmark building, catering for Bolton's student population, serving real ale and food (including breakfast *until 12.00)* 09.00-20.00. Family-friendly, *regular* events. Traditional pub games, sports TV and Wi-Fi. *Open 09.00-01.00 (Mon-Tue & Thu 23.00).*

6 The Barristers Bar 2-4 Churchgate, Bolton BL1 1HJ (01204 365174; www.facebook.com/BarristersBolton). Part of the Swan Hotel – a listed building dating from 1845 – this attractively panelled pub serves an excellent selection of real ales and food *L.* Live background Music *Thu-Sun.* Dog-friendly, courtyard seating. Wi-Fi. *Open Mon-Thu 10.00-00.00 (Thu 03.00) Fri-Sat 10.00-06.00 & Sun 09.00-02.00.*

Nob End

The two Ringley Locks lie hidden in the trees where the towpath is regained, across the main Kearsley Road and soon the navigation is again in water, perched above Prestolee, flanked by thin sandstone 'fencing' slabs. In parts the towpath is cobbled. Rounding a corner Nob End comes into view, heralded by the imposing Wellfield House and, upon crossing the striking Prestolee Aqueduct, the navigation arrives at the basin below the two sets of staircase locks. The aqueduct, locks, basins, bridges and waterway junction form a spectacular engineering ensemble, fully deserving to qualify in the forefront of any list of waterway wonders of the world, topped off with the contemporary twist of Liam Curtin's delightful Meccano bridge. The first ¾-mile of the Bolton Arm is in water and has in the past hosted several trailboat rallies, while the start of the Bury Arm is spacious and soon arrives at the site of a spectacular breach – dating from 1936 – and never repaired. Most of the length to Bury is in water, it being the last section in use and it hugs the contour, never far from the course of the Irwell, burbling along far below, often separated by only a thin screen of trees. Beyond Radcliffe, Elton Reservoir comes into view as trams rattle close by before the final evidence of the waterway vanishes in a short, shallow cutting.

WALKING AND CYCLING

North of A667 Kearley Road the towpath can be regained at the site of the two Ringley Locks and followed through to the basin below Prestolee Locks. Here a track on the left leads downhill to Wilson's Bridge (over the River Croal) and a 10-minute walk to Farnworth Railway Station. Uphill, the track leads to the junction of the Bolton and Bury Arms – the former being in water with a good towpath through to Moses Gate Country Park (*see* Walking & Cycling *page 171*).

The Bury Arm can be followed without difficulty through to the outskirts of the town, where it intersects the roadway into an industrial estate. Bear right and pass under Daisyfield Railway Viaduct and along Wellington Street to its junction with Bolton Road. This is close to the terminus of the navigation. To access the town (and public transport) turn right, cross the river and follow signs through the underpass to avoid the busy main road. National Cycle Route 6 uses the towpath between Radcliffe and Bank Top Bridge 80.

See also the Irwell Sculpture Trail (*page 174*) for another possible series of walks, which could be planned in conjunction with towpath exploration, to make up a circular perambulation.

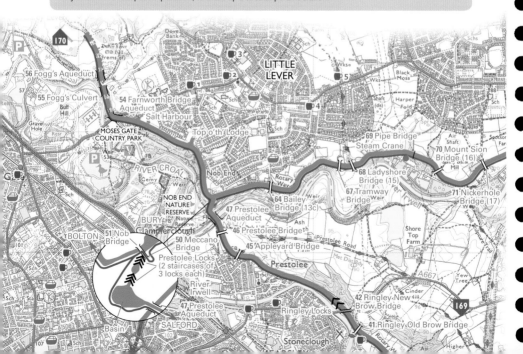

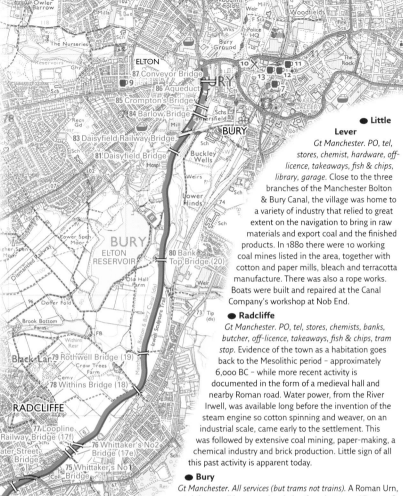

Gt Manchester. PO, tel,
stores, chemist, hardware, off-
licence, takeaways, fish & chips,
library, garage. Close to the three
branches of the Manchester Bolton
& Bury Canal, the village was home to
a variety of industry that relied to great
extent on the navigation to bring in raw
materials and export coal and the finished
products. In 1880 there were 10 working
coal mines listed in the area, together with
cotton and paper mills, bleach and terracotta
manufacture. There was also a rope works.
Boats were built and repaired at the Canal
Company's workshop at Nob End.

● **Radcliffe**
*Gt Manchester. PO, tel, stores, chemists, banks,
butcher, off-licence, takeaways, fish & chips, tram
stop.* Evidence of the town as a habitation goes
back to the Mesolithic period – approximately
6,000 BC – while more recent activity is
documented in the form of a medieval hall and
nearby Roman road. Water power, from the River
Irwell, was available long before the invention of the
steam engine so cotton spinning and weaver, on an
industrial scale, came early to the settlement. This
was followed by extensive coal mining, paper-making, a
chemical industry and brick production. Little sign of all
this past activity is apparent today.

● **Bury**
Gt Manchester. All services (but trams not trains). A Roman Urn,
containing small bronze coins dating from between AD 253-282,
was found immediately north of the present day town centre,
which has always been closely identified with the cotton industry,
together with its greatest son, Sir Robert Peel. Calico printing and light
engineering also figured as pillars of the area's industrial prowess, only
to decline in the second half of 20th C. Today, in common with many of the
prime textile producing areas of Lancashire, Bury seeks a new identity in retail,
the service industries and as a dormitory town for the nearby city of Manchester.
Bury Art Museum Moss Street, Bury BL9 0DR (0161 253 5878; www.buryartmuseum.
co.uk). Housed in a distinctive Edwardian building, that is a work of art in itself, this welcoming
and friendly establishment is the perfect place to enjoy art and find out more about the rich history of Bury
and the surrounding area. Also a showcase for international and local art. Shop and coffee shop. *Open Tue-Sat
10.00-17.00 (Sat 16.30).* Free.
Bury Castle Castle Armoury, Castle Street, Bury BL9 0LB. An early medieval, moated and fortified manor house,
dating from 1469. A leaflet detailing the history behind Bury Castle is available from the Tourist Information
Centre and all local libraries. *Open at any reasonable time.* Free.
Bury Market 1 Murray Road, Bury BL9 0BJ (0161 253 6520; www.burymarket.com). Dating from 1444, the
present day market robustly promotes itself as both 'World Famous' and 'Really Large' which, with its impressive
market hall and extensive spread of covered stalls, is rarely in dispute. Black pudding features prominently in any
catalogue of Bury's native provender. Market Hall *open Mon-Sat 09.00-17.00*; Fish and Meat Hall *open Mon-Sat
(not Tue afternoon) 09.00-17.00*; Open Market *Wed & Fri-Sat*.

Manchester Bolton & Bury Canal   Nob End

173

East Lancashire Railway Bolton Street Station, Bury BL9 0EY (0333 320 2830; www.eastlancsrailway.org.uk). An award-winning restored railway, complete with an excellent transport museum, offering a mainly steam-hauled service along the picturesque Irwell Valley. Shop and refreshments. Trains operate at *weekends and B Hols throughout the year and Apr-Sep, Wed-Fri.* Charge.

Fusilier Museum Moss Street, Bury BL9 0DF (0161 763 8950; www.fusiliermuseum.com). Home to the collection of the Lancashire Fusiliers and the Royal Regiment of Fusiliers – together they record more than 300 years of history and heritage. Shop and café (with Wi-Fi). *Open Mon-Sat 10.00-17.00 (Sat 16.00).* Charge.

Irwell Sculpture Trail (0161 253 5891; www.irwellsculpturetrail.co.uk). Winding its way from Bacup to Salford Quays and featuring over 70 artworks by locally, nationally and internationally renowned artists, this 33-mile trail links a series of clusters of thought provoking sculptures. Indeed, Bridge 76 on the Bury Arm – with its 'Water Made it Wet' sculpture – is a part of the trail. It passes through Bury (with a cluster in the town, together with a second one in Burrs Country Park, just to the north), Radcliffe (one cluster in the town with a second in Outwood Country Park to the south), Clifton Country Park (where the M60 intersects the canal) and thence south into Salford linking into clusters at Chapel Street and Ordsall. Visit the website for further information and to download a detailed map.

Ladyshore Bolton Countryside Service (01204 334343; www.woodlandtrust.org.uk/visiting-woods/wood/31610/ladyshore). Immediately south of Ladyshore Bridge 68. A picturesque site, sandwiched between the canal and the River Irwell, rich in wildlife.

Tourist Information Centre The Fusilier Museum, Moss Street, Bury BL9 0DF (0161 253 5111; www.visitbury.com/visitor-information/tourist-information-centre). Open Mon-Sat 10.00-17.00 (Sat 16.00).

Pubs and Restaurants (pages 164–165)

🍴✕ 1 **The Jolly Carter** 168 Church Street, Little Lever BL3 1BW (01204 577569; www.thejollycarter.com). Popular local serving real ale and appetising food *Mon-Fri L & Sat-Sun 12.00-20.00 (Sun 19.00).* Family-friendly, outside seating. Quiz *Sun*, karaoke *Fri.* Traditional pub games, sports TV and Wi-Fi. *Open 12.00-23.00 (Fri-Sat 00.00).*

🍴 2 **The New Inn** 56 Church Street, Little Lever BL3 1BE (01204 604747; www.newinnatlittlelever.co.uk). A sports orientated pub with 3D TV, serving real ale. *Regular* live music, newspapers, outside drinking area and traditional pub games. *Open Sun-Fri 12.00-23.30 (Fri 00.30) & Sat 11.00-00.30.*

🍴 3 **Henighans** 71 Lever Street, Little Lever BL3 1BA (01204 862664; www.henighans.com/little-lever). A warm, welcoming friendly atmosphere blends with well-kept real ales and food *available Fri-Sun 12.00-19.00.* Family-friendly, outside seating. *Regular* live music. Traditional pub games, newspapers, sports TV and Wi-Fi. *Open 12.00-01.00 (Fri-Sat 02.00).*

🍴 4 **The Queen Anne** 26 High Street, Little Lever BL3 1NB (01204 572640). Imposing, traditional local serving real ales. Dog- and family-friendly. Newspapers, sports TV, beer garden and traditional pub games. *Open Mon-Fri 16.00-23.00 (Fri 00.00) & Sat-Sun 12.00-00.00 (Sun 23.00).*

🍴 5 **The Stopes Tavern** 185 Stopes Road, Little Lever BL3 1NW (0161 723 4337; www.facebook.com/StopesTavern). Friendly community local serving real ale and food *Thu 17.00-200; Fri & Sun 12.00-18.00.* Dog- and child-friendly, garden. Traditional pub games and newspapers. *Open Mon-Thu 19.00-23.00 (Thu 17.00) & Fri-Sun 12.00-23.00.*

🍴 6 **The Bridge Tavern** 8 Blackburn Street, Radcliffe M26 1WW (0161 425 1252). Friendly community pub dispensing real ale and food *L and E.* Child- and *E.* Dog- and child-friendly, garden. Karaoke *Fri.* Traditional pub games, newspapers, sports TV and Wi-Fi. *Open Mon-Sat 11.00-00.00 (Fri-Sat 01.00) & Sun 12.00-00.00.*

🍴 7 **The Trackside Bar** Bolton Street Station, Bury BL9 0EY (0161 764 6461; www.facebook.com/thetrackside). Great ales combined with railway nostalgia, real cider with steam: up to 10 ciders and perries are available alongside their house beer. Dog- and family-friendly, platform seating. Food available *Sat-Sun 09.00-15.00. Regular* live music. *Open Mon-Thu 12.00-23.00 (Wed-Thu 11.00) Fri-Sat 11.00-00.00 (Sat 09.00) & Sun 09.00-23.00.*

🍴✕ 8 **The Lamb Inn** 533 Tottington Road, Woolfold, Bury BL8 1UB (0161 764 2714). Friendly, welcoming hostelry – with a landlord who is passionate about his beer – serving a range of real ales and real cider. Dog- and family-friendly, garden. Quiz alternate *Thu.* Traditional pub games, real fires, sports TV and Wi-Fi. *Open Mon-Fri 16.30-23.00 (Fri 00.00) & Sat-Sun 13.00-00.00 (Sun 22.30).*

🍴✕ 9 **The Black Bull** 8 Lowercroft Road, Bury BL8 2EY (0161 761 5961; www.theblackbullbury.co.uk) Award-winning and welcoming hostelry serving real ale and appetising food *Mon-Sat L and E & Sun 12.00-19.00.* Dog- and child-friendly, outside seating. Newspapers, real fires, sports TV and Wi-Fi. *Open 12.00-00.00 (Fri-Sat 01.00).*

✕🍷 10 **The Jewel in the Crown** 102 Bolton Street, Bury BL9 0LP (0161 764 2211; www.jewelinthecrownbury.co.uk). Award-winning Indian cuisine served *Mon-Sat 16.00-00.00 (Fri-Sat 00.30) & Sun 13.00-23.00.*

Also try: 🍴 11 **Wyldes** 4 Bolton Street, Bury BL9 0LQ (0161 797 2000; www.joseph-holt.com/pubs/view/wyldes); 🍴 12 **The Robert Peel** 10 Market Place, Bury BL9 0LD (0161 764 7287; www.jdwetherspoon.co.uk/home/pubs/the-robert-peel); and 🍴 13 **The Old White Lion** 6 Bolton Street, Bury BL9 0LQ (0161 764 2641; www.facebook.com/owlbury).

PEAK FOREST AND ASHTON CANALS

MAXIMUM DIMENSIONS
Length: 70'
Beam: 7'
Headroom: 6'

MANAGER
0303 040 4040;
www.canalrivertrust.org.uk/contact-us/ways-to-contact-us

MILEAGE
PEAK FOREST CANAL
WHALEY BRIDGE to:
Marple Junction: 6½ miles
Dukinfield Junction: 14½ miles
Locks: 16

ASHTON CANAL
DUCKINFIELD JUNCTION to:
Ducie Street Junction: 6½ miles
Locks: 18

THE PEAK FOREST CANAL

This canal runs from Whaley Bridge and Buxworth through Marple to the Ashton Canal at Dukinfield Junction. Authorised by Act of Parliament in 1794, it was aimed at providing an outlet for the great limestone deposits at Doveholes, south east of Whaley Bridge. However, since Doveholes is over 1000ft above sea level, the canal was terminated at Buxworth (Bugsworth as it was then known), and the line was continued up to the quarries by a 6½-mile tramway.
The canal was completed by 1800 except for the flight of locks at Marple, which were not built until 1804. A second, temporary, tramway bridged this gap in the meantime. Bugsworth soon became a busy interchange point where the wagons bringing the stone down from Doveholes tipped their load either into canal boats or into lime-kilns. This traffic, and the boats bringing coal *up* the canal for firing the kilns, accounted for the greatest proportion of the canal company's revenue.
The Peak Forest was also boosted by the opening of the Macclesfield Canal to Marple top lock in 1831, making it part of a new through route from Manchester to the Potteries. The Cromford & High Peak Railway was opened in 1831, joining up Whaley Bridge with the Cromford Canal on the far side of the Peak District.
By the early 1840s the Peak Forest Canal was suffering from competition from the Trent & Mersey Canal Company and two new railways. It was leased in perpetuity to the Sheffield, Ashton-under-Lyne & Manchester Railway, later the Great Central. In 1922 the Bugsworth traffic finished, while (through) traffic on the 'lower' Peak Forest Canal had disappeared by World War II. Along with the Ashton, full navigation was restored in 1974 and now the splendid Buxworth line is also open.

THE ASHTON CANAL

Authorised in 1792 and opened shortly afterwards, the Ashton was a strong rival of the Rochdale Canal – with which it connects in Manchester. The two canals were constructed simultaneously, partly to tap the big coal-producing area around Oldham. The Ashton also opened a new trade route from Manchester to the textile mills of Ashton, while the Rochdale served as a broad canal link over the Pennines between the Mersey and the rivers of Yorkshire. In 1831 completion of the narrow Macclesfield Canal made the Ashton part of a through route from Manchester to the Potteries.
The 1830s saw the peak of the Ashton Canal's prosperity. The canal company sold out to the forerunner of the Great Central Railway Company in 1846, who continued to maintain and operate the canal. Traffic declined in the present century and by 1962 it was unnavigable. A determined effort by the Peak Forest Canal Society, the IWA, local councils and the BWB (as was) resulted in its reopening in 1974.

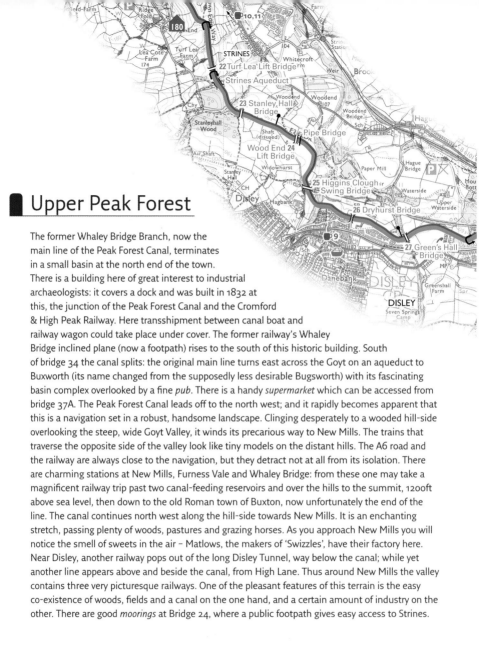

Upper Peak Forest

The former Whaley Bridge Branch, now the main line of the Peak Forest Canal, terminates in a small basin at the north end of the town. There is a building here of great interest to industrial archaeologists: it covers a dock and was built in 1832 at this, the junction of the Peak Forest Canal and the Cromford & High Peak Railway. Here transshipment between canal boat and railway wagon could take place under cover. The former railway's Whaley Bridge inclined plane (now a footpath) rises to the south of this historic building. South of bridge 34 the canal splits: the original main line turns east across the Goyt on an aqueduct to Buxworth (its name changed from the supposedly less desirable Bugsworth) with its fascinating basin complex overlooked by a fine *pub*. There is a handy *supermarket* which can be accessed from bridge 37A. The Peak Forest Canal leads off to the north west; and it rapidly becomes apparent that this is a navigation set in a robust, handsome landscape. Clinging desperately to a wooded hill-side overlooking the steep, wide Goyt Valley, it winds its precarious way to New Mills. The trains that traverse the opposite side of the valley look like tiny models on the distant hills. The A6 road and the railway are always close to the navigation, but they detract not at all from its isolation. There are charming stations at New Mills, Furness Vale and Whaley Bridge: from these one may take a magnificent railway trip past two canal-feeding reservoirs and over the hills to the summit, 1200ft above sea level, then down to the old Roman town of Buxton, now unfortunately the end of the line. The canal continues north west along the hill-side towards New Mills. It is an enchanting stretch, passing plenty of woods, pastures and grazing horses. As you approach New Mills you will notice the smell of sweets in the air – Matlows, the makers of 'Swizzles', have their factory here. Near Disley, another railway pops out of the long Disley Tunnel, way below the canal; while yet another line appears above and beside the canal, from High Lane. Thus around New Mills the valley contains three very picturesque railways. One of the pleasant features of this terrain is the easy co-existence of woods, fields and a canal on the one hand, and a certain amount of industry on the other. There are good *moorings* at Bridge 24, where a public footpath gives easy access to Strines.

BOAT TRIPS

Judith Mary II Canal Street, Whaley Bridge SK23 7LS (01663 732408/07540 895615; www.judithmary2.
co.uk). A long-established and fully equipped 70ft, 42-seater narrowboat available for private charter *all year*.
Also occasional public trips – telephone for details.
Phoenix is a day boat available for hire from Whaley Bridge Basin, Whaley Bridge SK23 7LS (07759
272632/07790 748860; www.phoenixdayboat.co.uk/narrow-boat-phoenix). For further details telephone
or visit the website.

NAVIGATIONAL NOTES

1 You will need an anti-vandal key for the locks and swing-bridges on the Ashton Canal. Bridge 1 on the Peak Forest also requires an anti-vandal key.
2 A Watermate key is required to operate bridge 25 and 30.
3 Bridges 22 and 24 are windlass operated.

WALKING AND CYCLING

The towpath is in good condition throughout. Peter Roger's Guide gives details of some walks and bicycle rides from Whaley Bridge – details at users. breathemail.net/ peter.rogers/whaley.htm. Details of local walks exploring Bugsworth (as was) Basin and the parish paths can be obtained from: PFCC, 41 Tatton Street, Knutsford, Cheshire, WA16 6AE or at users.iclway.co.uk/don. baines/maps& guides.htm. The Millennium Walkway (01663 743434/746904; www. visitpeakdistrict.com/New-Mills-Millenium-Walkway/details/?dms=3&feature=4&ven ue=6080107) which starts by the Heritage Centre in New Mills (see page 170) gives access to previously inaccessible parts of the gorge near New Mills. You can also obtain a series of leaflets from the centre giving full details of The Torrs Industrial Trail, The Bridges Trail, The Sett Valley Trail and The Waterside Way. The Goyt Way, which has an interpretation board at the canal terminus, and the Mid-Shires Way (from Buckinghamshire!) both pass through here.

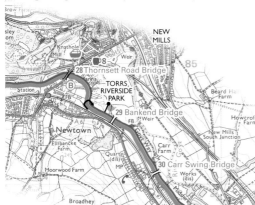

Boatyards

Ⓑ**Furness Vale Marina** The Moorings, Station Road, Furness Vale SK23 7QA (01663 747475), 🛏🚿♨D Pump out, long term mooring, winter storage, boat sales, chandlery, dry dock.
Ⓑ**TW Marine** Station Road, Furness Vale SK23 7QA (01663 745757; www.twmarine.co.uk). Marine engineers, chandlery.
Ⓑ **New Mills Marina** Hibbert Street, New Mills SK22 3JJ (01663 741310; www. canalmarinas.com/new-mills). ♨ D Gas, pump out, solid fuel, short- and long-term mooring, toilets, showers, launderette, 24hr CCTV. Wi-Fi. Holiday cottages to let.
Ⓑ **Trafalgar Marine Services Ltd** Victoria Works, Woodside Street, New Mills SK22 3HF (01663 747808; www.trafalgarmarineservices. co.uk). Traditional rope fender makers. Chandlery supplying rope, windlasses, chain, mooring accessories and rigging fittings. Day boat hire.

A SILK PURSE FROM A SOW'S EAR

The Ashton Canal is now a part of the Cheshire Ring, a superb 100-mile cruising circuit which can be comfortably completed in a week. Those with extra energy, or a day or two more, can add in a diversion along the Peak Forest Canal, and their efforts will reap just reward. The ability to cruise these waterways is due to those who campaigned between 1959 and 1974 to clear and restore canals that had become both an eyesore and a danger. Extensive lobbying resulted in the formation of the Peak Forest Canal Society, and with the staging of the 1966 IWA National Rally at Marple, restoration gained momentum. 'Operation Ashton', held over a weekend in September 1968, saw 600 waterway enthusiasts clear more than 2000 tons of rubbish from the canal. Local people were amazed, and began to realise that what had long been regarded as an eyesore and a danger could now become a valuable local amenity. *The corner had been turned*. Following a rally on the Rochdale Canal at Easter 1971, local authorities and the British Waterways Board (as it then was) decided to proceed with full restoration of the Ashton and Peak Forest Canals. We owe a great debt to all those involved.

Whaley Bridge
Derbs. PO, tel, stores, chemist, baker, takeaways, fish & chips, off-licence, library, garage, station. Built on a steep hill at the end of the canal, with good views across the Goyt valley, this is now a quiet and pleasant place, a new bypass having removed much of the traffic. The beautiful nearby hills are, however, more noteworthy than the town. There is also a useful cycle shop: The Bike Factory Vernon House, Beech Road, Whaley Bridge SK23 7BP (01663 735020; www.ukbikefactory.com). *Open Mon-Sat 09.00-17.30 (Thu 19.00).*

Cromford & High Peak Railway In the early 1820s a physical connection was planned between the Peak Forest Canal at Whaley Bridge and the Cromford Canal, way over to the south east on the other side of the Peak District, using a junction canal. However a waterway would have been impracticable through such mountainous terrain, and so a railway was constructed. Known as the Cromford & High Peak Railway, it was opened throughout in 1831, and was 33 miles long. With a summit level over 1200ft above sea level, this extraordinary standard-gauge goods line was interesting chiefly for its numerous slopes and inclined planes, up which the wagons were hauled by either stationary or tenacious locomotive steam engines (the steepest gradient on the line was 1 in 7). The C & HPR closed in 1967; now much of the route has been turned into a public footpath and bridleway. Around Whaley Bridge one may still see the remains of the short inclined plane (now a footpath) which brought the goods down the hill, then through the town to the wharf at the terminus of the Peak Forest Canal.

Toddbrook Reservoir Just south of Whaley Bridge. A very pleasant area for picnicking and walking. Private sailing club; fishing rights on this CRT reservoir exercised by an angling club (day tickets available).

Buxworth
Derbs. PO box, tel. The main feature in Buxworth is the fascinating old terminal basin system. This used to be a tremendously busy complex, and is of great interest to industrial archaeologists. The canal line to Bugsworth (as it was then known) was built to bring the canal as near as possible to the great limestone quarries at Doveholes, a plate tramway being constructed in 1799 via Chapel Milton to complete the connection. Known as the Peak Forest Tramway, this little line, 6½ miles long, brought the stone down the hills to Bugsworth, where it was transshipped into waiting canal boats. Throughout the history of the line, the wagons on the tramway

were drawn exclusively by horse-power – except for a 500yd inclined plane in Chapel-en-le-Frith, where the trucks were attached to a continuous rope so that the descending trucks pulled empty ones up the 1 in 7½ slope. The tramway was closed by 1926, and the sidings and basins at Buxworth became disused and overgrown, but are now fully restored and open to navigation. They should not be missed!

Furness Vale
Derbs. PO box, tel, fish & chips, takeaway. A main road (A6) village, useful for supplies.

New Mills
Derbs. PO, tel, stores, chemist, bank, baker, DIY, library, station. A mostly stone-built town on the Cheshire/ Derbyshire border; its industries include textile printing, engineering and engraving. A boatyard occupies old canal buildings to the east of bridge 28. There is also a useful cycle shop: Sett Valley Cycles 9 Union Road, New Mills SK22 3EL (01663 742629; www.settvalleycycles. co.uk). *Open Mon-Sat 09.00-18.00 (Sat 17.00).*

New Mills Heritage & Information Centre Rock Mill Lane, New Mills, High Peak SK22 3BN (01663 746904; www.newmillstowncouncil.org.uk/heritage. php). North of Thornsett Road Bridge (28). Located by the path leading down into the Torrs Gorge, next to the bus station. A splendid centre where you can see a display illustrating the history of the town, with a superb model. There is also a mock mine tunnel. Local books and walk details can be purchased in the shop, and there is also a café. The Millennium Walkway starts here. *Open Tue-Fri 10.30-16.00; Sat-Sun & B Hols 10.30-16.30 (winter 16.00).*

Disley
Cheshire. PO, tel, stores, chemist, bank, hardware, butcher, baker, takeaways, library, station. On the south bank of the canal. The centre of the village is quite pretty, spoilt slightly by the A6 traffic. The village is up the hill, south west of bridge 26. The attractive church stands among trees above the little village square. It was greatly renovated in the last century, but the ancient tower with the griffin leering down at passers-by dates from the 16th C. Vehicular and pedestrian access to Lyme Park (*see page 154*) is from the A6 near Disley, 1½ miles south west of Bridge 26. There is also a useful cycle shop: Freeride Cycles 18-20 Market Street, Disley SK12 2AA (01663 764444; www.freeridecycles.com). *Open Tue-Sat 10.00-17.30 (Tue 19.00).*

Pubs and Restaurants (pages 168–169)

🍺 1 **The Railway** 33–35 Market Street, Whaley Bridge SK23 7AA (07463 828655; www.facebook.com/therailwaywhaleybridge). Real ale in a fine straightforward Pub. Dog-friendly, traditional pub games. *Regular* live music. *Open 17.00-23.00 (Sat-Sun 12.00).*

🍺 2 **The Shepherds Arms** 7 Old Road, Whaley Bridge SK23 7HR (01663 308738). Once a farmhouse, this unspoilt gem of a pub serves real ales from its 17th-C stone-flagged taproom. Beer garden, open fires and traditional pub games. *Open 12.00-23.00 (Sat 00.00).*

🍺 3 **The Goyt Inn** 8 Bridge Street, Whaley Bridge SK23 7LR (01663 732710; www.facebook.com/goytinn). An attractive pub with an open fire and a garden, close to the canal basin and shops. Real ale is served. Dog-friendly, outside seating and real fires. *Open 16.30-23.00 (Sat-Sun 14.00).*

✕🍷 4 **Pear Tree Café** Baileys 29 Market Street, Whaley Bridge SK23 7AA (01663 734612; www.baileysrestaurant.co.uk). Seventy plus gins, excellent afternoon teas and memorable meals make this friendly restaurant well worth a visit. *Open Thu-Sat 12.00-15.00; Sun 12.30-16.00 & Tue-Sat 17.30-late; Sun 12.30-18.00 (last orders).*

🍺✕ 5 **The Navigation** Buxworth, High Peak SK23 7NE (01663 732072; www.navigationinn.co.uk). By the canal terminus, this is a superbly situated pub overlooking the old basins, beautifully decorated with some fine canal memorabilia, and with real fires *in winter*. It was built around 1794, and was once run by Pat Phoenix, *Coronation Street's* Elsie Tanner. A choice of real ale, along with meals served *daily* 12.00-20.30. Dog- and child-friendly, garden and play area. Traditional pub games. B&B. *Open Mon-Sat 11.00-00.00 (Mon-Tue 22.00) & Sun 11.00-23.00.*

🍺 6 **The Crossings Inn** Station Road, Furness Vale SK23 7QS (01663 744297). A friendly pub serving real ale. Dog-friendly, outside seating. *Open Mon-Thu 16.00-23.00; Fri 15.00-00.00 & Sat-Sun 12.00-00.00.*

🍺 7 **The Soldier Dick** 150-152 Buxton Road, Furness Vale SK23 7PH (01663 611010; www.soldierdick.co.uk/en-GB). Welcoming, friendly pub serving real ales and good value food *L and E*. Children welcome, open fires and a garden. B&B. *Open 12.00-23.00.*

🍺 8 **The Beehive** 67 Albion Road, New Mills SK22 3EY (01663 742087). A welcoming stone-built pub. Real ale and a good selection of bottled beers, mainly from local microbreweries. Upstairs cocktail and whisky bar. Dog- and family-friendly, outside seating. Traditional pub games, real fires, sports TV and Wi-Fi. *Open Mon-Thu 17.00-00.00; Fri-Sat 16.00-01.00 (Sat 15.00) & Sun 15.00-00.00.*

🍺 9 **The White Lion** 135 Buxton Road, Disley SK12 2HA (01663 762800). Village pub featuring a doggy dining room complete with blankets (and a meal for the price of a donation to a dogs trust). A wide selection of real ales are served, together with food *Tue-Sun (& B Hol Mon) 12.00-21.00 (Sun 20.00)*. Very dog-friendly, outside seating. Traditional pub games, newspapers, real fires and Wi-Fi. *Open Mon-Thu 12.00-23.00 (Mon 18.30) & Fri-Sun 12.00-00.30 (Sun 23.00).*

🍺 10 **The Sportsman** 105 Strines Road, Strines SK6 7GE (0161 427 2888; www.facebook.com/thesportsmanpubstrines). Perched on the side of the Goyt Valley, this pub has superb views across wooded countryside and serves real ales, together with food *Mon-Sat L and E & Sun 12.00-20.30*. Dog- and child-friendly, garden. Traditional pub games, real fires and sports TV. Camping. *Open 12.00-23.00.*

🍺 11 **The Crown Hawk** Green Road, Marple SK6 7HR (0161 427 2678; www.crownhawkgreen.pub). Friendly village pub, overlooking the green, dispensing real ales and food *12.00-20.30 (Sun 19.00)*. Dog- and family-friendly, garden. Wi-Fi. *Open 12.00-23.00. Fish & chips and takeaway (open Mon-Sat 08.00-15.00) nearby.*

Transshipment shed, Whaley Bridge

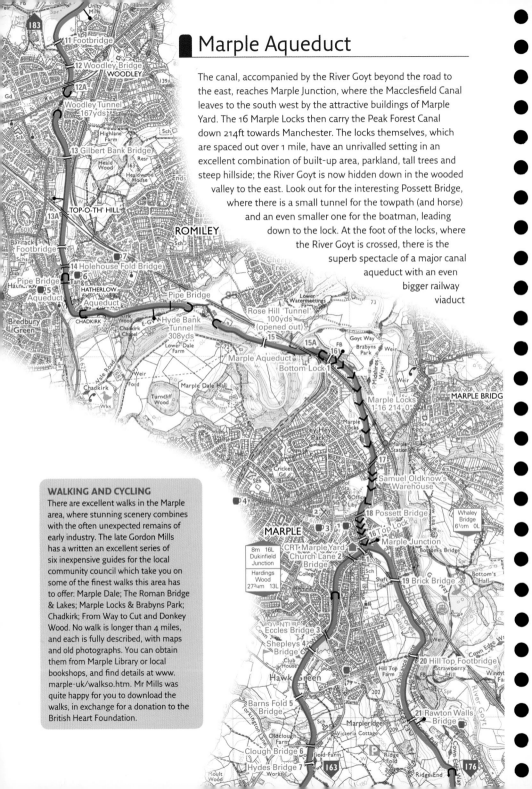

Marple Aqueduct

The canal, accompanied by the River Goyt beyond the road to the east, reaches Marple Junction, where the Macclesfield Canal leaves to the south west by the attractive buildings of Marple Yard. The 16 Marple Locks then carry the Peak Forest Canal down 214ft towards Manchester. The locks themselves, which are spaced out over 1 mile, have an unrivalled setting in an excellent combination of built-up area, parkland, tall trees and steep hillside; the River Goyt is now hidden down in the wooded valley to the east. Look out for the interesting Possett Bridge, where there is a small tunnel for the towpath (and horse) and an even smaller one for the boatman, leading down to the lock. At the foot of the locks, where the River Goyt is crossed, there is the superb spectacle of a major canal aqueduct with an even bigger railway viaduct

WALKING AND CYCLING

There are excellent walks in the Marple area, where stunning scenery combines with the often unexpected remains of early industry. The late Gordon Mills has a written an excellent series of six inexpensive guides for the local community council which take you on some of the finest walks this area has to offer: Marple Dale; The Roman Bridge & Lakes; Marple Locks & Brabyns Park; Chadkirk; From Way to Cut and Donkey Wood. No walk is longer than 4 miles, and each is fully described, with maps and old photographs. You can obtain them from Marple Library or local bookshops, and find details at www.marple-uk/walkso.htm. Mr Mills was quite happy for you to download the walks, in exchange for a donation to the British Heart Foundation.

alongside. West of here a narrow stretch was once Rose Hill Tunnel, long since opened out. The canal then traverses a wooded hillside before diving into Hyde Bank Tunnel, 308yds long. The towpath is diverted over the hill, passing a farm. On the other side, a couple of minor aqueducts lead the canal northwards, away from the Goyt Valley and past Romiley, Bredbury and Woodley, where there is a narrow 176yd-long tunnel, this time with the towpath continuing through it. There is a *swimming pool* close to the canal at Bridge 14.

NAVIGATIONAL NOTES

1 There is no mooring on the Marple flight since water levels in the pounds can fall dramatically when the locks are in use.
2 Hyde Bank Tunnel, although appearing wide, does not have sufficient clearance for two boats to pass. Make sure it is clear before you enter.

● **Marple**
Gt Manchester. All services. Once a famous hat-making centre, the town is most interesting by the canal. The town centre can be accessed from bridge 18.

● **Marple Locks**
The 16 locks at Marple were not built until 1804, four years after the rest of the navigation was opened. The 1-mile gap thus left was bridged by a tramway, while the Canal Company sought the cash to pay for the construction of a flight of locks. This was obviously a most unsatisfactory state of affairs, since the limestone from Doveholes had to be shifted from wagon to boat at Bugsworth Basin, from boat to wagon at Marple Junction, and back into boat again at the bottom of the tramway. Not surprisingly, a container system was developed – using iron boxes with a 2-ton payload – to ease the triple transshipment. However, this was no long-term solution, and when the necessary £27,000 was

forthcoming the company authorised construction of the flight of locks. Today they stand comparison with any flight on the network. Note especially Samuel Oldknow's superb warehouse, by lock 9, now tastefully converted to offices.

● **Marple Aqueduct**
Deservedly scheduled as an ancient monument, this three-arched aqueduct over the River Goyt is a very fine structure, in an exquisite setting almost 100ft above the river. Designed by Benjamin Outram, its construction utilises circular pierced shoulders above each arch to reduce the weight of the rubble filling whilst providing a decorative feature. Contrast and interest are further added by the use of two different colours of gritstone in the parapets and ledges.

● **Romiley**
Gt Manchester. All services. A useful place for supplies.

Pubs and Restaurants

●✕ **1 The Navigation** at Lock 13 9 Stockport Road, Marple SK6 6BD (0161 427 3817; www.robinsonsbrewery.com/navigationmarple). Useful for 'lock wheelers' (remember, there is no mooring on the flight!) A large comfortable pub serving real ale. Food is available *Mon-Fri L and E & Sat-Sun 12.00-20.00 (Sun 18.00).* Dog- and family-friendly, outside seating. Traditional pub games and sports TV. *Open 11.00-00.00 (Fri-Sat 01.00).*

✕✚ **2 No 48 Kitchen & Bar** 48 Stockport Road, Marple SK6 6AB (0161 427 1200; www.no48kitchenandbar.com). Spanish restaurant and tapas bar. *Open Tue-Sun 12.00-23.00 (Fri-Sat 00.00).*

● **3 The Hatters Arms** 81 Church Lane, Marple SK6 7AW (0161 427 1529; www.robinsonsbrewery.com/thehattersarms). Set in a terrace, this intimate little pub – with panelled walls and leaded lights – serves real ale. Children welcome *(until 19.00).* Traditional pub games. *Open 12.00-23.00 (Fri-Sat 00.00).*

● **4 The Railway** 223 Stockport Road, Marple SK6 6EN (0161 427 2146; www.robinsonsbrewery.com/railwayrosehill). Friendly pub, beside Rose Hill railway station, serving real ale and food

daily 12.00-14.00 (Sun 15.00). Children welcome. Garden, sports TV and Wi-Fi. *Open 11.45-00.00 (Fri-Sat 00.30).*

● **5 The Spread Eagle** Hatherlow, Romiley SK6 3DR (0161 494 5723; www.almond-pubs.co.uk/spread-eagle). A sympathetically renovated pub, dating from the 1770s, serving real ale and food *Mon-Fri L and E & Sat-Sun 12.00-21.00 (Sun 20.30).* Family-friendly, outside seating. Traditional pub games, real fires, sports TV and Wi-Fi. *Open 11.30-23.00 (Sun 22.30).*

● **6 The Duke of York Hotel** Stockport Road, Romiley SK6 3AN (0161 406 9988). A choice of real ale in an unspoilt 18th-C pub. Food is available *Tue-Fri L and E & Sat-Sun 12.00-21.00 (Sun 18.00).* Garden, real fires and Wi-Fi. *Open 12.00-23.00 (Wed &-Fri-Sat 23.30).*

●✕ **7 Platform One** 6 Stockport Road, Romiley SK6 4BN (0161 406 8686; www.facebook.com/platform.oneromiley). Formerly the Railway, this pub and wine bar serves a wide range of real ales, real cider and food *daily 12.00-20.00* (accessed via separate entrance – Platform 2). Quiz *Wed.* Family-friendly, outside seating. Wi-Fi. *Open Sun-Thu 12.00-22.30 & Fri-Sar 12.00-00.00.*

See also **Pubs and Restaurants** and **Boatyards** entries on page 164.

Hyde

The canal continues northward through a landscape which becomes less rural, but increasingly interesting. Bridge 6 is a pretty roving bridge, grown wider over the years. To the north, beyond the M67 motorway , the industrial tentacles of Hyde – Greater Manchester – ensnare the canal traveller, but the approach to Dukinfield Junction and Portland Basin is still very pleasant. The towpath is tidy, with plenty of grass, trees and seats. A lift bridge, a canal arm, an aqueduct over the River Tame and a stone roving bridge provide plenty of canal interest as you approach the junction, where the Ashton canal heads south-west into Manchester, and the Huddersfield Narrow canal starts its journey east across the Pennines (see page 65) to Huddersfield. Portland Basin was constructed to allow boats to make the sharp turn here, and was nicknamed the 'weavers rest', since so many weavers had reputedly drowned themselves here during hard times, such as the famine of 1860 and the depression of the 1930s. The warehouse which faces you across the junction, built in 1834, has been well restored. The Ashton Canal takes you into Manchester proper: this is still a fine, solid industrial section of waterway, still with a few steaming factories, tall chimneys and a good clear towpath. If you pass Dukinfield Junction in *mid-July*, you may see the colourful Tameside Canals Festival, which has been running successfully for many years now.

● **Ashton-under-Lyne**
Gt Manchester. All services. Walk north west from Portland Basin and you will find the church of St Michael, which was begun by Sir John de Assheton in the early 15th C and completed by his great grandson before 1516. The church is large, with a tall west tower rebuilt by Crowther in 1886–8. Particularly notable is the stained glass, depicting the Life of St Helena and dating from the 15th–16th C. A market was granted to the town in 1284, but by 1801 the population still numbered only 4800. It then expanded rapidly, due to the growth of cotton weaving in the area, and by 1851 totalled over 30,000.
Portland Basin Social & Industrial History Museum 1 Portland Place, Ashton-under-Lyne OL7 0QA (0161 343 2878; www.tameside.gov.uk/portlandbasin). This museum is housed in a superb reconstruction of a canal warehouse dating from 1834, at the junction of the Ashton, Peak Forest

and Huddersfield canals. It tells the rich story of Tameside's social, political and industrial history, drawing upon many different facets of local life. The museum features a 1920s street, working models, computer interactives, sound and film. The original waterwheel is restored to working order on the wharfside. Displays include topics such as textiles, hatting, printing, canals, coalmining, Chartism, education and politics. *Open Tue-Sun & B Hols 10.00-16.00 (Jul-Sep 17.00).* Café and shop. Free
Astley Cheetham Art Gallery Trinity Street, Stalybridge SK15 2BN (0161 338 6767; www.tameside.gov.uk/astleycheetham). Above Stalybridge Library, this gallery was built as a gift to the town in 1901. Exhibition programme of sculpture, textiles, painting and drawings, featuring work by prominent local artists and community groups. *Opening times vary* so visit the website for details. Free.
Stalybridge See page 58.

WALKING AND CYCLING
Pasture and fine woodland are a feature of Haughton Dale Nature Reserve, to the west of the canal near Hyde. Paths follow the River Tame here. Details from: Park Bridge Heritage Centre, The Stable, Park Bridge, Ashton-under-Lyne OL6 6D (0161 342 3055; www.tameside.gov.uk/parkbridge) which is the site a well-documented ironworks – a thriving family business for nearly 200 years. Café and Information Centre *open Thu-Sun 09.00-14.00.* Free.

Boatyards

Ⓑ**Portland Basin Marina** Lower Alma Street, Dukinfield SK16 4SQ (0161 330 3133; www.portlandbasinmarina.co.uk) 🛈 D Pump out, gas, overnight and long-term mooring, winter storage, crane, 100-year-old dry dock, day boat

hire, narrowboat hire, boat building and fitting out, engine repairs, chandlery, toilets, showers, books and maps, gifts, solid fuel, DIY facilities. Laundrette and supermarket close-by. *Emergency call out. Open Mon-Sat 09.00-17.00 & Sun 11.30-14.30.*

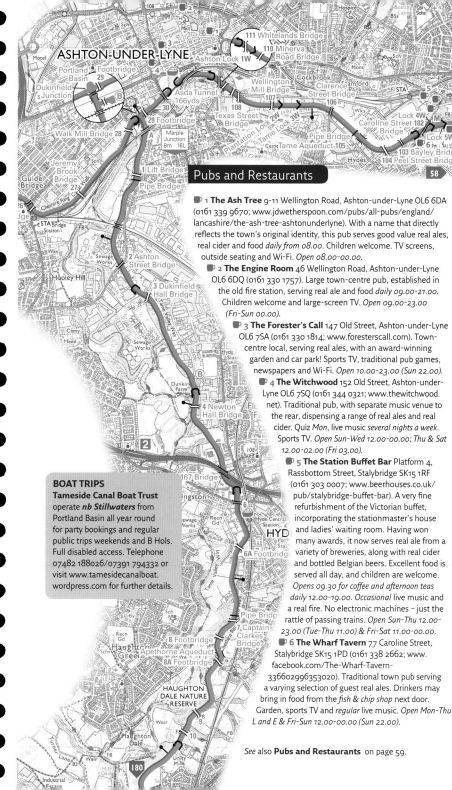

Pubs and Restaurants

58

1 The Ash Tree 9-11 Wellington Road, Ashton-under-Lyne OL6 6DA (0161 339 9670; www.jdwetherspoon.com/pubs/all-pubs/england/lancashire/the-ash-tree-ashtonunderlyne). With a name that directly reflects the town's original identity, this pub serves good value real ales, real cider and food *daily from 08.00*. Children welcome. TV screens, outside seating and Wi-Fi. *Open 08.00-00.00.*

2 The Engine Room 46 Wellington Road, Ashton-under-Lyne OL6 6DQ (0161 330 1757). Large town-centre pub, established in the old fire station, serving real ale and food *daily 09.00-21.00*. Children welcome and large-screen TV. *Open 09.00-23.00 (Fri-Sun 00.00).*

3 The Forester's Call 147 Old Street, Ashton-under-Lyne OL6 7SA (0161 330 1814; www.foresterscall.com). Town-centre local, serving real ales, with an award-winning garden and car park! Sports TV, traditional pub games, newspapers and Wi-Fi. *Open 10.00-23.00 (Sun 22.00).*

4 The Witchwood 152 Old Street, Ashton-under-Lyne OL6 7SQ (0161 344 0321; www.thewitchwood. net). Traditional pub, with separate music venue to the rear, dispensing a range of real ales and real cider. Quiz *Mon*, live music *several nights a week*. Sports TV. *Open Sun-Wed 12.00-00.00; Thu & Sat 12.00-02.00 (Fri 03.00).*

5 The Station Buffet Bar Platform 4, Rassbottom Street, Stalybridge SK15 1RF (0161 303 0007; www.beerhouses.co.uk/pub/stalybridge-buffet-bar). A very fine refurbishment of the Victorian buffet, incorporating the stationmaster's house and ladies' waiting room. Having won many awards, it now serves real ale from a variety of breweries, along with real cider and bottled Belgian beers. Excellent food is served all day, and children are welcome. *Opens 09.30 for coffee and afternoon teas daily 12.00-19.00. Occasional* live music and a real fire. No electronic machines – just the rattle of passing trains. *Open Sun-Thu 12.00-23.00 (Tue-Thu 11.00) & Fri-Sat 11.00-00.00.*

6 The Wharf Tavern 77 Caroline Street, Stalybridge SK15 1PD (0161 338 2662; www.facebook.com/The-Wharf-Tavern-336602996353020). Traditional town pub serving a varying selection of guest real ales. Drinkers may bring in food from the *fish & chip shop* next door. Garden, sports TV and *regular* live music. *Open Mon-Thu L and E & Fri-Sun 12.00-00.00 (Sun 22.00).*

See also **Pubs and Restaurants** *on page 59.*

BOAT TRIPS

Tameside Canal Boat Trust operate *nb Stillwaters* from Portland Basin all year round for party bookings and regular public trips weekends and B Hols. Full disabled access. Telephone 07482 188026/07391 794332 or visit www.tamesidecanalboat.wordpress.com for further details.

183

10' 9" Slaters Lower Lock 76
Grimshaw Lane Bridge
189
Railway Bridge
Hulme Hall Lane Bridge
Pipe Bridge
77 Anthony's Lock 9'7"
61
62
MILES PLATTING
8'9" Coalpit Middle 79
78 Coalpit Higher 11'1" Sta
7'11" Coalpit Lower 80
Varley Bridge
Philips Park Cemetery
FB
61
Clayton
8'6" Butler Lane Lock 81
Royle Bridge
New Viaduct Street
Forge Lane
Philips Park
Weir
VICTORIA STATION
Littleborough 16m 35L
Rochdale Canal
FB
Pipe Bridge
Bridge adto Bridge
7 4 5 7A en 8 9
National Cycling Centre
Sch
VELODROME
Clayton
Weir
6 Cambrian Street Bridge
Squash
Beswick Locks 4-7
6
9A
Ashton New Road Bridge
Union Street Bridge
82
5 Beswick Street Bridge
Regional Athletic
SPORT CITY
Etihad Stadium
Footbridge
10
Kitty Footbridge
4 Carruthers Street Bridge
New Islington Marina
62
8
9 Footbridge
ANCOATS
3
2 Ancoats Locks 1-3
24'0"
Sch
FB
Clayton Lane Bridge 11
10
11
37
Great Ancoats Street Bridge
MANCHESTER
Beswick
Clayton Locks 8-16
8'0"
Ancoats Lane Lock
82
Kitty Footbridge
Sch
66
Footbridge
Leech Street Bridge
Merchant's Wharf X
83 Brownsfield Lock
Store Street Aqueduct
Offices
Sch
Coll Ashburys Sta
Coll
Footbridge
London Road Bridge
3
MANCHESTER
Waters Meeting 4m 9L
Fairfield Junction 3¾m 18L
7'4" Dale Street Lock 84
Piccadilly Village
3 Great Ancoats Street Bridge
West Gorton
University
Jutland Street Bridge 2
Footbridge
Thomas Telford Basin

Droylsden

From start to finish, the Ashton Canal passes through a densely built-up area in which the canal is conspicuous as a welcome relief from the townscape which flanks it. Its clear water, excellent towpath, functional but dignified old bridges and the peace that generally surrounds it make it a haven for local school children, anglers, walkers and idlers, indeed for anyone who enjoys an environment that is quite separate from and unrelated to ordinary daily life. The rare pleasure, afforded only by an English canal, of stepping out of a city suburb into the peaceful and unpretentious atmosphere of the 18th C is once again, with continued restoration work, becoming available to all. At Fairfield Junction the top lock of the 18 which climb from Ducie Street Junction is encountered. It is a picturesque canal scene here with traditional buildings, including a shed dated 1833 standing over a canal arm, giving the area a quiet dignity. Descending the locks, you may wish to look out for the remains of several old canal arms: one of the more important was the 5-mile Stockport Branch, leaving from Clayton Junction, just below lock 11. The canal then falls through the remaining locks into Manchester. The surroundings are brightened by the well-cared-for Beswick flight of four locks, standing next to the new Stadium, where you could once see the extraordinary 'B of the Bang' sculpture, an explosion of spikes designed by Thomas Heathwick, to mark the success of the Commonwealth Games held here in 2002. Costing £1.42m – and Britain's tallest sculpture when completed in 2005 – it was beset by problems (largely from falling spikes) from the outset and its core was eventually melted down for scrap in 2012. The spikes remain in store! Large-scale redevelopment has been completed at Paradise Wharf and Piccadilly Village, making this final stretch unusually gentrified, with smart flats, basins and a crane. The Rochdale Canal, joined here, stretches from Ducie Street Junction for 33 miles over the Pennines to join the Calder & Hebble Navigation.

NAVIGATIONAL NOTES

1 You will need a handcuff lock key for the locks on this and the Peak Forest Canal.
2 CRT advise you to cruise the Ashton lower Rochdale Canals early in the morning, and avoid school holidays if possible. Moor only at recognised sites in this area, and do not offer anyone you do not know a ride on your boat. Keep the front doors locked.
3 Bridge 21 is very low.
4 Passage through locks 1–18 should be commenced *before 10.00*.

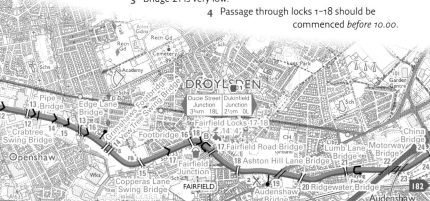

THE CHESHIRE RING – THEN AND NOW

This route has remained one of the most popular cruising circuits for many years now – a one-week trip encompassing parts of the Trent & Mersey, the Bridgewater, the Ashton, the Peak Forest and Macclesfield canals, passing through a wide and exciting variety of canalscape. Part of the journey includes a passage through central Manchester, a pleasant experience these days, but it was not always so . . .

The problem used to be timing your passage through the city so that the 'Rochdale Nine' locks were open, and your subsequent overnight mooring was a safe one! Local children preyed upon you as you tackled the Ancoats, Beswick and Clayton flights, leaping across the locks from one side to the other, begging lifts, and 'picking up' *anything* you might have left lying around . . .

The lock machinery was stiff, water supply uncertain, and the things which fouled your propeller defied description . . .

It is, thankfully, VERY different now, and the city passage is very attractive, interesting and enjoyable. Just take the usual precautions.

Pubs and Restaurants

🍺 1 **The Kings Head** 169 Market Street, Droylsden M43 7AY (0161 371 8194). Decorated with military memorabilia, this busy pub attracts a mixed clientele and serves real ale, together with food *L and E*. Traditional pub games, outdoor drinking area and sports TV. Dogs welcome. *Weekend* discos and Karaoke. Wi-Fi. *Open Mon-Sat 11.00-23.00 (Fri-Sat 00.00) & Sun 12.00-23.00.*

✗♌ 2 **The Pearl Restaurant Bar and Lounge** 119 Manchester Road, Audenshaw M34 5PY

(0161 301 5680.uk). Brightly decorated, upmarket Asian restaurant. *Open Mon-Sat 17.00-23.00 (Fri-Sat 01.00) & Sun 14.00-22.30.*

🍺 3 **The Jolly Angler** 47 Ducie Street, Manchester M1 2JW (0161 236 5307; www.hydesbrewery.com). A small, plain and friendly pub. Real ale. Café nearby. Regular Irish and folk music sessions. Children welcome. Mooring nearby but **don't** leave your boat here overnight. *Open Mon-Fri 17.30; Sat 12.00 & Sun L and E.*

See also **Pubs and Restaurants** on page 189.

Boatyards

ⓑ**Droylsden Marina** Lock Keepers Cottage, Droylsden M43 6GN (0161 330 3133; http://www.portlandbasinmarina.co.uk/services-offered/droylsden-marina). 🛶🛶🛶 Gas, secure pontoons for overnight and long-term moorings. There is also a new marina being Operated by **Portland Basin Marina**, Manchester. *See* page 182.

ⓑ**New Islington Marina** contact Urban Splash Timber Wharf, 16-22 Worsley Street, Castlefield, Manchester M15 4LD (0161 839 2999/0333 666 0000; www.urbansplash.co.uk). 🛶🛶🛶 Pump out, short- and long-term mooring, toilets, shower, laundry. Access from Rochdale Canal, south west of Union Street Bridge.

● **Fairfield**

Gt Manchester. PO, tel stores, chemist, off-licence, fish & chips, takeaway, garage, station. Immediately south of Fairfield Junction is a group of neat and tidy buildings around a fine chapel. This is an original Moravian settlement, established in 1785 by Benjamin Latrobe and consisting of tidy rows of cottages built in brick, intended to house the members of a self-contained community. The *post office, chemist and supermarket (open Mon-Sat 07.00-22.00 & Sun 10.00-16.00)* are north of the Marina in Droylesden.

National Cycling Centre Stuart Street, Manchester M11 4DQ (0161 223 2244www.nationalcyclingcentre. com). Access from the bridge, west of bridge 9, and in view from bridge 8, when climbing the locks. This is the National Cycling Centre, where the track is widely regarded as one of the finest and fastest in the world. There is a full programme of exciting cycle races staged in this magnificent stadium, which hosted the track events of the Commonwealth Games 2002. *See also* **Walking & Cycling.**

City of Manchester Stadium Ashton New Road, Manchester M11 3FF (0161 444 1894; www. stadiumguide.com/cityofmanchester). Now known as the Etihad Stadium and home to Manchester City Football Club. A wonderful 55,000 capacity stadium used for the 2002 Commonwealth Games. The foundation stone was laid by Tony Blair on the 17th of December 1999, and the stadium was built at a cost of £90 million.

● **Manchester**

All services. One of Britain's finest Victorian cities, a monument to 19th-C commerce and the textile boom, its size increasing remorselessly with the building of the canals, and later railways. Unfortunately virtually no early buildings survived the city's rapid growth, although there is an incredible wealth of Victorian architecture still to be seen, in spite of redevelopment. The town hall and surrounding streets are a particularly rich area. St Peter's Square, by the town hall, was the site of the 'Peterloo Massacre' in 1819, when a meeting demanding political reform was brutally dispersed by troops carrying drawn sabres. Eleven people were killed and many more were injured. The Free Trade Hall, once the home of the Hallé Orchestra, is a little further along the road. Built in 1856, it was badly damaged in World War II, but was subsequently re-built to its original Palladian design. There is theatre, ballet and cinema, art galleries, and a wealth of interesting buildings, Victorian shopping arcades, many pubs with a choice of good beer and a variety of restaurants just a short walk from the canal. Sporting facilities are excellent, partly as a consequence of Manchester being the venue for the 2002 Commonwealth Games. The new developments at Salford Quays, on the Manchester Ship Canal, are quite breathtaking.

Manchester Visitor Information Centre 1 Piccadilly Gardens, Manchester M1 1RG (0871 222 8223; www.visitmanchester.com). *Open Mon-Sat 09.30-17.00 & Sun 10.30-16.30.*

See pages 188 and 189 for details of Manchester attractions.

WALKING AND CYCLING

Keen cyclists might like to visit the magnificent National Cycling Centre (see above) for a 'Taster Session' where, for a very modest fee, you can hire a track bike and a helmet and ride the steeply banked circuit for an hour. Telephone 0161 223 2244 or visit www.nationalcyclingcentre.com for details and times.

Dulcie Street Junction (with Rochdale Canal)

ROCHDALE CANAL

MAXIMUM DIMENSIONS

Length: 72' 0"
Beam: 14' 2" (Locks 40, 41 & 47: 13' 6")
Headroom: 7' 6" (7' 1" under the M62 culvert)
Draught: 2' 6" (recommended by CRT as some
sections of the western end of the canal are only
dredged to 3' 3")

MILEAGE

MANCHESTER to:
Failsworth: 5 miles
Castleton: 11½ miles
Littleborough: 16½ miles
Todmorden: 22 miles
Hebden Bridge: 26½ miles
SOWERBY BRIDGE: 32 miles

MANAGER

0303 040 4040;
www.canalrivertrust.org.uk/contact-us/ways-
to-contact-us

The Rochdale Canal is one of three Pennine canal crossings. It was authorised by an Act of Parliament in 1794 and completed exactly ten years later. With wide locks it was able to handle barges, Humber keels and even small coasters, the latter sometimes trading between the Continent and Irish ports, using the River Mersey and the Irwell Navigation at the eastern end. However, the Achilles' heel of the waterway lay in its requirement for a copious supply of water at the summit pound, together with the sheer physical effort required to operate the three locks per mile that are averaged over the canal's relatively short length.

The boom years for the canal were in the 1820s and 1830s before the inevitable railway competition began to make an impression. Passenger carrying packet boats (Manchester to Rochdale: 13 miles and 41 locks in 7 hours) and fast, light-goods-carrying fly boats (20 tons transported from Manchester to Todmorden in 12 hours) were both successful enterprises in the early 1800s.

In 1887 the canal's fortunes appeared to take an upturn when the canal company bought its own boats. Traffic included cotton, grain, coal, wool, cement, salt and timber, and whilst end to end carriage steadily declined, shorter journeys continued to thrive. At the outbreak of World War I the canal company was still ordering new craft (powered by 25hp inverted compound steam engines) which were capable, loaded, of pulling a further two laden dumb barges. However, in 1921, as competition from the roads took its toll, the fleet ceased operation and traffic became spasmodic. The last loaded boat to trade over the canal's entire length was *nb Alice*, in April 1937, carrying 20 tons of wire from Manchester to Sowerby Bridge. The navigation was officially closed by an Act in 1952, except for the stretch connecting the Bridgewater and Ashton canals in Manchester. Restoration was commenced nearly 30 years ago and the canal society had not only succeeded in protecting nearly all its original line, but also re-opened 16 miles of the eastern end. It has also, in conjunction with the local authority-based Canal Trust, inspired the construction of Tuel Lane Lock and Tunnel.

Subsequently Canal & River Trust and its partners have completed restoration at a cost of £23 million, rebuilding locks, bridges and tunnels and completing many new structures. This investment has only been possible because of projected benefits to the local community over a number of years, totalling in the region of £200 million.

Central Manchester

Departing from Dale Street Basin, the canal begins its unremitting climb into the Pennines flanked by a series of not unattractive, although somewhat unusual, stone-filled gabions. Attractively painted cast iron bridges, reflecting the livery of past railway companies, regularly span the navigation as it heaves its way up past a series of abandoned, but still impressive, cotton mills. Moving steadily onwards and upwards the waterway is accompanied by a mix of urban housing, parkland and industry; the redeveloped Victoria Mill at Miles Platting is a most impressive example. Passing Newton Heath with its canalside *market* and handy *shops*, the canal soon reaches Failsworth where there is a collection of fine mill buildings, many now in their second or third incarnations. The section of the waterway west of the A62 bridge had been built over and part of a supermarket had to be demolished during restoration; the remaining portion together with a *PO, banks and a chemist* still lies to the north beside the new footbridge. Beyond Failsworth, and several more solid mill buildings, development starts to step back from the navigation as it enters a pleasantly tree-lined section. Between here and Littleborough, the line of the canal has been designated an SSSI in recognition of its importance as a site for certain rare aquatic plants, particularly floating water plantain (*Luronium natans*). The staked-out rectangles along sections of the waterway are 'in-channel reserves' designed to protect the plant's tendrils of floating oval leaves and delicate three-petalled white flowers. The white-clawed crayfish has also adopted the canal, living in the well-oxygenated water of the lock by-washes where they remain hidden from the prying eyes of their natural predators such as herons and mink.

NAVIGATIONAL NOTES

1 *See* Navigational Notes 1 & 2 on page 185.
2 Volunteers are often available to assist boaters up the Flight to Failsworth and are an invaluable source of local knowledge and information. Contact Canal & River Trust (0303 040 4040; www.canalrivertrust.org.uk/contact-us/ways-to-contact-us) for further information.

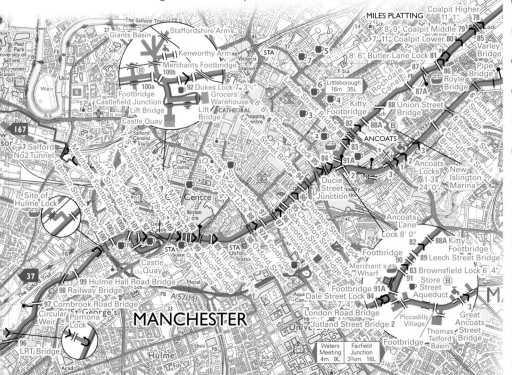

Pubs and Restaurants

✗♲ **1 Vivid Lounge** 149A Great Ancoats Street, Manchester M4 6DH (0161 272 8474; http://www.vividlounge.uk). Modern café/bar, serving everything from breakfast to a range of rustic home-cooked Thai dishes, using locally sourced produce. Waterside terrace. *Open Mon-Thu 11.00-23.00 & Fri-Sun 09.00-00.00 (Sun 23.00).*

🍺 **2 Port Street Beer House** 39-41 Port Street, Manchester M1 2EQ (0161 237 9949; www.portstreetbeerhouse.co.uk). Opened in 2011 in a former shop premises this pub has, arguably, the best selection of beers in Manchester – from real ales to over 100 bottled beers. Dog- and family-friendly *(daytime only)* outside seating. Traditional pub games, newspapers and Wi-Fi. *Open Mon-Fri 16.00-00.00 (Fri 14.00) & Sat-Sun 12.00-01.00 (Sun 00.00).*

🍺✗ **3 The Castle Hotel** 66 Oldham Street, Manchester M4 1LE (0161 237 9485; www. thecastlehotel.info). Dating from 1776, this Grade II listed building retains many of its original features and today majors on real ale, real cider and *regular* live music. Dog- and child-friendly *(during the day)* outside seating. Wi-Fi. *Open Mon-Sat 12.00-01.00 (Fri 02.00) and Sun 12.00-00.00.*

🍺 **4 The Crown & Kettle** 2 Oldham Road, Manchester M4 5FE (0161 236 2923; www.facebook.com/TheCrownandKettle). Dating from around 1800, this Grade II hostelry is famed for its ornate ceiling and striking chandeliers! Beyond the semi-ecclesiastical façade lie eight real ales and, often, an equal number of real ciders. No food but local pork pies are available at the bar. Dogs welcome; *regular* live music. Beer garden, sports TV and Wi-Fi. *Open Mon-Sat 12.00-23.00 (Fri-Sat 00.00) & Sun 12.00-22.30.*

🍺✗ **5 The Marble Arch Inn** 73 Rochdale Road, Manchester M4 4HY (0161 832 5914; www.marblebeers.com). A Grade II listed building with a sumptuous interior, featuring a barrel vaulted ceiling (to rival the Crown & Kettle above) with a decorative frieze, serving real ales from their own brewery. Equally highly-regarded food is available *daily 12.00-20.30 (Fri-Sun 20.00).* Also real cider. Dog- and child-friendly, outside seating. Real fires and Wi-Fi. *Open 12.00-23.00 (Fri-Sat 00.00).*

🍺 **6 Bar Fringe** 8 Swan Street, Manchester M4 5JN (0161 835 3815). A motorbike sits atop the entrance to this somewhat quirky, Belgian-style, urban pub, serving real ales and an excellent range of continental bottled and draught beers. Also real cider. Dog-friendly, outside seating. Wi-Fi. *Open 12.00-00.00 (Fri-Sat 00.30).*

🍺✗ **7 The Angel** 6 Angel Street, Manchester M4 4BQ (0161 833 4786; www.facebook.com/AngelPubMCR). A dining pub free from intrusive television, which showcases the work of local artists. The 10 handpumps ensure a mini beer festival on a weekly basis, with the beers changing with unprecedented frequency! Real cider and an excellent range of food available *daily 12.00-21.00.* Dog- and child-friendly *(until 20.00)* outside seating. Real fires and Wi-Fi. *Open 12.00-00.00.*

🍺✗ **8 The Millgate** Ashton Road West, Failsworth, Manchester M35 0ES (0161 681 8284; www.themillgatepub.co.uk). Carvery pub serving real ale and food *daily 12.00-20.* Family-friendly, garden and play area. Traditional pub games, sports TV and Wi-Fi. *Open 12.00-23.00 (Fri-Sat 23.30).*

🍺 **9 The Church Inn** 477 Oldham Road, Failsworth M35 0AA (0161 683 4076; www.churchinnfailsworth. robinsonsbrewery.com). Refurbished pub, east of Bridge 78B, serving real ale and food *daily 12.00-16.00.* Children welcome *until 20.00,* garden and play area. Karaoke *Sat-Sun.* Sports TV. *Open Sun-Thu 16.00-00.00 (Sun 12.00) & Fri-Sat 14.00-01.00.*

Map labels:
Holinwood Avenue Bridge 77
Henshaw Bridge 77A
193 Wks
Wrigley Head Bridge 78
Railway Bridge
78A
Failsworth Top Lock 65
9
78B
STA
78C
Liby
Back Lane Bridge 79
78D
FAILSWORTH
78
66 Tannersfield Highest Lock 9' 5"
Ridgefield Street Bridge
Tannersfield Middle Lock
Tannersfield Lowest Lock 67
80 Poplar Street Bridge
FB
80A Flash Street Footbridge
81 Droylesden Bridge
Newton Heath Footbridge
82A
NEWTON HEATH
Weirs
9'1" Shears Lock
10'4" Scotchman's Lock 72
10'1" Ten Acres Lock 73
83 Tenacres Bridge
74 Drunken Bridge Lock
Grimshaw Lane Bridge 83A
75 Slaters Higher Lock 10'4"
Railway Bridge
76 Slaters Lower Lock 10'9"
77 Anthony's Lock 9'7½"
84 Hulme Hall Lane Bridge
Philips Park Cemetery
BRADFORD
New Viaduct Street Bridge
Forge Lane Bridge
Ten Cent
Weirs
Nat
Squash
Beswick Locks 4-7
38'
184
Regional SPORT
Athletic Arena CITY
Pinfold Lock
Newton Heath Bridge
87

189

Manchester.
All services. One of Britain's finest Victorian cities, a monument to 19th-C commerce and the textile boom, its size increasing remorselessly with the building of the canals, and later the railways. Unfortunately virtually no early buildings survived the city's rapid growth, although there is an incredible wealth of Victorian architecture surviving, in spite of redevelopment. The town hall and surrounding streets are a particularly rich area (north of Oxford Street Bridge). St Peter's Square, by the town hall, was the site of the 'Peterloo Massacre' in 1819, when a meeting demanding political reform was brutally dispersed by troops carrying drawn sabres. Eleven people were killed and many more were injured. The Free Trade Hall, once the home of the Hallé Orchestra, is a little further along the road. Built in 1856, it was badly damaged in World War II, but was subsequently re-built to its original Palladian design. There is theatre, ballet and cinema, art galleries, and a wealth of interesting buildings, Victorian shopping arcades, many pubs with a choice of good beer and a variety of restaurants just a short walk from the canal. Sporting facilities are excellent, partly as a consequence of Manchester being the venue for the 2002 Commonwealth Games. The new developments at Salford Quays, on the Manchester Ship Canal, are quite breathtaking.
24 Hour Museum Guide Visit www.museumcrush.org to plan your day out and gain a unique perspective on the heritage of English cities. Non-commercial and free to use.
Bridgewater Hall Lower Mosley Street, Manchester M2 3WS (0161 907 9000; www.bridgewater-hall.co.uk). A visually striking hall – built beside the Rochdale Canal coal wharves and its junction with the Manchester & Salford Junction Canal (its name was almost as long as the waterway itself) – and home to the Hallé Orchestra, BBC Philharmonic, Manchester Camerata and an impressive pipe organ. The auditorium seats over 2000 for classical concerts, celebrity recitals, jazz and rhythm and blues music. Conducted tours of the auditorium and backstage can be pre-booked. Telephone for programme details.
East Lancashire Railway Bolton Street Station, Bury BL9 0EY (0333 320 2830; www.eastlancsrailway.org.uk). An award-winning restored railway offering a mainly steam-hauled service along the picturesque Irwell Valley. Shop and refreshments. Trains operate *at weekends and B Hols throughout the year and Apr-Sep, Wed-Fri*. Charge.
Greater Manchester Police Museum www.gmpmuseum.co.uk.

Home 2 Tony Wilson Place, Manchester M15 4FN (0161 200 1500; www.homemcr.org). Formed from the combined talents of the old Library and Cornerhouse theatres, this new venue is home to cinema, theatre, the arts and a whole range of events. Box office and bookshop *open daily 12.00-20.00* and food is available in either the bar or café *Mon-Sat 10.00-23.00 (Fri-Sat 00.00) & Sun 11.00-22.30*. Gallery *open Tue-Sun 12.00-20.00 (Sun 18.00)*.
Manchester Art Gallery Mosley Street, Manchester M2 3JL (0161 235 8888; www.manchesterartgallery.org). Outstanding collection of 19th-C Pre-Raphaelite paintings; works from 18th-C masters (Gainsborough, Reynolds and Stubbs); contemporary art and sculpture; fine examples of Dutch and Italian painting and an internationally renowned collection of decorative art (ceramics, metalwork, furniture and textiles). Also the Clore Interactive Gallery for 5–12 year olds and their families. Shop and Gallery Restaurant. *Open daily 10.00-17 (Mon 11.00)*. Free.
Manchester Cathedral Victoria Street, Manchester M3 1SX (0161 833 2220; www.manchestercathedral.org). Founded as a Chantry College in 1421, it became the cathedral for the newly formed diocese in 1847. 16th-C misericords render a humorous depiction of medieval life; carving in the choir stalls and canopies is exquisite as is the choir screen and the six bays that make up the nave, which are the widest of any church in England.
Manchester City Football Club Etihad Stadium, Manchester M11 3FF (0161 444 1894; www.mancity.com). Much the same as Manchester United really except the *opening times are Mon-Sat 09.00-17.00; Sun & B Hols 10.00-17.00*. Charge.
Manchester Jewish Museum 190 Cheetham Hill Road, Manchester M8 8LW (0161 834 9879; www.manchesterjewishmuseum.com). Beautifully restored, Grade II listed building opened in 1874 and now a museum but retaining the basic layout of a synagogue. Striking architecture, stained glass and the former Ladies Gallery containing the Permanent Exhibition which tells the 200-year old story of Manchester Jewry. Heritage Trails take place *monthly Mar-Oct*. Shop. *Open Sun-Fri (10.00-16.00 (Fri 13.00)*. Charge.
Manchester Museum University of Manchester, Oxford Road, Manchester M13 9PL (0161 275 2648; www.museum.manchester.ac.uk). This university museum helps to uncover the mysteries of Ancient Egypt, discover the world of neotropical frogs, tease out the intricacies of the human body and encourage you to marvel at the dinosaurs and other prehistoric beasts. Stunning displays and interactive exhibits. Shop and café. Open *daily 10.00-17.00*. Free.

Manchester United Football Club Sir Matt Busby Way, Old Trafford, Manchester M16 0RA (0161 868 8000; www.manutd.com). Museum charting the history of the club from 1878 to the present day, hall of fame and the trophy room. The tour visits the player's dressing rooms, takes in Sir Alex's dugout and lets you run down the players tunnel to the imaginary roar of the crowd. Shop and café. *Open 09.30–17.00.* Charge

Markets Piccadilly Gardens, Manchester (0161 234 5730; www.manchester.gov.uk/markets). Flower Market *Thu–Sat 10.00– 18.00;* French Market *once a month (usually 3rd week) Thu–Sat 10.00–18.00;* Farmers' Market *once a month (usually 2nd week) Fri–Sat 08.30–17.00.* Fashion Market, Tib Street *Sat 10.00–17.00.*

Museum of Science and Industry Liverpool Road, off Deansgate, Manchester M3 4FP (0161 832 2244; www.scienceandindustrymuseum. org.uk). Located on the site of the world's first passenger railway station, this exciting hands-on museum has 14 galleries covering everything from steam to space, transport to textiles, and includes a working steam train, a reconstructed Victorian sewer (complete with smells!) and an interactive science centre. Shop, café *(open at 08.00 – Sun 09.00)* and bistro. *Open daily 10.00–17.00.* Free.

Palace Theatre and Opera House Oxford Street, Manchester M1 6FT (0871 977 3801; www.manchestertheatres.com/palacetheatre. htm). Two of the most prestigious theatres in the Northwest, hosting the best in musicals, drama, opera and comedy. Visit the website for programme details.

Royal Exchange Theatre St Ann's Square, Manchester M2 7DH (0161 833 9833; www.royalexchangetheatre.co.uk). Theatre-in-the-round set in the recently restored Royal Exchange Centre. Visit the website for programme details.

Runway Visitor Park Sunbank Lane, Altrincham WA15 8XQ (0161 489 3932; www. book.manchesterairport.co.uk/manweb.nsf/ content/runwayvisitorpark). The chance to get a close-up of Concorde G-BOAC together with a selection of other aircraft and unrivalled views of the operational runways at Manchester Airport. Shop, snack bar, picnic and children's play areas. *Open 08.00-dusk.* Charge for entrance and car parking.

Smithills Hall Smithills Dean Road, Bolton BL1 7NP (01204 332377; www.boltonlams.co.uk/ historic-halls/smithills-history). Some of the finest examples of Medieval, Tudor and Victorian Architecture in the region exhibited in a Grade I listed building. Shop and refreshments. Guided tours. *Open Wed-Fri 10.00-16.00 & Sun 12.00-16.00.* Free.

Travel Metroshuttle is a free city centre bus-contact Traveline for details of this and all public transport information on 0871 200 2233 *open 07.00-20.00 (08.00 weekends).* For Metrolink Trams contact 0161 205 2000; www.metrolink. co.uk and for train travel 08457 48 49 50.

Whitworth Art Gallery University of Manchester, Oxford Road, Manchester M15 6ER (0161 275 7450; www.whitworth.manchester. ac.uk). Home to internationally renowned collections of British watercolours, textiles and wallpapers. Also an impressive range of paintings, drawings, sculptures and prints. Exhibitions and events throughout the year. Gallery Bistro (0161 275 7497) serving drinks, home-made cakes and light lunches *Mon-Sat 09.00-17.00 (Thu 21.00) & Sun 10.00-17.00. Shop. Gallery open daily 10.00-17.00 (Thu 21.00).*

Manchester Visitor Information Centre 1 Piccadilly Gardens, Manchester M1 1RG (0871 222 8223; www.visitmanchester.com). *Open Mon-Sat 09.30-17.00 & Sun 10.30-16.30.*

● **Rochdale Canal Corridor Regeneration** The £24m restoration of the waterway, part of which runs through Oldham and Rochdale, is seen as a core programme of restoration acting as a catalyst for areas and communities within the canal corridor. A study commissioned by British Waterways and the two local authorities came up with proposals which include a range of accessible canalside developments where people can live and work, a series of visitor attractions, a waterside network of safe green spaces and walking routes together with good maintenance and management marketed by a cross-section of public and private groups. The Rochdale Canal Strategy will also help to create a further 15,000 jobs, the construction or re-use of 627,000 sq yds of office, leisure and shopping floorspace as well as reclamation and recovery of 1484 acres of land. A comprehensive brief has been developed to maximise the potential the navigation has to offer the local community in terms of economic regeneration, leisure, transport, tourism and movement. Hopefully this holistic approach will ultimately succeed in eliminating many of the social problems that beset the area and, in their turn, detract from the boater's enjoyment of this historic section of newly restored waterway.

● **Ancoats Mills** (www.heritageworks.co.uk) Not far out of Ducie Street Basin the canal passes, on the off side, a collection of fine old cotton spinning mills. These are of national importance and include some of the earliest mills built in Manchester. Murray's Mills were constructed between 1798 and 1804 and Old Mill – built 1798 – is the city's oldest surviving mill and is of a non-fireproof design. Of slightly later construction is Sedgewick Mill (1818-20), while Paragon and Royal Mills were the last of a whole series of buildings on this site, being completed in 1912. They ceased production around 1960.

● **Newton Heath** *Gt Manchester. PO, tel, stores, chemist, butcher, baker, bank, hardware, takeaways, fish & chips, library, station.* A satellite to Failsworth, once engaged in cotton spinning and weaving and now a useful place to stop outside the city.

● **Failsworth**
Gt Manchester. PO, tel, stores, chemist, baker, hardware, fish & chips, takeaways, banks, library, garage, station. Virtually the most southerly outpost of the cotton industry in Rochdale and close to the crescent-shaped Lancashire coalfield, exploited around Ashton-under-Lyne. *Gas* is available 100yds east of 78C (0161 681 1563; www.embassygas.co.uk).

Pubs and Restaurants

🍺✕ 1 **Boat and Horses** Broadway, Chadderton, Oldham OL9 8AU (0161 681 2363; www.boatandhorsespub.co.uk). Originally dating from 1804, this pub had to be completely rebuilt in 1999 following serious foundation disturbance due to the construction of the M60. Today it serves real ales and food *daily 12.00-20.45 (Sun 20.00)*. There is a carvery *L and E Mon-Thu and all day Fri-Sun*. Breakfast is available *daily 09.00-11.30*. Family-friendly, garden and play area. Conservatory, sports TV and Wi-Fi. *Open 12.00-23.00 (Fri-Sat 00.00)*.

🍺 2 **The Minders Arms** 51 Joshua Lane, Middleton M24 2AY (0161 643 4964; www.jwlees.co.uk/venue/minders-arms-middleton). A friendly local, but a stone's throw from the brewery gates, serving real ale. Dog- and family-friendly, beer garden. Traditional pub games, newspapers and Wi-Fi. *Open Mon-Sat 12.00-23.00 (Fri-Sat 00.00) & Sun 12.00-22.00.*

🍺✕ 3 **The Rose of Lancaster** 7 Haigh Lane, Chadderton, Oldham OL1 2TQ (0161 624 3031; www.roseoflancaster.co.uk). Overlooking the canal, the River Irk and open countryside, this popular pub serves real ale and food *daily 12.00-21.15 (Sun 20.45)*. Conservatory restaurant and covered patio. Open fires, sports TV, traditional pub games and Wi-Fi. *Open 11.30 (Sun 12.00).*

🍺 4 **The Ship Inn** 693 Rochdale Road, Slattocks M24 2RN (0161 643 5871; www.slattocks.com/the-ship-inn). Dating from 1837, this pub offers real ale, canalside seating and traditional pub games. Moorings nearby. *Open 11.00-22.00 (Fri-Sat 23.00).*

🍺 5 **The Hopwood Arms** 753 Rochdale Road, Middleton M24 2RA (01706 359807; www.hopwoodpub.co.uk). Village pub at Slattocks Top Lock serving real ale and food *Mon-Fri L and E & Sat-Sun 12.00-19.00 (Sun 18.00)*. Family-friendly, garden. Traditional pub games, sports TV and Wi-Fi. *Open 12.00-00.00 (Sun 23.00).*

🍺 6 **Tandle Hill Tavern** 14 Thornham Lane, Slattocks M24 2SD (0161 376 4492). 1 mile east of Slattocks Top Lock, up the severely potholed Thornham Lane. It is well worth the walk to this unusually remote hostelry, to enjoy a pint (or two) of the house ale, Bumpy Lane. Frequented by farmers, locals and walkers, this pub caters for dogs and offers toasties by way of sustenance. Family-friendly. Real fires and a beer garden with real views. *Open Wed-Fri 17.00-22.00 (Fri 23.00) & Sat-Sun 12.00-22.30. Check opening times in winter or adverse weather.*

Climbing the Rochdale Canal out of Manchester

Slattocks

This stretch is a mix of industry and housing, with the navigation sometimes part buried in a leafy cutting. There is only one lock in the 3-mile length. Beyond Mills Hill there is an abrupt and welcome change as, on crossing the infant River Irk, the waterway bends around to confront a stone bridge and lock in a delightfully rural setting. As it gains height the navigation has partially looped back on itself and at Higher Boarshaw the locks are interspersed with two striking examples of the Manchester & Leeds Railway's bridges. Above the second bridge, as the waterway rounds a slight bend, the Pennines first come into full view and although still distant, herald the challenge yet to come – for which the compact flight of the six Slattocks Locks provides a telling overture!

Slattocks
Gt Manchester. PO box, tel, stores, garage. A long, narrow village. It is reputed to derive its name from a Northern-style amalgamation of the two words 'South Locks'. There is a small stores in the garage which is *open 24hrs.*

Boatyards

Ⓑ**New Islington Marina** contact Urban Splash Timber Wharf, 16-22 Worsley Street, Castlefield, Manchester M15 4LD (0161 839 2999/0333 666 0000; www. urbansplash.co.uk). 🚿🛊🧺 Pump out, short- and long-term mooring, toilets, shower, laundry. Access from Rochdale Canal, south west of Union Street Bridge. (*see* map on page 188)

See also Boatyard entries for the Bridgewater Canal pages 30 and 33.

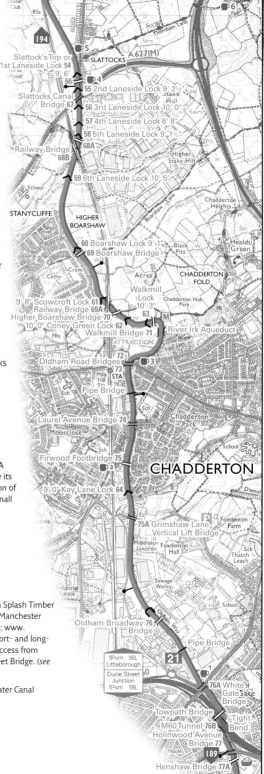

Rochdale

Above the locks there are fine open views as the waterway bends first towards the railway then swings back to duck under the motorway, in what was a road crossing over a farm lane. No provision was made for the canal, then derelict, when the M62 was constructed and to build one retrospectively, when the navigation was restored, would have been prohibitively expensive. The ingenious solution devised was to commandeer an existing culvert, divert the line of the waterway through it, relocate lock 53 south of the motorway to correct the levels, and provide an alternative approach to the farm. Above Castleton, the canal heads into Rochdale but skirts the town itself which used to be served by an arm below Moss Locks, now derelict. The main line maintains a discrete distance and retains its Pennine vistas, stretching out ahead in a wide arc. Passing through a shallow cutting in open moorland, the navigation arrives at the charming cluster of buildings at Clegg Hall: early 19th-C weavers' cottages, an old mill from the same era and the gaunt and newly renovated hall peeping out from behind the trees. Beyond, the waterway negotiates a series of new bridges – replacing previous infilling – and passing Little Clegg, a chemical works and Smithy Bridge station, arrives in Littleborough accompanied by the railway.

NAVIGATIONAL NOTES

1 The M62 culvert is only 14' 7'' wide with a maximum draught of 3' 3'' and an air draught of 7' 1''. All craft should proceed with extreme caution. Wide boats wishing to use this culvert must give *24 hrs notice* (0303 040 4040; www.canalrivertrust.org.uk/contact-us/ways-to-contact-us) as a floating towpath has been installed.
2 The new section under the A627(M) is made up of new narrow channel, a passing place and a 121yd tunnel. As there are short sightlines throughout, boaters should proceed with caution. The channel and tunnel are only 16' 6'' wide so wide boats must give way in the passing place between the two.
3 The new channel west of Well i'th Lane Bridge (approximately ½ mile east of the A627(M) Tunnel) is 20' wide but there is a tight curve at the eastern end. Care should be taken, especially by wide boats.

Pubs and Restaurants

There are further pubs in Castleton, together with an excellent selection in both Rochdale and Milnrow, rewarding a ¾-mile walk in either direction.

🍺 1 **The Blue Pits Inn** 842 Manchester Road, Castleton OL11 2SP (01706 632151; www.jwlees.co.uk/venue/blue-pits-inn). Welcoming, friendly pub – once used as a mortuary – and now serving real ale. Dog- and family-friendly, outside seating. Traditional pub games, sports TV and Wi-Fi. *Open 12.00-00.00.*

🍺 2 **The Midland Beer Co** 826 Manchester Road, Castleton OL11 3AW (01706 750873; www.facebook.com/Midland-Beer-Company-Castleton-263968833949637). A pool table, a jukebox with over 15,000 songs and real ale conspire to make this a friendly local. Outside seating and sports TV. *Open 12.00-00.00 (Fri-Sat 01.00).*

🍺 3 **The Crown & Shuttle** 170 Rochdale Road, Firgrove OL16 3BU (01706 648259; www.jwlees.co.uk/venue/crown-shuttle-inn). Friendly, traditional three-roomed pub serving real ale. Dog-friendly and outside seating. Traditional pub games, real fires, sports TV and Wi-Fi. *Open Mon-Fri 14.00-00.00 & Sat-Sun 12.00-00.00 (Sun 23.00).*

🍺 4 **The Hornet** Helmsman Lane, Kingsway, Rochdale OL16 4PS (01706 526099; www.hungryhorse.co.uk/pubs/greater-manchester/hornet). New, foody pub serving a real ale. Food *available all day,* including breakfast. Family-friendly, garden. Traditional pub games, sports TV and Wi-Fi. *Open 11.00-23.00.*

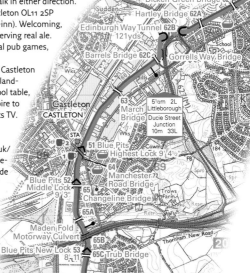

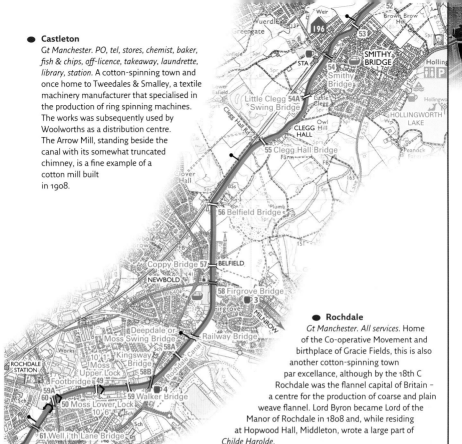

Castleton

Gt Manchester. PO, tel, stores, chemist, baker, fish & chips, off-licence, takeaway, laundrette, library, station. A cotton-spinning town and once home to Tweedales & Smalley, a textile machinery manufacturer that specialised in the production of ring spinning machines. The works was subsequently used by Woolworths as a distribution centre. The Arrow Mill, standing beside the canal with its somewhat truncated chimney, is a fine example of a cotton mill built in 1908.

Rochdale

Gt Manchester. All services. Home of the Co-operative Movement and birthplace of Gracie Fields, this is also another cotton-spinning town par excellence, although by the 18th C Rochdale was the flannel capital of Britain – a centre for the production of coarse and plain weave flannel. Lord Byron became Lord of the Manor of Rochdale in 1808 and, while residing at Hopwood Hall, Middleton, wrote a large part of *Childe Harolde*.

Touchstones Rochdale The Esplanade, Rochdale OL16 1AQ (01706 924492; www.link4life.org/centres/touchstones-rochdale). Four art galleries, museum, heritage gallery, tourist information centre and café. *Open Tue-Sat 10.00-17.00.* Free.

Rochdale Pioneers Museum 31 Toad Lane, Rochdale OL16 0NU (01706 524920; www.rochdalepioneersmuseum.coop). The Rochdale Society of Equitable Pioneers held their first meeting here on 15 August 1844 and 31 Toad Lane went on to become the world's first viable Co-operative shop. *Open Wed-Sat 10.30-16.00.*

St Chad's Parish Church Sparrow Hill, Rochdale OL16 1QT (01706 645014). There has been a church overlooking the town, perched on this site, for over 1,000 years and parts of the present tower date back to Saxon times, although there have been several different buildings over the centuries. There is a striking Burne-Jones stained-glass window in the tower and further glass by William Morris. The town stocks, dating from 1688, are within the church curtilage.

Milnrow

Gt Manchester. PO, tel, stores, chemist, butcher, baker, hardware, off-licence, takeaways, fish & chips, garage, station. Very much a centre for stone quarrying, open-cast and shaft mining, lying on the south east end of the crescent-shaped Lancashire coalfield. At Tunshill Farm there is a bank of old coking kilns and the remains of a fulling mill, with evidence of a paved pack-horse track and numerous local paths. Also six beehive coking ovens nearby. A mile east of Firgrove Bridge 58.

Ellenroad Engine House Steam Museum Elizabethan Way, Newhey, Rochdale OL16 4LE (07981 391603; www.sites.google.com/a/ellenroad.org.uk/www/www/home). Home to one of the world's largest working steam mill engine and the Whitelees beam engine. Café and picnic area. The engine house is *open Tue & Sun 11.00-15.00 and Sat before steaming 12.00-15.00.* Free – donations welcome. The engine is in steam *1st Sun in each month (except Jan) 11.00-16.00.* Charge. Reglar bus service from Rochdale terminus and Newhey railway station is nearby.

Rochdale Canal Rochdale

195

Summit

Leaving Littleborough, the canal climbs steadily upwards past the strung-out Courtaulds factory, leaving the industrial chimneys of Rochdale far behind. The transition between sheltered valley bottom, with its compact, functional towns, and the open moorland that the waterway now heads towards, is fairly abrupt. Above West Summit Lock two contrasting, though striking features planted on the landscape are the Steanor Bottom Toll House (at the intersection of two roads to the west) and the 763yd span of the high-voltage line totally straddling the valley here. The typical moorland of the area is an acid peat overlying gritstone, poor draining and therefore agriculturally unproductive. At Longlees Lock the remote summit pound finishes. This was once the site of both a chemical and a brick works. Now reverted to coarse grasses, rushes and mosses, this section of the waterway is a haven to birdlife that can include meadow pipit, snipe, sandpiper, wheatear, dunlin, curlew and redshank. The descent into Todmorden is as scenically exhilarating as it is physically exhausting and the extended views, both in front and behind, steadily give way to the valley's intimacy.

- **Smithy Bridge**
  Lancs. PO, tel, stores, chemist, butcher, baker, delicatessen, laundrette, takeaway, fish & chips, library, station.
- **Littleborough**
  Lancs. All services. Laundrette. A bustling little town, busy with visitors in summer though, strangely, without a market. Opposite the solid stone parish church is the excellent Coach House Heritage Centre – a local initiative to provide tourist information established in a grade II listed building. Just round the corner, in Victoria Street, are a good butcher and baker.
  Coach House Heritage Centre Lodge Street, Littleborough OL15 9AE (01706 378481; www.littleboroughcoachhouse. org). Community hub; café; exhibitions and gifts. Tourist information. *Open Mon-Sat 09.00-16.00 (Thu-Sat 20.00) & Sun 09.00-15.00.*
- **Summit**
  Lancs. PO box, tel. Once a bustling woollen weaving community, the village has played an important part in three very different forms of transport. It sits beside the summit level of the canal, a place of sustenance to the thirsty boater and source of the much-needed water supply for locks descending east and west. The railway burrows underneath in a tunnel 2869yds long – the longest rail tunnel in the world when built in 1839. Some 23 million bricks were used in its construction. In 1984 a petroleum-carrying goods train caught fire and burnt

uncontrollably in the tunnel for several weeks, smoke and flames belching from the ventilation shafts. It took £4 million and six months to re-open the tunnel to traffic.

Steanor Bottom Toll House Just to the north of the village and built in 1824 at the junction of the old and new routes to Littleborough.

● **Walsden**

W. Yorks. PO, tel, stores, takeaways, fish & chips, off-licence, library, station. Meaning 'Valley of the Welsh' this textile village, just outside Todmorden, offers the boater all the important forms of sustenance.

NAVIGATIONAL NOTES

From Mar-Oct The Summit Locks are locked *in the evening* and unlocked *in the morning*. This is necessary to maintain control of water supplies.

Pubs and Restaurants

● 1 **Tophams Tavern** 18 Smithybridge Road, Smithy Bridge OL15 8QF (01706 379922). Popular local serving real ale. *Open 16.00-00.00 (Sat-Sun 12.00).*

●✕ 2 **Rake Tapas Restaurant** 2 Blackstone Edge Old Road, Littleborough OL15 0JX (01706 379686; www.raketapas.co.uk). Home to the Hay Rake microbrewery this pub (formerly The Rake Inn) dispenses its own real ales and locally-sourced food, with tapas a speciality. Family-friendly, garden. Traditional pub games, real fires and Wi-Fi. B&B. *Open Mon-Sat 17.00-22.00 (Fri-Sat 00.00) & Sun 15.00-22.00.*

✕ 3 **The Cherry Tree Café** Lodge Street, Littleborough OL15 9AE (01706 378481; www. facebook.com/cherrytreelittleborough). Inexpensive home-made snacks and cakes, teas and coffees served in this friendly annexe to the Heritage Centre. *Open Mon-Wed 09.00-16.30 (Mon 16.00) Thu-Fri 09.00-16.30; Sat 09.00-20.00 & Sun 09.00-15.00.*

● 4 **The Red Lion Hotel** 6 Halifax Road, Littleborough OL15 0HB (01706 378195). Once a farmhouse, this very traditional old pub has been licensed since the 18th C to dispense a wide selection of regular and guest real ales. Also an excellent range of Belgian bottled beers and foreign ales. Dog-friendly. Live music *Wed* and quiz *Tue*. Traditional pub games, newspapers, sports TV and Wi-Fi. *Open Sun-Thu 14.00-00.00 (Sun 13.00) & Fri-Sat 12.30-01.00.*

✕♇ 5 **Waterside Bar and Restaurant** 1 Inghams Lane, Littleborough OL15 0AY (01706 376250; www.thewatersideexperience.co.uk). Modern bar-restaurant with an exciting menu offering Mediterranean options as well as modern British food. Meals served *Wed-Sat L and E (not Wed-Thu L) & Sun 12.00-18.00*. Children welcome; beautiful garden with decking overlooking the canal. Exciting *regular* theme nights. *Closed Mon-Tue.*

●✕ 6 **The Summit Inn** 140 Summit OL15 9QX (01706 379500; www.facebook.com/

summitinnlittleborough). Real ale is served in thus country pub high up in the Pennines together with home-cooked food *daily 12.00-20.00*. Dog- and family-friendly, garden. Live music *Fri* and Quiz *Sun*. Traditional pub games and real fires. *Open 12.00-23.00 (Fri-Sat 00.00).*

✕ 7 **Cotton Weavers Café** Gordon Rigg Garden Centre, Rochdale Road, Walsden OL14 7UB (01706 817722; www.gordonrigg.com/catalog/view/theme/ gordonrigg/docs/cotton-weavers-cafe-menu.pdf). Based in the garden centre, itself once a cotton mill, this friendly café serves an *all-day* breakfast, lunches and tea. Children's menu. *Open daily 09.00-16.00 (Sun 10.00).*

●✕ 8 **The Border Rose Inn** 772 Rochdale Road, Walsden OL14 7UA (01706 812142; www.facebook. com/TheBorderRoseInn). Busy, upmarket pub and restaurant serving a wide range of home-made food *L and E*. Also real ale. Dog- and child-friendly, beer garden. Sports TV. *Open Mon-Thu L and E & Fri-Sun 11.30-19.30 (closes at 19.30 every evening).*

✕ 9 **Grandma Pollard's Fish & Chips and Homemade Pies** Rochdale Road, Walsden OL14 7SL (01706 815769; www.grandmapollards.co.uk). Something of an institution in the area, this is a chippy and pie provider of great character. *Open Mon-Tue until 15.30 & Wed-Fri until 20.00.* Tony claims that 'his little legs need a rest' as his excuse for *staying closed over the weekend*. Nevertheless, his famous vanilla slices are well worth waiting for.

● 10 **The Shepherd's Rest** Lumbutts Road, Lumbutts, Todmorden OL14 6JJ (01706 813437; www.shepherdsrestinn.co.uk). Well worth the walk up onto the moors from Copperas Bridge 32, this isolated but welcoming pub, dispenses real ale and food – served in a dining area with spectacular views over the upper Calder valley – available *Mon-Thu 17.00-21.00; Thu 12.00-14.30 & Fri-Sun 12.00-21.30 (Sun 21.00).* Dog-friendly, garden. Real fires and Wi-Fi. *Open Mon-Tue 17.00-23.30 & Wed-Sun 12.00-23.30 (Sun 22.30).*

Todmorden

Now the descent begins in earnest with 17 locks in less than 3 miles and a spectacular railway crossing for good measure. A sweeping bend leads the waterway into the town with an immense brick retaining wall of massive proportions running all the way around the outside. The 'Great Wall of Tod' supports the railway embankment at this point and estimates of the total number of bricks used put the figure at more than 4 million. Beyond the compact town of Todmorden the countryside initially opens out revealing the disused Cross Stone Church, perched high on hills to the north of the navigation. Its badly blackened stonework is a reminder of the concentration of local industry, both past and present. Lobb Mill has finally been re-built (and turned into luxury apartments) while opposite Callis Lock there is a useful, boater-friendly *coal merchant* selling just about everything that is combustible. The waterway is now tucked tightly under a steep hillside covered by ancient deciduous woodland as the canal hugs the narrow valley bottom, interspersed, on the towpath side, with textile mills and dyeworks. The navigation approaches Hebden Bridge descending Stubbing (meaning a cleared area of woodland), Upper and Lower locks and passing gaily painted cottages, washing stretched like bunting across cobbled alleyways.

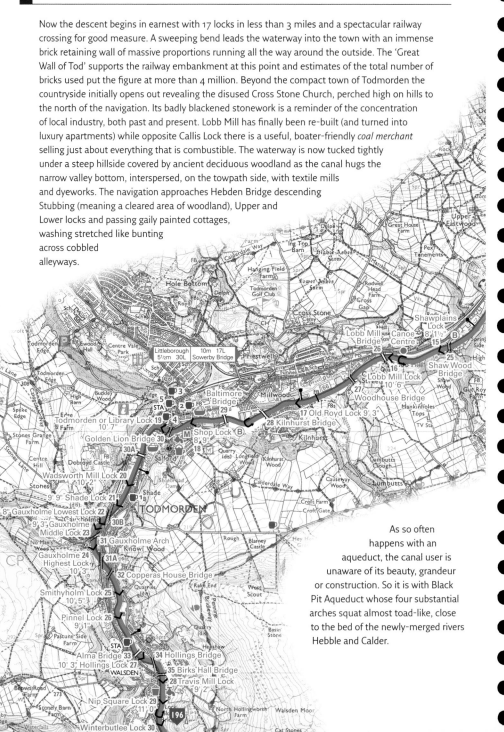

As so often happens with an aqueduct, the canal user is unaware of its beauty, grandeur or construction. So it is with Black Pit Aqueduct whose four substantial arches squat almost toad-like, close to the bed of the newly-merged rivers Hebble and Calder.

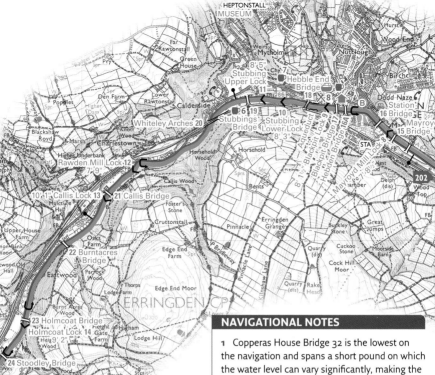

NAVIGATIONAL NOTES

1 Copperas House Bridge 32 is the lowest on the navigation and spans a short pound on which the water level can vary significantly, making the bridge very low at times. Proceed with caution.

2 Immediately below Lobb Mill Lock 17 there is a canoe centre. Approaching boaters are requested to sound their horn.

Boatyards

ⓑ **Mobile Boat Repairers** Sandworth Street, Todmorden OL14 6NP (01706 815103/07957 869641). Mobile welding, repairs to engines, gearboxes and generators, agents for RCR. *24hr emergency call out.*

ⓑ **Pickwell and Arnold** Unit 10, Nanholme Mill, Shaw Wood Road, Todmorden OL14 6DA (01706 812411; www.pickwellandarnold.co.uk). Below Shaw Plains Lock 15. Engine sales and repairs, boat building and repairs. *Emergency call out.*

ⓑ **Valley Fuels** Lower Underbank, Halifax Road, Charlestown HX7 6PH (01422 842284; www. facebook.com/valleyfuels). Opposite Callis Mill. Coal, seasoned logs, coke, sticks, charcoal, firelighters, stoves and spare parts. *Open Mon–Fri 10.00–17.30 and Sat 09.00–16.00. Also open Sun 12.00–15.00 when the frost comes!*

ⓑ **Bronte Boat Hire** New Road, Hebden Bridge HX7 8AD (01706 815103; www.bronteboathire. co.uk). 🛏🛏⚓ D E Gas, pump out, narrowboat hire, day boat hire, slipway, dry dock. *24hr emergency call out.*

CHARLESTOWN RAILWAY DISASTER

In 1912 there was a serious derailment on the Charlestown curve when the 14.25 Manchester to Leeds express left the track, having effectively shattered the alignment of the rails at this point. The accident, involving a 2-4-2 radial tank engine, occurred on the stretch of line just before the railway crosses the canal on Whiteley Arches. The inspector, Colonel Druit, found at the subsequent enquiry that while the 45mph line speed at this point was suitable for normal express running, it was too high for tank engines of this type. Indeed, he went on to question the suitability of tank engines per se – with their high centre of gravity and inherent instability – for sustained high-speed traction. The derailed locomotive, together with all its carriages, toppled down the embankment, coming to rest strewn across the grounds of the old Woodman Inn.

Todmorden

W. Yorks. All services. Laundrette. 19th C manufacturing success led to the concentration of wealth in the pockets of a few individuals whose ostentation was often manifested locally in civic and domestic architecture. Todmorden is fortunate, indeed, to have benefited greatly from the philanthropy of the Fielden family, whose legacy of good taste in buildings represents a feast in stone. Their choice of architect, in John Gibson of London, proved most successful. His work both echoes the solid vernacular building from a previous era, while introducing a further wealth of styles, which in turn complement the fine stone railway viaduct that dominates the town's centre. Simple classical building sits side by side with the richly ornate, a striking example of the latter being the elaborately pedimented town hall. Originally built astride the county boundary (moved in a later reorganisation) between Lancashire and Yorkshire, this Italian Renaissance style building is fronted by six sturdy pillars, surmounted by statuary depicting, on the one half, the agriculture and engineering of Yorkshire, while on the other various facets of cotton spinning in Lancashire. In contrast the Unitarian Church, erected by Joshua and Samuel Fielden, again to a design by Gibson, is pure Victorian Gothic revival and a fitting memorial to their father, John Fielden MP. His concern for his fellow man extended to Westminster and industrial reform, being largely responsible for the Ten Hours Act of 1847 which limited the maximum working day to ten hours for any person under 18 and any woman over 18.

Craft Centre Lever Street, Todmorden OL14 5QF (01706 818170). Small family-run centre: stalls, workshops and a tearoom.

Free Library Rochdale Road, Todmorden OL14 7LB. Typifies the many individual buildings in the town displaying the skills of the stone mason in conjunction with the philanthropy of local benefactors. The library was a gift from the local Co-operative Society in 1897 and its asymmetry is pleasing in a simple way. It gives a second name to Todmorden Lock beside it, namely Library Lock.

Hippodrome Theatre 83 Halifax Road, Todmorden OL14 5BB (01706 814875). A striking building of its period.

St Mary's Church Rochdale Road, Todmorden OL14 7BS. Built on land given to the town c. 1476 it still retains its 15th-C tower. Subsequently much altered, the present Gothic Revival chancel bears little relationship to the original, although it contains a pleasing carved oak screen and attractive stained-glass windows.

Stoodley Pike The original monument was erected in 1815 to commemorate the end of the Napoleonic Wars. However, weakened by lightning, it collapsed 40 years later and was replaced by the present 120ft high structure. Visible from the canal, as you approach the town, it makes the object of a bracing walk, rewarded by stunning views across Calderdale.

Tourist Information Centre 15 Burnley Road, Todmorden OL14 7BU (01706 818181; www. visittodmorden.co.uk). *Open Mon–Sat 10.00–16.00.*

ON YOUR TOD

It is said that the only man-made feature distinguishable on the Earth, when viewed from the moon, is the Great Wall of China. Clearly this must be due to its length rather than its – relatively speaking – minuscule width. For a guard detachment, patrolling some of its more remote lengths, it must have been a singularly lonely and, in some cases, solitary occupation. The 'Great Wall of Tod' – the name given to the canalside railway retaining wall before Library Lock – is unlikely to hold quite such long-standing historical significance. Nor will it become a talking point amongst future lunar cosmonauts. Owing its existence to the less than prosaic function of keeping 'railway out of t'cut' it still remains, nonetheless, one of the wonders of a more local world. Building with brick (well in excess of 4 million in this instance) in the Calder Valley, rather than the local gritstone, was largely down to the advent of the railway: a phenomenon repeated throughout many other areas of the country.

BIRD LIFE

The *Nuthatch* is recognised by its rounded, short-tailed appearance and its habit of descending tree trunks head-downwards, a trait unique in Britain to this species. The nuthatch has blue-grey upperparts, a black eyestripe, white cheeks and orange-buff underparts. The chisel-like bill is used to prise insects from tree bark and to hammer open acorns wedged in bark crevices. This woodland species has a falcon-like call. It nests in tree holes, often plastering the entrance with mud to reduce its diameter.

Pubs and Restaurants (pages 190–191)

🍺 1 **The Woodpecker** Rochdale Road, Shade, Gauxholme, Todmorden OL14 7NU (07957 992284; www.facebook.com/The-Woodpecker-Todmorden-800871486638346). End of terrace pub, incorporating an old slaughterhouse, this hostelry serves real ale. *Occasional* live music, disco and quiz *Sat*. Pool table. *Open Mon-Fri 15.00-23.00 & Sat-Sun 12.00-23.00*.

🍺 2 **The Pub** 3 Brook Street, Todmorden OL14 5AJ (01706 812145; www.thepubtodmorden. co.uk). Newly-opened micro-pub, established in an old café, dispensing real ale and real cider. More than 30 gins are also stocked. Dog-friendly, outside seating. *Open 12.00-21.00 (Fri-Sat 23.00)*.

🍺✕ 3 **The Polished Knob** 31 Burnley Road, Todmorden OL14 7BU (01706 810480; www. thepolishedknob.co.uk). Originally the Black Swan, and sporting a fine façade, this pub now serves real ales and food *Wed-Sun 12.00-16.00*. Live music *Wed* and *weekends*. Dog- and family-friendly, outside seating. Real fires, sports TV and Wi-Fi. *Open 11.00-23.00 (Fri-Sat 02.00)*.

🍺 4 **The Queen Hotel** Rise Lane, Todmorden OL14 7AA (01706 819917; www.thequeenhotel. org.uk). Built to serve the adjacent railway, and once linked to the platform by a footbridge this fine, stone-built hostelry – complete with moulded ceilings and oak-panelled walls – serves real ale and *lunchtime* snacks. There is also an *evening* carvery. B&B. *Open 11.00-23.00 (Sun 22.30)*.

🍺 5 **The White Hart** Station Approach, Todmorden OL14 (01709 811760; www. jdwetherspoon.com/pubs/all-pubs/england/west-yorkshire/the-white-hart-todmorden). Imposing mock-Tudor building replacing the 1728 original that once housed the local court. Today it dispenses real ale and food *daily 08.00-22.00*. Outside seating, children welcome, real fires and Wi-Fi. *Open 08.00-00.00 (Fri-Sat 01.00)*.

🍺✕ 6 **Stubbing Wharf** King Street, Hebden Bridge HX7 6LU (01422 844107; www.stubbing. co.uk). A good range of real ales are dispensed in this canalside, family pub, together with excellent food *daily 12.00-21.00*. Family-friendly, garden. Real fires and poolroom. Mooring. *Open 12.00-00.00 (Sun 23.00)*.

🍺 7 **The Fox and Goose** 7 Heptonstall Road, Hebden Bridge HX7 6AZ (01422 648052; www. foxandgoose.org). A community-owned, real ale pub that is serious about its beer and cider. Alongside its real ales, many from local microbreweries, is an excellent range of bottled continental lagers and ciders. Dogs welcome, hillside beer garden, open fires, traditional pub games and Wi-Fi. Quiz *Mon*. *Open Mon-Thu 12.00-23.00 (Mon 14.00) & Fri-Sun 12.00-01.00 (Sun 23.00)*.

✕ 8 **Greens Vegetarian Café** New Oxford House, 24 Albert Street, Hebden Bridge HX7 8AH (01422 843587; http://greensvegetariancafe.co.uk). Friendly establishment serving appetising vegetarian meals, homemade cake, tea and coffee. *Open Wed-Sun 11.00-15.00; B Hols & Fri-Sat 18.30-22.00*.

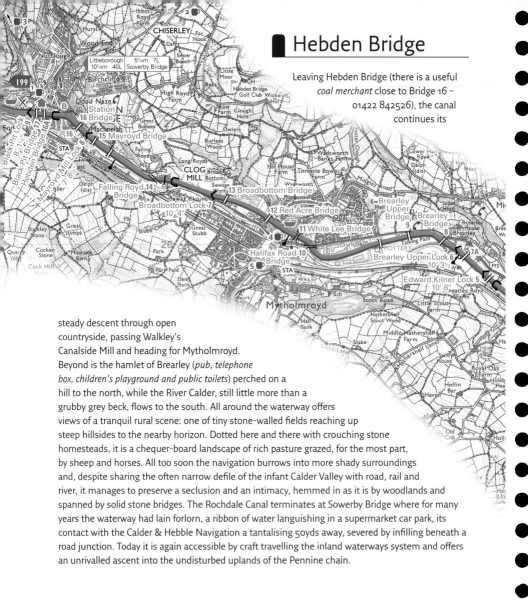

Leaving Hebden Bridge (there is a useful *coal merchant* close to Bridge 16 – 01422 842526), the canal continues its

steady descent through open countryside, passing Walkley's Canalside Mill and heading for Mytholmroyd. Beyond is the hamlet of Brearley (*pub, telephone box, children's playground and public toilets*) perched on a hill to the north, while the River Calder, still little more than a grubby grey beck, flows to the south. All around the waterway offers views of a tranquil rural scene: one of tiny stone-walled fields reaching up steep hillsides to the nearby horizon. Dotted here and there with crouching stone homesteads, it is a chequer-board landscape of rich pasture grazed, for the most part, by sheep and horses. All too soon the navigation burrows into more shady surroundings and, despite sharing the often narrow defile of the infant Calder Valley with road, rail and river, it manages to preserve a seclusion and an intimacy, hemmed in as it is by woodlands and spanned by solid stone bridges. The Rochdale Canal terminates at Sowerby Bridge where for many years the waterway had lain forlorn, a ribbon of water languishing in a supermarket car park, its contact with the Calder & Hebble Navigation a tantalising 50yds away, severed by infilling beneath a road junction. Today it is again accessible by craft travelling the inland waterways system and offers an unrivalled ascent into the undisturbed uplands of the Pennine chain.

Hebden Bridge

W.Yorks. All services. Developed as a settlement in late medieval times, providing both a meeting point of packhorse routes and a river crossing. However, it was not until the late 19th C, with the advent of steam power, the building of canal and railway, together with the mechanisation and centralisation of the textile industry, that the town attained its present size and layout. Displaying a variety and delicacy of stonework – towers, turrets and pediments at every turn – houses and mills peel off from the market square to straggle haphazardly up steep hillsides. The first bridge to cross the River

Hebden was wooden, dating from 1477 and replaced by the present stone packhorse bridge some 30 years later. This solid structure contrasts with the delicate ironwork of the cast iron Victorian road bridge, sited upstream beside the ornate council offices, which incorporate the original fire station. Double-decker housing and a diversity of religious non-conformism are also characteristic of this strikingly compact mill-town.

Hebden Bridge Alternative Technology Centre

Unit 7, Victoria Works, Victoria Road, Hebden Bridge HX7 8LN (01422 842121; www.alternativetechnology. org.uk). Working from a strong base within the local community, this charitable organisation – in making sustainability sustainable and simply irresistible – aims to provide inspiration, practical innovation, information and advice. By setting a stimulating and exciting example, it seeks to enable people to improve all aspects of their lives and environment. Permoculture garden, plastic pipe recycling, 'renewables' and shop. *Open Mon-Fri 10.00-16.00.*

Hardcastle Crags NT, Hollin Hall Office, Hebden Bridge HX7 7AP (01422 844518; www.nationaltrust.org.uk). Large tract of Trust-managed countryside, 1½ miles north of Hebden Bridge, easily accessible by bus. Rich in natural history and famous as the seat of the hairy wood ant. Regular events and guided walks – telephone for details. *Open all year.* Free.

Visitor and Canal Centre Butlers Wharf, New Road, Hebdon Bridge HX7 8AF (01422 843831; www.hebdenbridge.co.uk/tourist-info). *Open daily 10.00-17.00.*
Metro (0113 245 7676; www.wymetro.com). Contact for all local travel information or a selection of free timetables.

● **Heptonstall**
W. Yorks. PO, tel, stores. An extraordinary 'textile village', little changed over the centuries, set high on hills overlooking Hebden Bridge. Walk up the Buttress (beyond the packhorse bridge) or take a bus and visit this settlement barely touched by time. In one small area there is a ruined 15th-C church, its early Victorian replacement and the Octagonal Chapel, one of the oldest continually used Methodist churches in the world, dating from 1764. Also a 16th-C cloth market hall, school museum, a dungeon and David Hartley's (the infamous coiner) grave. There is also the grave of Sylvia Plath, American poet and wife of Ted Hughes. The village provides one of the most spectacular viewpoints in Calderdale.

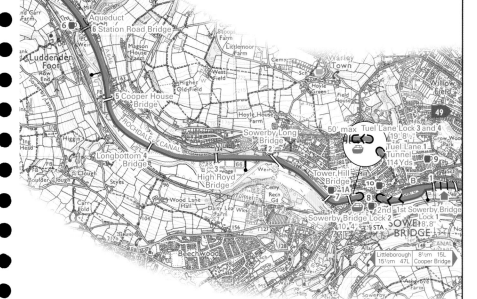

Heptonstall Museum Church Yard Bottom, Heptonstall, Hebden Bridge HX7 7PL (01422 843738; www.museums.calderdale.gov.uk/visit/heptonstall-museum). Depicts an old school classroom together with varying local history displays. *Open Mar-Oct, Sat-Sun & B Hols 11.00-16.00.* Free.

Cloth Hall Heptonstall. Built between 1545 and 1558 as a market for local handloom weavers to sell their cloth to dealers. It is now a *private* house.

Weavers' Square Church Yard Bottom, Heptonstall HX7 7PL. A unique area of stone depicting many types of Yorkshire paving.

● **Mytholmroyd**

W. Yorks. PO, tel, stores, chemist, hardware, takeaways, fish& chips, greengrocer, delicatessen, off-licence, laundrette, garage, station. Since the 11th C the ingredients of a farming and weaving community have existed in the area, confined largely to individual settlements above the marshy valley bottom. The site of the present village was initially a fordable crossing of the River Calder and, with the coming of the canal and the railway, developed as a focus for steam-powered textile production. Initially producers of cotton goods (with the canal as both supplier of raw materials and shipper of finished goods) the mills went on to manufacture worsted in the late 19th C, which in turn stimulated the growth of local dyeworks. Infamous as the base for the activities of David Hartley and the 'Coiners', Mytholmroyd was also the birthplace of Ted Hughes, the late Poet Laureate, and home to the annual Dock Pudding championships – *held in May.*

The Coiners of Cragg Vale Coining was the illicit manufacture of coins, often using metal filed or clipped away from the perimeter of genuine coins. This was melted down and cast into new coins with an appropriate design hammered onto the face and reverse sides. A new rim was then hammered onto the adulterated coin. On 10 November 1769 an excise man, William Dighton, who had been sent to curtail the activities of the Cragg Vale coiners, was murdered in Halifax by members of the gang. Loyalty was not a notable feature within coiner circles and the miscreants were quickly betrayed to the authorities in return for an enticing reward.

Dock Pudding Championships Dock Pudding is made from the weed *Polygonum bistorta* (sweet dock) and is not to be confused with the large coarse cow docks. Mixed with other ingredients and cooked to a variety of secret recipes, the finished product, looking not unlike a slimy, spinach concoction, is entered into a competition and judged on its culinary merits. Believed by many locals to be an essential spring medicine, efficacious in the cure of acne and as a cleanser of the blood.

● **Luddenden Foot**

W. Yorks. PO box, tel, stores, off-licence, takeaway, fish & chips, hardware, library. Centred around more recent lines of communication in the valley bottom, the village once featured the railway station where Branwell Brontë was booking clerk. Passengers arriving on one of the earliest passenger lines to be opened in Britain, were greeted with the cry of 'Foo-it! Foo-it!' as porters sought to differentiate this upstart settlement from the ancient, textile-producing village, perched on the hillside ½ mile above. Stores *open daily 07.00-23.00.*

● **Sowerby Bridge**

W. Yorks. All services. See page 54.

Boatyards

See Calder & Hebble Navigation page 54.

Brontë Boat Hire The Marina, Hebden Bridge HX7 8AD (01706 815103; www.bronteboathire.co.uk).

🚽🚿🔧D E Pump out, gas, engine repairs, coal, dry dock, slipway, maintenance, boat fitters, insurance repairs, mobile boat repairs, day hire boats.

Reflections in the Rochdale Canal as it passes through Hebden Bridge

Pubs and Restaurants (pages 202-203)

See also Calder & Hebble Navigation, page 55.

🍺There is a wide selection of pubs to choose from in Hebden Bridge and its environs, together with an even wider selection of real ales. ✕ The variety and diversity of tearooms, bistros, pizzerias, cafés and restaurants is equally copious!

🍺✕ 1 **The White Lion** Bridge Gate, Hebden Bridge HX7 8EX (01422 842197; www.whitelionhotel.net). A friendly and relaxed family pub with many interesting features set in a 17th-C listed building. An excellent selection of real ales and good food, made using fresh local ingredients, served *daily 12.00-21.00 (Sun 20.00)*. Children's room and riverside garden. Open fires *in winter*. B&B. *Open 11.00-23.00 (Sun 22.30)*.

These two pubs represents worthwhile walks or bus rides.

🍺 2 **The Hare & Hounds** Lane Ends, Wadsworth, Hebden Bridge HX7 8TN (01422 842671; www. hareandhounds.me.uk). Cosy pub serving real ale and tasty bar meals *Mon-Fri E; Sat-Sun all day*. Children and dogs welcome. Real fires and Wi-Fi. Beer garden with stunning views over the Calder Valley – close to the Pennine Way. Wi-Fi. B&B. *Hourly Halifax service bus no 593 during day or minibus H3 and H7 evenings and weekends*. Open Mon-Thu 18.00-22.00; Fri 17.00-23.00 & Sat-Sun 12.00-22.00.

🍺 3 **The White Lion** 58 Towngate, Heptonstall, Hebden Bridge HX7 7NB (01422 842027; www. whitelionheptonstall.co.uk). The perfect way to round off a visit to this historic, unspoilt village and its museum. Real ale and real cider are both dispensed in this old stone-built pub in the heart of the community. 170 gins and food available *Mon 12.00-15.00 & Tue-Sun 12.00-20.30 (Sun 18.30)*. Dog-friendly, beer garden. *Occasional* live music. Traditional pub games, newspapers and real fires. *Open 12.00-00.00*.

🍺✕ 4 **The Dusty Miller** Burnely Road, Mytholmroyd HX7 5LH (01422 885959/07840 939736; www. dustymillerinn.co.uk). Once the regular haunt of the Crag Vale Coiners. It is now a restaurant with rooms, serving real ale. Dog- and child-friendly, outside seating. Sports TV and Wi-fi. B&B. *Open 12.00-23.00*.

🍺 5 **The Shoulder of Mutton** 38 New Road, Mytholmroyd HX7 5DZ (01422 883165; www. shoulderofmuttonmytholmroyd.co.uk). Award-

winning hostelry that takes its beer and food seriously. An excellent selection of both regular and guest real ales are served; there are three cosy eating areas, portions are generous and the prices low. Tasty, home-cooked food available *Mon-Fri L and E & Sat-Sun 12.00-20.00 (Sun 19.00)*. Also real cider. Dog-friendly, outside seating and real fires. *Open 12.00-23.00*.

🍺 6 **The Old Brandy Wine** Station Road, Luddenden Foot HX2 6AD (01422 886173). Real ales are served in this ex-factory and working-man's club. Child- and dog-friendly, sports TV and traditional pub games. *Open Mon-Fri 16.00-00.00 (Fri 02.00) & Sat-Sun 12.00-02.00 (Sun 00.00)*.

🍺 7 **Hollins Mill** 12 Hollins Mill Lane, Sowerby Bridge HX6 2QG (01422 647410; www.facebook. com/Hollinsmillhub). Converted from an old joinery workshop, this pub eschews TV and loud music in favour of conversation, real ale and real cider. Outside seating, real fires and Wi-Fi. *Open Mon-Thu 16.00-23.00 & Fri-Sun 12.00-23.00 (Sun 22.30)*.

🍺 8 **Jubilee Refreshment Rooms** Station Road, Sowerby Bridge HX6 3AB (01422 648285; www. jubileerefreshmentrooms.co.uk). Created by two railway enthusiast, to represent a refreshment room from the golden days of rail travel, this bright, airy establishment serves real ale and hot and cold snacks *Mon-Sat 09.30-21.30 (Sat 21.00) & Sun 12.00-21.30*. Hot meals available *Mon-Sat 12.00-14.00*. The Whistlestop Window opens *Mon-Fri 06.45-09.30*. Outside seating, real fires and Wi-Fi. Dog-friendly.

🍺 9 **The Shepherd's Rest** 125 Bolton Brow, Sowerby Bridge HX6 2BD (01422 831937; www. ossett-brewery.co.uk/pubs/shepherds-rest-sowerby-bridge). Cosy pub with a flagged floor – dating from 1877 – with a large brick-arched fireplace, serving real ales. Quiz *Tue*. Traditional pub games, real fires, sports TV and Wi-Fi. *Open Mon-Thu 15.00-23.00 & Fri-Sun 12.00-23.30 (Sun 23.00)*.

🍺 10 **The Hogs Head Brew House & Bar** 1 Stanley Street, Sowerby Bridge HX6 2AH (01422 836585; www.hogsheadbrewhouse.co.uk). A comfortable brew pub (the brewery can be seen through a window in the bar area) serving eight real ales including five of their own. Dog-friendly and Wi-Fi. *Open Mon-Fri 15.00-23.00 (Fri 00.00) & Sat-Sun 12.00-00.00 (Sun 23.00)*.

NAVIGATIONAL NOTES

1 Tuel Lane Lock is only operated by Canal & River Trust staff. *From mid Mar-mid Nov a lock keeper is on site Fri-Mon from 8.30am, with the last passage late afternoon*. Outside these times, contact 0303 040 4040; www.canalrivertrust.org.uk/contact-us/ways-to-contact-us and give *24 hours* notice to make a booking.
2 Do not enter Tuel Lane Tunnel whilst boats are in the lock, or when the lock is emptying, as turbulence can cause a serious accident.

SANKEY CANAL

MAXIMUM DIMENSIONS

Length: 72' 0"
Beam: 16' 6½"
Draught: 6' 3" (as built)
Headroom: 21' 6" (as built)

MANAGER:

The three Local Authorities own the sections of canal
that pass through their boroughs.
Halton BC (0303 3334300)
Warrington BC (www.warrington.gov.uk)
St.Helens MBC (01744 676 789)
Canal & River Trust (0303 040 4040; enquiries.
northwest@canalrivertrust.org.uk) own a short
section at Blackbrook.

Sankey Canal Restoration Society
www.scars.org.uk

MILEAGE

WIDNES LOCK junction with the River Mersey to:
Fiddler's Ferry Lock: 3½ miles
Bewsey Lock: 6½ miles
Winwick Lock: 8 miles

Sankey Viaduct (Earlestown): 10½ miles
Old Double Locks (junction with Blackbrook Branch):
13 miles

ST HELENS: 15¼ miles

Although this is a long abandoned and, therefore,
un-navigable canal, it has a good towpath
throughout with the minimum of diversions.
However, the two lengths adjacent to the River
Mersey locks at Widnes and Fiddlers Ferry, are
dredged and act as moorings.

The Sankey Canal Restoration Society has produced
a useful towpath guide, containing additional
historical insight into the waterway, available from
colin.greenall@btinternet.com. This forms an
excellent companion to this guide.

Most bridges (and all the locks) shown on the
mapping date from the time before the canal was
abandoned. Many have since vanished or, in the
case of swing bridges, will have been converted to a
fixed structure.

To follow the Sankey Canal is to walk through history and the early annals of the Industrial Revolution,
its echoes reverberating off the distant Pennine foothills to this very day. This is a navigation conceived,
and for the most part constructed, before the completion Francis Egerton's Bridgewater Canal into the
Castlefields district of Manchester in 1765.

On 20th March 1755 an Act was passed authorising 'the making navigable of the Sankey Brook' together
with 'three several Branches thereof ...' although, in the face of anticipated landowner opposition, it
leaned heavily on a clause shared with the earlier Mersey & Irwell Act, 'to make such new Cuts, Canals,
Trenches or Passages for water, in, upon or through the lands or grounds adjoining or near onto the same
River or Three Several Branches aforesaid ... as they shall think proper and requisite.'

It was surveyed by Henry Berry (then the Liverpool Dock engineer) at the behest of the Common Council
of Liverpool, who recognised the escalating need for coal used in salt refining, sugar boiling, pottery
and glass manufacture, brewing and for domestic use. He was assisted by William Taylor, who had
recently surveyed the route for the still-born Salford to Worsley and Wigan canal, rejected by Parliament
due to pressure applied by affected landowners. Both men would have been perfectly aware that the
Sankey Brook was too small for practical navigation and, in the event, only a small portion of its bed was
ultimately used.

Work commenced on 5th September 1755, supervised by Berry (who was given two days a week leave by
his Liverpool employers) on a line connecting the Mersey at the Sankey Brook outlet, with collieries in the
Gerard's Bridge district of St Helens, and the first section opening two years later. By 1762 the line was
completed to Blackbrook (including construction of Old Double Locks – the first of their kind in Britain)
and by 1772 it had climbed the New Double Locks into the town of St Helens itself.

The Sankey Canal developed in tandem with the River Weaver Navigation, supplying coal for salt
production. In symbiotic exchange, salt returned to fuel the burgeoning chemical industry and its alkali-
dependant processes. Mixed with silica it also provided the basis for glass manufacture.

Access from the tidal Mersey was greatly helped by the westerly extension to the new Fiddler's Ferry Lock
in 1762 and further improved with the opening of a second extension into Widnes Dock in 1833.

Traffic was carried by the, then, ubiquitous Mersey Flat, which could be either bow- or horse-hauled, although the open nature of the terrain (and the reliance on swing bridges at crossing points) meant that sailing was perfectly feasible. Craft were generally in the order of 65' x 16' 6" although by the end of the 19th C, when cargoes included alkali, soap, silicate, river and silver sand, acid, tallow, manure, copper ore, salt and copper itself (but no longer coal) some vessels were as large as 68' x 16' 9" and carried up to 75 tons.

The navigation always enjoyed harmonious relationships with its railway partners and it was the complete absence of traffic that led to closure of the five-mile section above Newton Common Lock in 1931. Raw sugar continued to be carried to the Sankey Sugar Works in Earlestown until 1959 and, with its cessation, the waterway was finally abandoned in 1963.

▌Fiddler's Ferry

The Sankey Canal joins a large body of tidal water at both Fiddler's Ferry and Widnes and, whilst provide a safe mooring for blue-water boats, the navigation is somewhat divorced from the remainder of the inland canal system. However the Mersey, in its close proximity to the canal, is not without its own form of haunting beauty and, as one heads towards Sankey Bridges, the tandem waterways offer a joint haven to the teeming wildlife, under the sombre gaze of the dominant cooling towers. The boat club, pub and boatyards at Fiddler's Ferry Lock add interest, as did the occasional coal trains that once fed the hungry maws of the power station. Sankey Bridges marks the parting from the Trans Pennine Trail, with its increased towpath activity, as the canal now swings northwards past what was once an area of busy wharfs. This is also the point where the navigation originally entered the Mersey, before the two extensions westwards were constructed to prevent loaded boats from becoming stranded on a neap tide.

● **Widnes**
Cheshire. All services. The Industrial Revolution was a late arrival in the town (indeed it effectively spawned the town), coming with the opening of John Hutchinson's alkali factory in 1847, which produced soap, borax, soda ash and bleach and was ultimately to become a part of the giant ICI. Iron and copper were also smelted in the town earning it the description, in 1888, as 'the dirtiest, ugliest and most depressing town in England' in which 'the spring never comes hither ... there being no place in which it can manifest itself. The foul gases which, belched forth night and day from the many factories, rot the clothes, the teeth, and, in the end, the bodies of the workers, having killed every tree and every blade of grass for miles around.' Things improved after WWI and again following WWII, although there were still 45 major chemical factories recorded in the town in the late 1950's. Today it is a major multi-modal distribution centre and the chemical industry benefits from streamlined, modern production processes. Salmon are once again to be found in the Mersey.
Catalyst Science Discover Centre Gossage Building, Mersey Road, Widnes WA8 0DF (0151 420 1121; www.catalyst.org.uk). Unique, award-winning museum representing the area's chemical industry. Interactive exhibits and hands-on displays. 'Industry in view' is a computer and video based exhibition 100ft above the Mersey, embracing spectacular river views. Reconstructions and original film footage trace the development of the chemical industry from ancient times to the present day. Café with riverside views. Shop selling educational toys etc and activity guides for home-based experiments. *Open Tue-Sun (& Mon B Hol; daily during school holidays) 10.00-16.00.* Charge.
Mersey Gateway Visitor Centre Details as per Catalyst Science Discovery Centre. Set up to tell the story of Halton's iconic new bridge. Volunteers are on hand to answer questions on everything from local history and heritage, environment and ecology, to details of the bridge construction. Free.
Moore Nature Reserve Lapwing Lane, Moore WA4 6XE (01925 444689; www.facebook.com/moorenr). Occupying the land bounded by the Manchester Ship Canal and the River Mersey, the reserve is bisected by the route of the long-abandoned Latchford Canal. Taken in conjunction with Wigg Island (see below) to the east, it is possible to make up an excellent circular walk, travelling out (or vice versa) along the Sankey Canal from Widnes to Sankey Bridges, returning on the river's south bank through these interconnecting reserves, using Forrest Way Bridge and Silver Jubilee Bridge at either end to cross the Mersey.
Reel Cinema Venture Fields Leisure Park, Earle Road, Widnes WA8 0GY (0151 423 0424; www.reelcinemas.co.uk/widnes/out-now).
Spike Island. Now open parkland, ringed by the canal, with several items of industrial archaeological interest. Acknowledged as the

Spike Island, Widnes

birthplace of the British chemical industry, this long-abandoned wilderness was reclaimed as woodland, wetlands and green space between 1975 and 1982.
Wigg Island Off Astmoor Road, Runcorn WA7 1RR (01928 563803; www.woodlandtrust.org.uk/visiting-woods/wood/?woodId=33188&woodName=wigg-island-nature-reserve). The Reserve can be accessed *anytime* while the Visitor Centre itself is *open on selected days throughout the year*. Telephone for details. See also walk suggested under Moore Nature Reserve above.
Tourist Information Centre Details as per Catalyst Science Discovery Centre – *see page 207*.

● **Penketh**
Cheshire. PO, tel, stores, chemist, bank, takeaway, baker, off-licence, garage. Originally a small, rural community, Penketh developed on the back of the Mersey ferry crossing and the coming of the Sankey Canal. Industry was limited to boat building and a tannery. Today the town is dominated by the

massive coal-fired, Fiddler's Ferry power station, which is fed by the railway running parallel to the navigation.

● **Great Sankey**
Cheshire. PO box, tel, stores, chemist, off-licence, fish & chips, station. A predominantly rural community, touched by industrial development along the Sankey Canal to the south and, later, by the construction of RAF Burtonwood to the north. Today it is a residential suburb of Warrington.

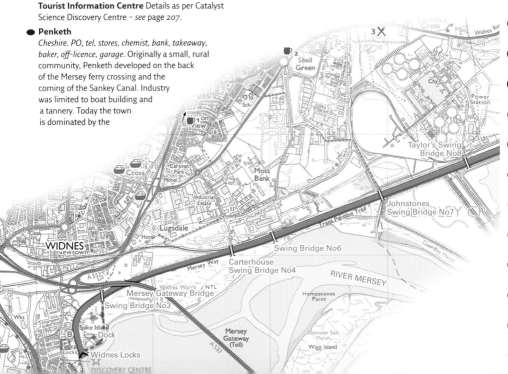

Pubs and Restaurants

🍺✕ 1 **The Eight Towers** Weates Close, Widnes WA8 3RH (0151 424 8063; www.eighttowerspub.co.uk). Friendly, family pub dispensing real ale and food *daily 12.00-21.00 (Sun 20.00).* Sports TV and beer garden. *Open 11.00-23.00 (Fri-Sat 00.00).*

🍺✕ 2 **The Ring O'Bells** Pit Lane, Widnes WA8 9LW (0151 424 6330; www.ringobellswidnes.co.uk). Popular town pub serving real ale and food *daily 12.00-20.30 (Fri-Sat 21.30).* Family-friendly, outside seating. Live music *Fri and Sat.* Sports TV and Wi-Fi. *Open 11.30-23.00 (Fri-Sat 00.00).*

✕🍷 3 **The Spice of India** Cuerdley Cross Inn, Cuerdley, Widnes Road, Widnes WA5 2XD (0151 424 9942; www. spiceofindiacuerdley.co.uk). Popular restaurant serving contemporary Indian food with a garden, children's play area and indoor children's fun house. Quiz *Sun.* Takeaway service. *Open daily 17.00-23.00 (Sun 15.00).*

🍺 4 **The Ferry Tavern** Station Road, Penketh WA5 2UJ (01925 791117; www.theferrytavern.com). First licensed in 1762 to provide sustenance for travellers using the nearby Mersey ferry, this hostelry still serves real ales and food *Fri E* (bookings only) *& Sat-Sun L and E.* Dogs, cyclists, walkers and families welcome. *Regular* live music and quiz *Sun. Open Mon E; Tue-Sat 12.00-23.00 (Fri-Sat 00.00) & Sun 12.00-22.30.*

🍺 5 **The Crown & Cushion** 1 Farnworth Rd, Warrington WA5 2RZ (01925 723184; www.facebook. com/Crownandcushionpenketh). Large modern pub serving real ale and food *daily 12.00-20.00.* Dog- and child-friendly, outside seating. Quiz *Mon.* Sports TV and Wi-Fi. *Open 12.00-01.00.*

🍺✕ 6 **The Red Lion** 164 Warrington Road, Warrington (01925 722185; www.facebook.com/ TheRedLionPenkethWarrington). Family pub, complete with indoor children's funhouse, serving real ale and food *Mon-Sat 09.00-22.00* (breakfast *from 09.00*). Beer garden, sports TV and Wi-Fi. *Open 12.00-23.00.*

🍺 7 **The Sloop** Liverpool Old Road, Sankey Bridges WA5 1DP (01925 634853). Just to east of the canal in Sankey Bridges, serving real ale. Dog-friendly, beer garden. Live music *Sat.* Real fires and Wi-Fi. *Open 12.00-00.00 (Fri 01.00).*

🍺 8 **The Black Horse** 272 Liverpool Old Road, Sankey Bridges WA5 1DZ (01925 635301). Reputed to be the town's oldest pub, and still dispensing real ale, this pub provides traditional pub games, newspapers, sports TV and Wi-Fi. Quiz *Tue. Open 11.30-23.00 (Sun 11.00).*

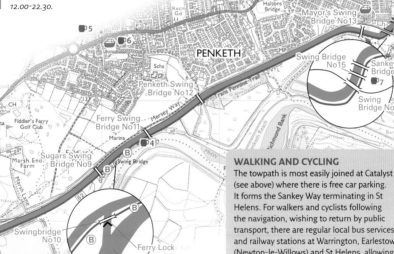

Boatyards

Ⓑ**West Bank Boat Club** Spike Island, Upper Mersey Road, Widnes WA8 0DE (www.sail-clubs.com/ en/i/1066/United-Kingdom/Cheshire/Widnes-/ Sailing-/-Yacht-Club/West-Bank-Boat-Club). Moorings.

Ⓑ**Fiddlers Ferry Boat Yard** Harbour Master, Penketh, Warrington WA5 2UJ (01925 727519/07876 767484; www.ferryboatyard.com). ⚓ Short- and long-term mooring, winter storage, boat sales and repairs, engine sales and repairs, cranage, slipway, chandlery, marine engineering. *Emergency call out (40 mile radius).*

WALKING AND CYCLING

The towpath is most easily joined at Catalyst (see above) where there is free car parking. It forms the Sankey Way terminating in St Helens. For walkers and cyclists following the navigation, wishing to return by public transport, there are regular local bus services and railway stations at Warrington, Earlestown (Newton-le-Willows) and St Helens, allowing a straightforward return journey to Widnes. The Mersey Way runs from the Liverpool suburb of Garston to Rixton, east of Warrington, closely following the estuary and the north bank of the Mersey, paralleling two artificial cuts from the long-forgotten Mersey & Irwell Navigation. Trans Pennine Trail Trans Pennine Trail Office, c/o Barnsley Council, PO Box 597, Barnsley S70 9EW (01226 772574; www.transpenninetrail. org.uk). This coast to coast route makes use of the towpath from Widnes to Sankey Bridges – for further details visit the website. The whole length of the Sankey Canal is now designated The Sankey Valley Trail.

Bewsey

Beyond Sankey Bridges the towpath crosses
both the navigation and then the busy A57 by
footbridges, before re-joining the waterway on its
west bank. It is a pleasant walk north through this part
of the Sankey Valley Park to the site of the first 'inland'
lock at Bewsey, where the path briefly makes use of the
east bank of the navigation. This is the point where the canal
utilised the Sankey Brook, as witnessed by the arrangement
of flood control sluices still visible beside the lock. A pleasant,
wooded section leads through *picnic* and play *areas* to the point
where the Brook is crossed by a footbridge, to the north of which
is the clear outline of Hulme Lock. A few hundred yards above the
lock is the old Winwick canal maintenance yard and dry dock, while
beyond the motorway (having skirted the scrapyard by following the
marked path), Winwick Lock is still very much in evidence.

● Warrington

Cheshire. All services. Founded by the Romans as an important Mersey
crossing point, the market town's subsequent prosperity, in the
Middle Ages, was established on textile and tool production.
As the river was made navigable with the coming of the
Industrial Revolution, so the town flourished with the
development of its brewing, tanning, textile and
steel wire industries. In the 1960's, the decline
of heavy industry coincided with growth
in technology, distribution and service
industries and, in 1968, Warrington was
designated a New Town. There is a useful
cycle shop 200yds north of Sankey Bridge
No 16 – D & M Cycles 2-4 Hood Lane,
Sankey Bridges WA5 1EJ (01925 653606;
www.dandmcycles.com).
Gullivers World Old Hall, Shackleton
Close, Warrington WA5 9YZ (01925
444888; www.gulliversfun.co.uk/
warrington). Over 90 rides, shows and
attractions for children aged 2-13, ranging
from playing around in the clown school
to log flumes and tree top swings. 50%
of attractions are under cover. Stage
and theatre shows. Picnic area. Five
restaurants and a gift shop. B&B. *Open
10.30 most days Apr-Aug; limited opening
Sep-Dec. Closing times vary.* Check website
for details. Charge.
Tenpin 10-15 Chetham Court, Winwick
Quay, Warrington WA2 8RF (0871 222
36 75; www.tenpin.co.uk/warrington).
Apart from the obvious bowling experience
there are also dodgems, lasers and karaoke.
Café. Open daily 10.00-23.00 (Fri-Sat 00.00).
Charge.
Museum and Art Gallery Museum Street,
Warrington WA1 1JB (01925 442399; www.
warringtonmuseum.co.uk). First opened in 1857,
and reputed to be one of the oldest museums in the
world, today visitors can view local and social history

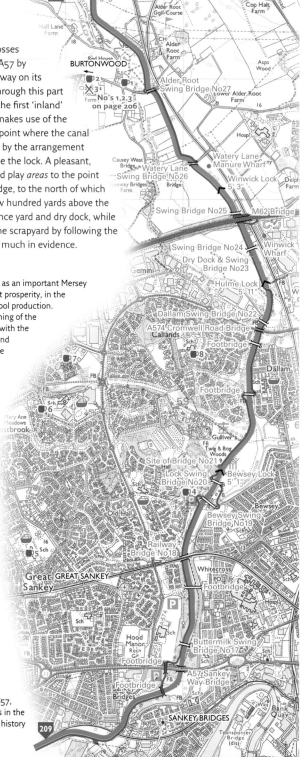

galleries with displays depicting the industries that shaped the town, which lays claim to its very own dinosaur. Also exhibits from contemporary artists and a Time Tunnel for younger visitors. *Open Mon-Sat 10.00-16.30 (Sat 16.00); closed B Hols.* Free.

Odeon Cinema 100 Westbrook Centre, Warrington, Cheshire WA5 8UD (0333 006 7777; www.film. list.co.uk/cinema/43044-odeon-warrington). Six screens. *Open daily 13.30-22.00 (Sat-Sun 10.30).* Charge.

Warrington Market Bank Street, Warrington WA1 2EN (01925 632571; www.warrington.gov. uk/info/200815/warrington_market). Award winning retail market with 200 stalls, home to 130 independent businesses, all located under one roof. *Open Mon-Sat 09.00-17.00.*

Tourist Information Centre Warrington Bus Interchange, Horsemarket Street, Warrington WA1 1TF (01925 428585; www.visitcheshire.com/ explore/warrington-p33851).

● **Bewsey**
Cheshire. PO, tel, stores, off-licence, takeaways, fish & chips. Founded around an estate originally owned by the monks of Titley Abbey, Essex who built a monastic grange known as Beausee – Beautiful Place. In 1264 the Grange came into the ownership of the Boteler family and was subsequently passed on to Robert Dudley, Earl of Leycester, in 1586. Following WWI, Bewsey was chosen for a new housing development and during WWII many Americans were stationed in the area, one family even occupying the Hall itself for a while. It is now flanked by the massive Gemini Retail Park, on its western boundary, home of this country's first IKEA.

Pubs and Restaurants

🍺 1 **The Lower Angel** 27 Buttermarket Street, Warrington Bank Quay, Warrington WA1 2LY (01925 652236). Opened in 1872 (and built next to what was then the Higher Angel), this traditional two-roomed pub is dedicated to the cause of serving an excellent range of real ales. Dogs (but not children) welcome, outside seating. Sports TV and Wi-Fi. *Open Mon-Sat 11.00-23.00 (Sat 00.00). & Sun 12.00-22.00.*

🍺 2 **The Tavern** 25 Church Street, Warrington WA1 2SS (01925 668817). The local 4T's brewery tap, offering an excellent selection of real ales, together with a wide range world bottled beers, malt whiskies, vodkas and brandy. Covered patio area, sports TV, traditional pub games and Wi-Fi. Dog and child-friendly *(until 20.00). Open Mon-Thu 16.00-00.00 (Wed-Thu 15.00) & Fri-Sun 12.00-00.00.*

🍺✕ 3 **The Bull's Head** 33 Church Street, Warrington WA1 2SX (07716 358945; www.facebook.com/The-Bulls-Head-149799616439). A rambling 17th-C pub, converted from a row of cottages, dispensing a rotating selection of real ales. Behind is one of the country's few remaining crown bowling greens. Dog-friendly, outside seating. Folk club *Sun.* Traditional pub games, sports TV and Wi-Fi. *Open 12.00-00.00 (Sun 23.00).*

🍺 4 **The Maltings** Bewsey Farm Close, Old Hall Road, Warrington WA5 9PB (01925 658952; www.facebook. com/maltingswarrington). Once a farmhouse and now enclosed within a new town development, this pub serves real ale and food *daily 12.00-21.00 (Sun 20.00).* Dog- and family-friendly. Garden, open fires and sports TV. *Regular* live music, traditional pub games and Wi-Fi. *Open 11.30-23.00 (Fri-Sat 00.00).*

🍺 5 **Chapelford Farm** Santa Rosa Boulevard, Chapelford WA5 3AG (01925 717732; www. chapelfordfarmpub.co.uk). An integral part of the Chapelford urban village, this family pub serves real ale and food *daily 11.00-21.00 (Fri-Sat 22.00).* A carvery is available *from 12.00.* Indoor children's play area, garden and Wi-Fi. Quiz *Tue. Open Mon-Thu 08.00-21.00 (Wed-Thu 22.00) & Fri-Sun 08.00-23.30 (Sun 23.00).*

🍺 6 **The Seven Woods** Westbrook Crescent, Westbrook WA5 8TE (01925 241036; www. sevenwoodspub.co.uk). Newly-built, food oriented pub, serving real ale with food available *daily 12.00-21.00 (Sun 20.00).* Family-friendly. Quiz *Sun.* Traditional pub games, sports TV and Wi-Fi. *Open Mon-Sat 11.00-23.00 (Fri-Sat 00.00) & Sun 12.00-23.00.*

🍺✕ 7 **Memphis Belle** Gemini Retail Park, Westbrook WA5 8WF (01925 712173; www. millerandcarter.co.uk/restaurants/north-west/ millerandcarterwarrington). Buried within a massive retail park, this modern pub serves food *Mon-Sat 11.00-23.00 & Sun 11.30-22.30.* Outside seating and Wi-Fi. *Open Mon-Sat 11.00-23.00 (Fri-Sat 00.00) & Sun 11.30-23.00.*

🍺 8 **Hoop & Mallet** Callands Road, Callands, Warrington WA5 9RJ (01925 419182; www. hoopandmallet.co.uk). Modern community pub serving real ales. Family-friendly, garden. Poker *Mon* and quiz *Tue.* Traditional pub games, sports TV and Wi-Fi. *Open Sun-Thu 12.00-23.00 (Thu 23.30) & Fri-Sat 12.00-00.00.*

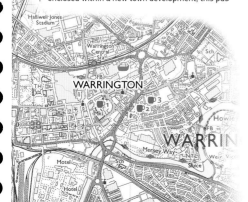

WALKING AND CYCLING
The Warrington Ranger Service (01925 571836) maintains a keen interest in the canal and its passage through Sankey Valley Park with an excellent series of interpretation boards.

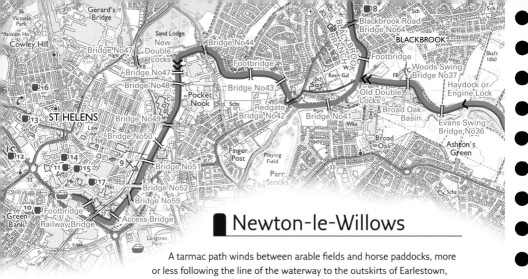

Newton-le-Willows

A tarmac path winds between arable fields and horse paddocks, more
or less following the line of the waterway to the outskirts of Earlestown,
where again the navigation becomes very much in evidence. Sleek Pendolino,
tilting trains, tear along the West Coast Main Railway Line: a reminder of the importance that this
area once played in the building of locomotives and rolling stock. Mucky Mountains, beside Bradley
(or Bradleigh) Stone Swing Bridge, bears witness to the chemical works that were once so prevalent
along the canal, while the site of the Sankey Sugar factory was on the off side, just south of the
Sankey (or Earlestown) Viaduct, beyond which repose the remains of Newton Common Lock. Above
Old Double Locks lies the Blackbrook Branch, which is a 'must' to visit: there is lots to see and the
interpretation is excellent. The final stretch into St Helens is via the New Double Locks, which were
re-gated not so long ago. Beyond, a series of footpaths more or less follow the original line of the
canal, into the centre of St Helens, to the point where the navigation was terminated in 1898.

● Burtonwood

*Cheshire. PO, tel, stores, fish & chips, takeaway,
library.* Brewing, mining and flying vie with one
another as heralds of the village's reputation. The
Burtonwood brewery was established in 1867 and
embarked on a joint venture with Thomas Hardy
in 1998. Today Brakspear ales compose the main
output. The USAF occupied the airfield (the largest
base in Europe) from 1942-1958 and coal mining
once dominated the area.

● Newton-le-Willows

Merseyside. All services. Technically the area
surrounding the canal is Earlestown, with Newton-
le-Willows (once known as Newton in Makerfield
and still an attractive Georgian town) lying a little
way to the east. As growing industrialisation
focused around the canal and the important railway
junction, so amenities and the administrative centre
moved west to their present location, although
the station still bears the correct appellation. Both
Newton-le-Willows and Earlestown stations lie on
the original Liverpool & Manchester Railway line
and the original station buildings are the oldest
examples of railway architecture in the world. The
unfortunate MP for Liverpool - William Huskisson
- was fatally injured at nearby Parkside on the
inaugural run of George Stephenson's Rocket. A
little over 130 years later Parkside Colliery, with an

expected lifespan of around a century, was opened,
only to close in 1992.
The impressive Sankey Viaduct, spanning both
the canal and Sankey Brook, was the world's first
passenger carrying railway viaduct and its eastern
approach arches housed the Viaduct Foundry, later
to become the London & North Western Railway's
principal waggon building works. To the immediate
south of the suburb of Wargrave lay the Vulcan
Foundry, originally opened as Charles Tayleur & Co Ltd
in 1832, building girders and similar ironwork for the
newly opened Liverpool & Manchester Railway.
As the Vulcan Foundry Ltd, the company went on to
build thousands of locomotives before closure in the
hands of English Electric and its successors in 2002.
In the early days Robert Stevenson held a stake in
the company, acknowledging that it was cheaper and
easier to build locomotives for the fledgling railway on
its doorstep, rather than in distant Newcastle on Tyne
- his then, home-base. Over the company's illustrious
170-year history, more than 60% of its locomotive
output was shipped abroad, although its contribution
to the home market was significant, including
construction of the Class 55, Deltic. Some 630 homes
are being built on the site, now totally bulldozed, the
past work force's Vulcan Village the only clue to the
area's faded glory.
The Sankey Sugar Company, situated beside the canal,

WALKING AND CYCLING
Between Double Rail Swing Bridge No 33 and Broad Oak Basin the original towpath can, in places, be confused with other paths that radiate out through this area of rough ground. Ensure that you follow the line of the canal to Broad Oak Basin (now almost lost in the undergrowth) and then bear right, picking up the now clearly defined towpath and dry canal bed, leading to Old Double Locks. At the top of the locks it is well worth bearing right along the Blackbrook Branch to visit the Sankey Valley Visitor Centre.
To follow the navigation through to St Helens, turn left along the edge of the playing fields to join Boardman's Lane and then right to its junction with Park Road, where you should turn left. On crossing the Sankey Brook you will again see the canal and towpath, stretching away at right angles to the road on your right.

was another significant local employer, and it was waterborne supplies of raw materials and fuel oil that kept the southern portion of the navigation open until 1959. Today, little industry remains in the area, although Nicholls Foods – manufacturers of the ubiquitous Vimto – are still in full production in the town, their factory clearly visible from the West Coast Main Line.

St Helens
Merseyside. All services. The growth and prosperity of St Helens came about as a result of coal mining and glassmaking during the 18th - and 19th C, together with a thriving cotton and linen industry, kept busy by sail making until the mid-19th C. The town is home to some 170 listed buildings. Amongst the most impressive are St Mary's Lowe House, the red brick Gamble Institute (where the Central Library is based), the Beechams Clock Tower and The Friends Meeting House. Today glass manufacture still dominates the town.

Cineworld Chalon Way West, St Helens, WA10 1BF (0871 200 2000; www.cineworld.co.uk). Eleven screen cinema in the town centre.

Citadel Arts Centre 39 Waterloo Street, St Helens WA10 1PX (01744 735436; www.citadel.org.uk). A rare survivor of the early British music hall and dating from 1861, the Citadel today plays host to a wide range of community and arts events. See the website for programme details. *Open Mon-Fri 12.00-16.00.*

North West Museum of Road Transport The Old Bus Depot, 51 Hall Street, St Helens WA10 1DU (01744 451681; www.nwmort.co.uk). A unique and extensive collection of vintage buses forms the centrepiece of this recently refurbished museum. Shop. *Open Feb-Dec, Sat-Sun & B Hols 11.00-16.00. Charge.* Free vintage bus rides *at events and first weekend of the month.*

Queens Park Health and Fitness Centre Boundary Road, St Helens WA10 2LT (01744 671717; www.goactive.sthelens.gov.uk/facilities/queens-park-health-fitness.aspx). *Open Mon-Fri 07.30-21.30 & Sat-Sun 09.00-16.30. Charge.*

Sankey Valley Heritage Visitor Centre Blackbrook Road, St Helens WA11 0AB (01744 677772; www.visitliverpool.com/things-to-do/sankey-valley-country-park-and-trail-p8977). Arguably the industrial heart of the Sankey Canal and its original terminus. Today a team of knowledgeable, helpful and friendly rangers oversee the country park, a series of trails benefiting from excellent interpretation, and a centre packed with useful information. Much work has been carried out in conjunction with the Sankey Canal Restoration Society to uncover the area's rich industrial past, which has exposed, amongst other industries, evidence of the Stanley Iron Slitting Mill. The centre carries an excellent range of publications on the area, most of them free, including information on a variety of fascinating trails and walks.

Smithy Heritage Centre Kiln Lane, St Helens WA10 4RA (01744 730744; www.smithyheritagecentre.org.uk). The Centre hosts temporary exhibitions on a wide range of topics, while the permanent displays are dedicated to the heritage of the building and its place at the heart of the history of Eccleston. The skills of the blacksmith, wheelwright, farrier and farmer are celebrated with original artefacts and images. *Open Easter-Sep, Sat-Sun 13.00-16.00. Free.*

Theatre Royal Corporation Street, St Helens WA10 1LQ (01744 756000; www.

sthelenstheatreroyal.com). Vibrant regional theatre with a varied programme. Bar. Booking office *open Mon-Sat 10.00-17.00 and an hour* before performances.

The World of Glass Chalon Way East, St Helens WA10 1BX (01744 22766; www.worldofglass.com). Watch glass making; join a glass blowing course or step into St Helens' Victorian past. Also a variety of changing exhibitions. Shop and canalside café. *Open Mon-Sat, Mar-Oct 10.00-17.00 & Nov-Feb 10.00-16.00. Closed B Hols.* Charge.

Tourist Information Centre The World of Glass, Chalon Way East, St Helens WA10 1BX (01744 755150; www.visit-sthelens.com).

Pubs and Restaurants (pages 204-205)

▣✕ 1 **Fiddle i' th Bag Inn** Alder Lane, Burtonwood WA5 4BJ (01925 225442). Close to the line of the old towpath, this pub-cum-museum is packed with curiosities, oddities and WWII memorabilia. It also serves real ale and food *Mon-Fri L and E & Sat-Sun 12.00-20.30 (Sun 18.30).* Garden and newspapers. *Open Mon-Fri L and E & Sat-Sun 12.00-23.00.*

▣ 2 **The Chapel House** Chapel Lane, Burtonwood WA5 4PT (01925 225607). Serving a selection of real ales, this village local also hosts *Sat* live music. Dog- and child-friendly, garden. Traditional pub games and Wi-Fi. *Open 12.00-00.00 (Fri-Sat 01.00).*

✕ 3 **Woody Delicious Sandwich Bar** 5a Clay Lane, Burtonwood WA5 4HH (01925 228998; www.facebook. com/pages/Woody-Delicious-160977950594761). Serving a tasty selection of takeaway food *Mon-Fri 06.30-14.30; Sat 07.00-14.00 & Sun 08.00-13.00.*

▣ 4 **The Wargrave Inn** 448 Wargrave Road, Earlestown, Newton-le-Willows WA12 8RT (01925 221922). Welcoming local, dog- and child-friendly, serving real ale and *open Mon-Fri 13.00-00.00 & Sat-Sun 12.00-00.00 (Sun 23.00).* Traditional pub games, newspapers, sports TV and Wi-Fi. Covered children's play area.

▣ 5 **The Victoria Inn** Wargrave Road, Earlestown, Newton-le-Willows WA12 8EP (01925 224493). Homely pub, benefiting from a recent makeover, serving real ale and freshly cooked, homemade food *daily Mon-Sat L and E & Sun 12.00-20.00.* Family-friendly, garden, sports TV and Wi-Fi. *Open 12.00-00.00.*

▣✕ 6 **The Pied Bull Hotel** 54 High Street, Newton-le-Willows WA12 9SH (01925 224549; www.piedbull.com). Family-orientated pub offering real ale and food *Mon-Fri L and E & Sat-Sun 12.00-19.00.* Family-friendly, garden. Wi-Fi. B&B. *Open 12.00-00.00 (Sun 23.00).*

▣ 7 **The Nine Arches** 3 Legh Street, Earlestown WA12 9NE (01925 224409; www.jdwetherspoon.com/pubs/all-pubs/england/merseyside/the-nine-arches-newton-le-willows). Originally a chapel and named after the nearby Sankey Viaduct, this pub serves real ales and food *daily 08.00-22.00.* Family-friendly, outside seating. Wi-Fi. *Open 08.00-00.00 (Fri-Sat 01.00).*

▣ 8 **The Ship Inn** 275 Blackbrook Road, Blackbrook, St Helens WA11 0AB (01744 28909). Handy for the Visitor Centre, this pub serves real ale and food *daily 12.00-20.00.* Children welcome, outside seating and large-screen TV. Quiz *Thu* and live entertainment *at the weekend. Open 11.00-23.00.*

✕⛾ 9 **La Casa Vieja** 6-12 Bickerstaffe Street, St Helens WA10 1DH (01744 454613; www.lacasavieja.co.uk). Sophisticated, yet relaxed, tapas restaurant and bar serving authentic, affordable Spanish food *Mon-Sat L and E.* Children welcome.

▣ 10 **The Phoenix Inn** 34 Canal Street, St Helens WA10 3LL (01744 751890). Built in 1903, this welcoming hostelry has its name picked out in glass mosaic sourced from the nearby Pilkington factory, and serves well-kept, competitively priced real ales and real cider. Outdoor drinking area and traditional pub games. Sports TV and Wi-Fi. *Open Mon-Thu 14.00-23.00 & Fri-Sun 12.00-01.00 (Sun 23.00).*

▣✕ 11 **The Nelson** Bridge Street, St Helens WA10 1NU (07746 940798; www.facebook.com/The-Nelson-Chippery-StHelens-390248194512335). Busy, town-centre pub, with its own in-house fish and chip shop, serving real ales. *Open daily 11.00-23.00* – fish & chips *Mon-Sat 11.00-17.00 (Fri-Sat 19.00).*

▣ 12 **The Cricketers Arms** 64 Peter Street, St Helens WA10 2EB (01744 361846). Friendly local hostelry, supporting local microbreweries, with at least seven handpumps. Also real cider and over 100 gins. Dog- and Family-friendly, beer gardens. Traditional pub games, real fires, sports TV and Wi-Fi. *Open 12.00-23.00 (Fri-Sat 01.00).*

▣✕ 13 **The News Room** 89 Duke Street, St Helens WA10 2JG (01744 322129; www.facebook.com/thenews.room.37). Family-run café bar with a welcoming, friendly atmosphere, serving a range of ales from local micro-breweries, together with many different Belgian and foreign bottled beers. *Open Mon-Thu 17.00-23.00; Fri-Sat 16.00-00.00 (Sat 13.00) & Sun 13.00-23.00.*

▣ 14 **The Sefton Arms** 1-7 Baldwin Street, St Helens WA10 1QA (01744 22065; www.greatukpubs.co.uk/theseftonarms). Playing host to regular bands, this large one-room pub serves real ales and food *daily 10.00-19.00 (Sun 12.00).* Sports TV and outside seating. *Open 11.00-23.00 (Fri-Sat 03.00).*

▣ 15 **The Market Tavern** 26-28 Bridge Street, St Helens WA10 1NW (01744 757313; www.facebook.com/st.helens). Popular town centre pub serving real ale and real cider. Sports TV and outside drinking area. *Open daily 11.00-23.00.*

▣ 16 **The Turks Head** 49 Morley Street, St Helens WA10 2DQ (01744 751289; www.facebook.com/theturksheadsthelens). Brewery Tudor, with etched glass, this hostelry serves a choice of a dozen real ales, real cider and a range of draught and bottled continental beers. Food is available *Thu-Sun;* jazz on *Thu* and a Quiz *Tue.* Open fires, sports TV and traditional pub games. *Open Mon-Fri 14.00-23.00 & Sat-Sun 12.00-00.30.*

▣ 17 **The Glass House** 5 Market Street, St Helens WA10 1NE (01744 762310; www.jdwetherspoon.com/pubs/all-pubs/england/merseyside/the-glass-house-st-helens). Within a stone's throw of the World of Glass Museum, this pub serves real ale, real cider and food *from 08.00.* Children welcome, large screen TV, outside seating area and Wi-Fi. *Open daily 08.00-23.00 (Sun 10.15).*

▌ TRENT & MERSEY CANAL

MAXIMUM DIMENSIONS

Derwent Mouth to Horninglow Basin, Burton upon Trent
Length: 72' 0"
Beam: 14' 0"
Headroom: 7' 0"
Stenson Lock is very tight for 14ft beam craft and Weston Lock is tight for boats of 72ft length.

Burton upon Trent to south end of Harecastle Tunnel
Length: 72' 0"
Beam: 7' 0"
Headroom: 6' 3"

Harecastle Tunnel
Length: 72' 0"
Beam: 7' 0"
Headroom: 5' 9"

North end of Harecastle Tunnel to Croxton Aqueduct
Length: 72' 0"
Beam: 7' 0"
Headroom: 7' 0"

Croxton Aqueduct to Preston Brook Tunnel
Length: 72' 0"
Beam: 8' 2"
Headroom: 6' 3"

MANAGER:

0303 040 4040
www.canalrivertrust.org.uk/contact-us/ways-to-contact-us

MILEAGE

DERWENT MOUTH to:
Swarkestone Lock: 7 miles
Willington: 12¼ miles
Horninglow Wharf: 16½ miles
Barton Turn: 21¼ miles
Fradley, junction with Coventry Canal: 26¼ miles
Great Haywood, junction with Staffordshire & Worcestershire Canal: 39 miles
Stone: 48½ miles
Stoke Top Lock, junction with Caldon Canal: 58 miles
Harding's Wood, junction with Macclesfield Canal: 63¾ miles
King's Lock, Middlewich, junction with Middlewich Branch: 76¼ miles
Anderton Lift, for River Weaver: 86½ miles

PRESTON BROOK north end of tunnel and Bridgewater Canal: 93½ miles

Locks: 76

This early canal was originally conceived partly as a roundabout link between the ports of Liverpool and Hull, while passing through the busy area of the Potteries and mid-Cheshire, and terminating either in the River Weaver or in the Mersey. Its construction was promoted by Josiah Wedgwood (1730–95), the famous potter, aided by his friends Thomas Bentley and Erasmus Darwin. In 1766 the Trent & Mersey Canal Act was passed by Parliament, authorising the building of a navigation from the River Trent at Shardlow to Runcorn Gap, where it would join the proposed extension of the Bridgewater Canal from Manchester.

The ageing James Brindley was appointed engineer for the canal. Construction began at once and in 1777 the Trent & Mersey Canal was opened. In the total 93 miles between Derwent Mouth and Preston Brook, the Trent & Mersey gained connection with no fewer than nine other canals or significant branches.

By the 1820s the slowly-sinking tunnel at Harecastle had become a serious bottle-neck, so Thomas Telford recommended building a second tunnel beside the old one. His recommendation was eventually accepted by the company and the new tunnel was completed in under three years, in 1827. Although the Trent & Mersey was taken over in 1845 by the new North Staffordshire Railway Company, the canal flourished until World War I.

Look out for the handsome cast iron mileposts, which actually measure the mileage from Shardlow, not Derwent Mouth. There are 59 originals, from the Rougeley and Dixon foundry in Stone, and 34 replacements, bearing the mark of the Trent & Mersey Canal Society – T & MCS 1977.

Harding's Wood Junction

At the north end of Harecastle Tunnel (2926yds long) the navigation passes Kidsgrove station and a coal yard; there is also a *shower* in the facilities block beside the north tunnel portal. Beyond is Harding's Wood and the junction with the Macclesfield Canal, which crosses the T & M on Poole Aqueduct. There are *showers, laundry facilities and toilets* at the CRT yard at Red Bull. The canal continues to fall through a heavily locked stretch sometimes called 'heartbreak hill' but known to the old boatmen as the

Pubs and Restaurants

🍺 1 **The Blue Bell** 25 Hardingswood, Kidsgrove ST7 1EG (01782 774052; www.bluebellkidsgrove.co.uk). Canalside, at Hardings Wood Junction. Friendly, quiet, one-bar local, winnner of many CAMRA awards. Real ale, plus a range of specialist bottled beers, including many from Belgium, plus real cider and perry. No juke box, pool table or gaming machines. Note the trapdoor in the lounge ceiling. Well-behaved children welcome *until 21.00.* Dogs welcome. Snacks are available *at weekends. Open Tue–Fri 19.30–23.00; Sat 13.00–16.00, 19.30–23.00; Sun 12.00–22.30 (all day during summer). Closed Mon.*

🍺✕ 2 **The Red Bull Hotel** Congleton Road South, Church Lawton ST7 3AJ (01782 782600; www. robinsonsbrewery.com/redbullchurchlawton) By Lock 43. Popular pub close to Hardings Wood Junction, serving real ale and bar meals, including fish dishes *Mon–Fri L and E & Sat–Sun 12.00–21.00 (Sun 20.00).* Family-friendly, garden. *Occasional* live music. Moorings. *Open daily 12.00–23.00 (Sun 22.30).*

🍺 3 **The Broughton Arms** Mill Mead, Rode Heath ST7 3RU (01270 883203; www.broughtonarmspub. co.uk). Canalside at Rode Heath. Friendly family pub, with comfortable bars and canalside seating. Range of real ale. Food available in bar and dining area *L and E.* Children welcome away from the bar. Wi-Fi. Dog-friendly, waterside garden. *Open daily 12.00–23.00 (Fri–Sat 00.00).*

🍺 4 **The Royal Oak** 41 Sandbach Road, Rode Heath ST7 3RW (01270 875670). Spacious, roadside pub, close to the navigation serving a selection of real ales and food *L and E.* Dog- and child-friendly, garden. Sports TV and Wi-Fi. *Open daily 11.30–23.00 (Sun 11.00).*

Lock 52, one of the 'Lawton Treble Locks'

'Cheshire Locks'. Two minor aqueducts are encountered, and most of the locks are narrow pairs – the chambers side by side.

● **Kidsgrove**
Staffs. All services. Originally an iron and coal producing town, Kidsgrove was much helped by the completion of the Trent & Mersey Canal. James Brindley is buried here.

● **Rode Heath**
Cheshire. PO, tel, stores, off-licence, takeaway. A useful shopping area right by bridge 140.
Rode Heath Rise ST7 3QD Once the site of a salt works, it has now been landscaped and restored as a wildflower meadow. Telephone (01260 297237/01625 383777) for further information.

NAVIGATIONAL NOTES

HARECASTLE TUNNEL Do not enter in an unpowered craft. With the complete removal of the towpath, headroom is no longer the problem it once was. A one-way system operates, so follow the instructions of the tunnel keepers. *For updated tunnel opening times, telephone 0303 040 4040.*

Boatyards

Ⓑ**David Smithson** Liverpool Road, Kidsgrove ST7 1EA (01782 787887; www.davidsmithson.co.uk/index.html). Near Bridge 132. **D** Gas, solid fuel, caravan fittings which can be used as chandlery. Also bicycles and bicycle spares for sale. Moorings at Kinnersley Wharf.

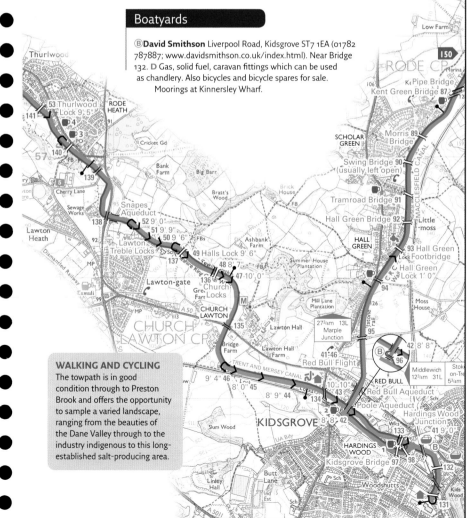

WALKING AND CYCLING
The towpath is in good condition through to Preston Brook and offers the opportunity to sample a varied landscape, ranging from the beauties of the Dane Valley through to the industry indigenous to this long-established salt-producing area.

Wheelock

The canal now descends the Wheelock flight of eight locks, which are the last paired locks one sees when travelling northwards. The countryside continues to be quiet and unspoilt but unspectacular. The pair of locks half-way down the flight is situated in the little settlement of Malkin's Bank, overlooked by terraced houses. The boatman's co-op used to be here, in the small terrace of cottages. The adjoining boatyard now specialises in the restoration of traditional working boats. At the bottom of the flight is the village of Wheelock (*toilets* and *shower*); west of here the navigation curls round the side of a hill before entering the very long-established salt-producing area that is based on Middlewich. The 'wild' brine pumping and rock-salt mining that has gone on hereabouts has resulted in severe local subsidence; the effect on the canal has been to necessitate the constant raising of the banks as lengths of the canal bed sink. This of course means that the affected lengths tend to be much deeper than ordinary canals. Non-swimmers beware of falling overboard. The navigation now begins to lose the rural character it has enjoyed since Kidsgrove. Falling through yet more locks, the canal is joined by a busy main road (useful for *fish & chips*, west of Kings Lock; and *Chinese takeaway*, west of bridge 166) which accompanies it into an increasingly flat and industrialised landscape, past several salt works and into Middlewich, where a branch of the Shropshire Union leads off westwards towards that canal at Barbridge. The first 100yds or so of this branch is the Wardle Canal, claimed to be the shortest canal in the country.

- **Wheelock**
  Cheshire. Tel, stores, off-licence, fish & chips, takeaway. Busy little main road village on the canal.
- **Sandbach**
  Cheshire. PO, tel, stores, garage, chemist, takeaways, bank, fish & chips, station (distant). 1¹/₂ miles north of Wheelock. An old market town that has maintained its charm despite the steady growth of its salt and chemical industries. After walking from the canal you can refresh yourself with a pint of real ale from any of the seven pubs visible from the seat in the market place. From the canal, the railway station is best accessed from Elton Moss Bridge 160.
  Ancient Crosses In the cobbled market place on a massive base stand two superb Saxon crosses, believed to commemorate the conversion of the

area to Christianity in the 7th C. They suffered severely in the 17th C when the Puritans broke them up and scattered the fragments for miles. After years of searching for the parts, George Ormerod succeeded in re-erecting the crosses in 1816, with new stone replacing the missing fragments.
St Mary's Church High Street, Sandbach CW11 1AN. A large, 16th-C church with a handsome battlemented tower. The most interesting features of the interior are the 17th-C carved roof and the fine chancel screen.
The Old Hall Hotel High Street, Sandbach CW11 1AL. An outstanding example of Elizabethan half-timbered architecture, which was formerly the home of the lord of the manor, but is now used as an hotel.

Boatyards

Ⓑ**Malkins Bank Canal Services** The Boatyard, Betchton Road, Malkins Bank, Sandbach CW11 4XN (01270 764595). ⚓ Long-term mooring, boat building and historic boat restoration, boat repairs, will help with breakdowns where possible.

Ⓑ**The Northwich Boat Company** Kings Lock Boatyard, Booth Lane, Middlewich CW10 0JJ (01270 760160/07970 151996; www.thenorthwichboat.com). D Pump out, gas, boat repairs, boat building and fitting out, new and used boat sales, boatshare sales and management.

Pubs and Restaurants

XΨ **1 Barchetta Restaurant** 464a Crewe Road, Wheelock CW11 3RL (01270 314183; www.barchettarestaurant.co.uk). Established in a canalside mill building, this independent, family-run restaurant uses fresh local ingredients to create authentic Italian and Mediterranean dishes. *Open Mon-Sat 17.00-21.00 & Sun 12.00-20.00.*

2 The Cheshire Cheese 466-468 Crewe Road, Wheelock CW11 3RL (01270 346600; www.cheshirecheesewheelock.co.uk). Heavily-beamed, canalside pub serving real ale and a range of meals and snacks *daily 12.00-20.00.* Family-friendly, garden. Quiz *Sun.* Traditional pub games and real fires. *Open daily 12.00-23.00 (Fri-Sat 00.00).*

XΨ **3 The Shampaan** 504 Crewe Road, Wheelock CW11 3RL (01270 753528/753511; www.shampaan.com). Authentic South Asian cuisine to eat in or takeaway. Children welcome. *Open daily 17.00-23.00.*

4 The Market Tavern 8 The Square, Sandbach CW11 1AT (01270 762099; www.themarkettavern-sandbach.co.uk). Opposite the crosses. Lively, old, traditional town pub, dating from 1680, dispensing a good selection of real ales. Large beer garden. Children welcome. Folk club *Tue* and live bands *Sat. Open L and E Sun-Fri & Sat 11.00-23.00.*

5 The Lower Chequer Inn Crown Bank, Sandbach CW11 1DB (01270 750214). Delightful 16th-C, timber-framed hostelry serving an excellent range of real ale. Food available *Tue-Fri E; Sat L and E & Sun 12.00-18.00.* Dog-friendly, patio. Real fires, sports TV and Wi-Fi. *Open Tue-Fri 17.00-23.00 (Fri 16.00) & Sat-Sun 12.00-23.00 (Sun 20.00).*

X 6 The Old Hall High Street, Sandbach CW11 1AL (01270 758170; www.brunningandprice.co.uk/oldhall). Microbreweries are well represented in this stunning, Grade 1 listed, timber-framed building recently completely restored to a very high standard, displaying it's wood panelling and Tudor fireplace to perfection. Family-friendly and garden – dogs on a leash welcome. Food available *Mon-Fri 10.00-21.30 (Fri 22.00) & Sat-Sun 09.00-22.00 (Sun 21.00).* Real fires. *Open Mon-Fri 10.00-23.00 & Sat-Sun 09.00-23.00 (Sun 21.00).*

7 The Fox Inn London Road, Elworth CW11 3BF (01270 761641; www.thefoxinnsandbach.com/index). Welcoming, multi-roomed, Grade II listed pub serving real ale and food *daily 12.00-20.00 (Sun 18.00).* Family-friendly, garden. Newspapers and sports TV. *Open Mon-Sat 12.00-23.30 (Thu-Sat 00.30) & Sun 12.00-23.00.*

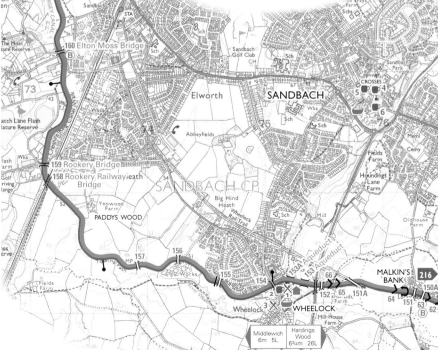

Middlewich

The Trent & Mersey skirts the centre of the town, passing lots of moored narrowboats and through three consecutive narrow locks, arriving at a wide (14ft) lock (which has suffered from subsidence) with a pub beside it. This used to represent the beginning of a wide, almost lock-free navigation right through to Preston Brook, Manchester and Wigan (very convenient for the salt industry when it shipped most of its goods by boat), but Croxton Aqueduct had to be replaced many years ago, and is now a steel structure only 8ft 2in wide. The aqueduct crosses the River Dane, which flows alongside the navigation as both water courses leave industrial Middlewich and move out into fine open country. Initially, this is a stretch of canal as beautiful as any in the country. Often overhung by trees, the navigation winds along the side of a hill as it follows the delightful valley of the River Dane. There are pleasant moorings with *picnic tables and barbecue facilities*, created by the Broken Cross Boating Club in old clay pits, just north of bridge 176, on the off-side. The parkland on the other side of the valley encompasses Bostock Hall, a Georgian house rebuilt in 1775 to a design thought to have been by Samuel Wyatt: it has now been converted into apartments. At Whatcroft Hall (privately owned), the canal circles around to the east, passing under a railway bridge before heading for the industrial outskirts of Northwich and shedding its beauty and solitude once again.

NAVIGATIONAL NOTES

There are several privately owned wide 'lagoons' caused by subsidence along this section of the Trent & Mersey, in some of which repose the hulks of abandoned barges and narrowboats, lately being salvaged. Navigators should be wary of straying off the main line, since the off-side canal bank is often submerged and invisible just below the water level.

Boatyards

Ⓑ**Kings Lock Chandlery** Booth Lane, Middlewich CW10 0JJ (01606 737564; www.kingslock.co.uk). D Gas, overnight mooring, long-term mooring, slipway, engine sales and repairs, boat repairs, Webasto dealer, chandlery (including mail order), books, maps, gifts, solid fuel, Vetus dealer.

Ⓑ**Andersen Boats** Wych House, St Anne's Road, Middlewich CW10 9BQ (01606 833668/07771 693981; www.andersenboats.com). Pump out, gas, narrowboat hire, books and maps. Useful DIY shop nearby.

Pubs and Restaurants

⬤✕ **1 The Kings Lock Inn** 1 Booth Lane, Middlewich CW10 0JJ (01606 836894; www.kingslockinn.com). Traditional, canalside hostelry, that once provided facilities and stabling for boating families. This so-called 'stack pub' – being built on two levels – today sells real ale, real cider and serves food *Mon-Sat 12.00-20.30 (Fri-Sat 21.00) & Sun 12.00-18.00*. Dog- and family-friendly, garden. *Monthly live music, real fires and Wi-Fi. Open Tue-Sun 12.00-23.00.*

⬤✕ **2 The Boars Head** Kinderton Street, Middlewich CW10 0JE (01606 833191; www. theboarsheadhotel.co.uk). Large rambling pub and restaurant offering real ale and food *L and E, daily*. Family-friendly, garden. B&B. *Open daily 12.00-23.00 (Sun 22.30).*

⬤ **3 The Golden Lion** 61 Chester Road, Middlewich CW10 9ET (01606 737163; www. goldenlionmiddlewich.co.uk). *Open all day* – at the top of the town at the junction between Chester Road and Newton Bank. Now a free house, dispensing real ale and traditional pub food *L and E*. Dog- and child-friendly, garden. Real

fires and sports TV. B&B. *Open Mon-Thu 15.00-00.00 & Fri-Sun 12.00-01.00 (Sun 00.00).*

⬤ **4 The Cheshire Cheese** Lewin Street, Middlewich CW10 9AX (01606 832097). Friendly, traditional establishment serving real ale. Dog-friendly, large garden. Sports TV. *Open Mon-Fri 15.00-23.00 (Thu-Fri 01.00) & Sat-Sun 12.00-01.00 (Sun 23.00).*

⬤ **5 The Newton Brewery Inn** 68 Webb Lane, Middlewich CW10 9DN (01606 832335). ¼ mile south of the Big Lock pub. Small friendly pub with attractive garden running down to the towpath. Real ale served. Dog-friendly. *Open from 16.00 (Sat-Sun 12.00) until late.*

⬤✕ **6 The Big Lock** Webbs Lane, Middlewich CW10 9DN (01606 833489; www.thebiglockpub.com). Canalside. Variously a bottle-making factory and canal-horse stables, this pub now serves real ale and a large menu of popular pub food. Freshly prepared meals available *Mon-Sat 12.00-21.00 (Fri-Sat 21.30) & Sun 12.00-20.30*. Family- and dog-friendly, garden. Wi-Fi. *Open from 11.30 (Sun 12.00) until late.*

⬤ **Middlewich**

Cheshire. PO, tel, stores, chemist, butcher, baker, off-licence, fish & chips, takeaways, library, garage. A town that since Roman times has been dedicated to salt extraction. Most of the salt produced here goes to various chemical industries. Subsidence from salt extraction has prevented redevelopment for many years, but a big renewal scheme is now in progress. The canalside area is a haven of peace below the busy streets. There is an interesting town trail depicting Roman Middlewich as a Romano-British saltworks settlement in the period 150-250 AD. Interpretation boards can be found on the towpath north of Bridge 172 and beside the Newton Brewery Inn.

St Michael's Church High Town, Middlewich CW10 9AN (01606 738005). A handsome medieval church which was a place of refuge for the Royalists during the Civil War. It has a fine interior with richly carved woodwork.

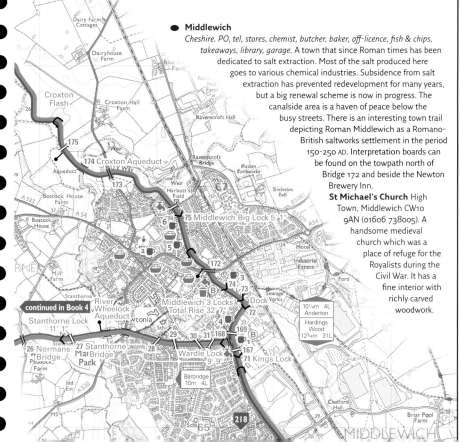

continued in Book 4

Anderton Lift

The outlying canal settlement of Broken Cross acts as a buffer between the beauty and solitude of the Dane Valley and the industrial ravages around Northwich. Beyond is another length in which salt mining has determined the nature of the scenery.

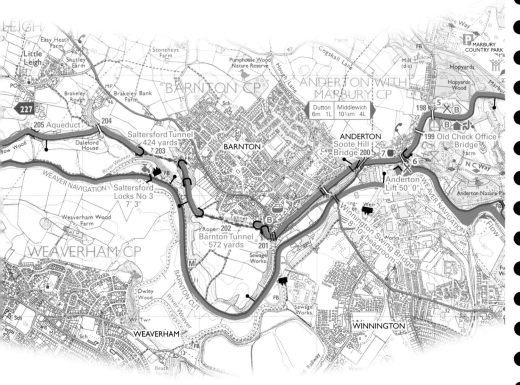

Part of it is heavily industrial, with enormous Tata Chemical works dominating the scene; much of it is devastated but rural (just), some of it is nondescript, and some of it is superb countryside. Donkey engines can still be seen in surrounding fields pumping brine. Leaving the vicinity of Lostock Gralam and the outskirts of Northwich, one passes Marston and Wincham where there is *gas and solid fuel* available ¼ mile north east of Bridge 193. Just west of the village, one travels along a ½-mile stretch of canal that was only cut in 1958, as the old route was about to collapse into – needless to say – underground salt workings. Beyond the woods of Marbury Country Park (attractive short-stay *moorings*) and before Bridge 198, there are a full range of facilities including *toilets and showers*, followed by Anderton – the short entrance canal to the famous boat lift down into the Weaver Navigation is on the left. Gas is available 100yds south of Bridge 200. The main line continues westwards, winding along what is now a steep hill and into Barnton Tunnel. There is a useful *range of shops*, up the hill from the east end of the tunnel, including a *PO, tel, stores, butcher, takeaways and an off-licence*. You then emerge onto a hillside overlooking the River Weaver, with a marvellous view straight down the huge Saltersford Locks. Now Saltersford Tunnel is entered: beyond it you are in completely open country again. There are good moorings in the basins to the east of both tunnels.

NAVIGATIONAL NOTES

1 Saltersford Tunnel is crooked, affording only a brief glimpse of the other end. It is subject to timed passage. Northbound, on the hour to 20 min past; southbound half past the hour to 10 mins to the hour. Two boats cannot pass in this or Barnton Tunnel, so make sure they are clear before proceeding.

2 *See* notes on page 177 covering use of the Anderton Boat Lift.

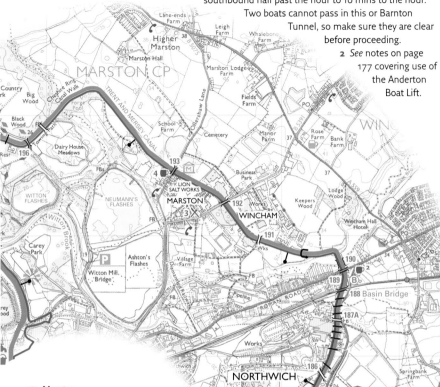

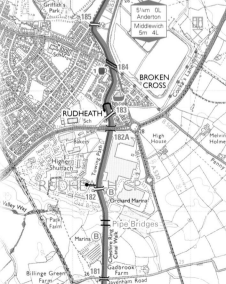

● **Marston**

Cheshire. Tel. A salt-producing village, suffering badly from its own industry. The numerous gaps in this village are caused by the demolition or collapse of houses affected by subsidence. Waste ground abounds.

Lion Salt Works Offershaw Lane, Marston CW9 6ES (01606 275066; www.lionsaltworks.westcheshiremuseums.co.uk). Beside the canal at bridge 193. The Thompson family established an open pan salt works in Marston in 1842, producing fishery salt, bay salt, crystal salt and lump salt. The salt was pumped as wild brine from 45yds beneath the works and evaporated in a large iron pan. The crystals thus formed were raked into tubs to form blocks, and subsequently dried in brick stove houses, before being exported (with the first part of the journey by canal) to India, Canada and West Africa. The Works closed in 1986 and after an extensive £8 million restoration project, finally re-opened to the public in 2015. Café, shop, butterfly garden and play area. *Open Tue-Sun & B Hol Mon 10.30-17.00 (Nov-Jan 16.00).* Charge (for museum only).

Marbury Country Park Comberbach CW9 6AT (01606 77741; www.visitcheshire.com/things-to-do/marbury-country-park-p32091). Two-hundred-acre park occupying the landscaped gardens of the former Marbury Hall and estate, once the home of the Barry and Smith-Barry families. Overlooking Budworth Mere, the house was demolished in 1968 and the much-neglected gardens restored to their former glory by Cheshire County Heritage and Recreation service. The Information Centre ($\frac{1}{2}$ mile north of bridge 196) houses a display of Marbury's wildlife and history, including its use as a POW camp during World War II. Visitor's moorings and picnic area.

● **Anderton Lift**
Lift Lane, Anderton CW9 6FW (01606 786777; www.canalrivertrust.org.uk/places-to-visit/anderton-boat-lift-visitor-centre). An amazing and enormous piece of machinery built in 1875 by Leader Williams (later engineer of the Manchester Ship Canal) to connect the Trent & Mersey to the flourishing Weaver Navigation, 50ft below. As built, the lift consisted of two water-filled tanks counterbalancing each other in a vertical slide, resting on massive hydraulic rams. It worked on the very straightforward principle that making the ascending tank slightly lighter – by pumping a little water out – would assist the hydraulic rams (which were operated by a steam engine and pump) in moving both tanks, with boats in them, up or down their respective slide. In 1908 the lift had to have major repairs, so it was modernised at the same time. The troublesome hydraulic rams were done away with; from then on each tank – which contained 250 tons of water – had its own counterweights and was independent of the other tank. Electricity replaced steam as the motive power. One of the most fascinating individual features of the canal system, it draws thousands of sightseers every year. Restoration to full working order is now complete, following the original 1875 hydraulic design, using oil as the motive force rather than the chemically contaminated water that was the cause of the 1908 failure. The more recent counter balance weights, together with their ungainly supporting structure, have been retained to demonstrate the engineering development of the lift.

● **Northwich**
Cheshire. All services. Regular buses from Barnton. A rather attractive town at the junction of the Rivers Weaver and Dane. (The latter brings large quantities of sand down into the Weaver Navigation, necessitating a heavy expenditure on dredging.) As in every other town in this area, salt has for centuries been responsible for the continued prosperity of Northwich. The Weaver Navigation has of course been another very prominent factor in the town's history, and the building and repairing of barges, narrowboats, and small seagoing ships has been carried on here for over 200 years. Nowadays this industry has been almost forced out of business by foreign competition, and the last private shipyard on the river closed down in 1971. (This yard – Isaac Pimblott's – used to be between Hunt's Locks and Hartford Bridge. Their last contract was a tug for Aden.) However, the big CRT yard in the town continues to thrive; some very large maintenance craft are built and repaired here. The wharves by Town Bridge are empty, and are an excellent temporary mooring site for anyone wishing to visit the place. The town centre is very close; much of it has been completely rebuilt however, signs of decay are already beginning to creep in. There is now an extensive shopping precinct. Although the large number of pubs has been whittled down in the rebuilding process, there are still some pleasant old streets. The Weaver and the big swing bridges across it remain a dominant part of the background.

Tourist Information Centre 1 The Arcade, Northwich CW9 5AS (0300 123 8123; www. visitcheshire.com/visitor-information/visitor-information-centres). *Open Mon-Fri 08.30-17.00.*

Weaver Hall Museum and Workhouse 162 London Road, Northwich CW9 8AB (01606 271640; www.weaverhall.westcheshiremuseums.co.uk). The history of the salt industry from Roman times to the present day, housed in the town's former workhouse. Look out for the remarkable model ship, made from salt of course. Shop and coffee shop. *Open Jan-Oct Tue-Fri; B Hols and during school holidays, 10.00-17.00 & Nov-Dec 10.00-16.00. Sat-Sun, Jan-Oct 14.00-17.00 & Nov-Dec 13.00-16.00.* Charge.

NAVIGATIONAL NOTES

1 The Anderton Boat Lift is available for use 7 days a week and pre-booked passage is essential by telephoning 01606 786777. Visit the website (www.canalrivertrust.org.uk/anderton) for more information.

2 Boaters should be careful to differentiate between the the holding moorings at the top and bottom of the lift, which are solely for lift use, and the visitor moorings.

Boatyards

⑧Park Farm Marina Davenham Road, Rudheath, Northwich CW9 7RY (01606 44672; www.parkfarm-marina.co.uk). Short- and long-term mooring.

⑧Orchard Marina & Boat Builders Ltd School Road, Gadbrook Park, Rudheath, Northwich CW9 7RG (01606 42082; www.orchardmarina.com). Beside bridge 182. 🛉🛉⚓D Gas, boat building, short- and long-term moorings, dry dock, boat and engine repairs, boat fitting out, boat and engine sales, DIY facilities, books, maps, solid fuel, toilets, showers, laundrette. *Emergency call out.*

⑧Colliery Narrowboat Co Wincham Wharf, 220 Manchester Road, Lostock Gralam, Northwich CW9 7NT (01606 44672). Overnight and long-term mooring, crane, winter storage, boat building, boat sales, boat and engine repairs, wet dock, DIY facilities, toilets.

⑧Olympus Narrow Boats Wincham Wharf, 220 Manchester Road, Lostock Gralam, Northwich CW9 7NT (01606 43048; www.narrowboats.org/canal-service/809/olympus+narrowboats). ⚓D Gas, narrowboat fitting out, boat repairs, dry dock, wet dock.

⑧ABC Leisure Group Anderton Marina, Uplands Road, Anderton CW9 6AJ (01606 79642; www.andertonmarina.com). 🛉🛉⚓D Pump out, gas, narrowboat hire, overnight mooring, long-term mooring, slipway, boat sales, engine sales and repairs, boat painting, covered wet docks for hire, chandlery, gifts, restaurant, telephone, toilets.

⑧Uplands Marina Uplands Road, Anderton CW9 6AQ (01606 782986/07931 323747; www.uplandsmarina.co.uk). ⚓ D Overnight and long-term mooring, boat sales and repairs, boat fitting out, winter storage, slipway, wet dock, gas, coal, chandlery.

BIRD LIFE

The *Kingfisher* is a dazzlingly attractive bird, but its colours often appear muted when the bird is seen sitting in shade or vegetation. It has orange-red underparts and mainly blue upperparts; the electric blue back is seen to the best effect when the bird is observed in low-level flight speeding along a river. It is invariably seen near water and uses overhanging branches to watch for fish. When a feeding opportunity arises, the Kingfisher plunges headlong into the water, catching its prey in its bill: the fish is swallowed whole. Kingfishers nest in holes excavated in the river bank.

Pubs and Restaurants (pages 164–165)

◖🗙 1 The Old Broken Cross Broken Cross Place, Middlewich Road, Rudheath CW9 7EB (01606 333111; www.oldbrokencross.co.uk). Once a row of canalside cottages, this establishment now serves real ale and food *daily 12.00-20.00 (Sun 18.00).* Dog- and child-friendly, garden. Traditional pub games, real fires, sports TV and Wi-Fi. *Open daily 12.00-23.30 Fri-Sat 00.00).*

◖🗙 2 The Boatyard Bistro & Bar Wincham Wharf, 216 Manchester Road, Lostock Gralam CW9 7NT (01606 333282). A converted mill, still with its original water wheel, serving real ale and high-quality food, sourced from local ingredients, *Tue-Thu 17.00-21.00 & Fri-Sun L and E.* Family-friendly, canalside terrace. Real fires and Wi-Fi. *Open Tue-Thu 17.00-23.00 & Fri-Sun 12.00-23.00.*

🗙 3 The Crusty Cob 37 Chapel Street, Wincham CW9 6DA (07555 517659). ¼ mile west of Bridge 192. Breakfast, snacks, filled rolls, sandwiches, hot and cold drinks. Eat in or takeaway. Dog-friendly. *Open Mon-Fri 08.00-14.00 & Sat 08.30-12.00.*

◖ 4 The Salt Barge Ollershaw Lane, Marston CW9 6ES (01606 43064; www.thesaltbargemarston.co.uk). Deceptively large pub with a friendly atmosphere, neatly divided into cosy areas, and with an inviting family room. Real ales and good food available

Mon-Sat L and E & Sun 12.00-20.00. Dog- and family-friendly, garden. Live music *Fri.* Traditional pub games, newspapers, real fires and Wi-Fi. B&B. *Open Mon-Wed L and E & Thu-Sun 12.00-23.00 (Fri 00.00).*

🗙♀ 5 The Moorings Anderton Marina, Uplands Road, Anderton CW9 6AJ (01606 79789; www.mooringsrestaurant.co.uk). Canalside seating. Boaters please moor outside the basin. Small, independent restaurant and bar overlooking Anderton Marina and the Trent & Mersey Canal. *Closed 17.00–18.30.* Wide variety of food with emphasis on fresh fish and fresh produce, served *L and E (not Mon & Sun E or Tue all day).* Children and dogs welcome. Patio and terrace.

🗙 6 Anderton Boat Lift Coffee Shop Lift Lane, Anderton, Northwich CW9 6FW (01606 786777; www.andertonboatlift.co.uk). Café inside the Lift Operations Centre serving tea, coffee, hot and cold snacks, ice creams, etc. Children welcome. *Open as per the Lift Centre.*

◖🗙 7 The Stanley Arms Old Road, Anderton CW9 6AG (01606 75059). Friendly real ale pub where children and dogs are welcome. Food available *daily 12.00-20.00 (Wed-Sat 21.00).* Garden, traditional pub games, real fires and Wi-Fi. *Open 12.00-23.00 (Sun 22.30).*

225

Dutton

This, the northernmost stretch of the Trent & Mersey, is a very pleasant one and delightfully rural. Most of the way the navigation follows the south side of the hills that overlook the River Weaver. From about 60ft up, one is often rewarded with excellent views of this splendid valley and the very occasional large vessels that ply up and down it. At one point one can see the elegant Dutton railway viaduct in the distance; then the two waterways diverge as the Trent & Mersey enters the woods preceding Preston Brook Tunnel. There is a stop lock south of the tunnel just beyond a pretty covered dry dock; there are often fine examples of restored working boats moored here. At the north end of the tunnel a notice announces that from here onwards one is on the Bridgewater Canal (*see Nicholson Guide 5 – North West & the Pennines*). There are good moorings north of bridge 213, and to the south of Dutton stop lock.

NAVIGATIONAL NOTES

1 Access to Preston Brook Tunnel is restricted to *northbound on the hour to 10 minutes past the hour; southbound on the 1/2 hour to 20 mins to the hour.*

2 North of Preston Brook Tunnel you are on the Bridgewater Canal, which is owned by the Manchester Ship Canal Company (Peel Ports) and is described in detail in *Nicholson Guide 5 – North West & the Pennines*.

3 A Canal & River Trust (CRT) licensed crafts are permitted up to 7 consecutive days free navigation on the Bridgewater Canal, with no return within any 28-day period (without a permit). Any return within 28 days from the date of leaving, whether leaving after 3 days, 5 days or up to 7 days, will required a permit. A 7-day permit is available which applies to Bridgewater craft on CRT waters and CRT craft on the Bridgewater Canal or there is a return permit (valid for 3 days) to transit for a reduced fee of £20. Permits can be purchased on the Bridgewater Canal website (www.bridgewatercanal.co.uk) by telephoning 0161 855 6400 or from an enforcement officer.

Pubs and Restaurants

🍺✕ **1 The Leigh Arms** Willow Green Lane, Little Leigh, Northwich CW8 4QT (01606 853327; www.leighharms.co.uk). ¼ mile south of bridge 208, overlooking the Weaver and Acton Swing Bridge. Attractive old coaching inn with large restaurant area serving real ales and an extensive menu of home-made food *Mon-Thu L and E & Fri-Sun 12.00-20.45 (Sun 17.00). Kitchen may close earlier in winter)*. Real cider. Dog- and family-friendly, garden and play area. Traditional pub games, live music *Thu*, newspapers and Wi-Fi. Moorings nearby. *Open 12.00-23.00 (Sun 22.30)*.

🍺✕ **2 The Hollybush** Warrington Road, Little Leigh, Northwich CW8 4QY (01606 853196; www.thehollybush.net). ¼ mile north of bridge 209. Listed, timber-framed building, one of the oldest farmhouse pubs in the country, with unique charm and character. Wide range of interesting, home-cooked food served in bar and restaurant *Mon-Sat L and E & Sun 12.00-19.00*. Children welcome. Garden with children's play area, including bouncy castle. Traditional pub games. Quiz night *Sun*. Real fires and Wi-Fi. B&B. *Open Mon-Fri L and E & Sat-Sun 12.00-23.00*.

🍺✕ **3 The Riverside** Warrington Road, Acton Bridge, Northwich CW8 3QD (01606 852310; www.riversideinnpub.co.uk). Large open-plan, riverside pub, serving real ale and food *daily 12.00-22.00 (Sun 20.00)*. *Sun* Carvery. Family-friendly, garden. Wi-Fi. Open *daily 12.00-22.00 (Sun 21.00)*.

Boatyards

Ⓑ **Black Prince Holidays** Bartington Wharf, Acton Bridge, Northwich CW8 4QU (01606 852945; www.black-prince.com). 🚿♨D E Pump out, gas, narrowboat hire, day-hire craft, long-term mooring, engine repairs, books, maps and gifts, coal, ice cream.

Ⓑ **Dutton Dry Dock** 3 Tunnel End, Dutton, Warrington WA4 4LA (01928 717273; www.claymoore.co.uk). Dry dock, historic boat repairs, boat blacking, boat repairs, engineering and machine shop, vintage engine repairs.

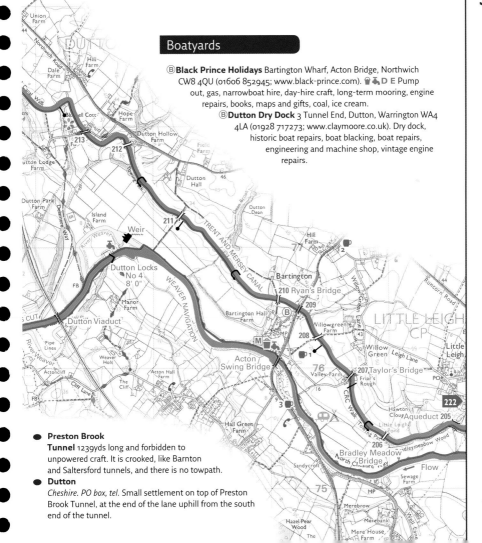

● **Preston Brook**
Tunnel 1239yds long and forbidden to unpowered craft. It is crooked, like Barnton and Saltersford tunnels, and there is no towpath.
● **Dutton**
Cheshire. PO box, tel. Small settlement on top of Preston Brook Tunnel, at the end of the lane uphill from the south end of the tunnel.

INDEX